ENCYCLOPAEDIA OF POLITICAL SCIENCE

ENCYCLOPAEDIA OF POLITICAL SCIENCE

A.K. Dixit

CYBER TECH PUBLICATIONS
4264/3, Ansari Road, Daryaganj, New Delhi-110002 (India)
Ph.: 011-23244078, 011-43559448 Fax: 011-23280028
E-Mail: cyberpublicationsdelhi@yahoo.com
Website: www.cybertechpublications.com

ENCYCLOPAEDIA OF POLITICAL SCIENCE

A.K. Dixit

First Edition 2010

Published by :

G.S. Rawat for **Cyber Tech Publications**

4264/3, Ansari Road, Daryaganj, New Delhi-110002 (India)

Ph.: 011-23244078, 011-43559448 Fax: 011-23280028

E-Mail: cyberpublicationsdelhi@yahoo.com

Website: www.cybertechpublications.com

Printed at: Asian Offset Printers, Delhi-53

Preface

Society enables man to achieve talents and qualities by virtue of which he can make progress and achieve superiority over other living beings. Civics helps to resolve social conflicts in society and help man to live in harmony with other fellow beings. However, the word civics is derived from the Latin word 'civis' that means 'a citizen'. Another Latin word 'Civitas' means 'city state'. Both these words have given birth to the social science known as 'Civics'. In fact, civics is actually the social science, however in certain respects it forms a part of political science. Civics is an old subject and previously it was taught along with history and political science. It was introduced as separate subject only in the nineteenth century. Thus, Civics is that branch of human knowledge which deals with rights and duties of man living as a member of a group of people politically organized. Whereas the subject which deals with man in relation to the state and government is known as *political science.* Political science is a branch of study which is concerned with political aspect of man's life in society as distinct from the economic, philosophical, ethical and other aspects.

There is a respectable impulse—indeed an honored tradition—in political science that urges political scientists to stay "relevant" to contemporary problems. I am prepared to guess that fully half the research agenda of the discipline—maybe more—is generated in response to various current events: wars, elections, laws, crime rates, scandals, press releases, those sorts of things. In this volume we are happy to present at least one example of a review of literature that follows the news pretty closely.

This work contains highly useful information on diverse core issues of civics and political science with special emphasis on teaching aspect of the subject. Researchers, teachers and students will be immensely benefited by this.

—*Author*

Preface

Contents

Preface

1. Introduction 1
2. Political Philosophy 17
3. Organs of Government 52
4. Political Culture 100
5. Power, Authority and Legitimacy 113
6. Revolution: Theory and Types 141
7. Modern Indian Thought 190
8. Greek Political Thought 206
9. Contemporary Political Thought 238

Bibliography 262

Index 263

CHAPTER

1

INTRODUCTION

While the study of politics is first found in ancient Greece and ancient India, political science is a late arrival in terms of social sciences. However, the discipline has a clear set of antecedents such as moral philosophy, political philosophy, political economy, history, and other fields concerned with normative determinations of what ought to be and with deducing the characteristics and functions of the ideal state. In each historic period and in almost every geographic area, we can find someone studying politics and increasing political understanding.

ANCIENT INDIA

In ancient India, the study of politics can be traced back to several Vedic Sanskrit texts: Rig-Veda (c. 1500-1200 BC), the Samhitas (c. 1200-900 BC), and the Brahmanas (c. 1200-900 BC). The study of politics is also found in the Buddhist Pali Canon (c. 6th century BC). Chanakya (c. 350-275 BC) was a professor of political science at Takshashila University, and later the Prime Minister of Mauryan emperor Chandragupta Maurya. Chanakya is regarded as one of the earliest known political thinkers, economists and king-makers, and is also known as the Indian Machiavelli. He wrote the Arthashastra, which was one of the earliest treatises on political thought, economics and social order, and can be considered a precursor to Machiavelli's The Prince. It discusses monetary and fiscal policies, welfare, international relations, and war strategies in detail, among other topics on political science.

ANCIENT GREECE

The antecedents of western politics trace their roots back even earlier than Plato and Aristotle, particularly in the works of Homer, Hesiod, Thucydides, Plato, Xenophon, and Euripides. Later, Plato analyzed political systems and abstracted their analysis from more literary-and history-oriented studies and applied an approach we would understand as closer to philosophy. Similarly, Aristotle built upon Plato's analysis to include historical empirical evidence in his analysis.

ROMAN EMPIRE

During the rule of Rome, famous historians such as Polybius, Livy and Plutarch documented the rise of the Roman Republic, and the organization and histories of other nations, while statesman like Julius Caesar, Cicero and others provided us with examples of the politics of the republic and Rome's empire and wars. The study of politics during this age was oriented toward understanding history, understanding methods of governing, and describing the operation of governments.

MEDIEVAL EUROPE

With the fall of the Roman Empire, there arose a more diffuse arena for political studies. The rise of monotheism and particularly for the Western tradition, Christianity, brought to light a new space for politics and political action. During the Middle Ages, the study of politics was widespread in the churches and courts. Works such as Augustine of Hippo's The City of God synthesized current philosophies and political traditions with those of Christianity, redefining the borders between what was religious and what was political. Most of the political questions surrounding the relationship between church and state were clarified and contested in this period.

ISLAMIC WORLD

In the Middle East and later other Islamic areas, works such as the Rubaiyat of Omar Khayyam and Epic of Kings by Ferdowsi provided evidence of political analysis, while the Islamic Aristotelians such as Avicenna and later Maimonides and Averroes, continued Aristotle's tradition of analysis and empiricism, writing commentaries on Aristotle's works.

EUROPEAN RENAISSANCE

During the Italian Renaissance, Niccolò Machiavelli established the emphasis of modern political science on direct empirical observation of political institutions and actors in The Prince. Later, the expansion of the scientific paradigm during the Enlightenment further pushed the study of politics beyond normative determinations.

POLITICAL HISTORY

Political history is the narrative and analysis of political events, ideas, movements, and leaders. It is usually structured around the nation state. The first "scientific" political history was written by Leopold von Ranke in Germany in the 19th century. His methodologies profoundly affected the way historians critically examine sources; see historiography for a more complete analysis of the methodology of various approaches to history. According to Hegel, Political History "is a concept of the state with a moral and spiritual force beyond the marerial interests of its subjects: it followed that the state was the main agent of historical change."

DIPLOMATIC HISTORY

Sometimes referred to as "Rankian History", diplomatic history focuses on politics, politicians and other high rulers and views them as being the driving force of continuity and change in history. It is the study of the conduct of international relations between states or across state boundaries. This is the most common form of history and is often the classical and popular belief of what history should be. Although history which might be classified as diplomatic history has been written for as long as history has been in existence -Thucydides, certainly, is among other things, highly concerned with the relations among states -the modern form of diplomatic history was codified in the 19th century by Leopold von Ranke, a German historian. Ranke wrote largely on the history of Early Modern Europe, using the diplomatic archives of the European powers (particularly the Venetians) to construct a detailed understanding of the history of Europe wie es eigentlich gewesen ("as it actually happened.") Ranke saw diplomatic history as the most important kind of history to write because of his idea of the "Primary of Foreign Affairs" (Primat der Aussenpolitik), arguing that the concerns of international relations drive the internal development of the state. Ranke's understanding of diplomatic history relied on the large number of official documents produced by modern western governments as sources.

Ranke's understanding of the dominance of foreign policy, and hence an emphasis on diplomatic history, remained the dominant paradigm in historical writing through the first half of the twentieth century. This emphasis, combined with the effects of the War Guilt Clause in the Treaty of Versailles (1919) which ended the First World War, led to a huge amount of historical writing on the subject of the origins of the war in 1914, with the involved governments printing huge, carefully edited, collections of documents and numerous historians writing multi-volume histories of the origins of the war. In general, the early works in this vein, including Fritz Fischer's controversial (at the time) 1961 thesis that German goals of "world power" were the principal cause of the war, fit fairly comfortably into Ranke's emphasis on Aussenpolitik. In the course of the 1960s, however, some German historians (notably Hans-Ulrich Wehler and his cohort) began to rebel against this idea, instead suggesting a "Primacy of Domestic Politics" (Primat der Innenpolitik), in which the insecurities of (in this case German) domestic policy drove the creation of foreign policy. This led to a considerably body of work interpreting the domestic policies of various states and the ways this influenced their conduct of foreign policy.

At the same time, the middle of the twentieth century began to see a general de-emphasis on diplomatic history. The French Annales school had already put an emphasis on the role of geography and economics on history, and of the importance of broad, slow cycles rather than the constant apparent movement of the "history of events" of high politics. The most important work of the Annales school, Fernand Braudel's The Mediterranean and the Mediterranean World in the Age of Philip II, contains a traditional Rankean diplomatic history of Philip II's Mediterranean policy, but only as the third and shortest section of a work largely focusing on the broad cycles of history in the longue durée ("long term"). The Annales were broadly influential, leading to a turning away from diplomatic and other forms of political history towards an emphasis on broader trends of economic and environmental change. In the 1960s and 1970s, an increasing emphasis on giving a voice to the voiceless and writing the history of the underclasses, whether by using the quantitative statistical methods of social history or the more qualitative assessments of cultural history, also undermined the centrality of diplomatic history to the historical discipline. Nevertheless, diplomatic history has always remained a historical field with a great interest to the general public, and considerable amounts of work are still done in the field, often in much the same way that Ranke pioneered in the middle years of the 19th century.

HISTORIOGRAPHY

Historiography is the study of the practice of history. This can take many forms, including the study of historical method and the historical development of history as an academic discipline. The term can also be used to refer a specific body of historical writing. For instance, "medieval historiography during the 1960s" can be taken to mean the methodological approaches and ideas about medieval history present in written history during that decade. As a meta-analysis of descriptions of the past, this third conception can relate to the first two in that the analysis usually focuses on the narratives, interpretations, worldview, use of evidence, or method of presentation of other historians.

Defining Historiography

Conal Furay and Michael J. Salevouris define "historiography" as "the study of the way history has been and is written -the history of historical writing... When you study 'historiography' you do not study the events of the past directly, but the changing interpretations of those events in the works of individual historians." (The Methods and Skills of History: A Practical Guide, 1988, p. 223. Although questions of method have concerned historians since Thucydides, many trace the modern study of historiography to E. H. Carr's 1961 work What is History?. Carr challenged the traditional belief that the study of the methods of historical research and writing were unimportant. His work remains in print to this day, and is used in many postgraduate programs of study in the English-speaking world. Historiography is often political in nature. For example, the Dunning school of historiography, which was sympathetic to former slave owners and leaders of the Confederacy, contended that black people, particularly former slaves, should neither be permitted to vote nor bear arms.

In the 1960s, historiography corrected the racism of the Dunning School viewpoint, and history that included the viewpoint of African Americans who had been disenfranchised by the Jim Crow political and economic system that grew up alongside the powerful Dunning School and its way of telling history from the viewpoint of former slave owners. Mid-twentieth century historians also focused on primary sources to reveal previously excluded roles of women, minorities, and labor from earlier histories of the United States.

According to these historiographers, historians in the 1930s and 1940s had a bias toward wealthy and well-connected white males. Some historians from that point onward devoted themselves to what they saw as more accurate representations of the past, casting a light on those who had been previously disregarded as non-noteworthy. The study of historiography demands a critical approach that goes beyond the mere examination of historical fact. Historiographical studies consider the source, often by researching the author, his or her position in society, and the type of history being written at the time.

Basic Issues Studied in Historiography

Some of the common questions of historiography are:

- Who wrote the source (primary or secondary)?

- For primary sources, we look at the person in his or her society, for secondary sources, we consider the theoretical orientation of the approach for example, Marxist or Annales School, ("total history"), political history, etc.
- What is the authenticity, authority, bias/interest, and intelligibility of the source?
- What was the view of history when the source was written?
- Was history supposed to provide moral lessons?
- What or who was the intended audience?
- What sources were privileged or ignored in the narrative?
- By what method was the evidence compiled?
- In what historical context was the work of history itself written?

Issues engaged in so-called critical historiography includes topics such as:

- What constitutes an historical "event"?
- In what modes does a historian write and produce statements of "truth" and "fact"?
- How does the medium (novel, textbook, film, theatre, comic) through which historical information is conveyed influence its meaning?
- What inherent epistemological problems does archive-based history contain?
- How does the historian establish their own objectivity or come to terms with their own subjectivity?
- What is the relation of historical theory to historical practice?
- What is the "goal" of history?
- What is history?

The History of Written History

Understanding the past appears to be a universal human need and the telling of history has emerged independently in civilisations around the world. What constitutes history is a philosophical question. For the purposes of this survey it is written history recorded in a narrative format for the purpose of informing future generations about events. The earliest critical historical thought emerged in Greece, a development which would be an important influence on the writing of history elsewhere in the world.

EARLY WESTERN HISTORIOGRAPHY

Written history appeared first with the ancient Greeks, whose historians greatly contributed to the development of historical methodology. The very first historical work were The Histories composed by Herodotus of Halicarnassus (484 BC-ca.425 BC), who became later known as the 'father of history' (Cicero). Herodotus personally conducted research into the history of various Mediterranean cultures, and attempted to distinguish between more and less reliable accounts. His research confirmed for him the belief that divinity plays a crucial role in the determination of historical events. Thucydides, on the other hand, largely eliminated divine causality from his account of the war between Athens and Sparta, and the same holds true for his successors, such as Xenophon and Polybius.

Reports exist of other near-eastern histories, such as that composed by the Phoenician historian Sanchuniathon; but his very existence is considered semi-fabled and writings attributed to him are fragmentary, known only through the later historians Philo of Byblos and Eusebius, who asserted that he wrote before even the Trojan war. Concerning the Bible, there is considerable debate about its historiographical character. To some scholars the use of a divinity to provide historical explanations contradicts the basic aim of any truly historical work, namely to provide rational explanations for events. Others argue that the Biblical search for an underlying cause of historical events is itself a characteristic of historiographical research, and point moreover to the Bible's frequent recourse to double-causation, whereby events are attributed to both human and divine causation. Controversy over this issue is complicated by the fact that the Bible is seen as an inspired text by many members of Western society today. Writing history was popular among Christian monks in the Middle Ages. They wrote about the history of the Church and of their patrons, the dynastic history of the local rulers. History was written about states or nations during the Renaissance. The study of history changed during the Enlightenment and Romanticism. Voltaire described the history of certain ages that were important according to him, instead of describing events in a chronological order. History became an independent discipline. It was not called philosophia historiae anymore, but merely history (historiae).

Chinese Historiography

The writing of history in China began with the work of Sima Qian around 100 BC. Its scope extends as far back as the 16th century BC. Traditionalist Chinese historiography describes history in terms of dynastic cycles. In this view, each new dynasty is founded by a morally righteous founder. Over time, the dynasty becomes morally corrupt and dissolute. Eventually, the dynasty becomes so weak as to allow its replacement by a new dynasty.

Islamic Historiography

Islamic historiography began developing with the reconstruction of Muhammad's life in the centuries following his death. Due to numerous conflicting narratives regarding Muhammad and his companions from various sources, it was necessary to verify which sources were more reliable. In order to evaluate these sources, various methodologies were developed, such as the "science of biography", "science of Hadith" and "Isnad" (chain of transmission). These methodologies were later applied to other historical figures in the Islamic World. Famous Muslim historians included Urwah (d. 712), Ibn Ishaq (d. 768), Al-Waqidi (745 -822), Ibn Hisham (d. 834), Al-Tabari (838 -923), Ibn Khaldun (1332 -1406) and Ibn Hajar (1372 -1449) among others.

Ilm ar-Rijal (Arabic) is the "science of biography" especially as practiced in Islam, where it was first applied to the sira, the life of the prophet of Islam, Muhammad, and then the lives of the four Rightly Guided Caliphs who expanded Islamic dominance rapidly. Since validating the sayings of Muhammad is a major study ("Isnad"), accurate biography has always been of great interest to Muslim biographers, who accordingly became experts at sorting out facts from accusations, bias from evidence, etc., and were renowned throughout the known world for their honesty in recording history. Modern practices of scientific citation and historical method owe a great deal to the rigor of the Isnad tradition of early Muslims. The earliest surviving Islamic biography is Ibn Ishaq's Sirat Rasul Allah, written in the 8th century. The "science of Hadith" is the process that Muslim scholars use to evaluate Hadith. The classification of Hadith into Sahih (sound), Hasan (good) and Da'if (weak) was firmly established by Ali ibn al-Madini (161 AH -234 AH). Later, al-Madini's student Muhammad al-Bukhari (810 -870) authored a collection that he believed contained only Sahih Hadith, which is now known as the Sahih Bukhari.

Modern Historiography

Modern historiography began with Ranke in the 19th century, who was very critical on the sources used in history. He was opposed to analyses and rationalizations. His adagium was writing history the way it was. He wanted eyewitness accounts and wanted an emphasis on the point of view of the eyewitness. Hegel and Marx introduced the change of society in history. Former historians had focused on cyclical events of the rise and decline of rulers and nations. A new discipline emerged in the late nineteenth century that analyzed and compared these perspectives on a larger scale and that discipline was sociology. The French Annales School radically changed history during the 20th century. Fernand Braudel wanted history to become more scientific by demanding more mathematical evidence in history, in order to make the history discipline less subjective. Furthermore, he added a social-economic and geographic framework to answer historical questions. Other French historians, like Philippe Ariès and Michel Foucault described history of daily life topics as death and sexuality. They wanted history to be written about all topics and that all questions should be asked.

In the 1970s, some historians began to focus on case-studies. Case studies describe particular aspects of history in a thorough fashion, to describe history as it was or to measure it precisely. Several well chosen case studies can enhance or change the major picture and can bring more truth to the answers of the questions that the Annales School likes to ask. However, because case studies focus so narrowly on particular pieces of place and time, i.e., the living conditions of female agricultural workers in 15th century Sussex, their findings cannot always be applied to broader sets of data i.e., using the data from the Sussex study to postulate about conditions in Kent, or France, or in seventeenth century Sussex. Case studies are best used in addition to raw data and primary sources. In the 1980s, American historians compared the differences and similarities between different world regions and to come to new concepts to describe them in the study of World History.

DIPLOMACY

Diplomacy is the art and practice of conducting negotiations between representatives of groups or states. It usually refers to international diplomacy, the conduct of international relations through the intercession of professional diplomats with regard to issues of peace-making, culture, economics, trade, and war. International treaties are usually negotiated by diplomats prior to endorsement by national politicians. The word stems from the Greek word "diploma", which literally means 'folded in two'. In ancient Greece, a diploma was a certificate certifying completion of a course of study, typically folded in two. In the days of the Roman Empire, the word diploma was used to describe official travel documents, such as passports and passes for imperial roads, that were stamped on double metal plates. Later, the meaning was extended to cover other official documents such as treaties with foreign tribes. In the 1700s the French called their body of officials attached to foreign legations the corps "diplomatique". The word "diplomacy" was first introduced into the English language by Edmund Burke in 1796, based on the French word "diplomatie". In an informal or social sense, diplomacy is the employment of tact to gain strategic advantage, one set of tools being the phrasing of statements in a non-confrontational, or polite manner.

Diplomats and Diplomatic Missions

A diplomat is someone involved in diplomacy; the collective term for a group of diplomats from a single country who are resident in another country is a diplomatic mission. Ambassador is the most senior diplomatic rank; a diplomatic mission headed by an ambassador is known as an embassy. The collective body of all diplomats of particular country is called that country's diplomatic corps.

History

The ability to practice diplomacy is one of the defining elements of a state, and diplomacy has been practiced since the first city-states were formed millennia ago. For most of human history diplomats were sent only for specific negotiations, and would return immediately after their mission concluded. Diplomats were usually relatives of the ruling family or of very high rank in order to give them legitimacy when they sought to negotiate with the other state. One notable exception involved the relationship between the Pope and the Byzantine Emperor; papal agents, called apocrisiarii, were permanently resident in Constantinople. After the 8th century, however, conflicts between the Pope and Emperor (such as the Iconoclastic controversy) led to the breaking of close ties.

Modern diplomacy's origins are often traced to the states of Northern Italy in the early Renaissance, with the first embassies being established in the thirteenth century. Milan played a leading role, especially under Francesco Sforza who established permanent embassies to the other city states of Northern Italy. It was in Italy that many of the traditions of modern diplomacy began, such as the presentation of an ambassadors credentials to the head of state. From Italy the practice was spread to the other European powers. Milan was the first to send a representative to the court of France in 1455. However, Milan refused to host French representatives fearing espionage and that the French representatives would intervene in its internal affairs. As foreign powers such as France and Spain became increasingly involved in Italian politics the need to accept emissaries was recognized. Soon the major European powers were exchanging representatives.

Spain was the first to send a permanent representative; it appointed an ambassador to the Court of England in 1487. By the late 16th century, permanent missions became customary. The Holy Roman Emperor, however, did not regularly send permanent legates, as they could not represent the interests of all the German princes (who were in theory subordinate to the Emperor, but in practice independent).

During that period the rules of modern diplomacy were further developed. The top rank of representatives was an ambassador. At that time an ambassador was a nobleman, the rank of the noble assigned varying with the prestige of the country he was delegated to. Strict standards developed for ambassadors, requiring they have large residences, host lavish parties, and play an important role in the court life of their host nation. In Rome, the most prized posting for a Catholic ambassador, the French and Spanish representatives would have a retinue of up to a hundred. Even in smaller posts, ambassadors were very expensive. Smaller states would send and receive envoys, who were a rung below ambassador. Somewhere between the two was the position of minister plenipotentiary. Diplomacy was a complex affair, even more so than now. The ambassadors from each state were ranked by complex levels of precedence that were much disputed. States were normally ranked by the title of the sovereign; for Catholic nations the emissary from the Vatican was paramount, then those from the kingdoms, then those from duchies and principalities. Representatives from republics were considered the lowest of the low. Determining precedence between two kingdoms depended on a number of factors that often fluctuated, leading to near constant squabbling.

Ambassadors, nobles with little foreign experience and no expectation of a career in diplomacy, needed to be supported by large embassy staff. These professionals would be sent on longer assignments and would be far more knowledgeable than the higher-ranking officials about the host country. Embassy staff would include a wide range of employees, including some dedicated to espionage. The need for skilled individuals to staff embassies was met by the graduates of universities, and this led to a great increase in the study of international law, modern languages, and history at universities throughout Europe. At the same time, permanent foreign ministries began to be established in almost all European states to coordinate embassies and their staffs. These ministries were still far from their modern form, and many of them had extraneous internal responsibilities. Britain had two departments with frequently overlapping powers until 1782. They were also far smaller; France, which boasted the largest foreign affairs department, had only some 70 full-time employees in the 1780s.

The elements of modern diplomacy slowly spread to Eastern Europe and Russia, arriving by the early eighteenth century. The entire edifice would be greatly disrupted by the French Revolution and the subsequent years of warfare. The revolution would see commoners take over the diplomacy of the French state, and of those conquered by revolutionary armies. Ranks of precedence were abolished. Napoleon also refused to acknowledge diplomatic immunity, imprisoning several British diplomats accused of scheming against France. After the fall of Napoleon, the Congress of Vienna of 1815 established an international system of diplomatic rank. Disputes on precedence among nations (and therefore the appropriate diplomatic ranks used) persisted for over a century until after World War II, when the rank of ambassador became the norm.

Diplomatic traditions outside of Europe were very different. A feature necessary for diplomacy is the existence of a number of states of somewhat equal power, as existed in Italy during the Renaissance, and in Europe for much of the modern period. By contrast, in Asia and the Middle East, China and the Ottoman Empire were reluctant to practice bilateral diplomacy as they viewed themselves to be unquestionably superior to all their neighbours. The Ottomans, for instance, would not send missions to other states, expecting representatives to come to Constantinople. It would not be until the nineteenth century that the Empire established permanent embassies in other capitals. As European power spread around the world in the eighteenth and nineteenth century so too did its diplomatic system.

Diplomatic Strategy

Real world diplomatic negotiations are very different from intellectual debates in a university where an issue is decided on the merit of the arguments and negotiators make a deal by splitting the difference. Though diplomatic agreements can sometimes be reached among liberal democratic nations by appealing to higher principles, most real world diplomacy is heavily influenced by raw power. The interaction of strength and diplomacy can be illustrated by a comparison to labor negotiations. If a labor union isn't willing to strike, then the union isn't going anywhere because management has absolutely no incentive to agree to union demands. On the other hand, if management isn't willing to take a strike, then the company will be walked all over by the labor union, and management will be forced to agree to any demand the union makes. The same concept applies to diplomatic negotiations. Good diplomacy and strength go together.

Diplomatic Immunity

The sanctity of diplomats has long been observed. This sanctity has come to be known as diplomatic immunity. While there have been a number of cases where diplomats have been killed, this is normally viewed as a great breach of honour. Genghis Khan and the Mongols were well known for strongly insisting on the rights of diplomats, and they would often wreak horrific vengeance against any state that violated these rights. This was shown when, having sent an ambassador to Persia, Genghis Khan received his ambassador's head sent by the Persians. Because of this act the Mongols invaded the whole of Persia, leading to even larger invasions by Khan in the future.

Diplomatic rights were established in the mid-seventeenth century in Europe and have spread throughout the world. These rights were formalized by the 1961 Vienna Convention on Diplomatic Relations, which protects diplomats from being persecuted or prosecuted while on a diplomatic mission. If a diplomat does commit a serious crime while in a host country s/he may be declared as persona non grata (unwanted person). Such diplomats are then often tried for the crime in their homeland. Diplomatic communications are also viewed as sacrosanct, and diplomats have long been allowed to carry documents across borders without being searched. The mechanism for this is the so-called "diplomatic bag" (or, in some countries, the "diplomatic pouch"). In recent years, however, signals intelligence has led to this use of diplomatic bags being largely discarded. In times of hostility, diplomats are often withdrawn for reasons of personal safety, as well as in some cases when the host country is friendly but there is a perceived threat from internal dissidents. Ambassadors and other diplomats are sometimes recalled temporarily by their home countries as a way to express displeasure with the host country. In both cases, lower-level employees still remain to actually do the business of diplomacy.

Diplomats as a Guarantee

The Middle East and other parts of the world had a very different tradition. In the Ottoman Empire, the diplomats of Persia and other states were seen as a guarantee of good behaviour. If a nation broke a treaty or if their nationals misbehaved the diplomats would be punished. Diplomats were thus used as an enforcement mechanism on treaties and international law. To ensure that punishing a diplomat mattered rulers insisted on high-ranking figures. This tradition is seen by supporters of Iran as a legal basis of the 1979 Iranian hostage crisis. In imitation of alleged previous practices supporters of the Iranian Revolution attempted to punish the United States for its alleged misdeeds by holding their diplomats hostage. Diplomats as a guarantee were also employed sometimes in pre-modern Europe and other parts of Asia.

Diplomacy and Espionage

Diplomacy is closely linked to espionage or gathering of intelligence. Embassies are bases for both diplomats and spies, and some diplomats are essentially openly-acknowledged spies. For instance, the job of military attachés includes learning as much as possible about the military of the nation to which they are assigned. They do not try to hide this role and, as such, are only invited to events allowed by their hosts, such as military parades or air shows. There are also deep-cover spies operating in many embassies. These individuals are given fake positions at the embassy, but their main task is to illegally gather intelligence, usually by coordinating spy rings of locals or other spies. For the most part, spies operating out of embassies gather little intelligence themselves and their identities tend to be known by the opposition. If discovered, these diplomats can be expelled from an embassy, but for the most part counter-intelligence agencies prefer to keep these agents in situ and under close monitoring. The information gathered by spies plays an increasingly important role in diplomacy. Arms-control treaties would be impossible without the power of reconnaissance satellites and agents to monitor compliance. Information gleaned from espionage is useful in almost all forms of diplomacy, everything from trade agreements to border disputes.

Diplomatic Recognition

Diplomatic recognition is an important factor in determining whether a nation is an independent state. Receiving recognition is often difficult, even for countries which are fully sovereign. For many decades after becoming independent, even many of the closest allies of the Dutch Republic refused to grant it full recognition. Today there are a number of independent entities without widespread diplomatic recognition, most notably the Republic of China, or Taiwan. Since the 1970s, most nations have stopped officially recognizing the ROC's existence on Taiwan, at the insistence of the People's Republic of China. Currently, the United States and other nations maintain informal relations through de facto embassies, with names such as the American Institute in Taiwan. Similarly, Taiwan's de facto embassies abroad are known by names such as the Taipei Economic and Cultural Representative Office. This was not always the case, with the US maintaining official diplomatic ties with Taiwan until 1979, when these relations were broken off as a condition for establishing official relations with China.

The Palestinian Authority has its own diplomatic service, however Palestinian representatives in most Western countries are not accorded diplomatic immunity, and their missions are referred to as Delegations General. Other unrecognized countries include Abkhazia, Transnistria, Somaliland, Nagorno Karabakh, and the Turkish Republic of Northern Cyprus. Nagorno Karabakh is the part of Azerbaijan Republic. Lacking the economic and political importance of Taiwan, these nations tend to be much more diplomatically isolated. Though used as a factor in judging sovereignty, Article 3 of the Montevideo Convention states, "The political existence of the state is independent of recognition by other states."

Informal Diplomacy

Informal diplomacy (sometimes called Track II diplomacy) has been used for centuries to communicate between powers. Most diplomats work to recruit figures in other nations who might be able to give informal access to a country's leadership. In some situations, such as between the United States and the People's Republic of China a large amount of diplomacy is done through semi-formal channels using interlocutors such as academic members of thinktanks. This occurs in situations where governments wish to express intentions or to suggest methods of resolving a diplomatic situation, but do not wish to express a formal position. Track II diplomacy is a specific kind of informal diplomacy, in which non-officials (academic scholars, retired civil and military officials, public figures, social activists) engage in dialogue, with the aim of conflict resolution, or confidence-building. Sometimes governments may fund such Track II exchanges. Sometimes the exchanges may have no connection at all with governments, or may even act in defiance of governments; such exchanges are called Track III.

POLITICAL FREEDOM

Political freedom is the right, or the capacity, of self-determination as an expression of the individual will.

Types

The concept of political freedom is closely allied with the concepts of civil liberties and human rights. Most democratic societies are characterized by various freedoms which are afforded the legal protection of the state. Some of these freedoms include (in alphabetical order):

- Freedom of assembly

- Freedom of association
- Freedom from government sanctioned discrimination
- Freedom of education
- Freedom of movement (or travel)
- Freedom of the press
- Freedom of religion (or belief)
- Freedom of speech
- Freedom of thought.

Views

Various groups along the political spectrum naturally differ on what they believe constitutes "true" political freedom. Friedrich Hayek famously noted that "liberty" and "freedom" have probably been the most abused words in recent history.

In libertarianism, freedom is defined in terms of interference with the individual pursuit of happiness either by government or other persons, where interference is defined as unreasonably preventing others from realising their will in their chosen course of action or in their use of things. Contrary to popular belief, libertarians are not pro-business. Rather, they simply oppose interference in any consenting acts between adults, including capitalist acts. Generally businesses favour regulations that protect them from competition, which requires many restrictions on consenting capitalist acts between adults. Libertarians call for freedom from coercion, governmental and civilian, in social, political, and economic matters. On the other hand, those on the political left place more emphasis on freedom as the ability of the individual to realize one's own potential and pursuit of happiness. Freedom in this sense may include freedom from want, poverty, deprivation, or oppression.

Many anarchists with the exception of individualist anarchists, anarcho-capitalists, and particularly anarchists that don't qualify their type of anarchism see negative and positive liberty as complementary concepts of freedom. Anarchists that recognize the concepts of negative and positive liberty tend to be left-leaning anarchists such as communist anarchists. Some treat freedom as if it were almost synonymous with democracy, while others see conflicts or even opposition between the two concepts. E.g. some argue that Iraq was free under Paul Bremer, because it was a rational, humanist, non-subjugating government, long before elections were held. While some thought that Iraq was free under Saddam because Iraq was not a colony.

Environmentalists often argue that political freedoms should include some social constraint on use of ecosystems. They maintain there is no such thing, for instance, as "freedom to pollute" or "freedom to deforest" given the downstream consequences. The popularity of SUVs, golf, and urban sprawl has been used as evidence that some ideas of freedom and ecological conservation can clash. This leads at times to serious confrontations and clashes of values reflected in advertising campaigns, e.g. that of PETA regarding fur. There have been numerous philosophical debates over the nature of freedom, the claimed differences between various types of freedom, and the extent to which freedom is desirable. Determinists argue that all human actions are predetermined and thus freedom is an illusion. Isaiah Berlin saw a distinction between negative liberty and positive liberty. In jurisprudence, freedom is the right to autonomously determine one's own actions; generally it is granted in those fields in which the subject has no obligations to fulfil or laws to obey, according to the interpretation that the hypothetical natural unlimited freedom is limited by the law for some matters.

Recent Trends

In modern times the expansion of "freedom" around the world is considered by some to be synonymous with increased participation in democratic political systems. In the 20th Century, the world observed a great reverse in terms of political situation, since the revolutionary struggles in areas of the world suddenly succeeded in establishing freedom from foreign colonialists and domination, at least in places like Africa, even though others may argue that the Cold War caused most of these new states to become puppet states for various regimes such as in Latin America, Africa, and Asia.

FREEDOM OF ASSEMBLY

Freedom of assembly is the freedom to associate with, or organize any groups, gatherings, clubs, or organizations that one wishes. It is held to be a key right in liberal democracies, whereby citizens may form or join any political party, special interest group, or union without government restrictions. In legal systems without freedom of assembly, certain political parties or groups can be banned with harsh penalties for any members. Public protests against the government are usually banned as well.

Tiered Rights

In legal or political systems where rights tend to be ranked in a hierarchy, or "tiered", such that some rights are considered more worthy of protection by the state than others, freedom of assembly is generally located on the top tier. However, the very concept of assigning relative value to rights by way of tiers tends to be controversial. Those who consider the right of assembly to exist on the "top" tier will sometimes concede that the state may legitimately ban groups which support terrorism or violence. This makes freedom of assembly closely linked with notions of freedom of speech. Thus, while one can be allowed to advocate the murder of the President, one is not necessarily allowed to be a member of a group that seeks to achieve this goal. The freedom of assembly in order to protest sometimes conflicts with laws intended to protect public safety, even in democratic countries: in many cities, the police are authorized by law to disperse any crowd (including a crowd of political protesters) which threatens public safety, or which the police cannot control.

The idea is to prevent rioting. Often local law requires that a permit must be obtained in advance by protest organizers if a protest march is anticipated; the permit application can be denied. Sometimes this bureaucratic power is abused by lawmakers if the protest is not a popular one in the community or with the local government, with the permit process in some cities taking a great deal of time, organization, and even money required before a permit is issued --and then, when issued, time and location restrictions are sometimes added. From time to time, local permit laws collide in court with the freedoms of assembly and of speech, such as in February 2003 when protests were anticipated over the exclusion of women from membership at the Augusta National Golf Club where golf's Masters Tournament is played every year.

The Richmond County, Georgia county commission implemented a new rule requiring 20 days of advance notice before a protest, and giving the county sheriff the power to approve or deny permits, and to dictate the location of demonstrations. The sheriff turned down a permit to protest in front of the golf club but approved a protest half a mile away. Two courts upheld the ordinance granting the sheriff this power.

FREEDOM OF ASSOCIATION

Freedom of association is a Constitutional (legal) concept based on the premise that it is the right of free adults to mutually choose their associates for whatever purpose they see fit. This concept has been included in several national constitutions, including the United States Constitution, the European Convention on Human Rights, and Canada's Charter of Rights.

United States

While the United States Constitution's First Amendment identifies the rights to assemble and to petition the government, the text of the First Amendment itself does not make specific mention of a right to association. Nevertheless, the United States Supreme Court has held that the freedom of association is an essential part of the Freedom of Speech because, in many cases, people can only engage in effective speech when they join together with others. The Supreme Court has found the Constitution to protect the freedom of association in two cases:

1. *Intimate Associations:* A fundamental element of personal liberty is the right to choose to enter into and maintain certain intimate human relationships. These intimate human relationships are known as "intimate associations." The paradigmatic "intimate association" is the family.
2. *Expressive Associations:* Expressive associations are groups that engage in activities protected by the First Amendment-speech, assembly, petitioning government for a redress of grievances, and the free exercise of religion. Because the role of these relationships is central to safeguarding individual freedoms, they may receive protection from undue intrusion by the State. Thus, there is a constitutional freedom to associate as a means of preserving other individual liberties.

Limitation

However, the implicit First Amendment right of association is not a general right of association. For example, it is illegal in the United States to consider race in the making and enforcement of private contracts other than marriage or taking affirmative action. This limitation of freedom of association results from Section 1981 of Title 42 of the Civil Rights Act, as weighed against the First Amendment according to the court decision Runyon v. McCrary, 427 U.S. 160 (1976).

The holding of Runyon is that the defendant private schools were free to express and teach their views, such as white separatism, but could not discriminate on the basis of race in the provision of services to the general public. So if the plaintiff African-American children wished to attend such private schools, and were clearly qualified in all respects (but race) and were able to pay the fees, and were willing to attend despite the fact that the schools strongly disliked them, then the schools were required by Section 1981 to admit them. The general rule to be drawn from this is that the First Amendment protects the right to express, including expression of racial discrimination, but people may not practice such ideas even within private associations. This doctrine rests on the interpretation of a private contract as a "badge" of slavery when either party considers race in choosing the other. The phrase "badges... of slavery" is from the Circuit Court decision 109 U.S. 3 (1883) upholding the power of Congress to pass laws under the Thirteenth Amendment to the United States Constitution compensating for the legacy of slavery.

Libertarian

Freedom of association is a term popular in libertarian literature. It is used to describe the concept of absolute freedom to live in a community or be part of an organization whose values or culture are closely related to what one wants; or on a more basic level, to associate with any individual one chooses. The right-libertarian (or "free market capitalist," "minarchist") concept of freedom of association is often rebuked from a moral/ethical context. Under laws in such a system, businessowners could refuse custom to anyone for whatever reason. Opponents argue that such practices are regressive and would lead to greater prejudice within society. Those right-libertarians sympathetic to freedom of association, such as Richard Epstein, in a case of refusing service, a case of the freedom of contract, respond that unjustified discrimination incurs a cost and therefore a competitive disadvantage.

Workers' Freedom of Association

To most of the world, the freedom of association is a right identified under international labor standards as the right of workers' to organize and collectively bargain. The freedom of association is recognized as a fundamental human right by a number of human rights documents, including the Universal Declaration of Human Rights and International Labor Organization Convention C87 and Convention C98 --two of the eight fundamental, core international labor standards.

CHAPTER

2 POLITICAL PHILOSOPHY

Political philosophy is the study of fundamental questions about the state, government, politics, liberty, justice, property, rights, law and the enforcement of a legal code by authority: what they are, why (or even if) they are needed, what makes a government legitimate, what rights and freedoms it should protect and why, what form it should take and why, what the law is, and what duties citizens owe to a legitimate government, if any, and when it may be legitimately overthrown-if ever. In a vernacular sense, the term "political philosophy" often refers to a general view, or specific ethic, belief or attitude, about politics that does not necessarily belong to the technical discipline of philosophy. Three central concerns of political philosophy have been the political economy by which property rights are defined and access to capital is regulated, the demands of justice in distribution and punishment, and the rules of truth and evidence that determine judgments in the law.

HISTORY OF POLITICAL PHILOSOPHY

Ancient Period

As an academic discipline, Western political philosophy has its origins in ancient Greek society, when city-states were experimenting with various forms of political organization including monarchy, tyranny, aristocracy, oligarchy, and democracy. The first classic work of political philosophy is Plato's The Republic, which was followed by Aristotle's Politics. Roman political philosophy was influenced by the Stoics, and the Roman statesman Cicero wrote on political philosophy. Independently, Confucius, Mencius, Mozi and the Legalist school in China, and the Laws of Manu and Chanakya and in India, all sought to find means of restoring political unity and stability; in the case of the former three through the cultivation of virtue, in the last by imposition of discipline. In India, Kautilya, in his Arthashastra, developed a viewpoint which recalls both the Legalists and Machiavelli. Ancient Chinese and Indian civilization resembled Greek in that there was a unified culture divided into rival states. In the case of China, philosophers found themselves obliged to confront social and political breakdown, and seek solutions to the crisis that confronted their entire civilization.

The early Christian philosophy of Augustine of Hippo was by and large rewrite of Plato in a Christian context. The main change that Christian thought brought was to moderate the

Stoicism and theory of justice of the Roman world, and emphasize the role of the state in applying mercy as a moral example. Augustine also preached that one was not a member of his or her city, but was a citizen of the City of God. Augustine's The City of God is an influential work of this period that refuted the thesis, after the First Sack of Rome, that the Christian view could be realized on Earth at all -a view many Christian Romans held.

Islamic Period

The rise of Islam, based on both the Qur'an and Muhammad strongly altered the power balances and perceptions of origin of power in the Mediterranean region. Early Muslim philosophy emphasized an inexorable link between science and religion, and the process of ijtihad to find truth -in effect all philosophy was "political" as it had real implications for governance. This view was challenged by the Mutazilite philosophers, who held a more Greek view and were supported by secular aristocracy who sought freedom of action independent of the mosque. By the medieval period, however, the Asharite view of Islam had in general triumphed. Islam was widely exposed to the writings of both Plato and Aristotle, however the main political writing from the Greeks that Islam encountered was Plato's Republic. The West and Christianity were exposed to both the Republic and Aristotle's Politics. Many credit this as to why the Middle East and the West developed differently "politically speaking".

Islamic "political philosophy", was, indeed, rooted in the very sources of Islam i.e. the Qur'an and the Sunna, the words and practices of the Prophet. However, in the Western thought, it is generally known that it was a specific area peculiar merely to the great philosophers of Islam: Kindi, Farabi, Ibni Sina, Ibn-i Bacce and Ibni Rusd. So, the political conceptions of Islam such as kudrah, sultan, ummah, cemaa -and even the "core" terms of the Qur'an, i.e. ibada, din, rab and ilah-should be taken as the very basis of an analysis. Hence, not only the ideas of the "Muslim political philosophers" but also many other "jurists" and "ulama" posed "political" ideas and even "theories." For example, the ideas of Hawarij in the very early years of Islamic history on Hilafa and Ummah, or that of Shia on the concept of Imamah deserve to be named as the proofs of "political" thought. In fact, the clashes between the Ehl-i Sunna and Shia in VII. and VIII. centuries had a genuine political character. Muslim "political philosophy" did not ceased in the classical period. Despite the fluctuations in its original character during the medieval period, it has lasted even in the modern era. Especially with the emergence of "Islamic radicalism" as a "political" movement, political thought has revived in Muslim world. The political ideas of Abduh, Afgani, Kutub, Mawdudi, Shariati and Khomeini has caught on an ethusiasm in especially Muslim youth in 20th century.

Medieval Period

Medieval political philosophy in Europe was heavily influenced by Christian thinking. It had much in common with the Islamic thinking in that the Roman Catholics also subordinated philosophy to theology. Perhaps the most influential political philosopher of the medieval period was St. Thomas Aquinas who helped reintroduce Aristotle's works, which had been preserved in the interim only by the Muslims. Aquinas's use of them set the agenda for scholastic political philosophy, and dominated European thought for centuries. The most influential work, however, was that which ended this period, that being Niccolò Machiavelli's The Prince, 1532. It is that work, and The Discourses, a rigorous analysis of the classical period, from which modern political philosophy is largely derived. Machiavelli was a republican, although he is falsely identified as the founder of a much harsher view of politics.

ENLIGHTENMENT PERIOD

During the Enlightenment period, new theories about what the human is and reality, along with the discovery of other societies in the Americas, and the changing needs of political societies (especially in the wake of the English Civil War, the American Revolution and the French Revolution) led to new questions and insights by such thinkers as Jean-Jacques Rousseau, Thomas Hobbes, Montesquieu and John Locke -known by most for his influential theory of the social contract. These theorists were driven by two basic questions: by what right or need do people form "states," and what is the best form for a "state." These large questions involved a conceptual distinction between "state" and "government." Basically, "state" refers to a set of enduring institutions through which power is distributed and its use justified. "Government" refers to a specific group of people who occupy these institutions, and exercise particular policies. This conceptual distinction continues to operate in political science, although some political scientists, philosophers, historians and cultural anthropologists have argued that most political action in any given society occurs outside of its state, and that there are societies that are not organized into states which nevertheless must be considered politically.

Political and economic relations were drastically changed by these views as the guild was subordinated to free trade, and Roman Catholic dominance of theology was increasingly challenged by Protestant churches subordinate to each nation-state and which preached in the "vulgar" or native language of each region. In the Ottoman Empire, these reforms did not take place and these views did not spread until much later. Also, there was no contact with the New World and the advanced civilizations of the Aztec, Maya, Inca, Mohican, Delaware, Huron and especially the Iroquois, who gave a great boost to Christian thought and in many cases actually inspired some of the institutions adopted in the United States: for example, Benjamin Franklin was a great admirer of some of the methods of the Iroquois Confederacy, and much of early American literature emphasized the political philosophy of the natives.

INDUSTRIALIZATION AND THE EARLY MODERN AGE

The industrial revolution produced a parallel revolution in political thought. Urbanization and capitalism greatly reshaped society. During this same period, the socialist movement began to form. In the mid-19th century, Marxism was developed, and socialism in general gained increasing popular support, mostly from the urban working class. By the late 19th century, socialism and trade unions were established members of the political landscape. In addition, the various branches of anarchism and syndicalism also gained some prominence. In the Anglo-

American world, anti-imperialism and pluralism began gaining currency at the turn of the century. World War I was a watershed event in human history. The Russian Revolution of 1917 (and similar, albeit less successful, revolutions in many other European countries) brought communism -and in particular the political theory of Leninism, but also on a smaller level Luxembourgism (gradually) -on the world stage. At the same time, social democratic parties won elections and formed governments for the first time, often as a result of the introduction of universal suffrage. In response to the sweeping social changes that occurred in the years after the war, ultra-reactionary ideologies such as fascism began to take shape. In particular, the rise of the Nazis in Germany would later lead to the Second World War.

All political thought was deeply affected by the Great Depression, which led many theorists to reconsider the ideas they had previously held as axiomatic. In the United States, President Franklin D. Roosevelt introduced the New Deal. In Europe, both the extreme left and the extreme right gained increasing popularity.

CONTEMPORARY POLITICAL PHILOSOPHY

After World War II political philosophy moved into a temporary eclipse in the Anglo-American academic world, as analytic philosophers expressed skepticism about the possibility that normative judgments had cognitive content, and political science turned toward statistical methods and behavioralism. The 1950s saw pronouncements of the 'death' of the discipline, followed by debates about that thesis. A handful of continental European emigres to Britain and the United States-including Hannah Arendt, Karl Popper, Friedrich Hayek, Leo Strauss, Isaiah Berlin, Eric Voegelin and Judith Shklar-encouraged continued study in the field, but in the 1950s and 60s they and their students remained somewhat marginal in their disciplines. Communism remained an important focus especially during the 1950s and 60s. Zionism, racism and colonialism were important issues that arose. In general, there was a marked trend towards a pragmatic approach to political issues, rather than a philosophical one. Much academic debate regarded one or both of two pragmatic topics: how (or whether) to apply utilitarianism to problems of political policy, or how (or whether) to apply economic models (such as rational choice theory) to political issues. The rise of feminism and the end of colonial rule and of the political exclusion of such minorities as African Americans in the developed world has led to feminist, postcolonial, and multicultural thought becoming significant.

In Anglo-American academic political philosophy the publication of John Rawls's A Theory of Justice in 1971 is considered a milestone. Rawls used a thought experiment, the original position, in which representative parties choose principles of justice for the basic structure of society from behind a veil of ignorance. Rawls also offered a criticism of utilitarian approaches to questions of political justice. Robert Nozick's book Anarchy, State, and Utopia (1974) responded to Rawls from a libertarian perspective. Contemporary with analytic ethics-oriented work in Anglo-American thought, within Europe several new lines of philosophy directed at critique of existing societies arose between the 1950s and 1980s. Many of these took elements of Marxist economic analysis, but combined them with a more cultural or ideological emphasis. Out of the

Frankfurt School, thinkers like Herbert Marcuse, Theodor W. Adorno, Max Horkheimer, and Jürgen Habermas combined Marxian and Freudian perspectives. Along somewhat different lines, a number of other continental thinkers-still largely influenced by Marxism-put new emphases on structuralism and on a "return to Hegel". Within the (post-) structuralist line (though mostly not taking that label) are thinkers such as Gilles Deleuze, Michel Foucault, Claude Lefort, and Jean Baudrillard. The Situationists were more influenced by Hegel; Guy Debord, in particular, moved a Marxist analysis of commodity fetishism to the realm of consumption, and looked at the relation between consumerism and dominant ideology formation. Another debate developed around the (distinct) criticisms of liberal political theory made by Bernard Williams and Charles Taylor. The liberalism-communitarianism debate is often considered valuable for generating a new set of philosophical problems, rather than a profound and illuminating clash of perspectives. Today some debates regarding punishment and law center on the question of natural law and the degree to which human constraints on action are determined by nature, as revealed by science in particular. Other debates focus on questions of cultural and gender identity as central to politics.

INFLUENTIAL POLITICAL PHILOSOPHERS

A larger list of political philosophers is intended to be closer to exhaustive. Listed below are a few of the most canonical or important thinkers, and especially philosophers whose central focus was in political philosophy and/or who are good representatives of a particular school of thought.

- *Confucius:* The first thinker to relate ethics to the political order.
- *Chanakya:* Founder of an independent political thought in India, laid down rules and guidelines for social, law and political order in society.
- *Mozi:* Eponymous founder of the Mohist school, advocated a strict utilitarianism.
- *Socrates/Plato:* Named their practice of inquiry "philosophy", and thereby stand at the head of a prominent (often called "Western") tradition of systematic intellectual analysis. Set as a partial basis to that tradition the relation between knowledge on the one hand, and a just and good society on the other. Socrates is widely considered founder of Western political philosophy, via his spoken influence on Athenian contemporaries; since Socrates never wrote anything, much of what we know about him and his teachings comes through his most famous student, Plato.
- *Aristotle:* Wrote his Politics as an extension of his Nicomachean Ethics. Notable for the theories that humans are social animals, and that the polis (Ancient Greek city state) existed to bring about the good life appropriate to such animals. His political theory is based upon an ethics of perfectionism (as is Marx's, on some readings).
- *Mencius:* One of the most important thinkers in the Confucian school, he is the first theorist to make a coherent argument for an obligation of rulers to the ruled.
- *Han Feizi:* The major figure of the Chinese Fajia (Legalist) school, advocated government that adhered to laws and a strict method of administration.

- *Niccolò Machiavelli:* First systematic analyses of: (1) how consent of a populace is negotiated between and among rulers rather than simply a naturalistic (or theological) given of the structure of society; (2) precursor to the concept of ideology in articulating the epistemological structure of commands and law.
- *Thomas Hobbes:* Generally considered to have first articulated how the concept of a social contract that justifies the actions of rulers (even where contrary to the individual desires of governed citizens), can be reconciled with a conception of sovereignty.
- *Baruch Spinoza:* Set forth the first analysis of "rational egoism" in which the rational interest of self is conformance with pure reason. To Spinoza's thinking, in a society in which each individual is guided of reason, political authority would be superfluous.
- *John Locke:* Like Hobbes, described a social contract theory based on citizens' fundamental rights in the state of nature. He departed from Hobbes in that, based on the assumption of a society in which moral values are independent of governmental authority and widely shared, he argued for a government with power limited to the protection of personal property. His arguments may have been deeply influential to the formation of the United States Constitution.
- *Baron de Montesquieu:* Analyzed protection of liberty by a "balance of powers" in the divisions of a state.
- *David Hume:* Hume criticized the social contract theory of John Locke and others as resting on a myth of some actual agreement. Hume was a realist in recognizing the role of force to forge the existence of states and that consent of the governed was merely hypothetical.
- *Jean-Jacques Rousseau:* Analyzed the social contract as an expression of the general will, and controversially argued in favor of absolute democracy where the people at large would act as sovereign.
- *Immanuel Kant:* Argued that participation in civil society is undertaken not for self-preservation, as per Thomas Hobbes, but as a moral duty. First modern thinker who fully analyzed structure and meaning of obligation. Argued that an international organization was needed to preserve world peace.
- *Adam Smith:* Often said to have founded modern economics; explained emergence of economic benefits from the self-interested behavior ("the hidden hand") of artisans and traders. While praising its efficiency, Smith also expressed concern about the effects of industrial labor (e.g. repetitive activity) on workers. His work on moral sentiments sought to explain social bonds outside the economic sphere.
- *Edmund Burke:* Irish member of the British parliament, Burke is credited with the creation of conservative thought. Burke's Reflections on the Revolution in France is the most popular of his writings where he denounced the French revolution. Burke was one of the biggest supporters of the American Revolution.
- *John Adams:* Enlightenment writer who defended the American cause for independence. Adams was a Lockean thinker, who was appalled by the French revolution. Adams is

known for his outspoken commentary in favor of the American revolution. He defended the American form of republicanism over the French liberal democracy. Adams is considered the founder of American conservative thought.

- *Thomas Paine:* Enlightenment writer who defended liberal democracy, the American Revolution, and French Revolution in Common Sense and The Rights of Man.
- *Jeremy Bentham:* The first thinker to analyze social justice in terms of maximization of aggregate individual benefits. Founded the philosophical/ethical school of thought known as utilitarianism.
- *John Stuart Mill:* A utilitarian, and the person who named the system; he goes further than Bentham by laying the foundation for liberal democratic thought in general and modern, as opposed to classical, liberalism in particular. Articulated the place of invididual liberty in an otherwise utilitarian framework.
- *Karl Marx:* In large part, added the historical dimension to an understanding of society, culture and economics. Created the concept of ideology in the sense of (true or false) beliefs that shape and control social actions. Analyzed the fundamental nature of class as a mechanism of governance and social interaction.
- *John Dewey:* Co-founder of pragmatism and analyzed the essential role of education in the maintenance of democratic government.
- *Antonio Gramsci:* Instigated the concepts hegemony and social formation. Fused the ideas of Marx, Engels, Spinoza and others within the so-called dominant ideology thesis (the ruling ideas of society are the ideas of its rulers).
- *Herbert Marcuse:* One of the principle thinkers within the Frankfurt School, and generally important in efforts to fuse the thought of Freud and Marx. Introduced the concept of repressive desublimation, in which social control can operate not only by direct control, but also by manipulation of desire. Analyzed the role of advertising and propaganda in societal consensus.
- *Friedrich Hayek:* Advanced an analysis under which any collectivism could only be maintained by a central authority. Advocated free-market capitalism in which the sole role of the state was to maintain the rule of law.
- *Hannah Arendt:* Analyzed the roots of totalitarianism and introduced the concept of the "banality of evil" (how ordinary technocratic rationality comes to deplorable fruition). Brought distinctive elements of and revisions to the philosophy of Martin Heidegger into political thought.
- *Leo Strauss:* Strauss is known for his writings on the classical and modernity philosophers and denouncement of the modern politics.
- *John Rawls:* Revitalised the study of normative political philosophy in Anglo-American universities with his 1971 book A Theory of Justice, which uses a version of social contract theory to answer fundamental questions about justice and to criticise utilitarianism.

- *Robert Nozick:* Criticized Rawls, and argued for Libertarianism, by appeal to a hypothetical history of the state and the real history of property.

BUREAUCRATIC POLITICS

Bureaucratic politics theories or explanations of why particular public policy decisions got made the way they did stress the motivation by the relevant officials in the government bureaucracy to protect or promote their own agency's special interests (in competition with other agencies) as a major motivating factor in shaping the timing and the content of government decisions. Each bureau (or other governmental sub-division) continually strives to maximize its budget and its authorized manpower, as well as to protect or extend its operating autonomy and discretion in decision-making in the area of its assigned responsibilities. Often this can be most readily accomplished by lobbying for an expansion of the scope of the bureau's responsibilities that are prescribed by Congress or the legislature. Because bureaucratic agencies are in competition with each other for budget shares and for personnel allocations as well as for gaining responsibility for juicy new programs justifying expansion, the policies and policy recommendations generated in the executive branch of the government and passed on to both the chief executive and the legislative authorities are often better understood as the by-product of bureaucratic turf-battles and expedient compromises between bureaucratic chieftains than as the product of reasoned analysis of how most effectively and efficiently to carry out the policy commitments of the elected chief executive or to serve the public interest.

BUREAUCRACY

In ordinary usage, "bureaucracy" refers to a complex, specialized organization (especially a governmental organization) composed of non-elected, highly trained professional administrators and clerks hired on a full-time basis to perform administrative services and tasks. Bureaucratic organizations are broken up into specialized departments or ministries, to each of which is assigned responsibility for pursuing a limited number of the government's many official goals and policies -those falling within a single relatively narrow functional domain. The departments or ministries are subdivided into divisions that are each assigned even more specialized responsibilities for accomplishing various portions or aspects of the department's overall tasks, and these divisions are in turn composed of multiple agencies or bureaus with even more minutely specialized functions (and their own subdivisions). Bureaucratic organizations always rely heavily on the principle of hierarchy and rank, which requires a clear, unambiguous chain of command through which "higher" officials supervise the "lower" officials, who of course supervise their own subordinate administrators within the various subdivisions and sub-subdivisions of the organization.

Bureaucratic organizations are typically charcterized by great attention to the precise and stable delineation of authority or jurisdiction among the various subdivisions and among the officials who comprise them, which is done mainly by requiring the organization's employees to operate strictly according to fixed procedures and detailed rules designed to routinize nearly all decision-making. Some of the most important of these rules and procedures may be specified in laws or decrees enacted by the higher "political" authorities that are empowered to set the official goals and general policies for the organization, but upper-level (and even medium-level) bureaucrats typically are delegated considerable discretionary powers for elaborating their own detailed rules and procedures. Because the incentive structures of bureaucratic organizations largely involve rewarding strict adherence to formal rules and punishing unauthorized departures from standard operating procedures (rather than focussing on measureable individual contributions toward actually attaining the organization's politically assigned goals), such organizations tend to rely very heavily upon extensive written records and standardized forms, which serve primarily to document the fact that all decisions about individual "cases" were taken in accordance with approved guidelines and procedures rather than merely reflecting the personal preferences or subjective judgment of the individual bureaucrat involved.

The classic social scientific analysis of bureaucracy was that of the pioneer sociologist Max Weber in his 1922 book Economy and Society. Weber, like the good German he was, believed that a permanent, well-educated, conscientious, "non-partisan," Prussian-style bureaucracy professionally committed to implementing whatever decisions the legitimate rulers of the state might arrive at was the best organizational form yet discovered for the rational and efficient pursuit of collective social goals in a modern society with a specialized and highly complex division of labor. In his writings, Weber devoted considerable attention to showing ways in which the gradual evolution of modern bureaucratic methods and values helped to remove the formidable obstacles to economic development, social advancement and political stability that had been inherent in the much less professionalized and systematized practices of government administration in feudal Europe and most other premodern societies.

While most other social scientific students of bureaucracy have recognized the historical importance of bureaucratic organizational techniques in creating the powerful, centralized nation-states (and other very large organizations such as modern business corporations and labor unions) that predominate in the industrialized world of the 20th century, it is fair to say that they have generally been considerably less one-sidedly approving of bureaucracy than Weber was. Despite their many advantages for dealing efficiently and effectively with routine, recurring problems in a fairly stable and predictable environment, bureaucratic methods also have their dark side. Hired and promoted largely on the basis of educational credentials and seniority within the organization and protected by civil service personnel practices designed to provide a high degree of job security, bureaucratic officials tend to be very well insulated from responsibility for the external consequences of their decisions and actions as long as they stay formally within prescribed procedures. Such sociologists as Robert K. Merton and Michel Crozier have shown that pressures on officials to conform to fixed rules and detailed procedures, when added to the narrow responsibilities of highly specialized agencies for pursuing only a select few of the many objectives that government has set, quite regularly leads bureaucrats to become defensive, rigid, and completely unresponsive to the urgent individual needs and concerns of the private citizens and outside organizations with which they come into professional contact. ("That's not my department. I cannot help you.")

Because the salaries and promotion prospects of officials working in large bureaucracies seldom depend upon measurable success or efficiency by the organization in achieving its larger goals (which are often especially difficult to measure in government agencies and other non-profit oriented organizations that lack a clear "bottom line") and because any departure from established routines always requires permission from remote higher levels of the hierarchy, large bureaucratic organizations tend to be very slow and cumbersome in making important policy decisions (the "buck-passing" phenomenon) and are especially dull-witted in recognizing and responding to the consequences of major changes in economic, social and technological conditions and circumstances outside the organization itself. In other words, individual officials working under bureaucratic incentive systems frequently find it to be in their own best interests to adhere rigidly to internal rules and formalities in a ritualistic fashion, behaving as if "proper procedure" were more important than the larger goals for serving their clients or the general public that they are supposedly designed to accomplish (the "red tape" phenomenon).

INCENTIVE

Something that provides a motive for a person to choose a particular course of action. Organized cooperative activities in a social setting --such as cooperation for the purpose of economic production --depends upon each of the participants having some sort of incentive to behave in the required cooperative fashion. Different societies (and even different organizations within the same society) vary considerably in the nature of the incentive systems upon which they characteristically rely to organize their common projects. Incentives may be classified according to a number of different schemes, but one of the more useful classifications subdivides incentives into three general types: moral incentives, coercive incentives and remunerative incentives.

- A person has a moral incentive to behave in a particular way when he has been taught to believe that it is the "right" or "proper" or "admirable" thing to do. If he behaves as others expect him to, he may expect the approval or even the admiration of the other members of the collectivity and enjoy an enhanced sense of acceptance or self-esteem. If he behaves improperly, he may expect verbal expressions of condemnation, scorn, ridicule or even ostracism from the collectivity, and he may experience unpleasant feelings of guilt, shame or self-condemnation.
- A person has a coercive incentive to behave in a particular way when it has been made known to him that failure to do so will result in some form of physical aggression being directed at him by other members of the collectivity in the form of inflicting pain or physical harm on him or his loved ones, depriving him of his freedom of movement, or perhaps confiscating or destroying his treasured possessions.
- A person has a remunerative incentive to behave in a particular way if it has been made known to him that doing so will result in some form of material reward he will not otherwise receive. If he behaves as desired, he will receive some specified amount of a valuable good or service (or money with which he can purchase whatever he wishes) in exchange.

All known societies employ all three sorts of incentives to at least some degree in order to evoke from its members the necessary degree of cooperation for the society to survive and flourish. However, different societies differ radically in the relative proportions of these different kinds of incentives used within their characteristic mix of incentives. "Primitive" or "traditional" cultures such as those of hunter-gatherers tend to rely very heavily on moral incentives and make relatively little use of coercive and remunerative incentives to sustain social cooperation. More "advanced" or "modern" societies built around a much more specialized and complex division of labor tend to make much greater use of both coercive and remunerative incentives in organizing social activities, while still relying in very important ways upon moral or normative incentives. Among the more "advanced" societies, liberal societies try to rely as much as possible on remunerative and moral incentives in preference to the use of coercive incentives, while authoritarian and totalitarian societies display much less reluctance to resort to coercive incentives in securing social cooperation.

STATE

1. A specialized type of political organization characterized by a full-time, specialized, professional work force of tax-collectors, soldiers, policemen, bureaucrats and the like that exercises supreme political authority over a defined territory with a permanent population, independent from any enduring external political control and possessing a local predominance of coercive power (always supplemented with moral and remunerative incentives as well) great enough to maintain general obedience to its laws or commands within its territorial borders. The first known states were created in ancient times in Egypt, Mesopotamia, India, China, Mexico and Peru, but it is only in relatively modern times that states have almost completely displaced alternative "stateless" forms of political organization of societies all over the planet. (Roving bands of hunter-gatherers and even fairly sizable and complex tribal societies based on herding or agriculture have existed without any full-time specialized state organization, and these "stateless" forms of political organization have in fact prevailed for all of the prehistory and much of the history of the human species.)
2. One of the component territorial political units in a larger federal state that are so called because, although they actually fall short of full independent statehood or sovereignty, they still possess a very large degree of autonomy in decision-making with respect to most of their internal affairs and are thus also legally allowed to exercise various forms of coercion over their regional populations.

Nation State

A form of state in which those who exercise power claim legitimacy for their rule partly or solely on the grounds that their power is exercised for the promotion of the distinctive interests, values and cultural heritage of a particular nation whose members ideally would constitute all, or most of, its subject population and all of whom would dwell within the borders.

Nation

A large aggregation or agglomeration of people sharing a common and distinctive racial, linguistic, historical and/or cultural heritage that has led its members to think of themselves as belonging to a valued natural community sharing a common destiny that ought to be preserved forever.

Nationalism

An ideology, or rather a whole category of similar ideologies, based on the premise that each nation (or at least the ideologist's own nation) constitutes a natural political community whose members should all live together under the authority of "their own" independent nation state. When the people of one nation live in large numbers in a multi-ethnic state or in states with government(s) dominated by political elites drawn from another nationality, nationalism often becomes an ideology justifying rebellion or secession in order to create or recreate a nation state for the heretofore subjugated nation. When substantial numbers of people seen as belonging to the nation live outside the borders of their own nation state, nationalism often becomes an ideology justifying an aggressive foreign policy striving to expand the state's borders to include them. Nationalist ideologies usually claim that their respective nation possess special national characteristics or virtues that make them morally and intellectually superior to all other nations and should qualify their nation state for a special or privileged role in the world at large.

Ideology

A comprehensive and coherent set of basic beliefs about political, economic, social and cultural affairs that is held in common by a sizable group of people within a society. Such interrelated ideas and teachings purport both to explain how political, economic, social and cultural institutions really do work and also to prescribe how such institutions ought ideally to operate. Conservative ideologies seek to demonstrate a close correspondence between "the way things are" and "the way things ought to be," thus legitimizing the existing order in the eyes of those who can be convinced to believe in the ideology. Radical and revolutionary ideologies, on the other hand, set unconventional, higher, or even utopian standards with regard to what would constitute a legitimate and supportable social-economic-political system and then demonstrate in detail that the existing order does not even come close to meeting these standards, thereby de-legitimizing the existing system and helping mobilize believers in the ideology for concerted action to reform or overthrow the existing order. (In addition to their descriptive and prescriptive functions about existing and ideal social orders, ideologies may also include more specialized doctrines regarding the most suitable political strategies and tactics to be pursued by believers in their efforts to shore up or undermine the existing order.)

One useful way of categorizing ideologies from a political point of view focusses on differences in the ideologies' prescriptions for how much the government ought to be involved in directing or regulating economic, social and cultural affairs and how much individuals or voluntary organizations ought to be left alone to make their own (widely varied) decisions in these spheres of life. In this course, for example, we frequently employ a two-dimensional classification of ideologies proposed by Maddox and Lilie that is based on assessing people's preferences for government regulation versus non-regulation in:

1. Economic decisions
2. Non-economic or life-style decisions.

It should be noted that the term "ideology" often has a somewhat derogatory flavor, especially in Anglo-American societies, because it often carries the implication that "ideological" thought is unduly biased, dogmatic and distorted, an obstacle rather than an aid in perceiving how the world "really" works. ("You, sir, are an ideologue. I, on the other hand, am a pragmatic man of reason who sees things the way they really are.")

Legitimacy

The principle that indicates the acceptance of the decisions of government leaders and officials by (most of) the public on the grounds that these leaders' acquisition and exercise of power has been in accordance with the society's generally accepted procedures and political or moral values. Legitimacy may be conferred upon power holders in a variety of ways in different societies, usually involving solemn formal rituals of a religious or quasi-religious nature --royal birth and coronation in monarchies, popular election and "swearing in" in democracies and so on. "Legitimate" rulers typically require less use of physical coercion to enforce their decisions than rulers lacking in legitimacy, because most of the people are apt to feel a moral obligation to obey the former but not the latter. Consequently, people who gain or hold power by illegitimate means tend to work very hard to discover or create ways of endowing themselves with legitimacy after the fact, often by inventing a new ideology or religion and attempting to indoctrinate the people with its legitimating formulas through various forms of propaganda, thus creating moral incentives for the citizenry to obey their government.

Propaganda

Persuasive communications directed at a specific audience that are designed to influence the targeted audience's opinions, beliefs and emotions in such a way as to bring about specific, planned alterations in their behavior. The information communicated by the propagandist may be true or false, the values appealed to may be sincerely held by the propagandist or cynically manipulated, and the presentation may be either logically and dispassionately argued or rhetorically tailored to arouse the most irrational emotions and prejudices -but the message content of propaganda is always deliberately selected and slanted to lead the audience toward a predetermined mindset that benefits the cause of the propagandist.

Socialism

A class of ideologies favoring an economic system in which all or most productive resources are the property of the government, in which the production and distribution of goods and services are administered primarily by the government rather than by private enterprise, and in which any remaining private production and distribution (socialists differ on how much of this is tolerable) is heavily regulated by the government rather than by market processes. Both democratic and non-democratic socialists insist that the government they envision as running the economy must in principle be one that truly reflects the will of the masses of the population (or at least their "true" best interests), but of course they differ considerably in their ideas about what sorts of political institutions and practices are required to ensure this will be so. In practice, socialist economic principles may be combined with an extremely wide range of attitudes toward personal freedom, civil liberties, mass political participation, bureaucracy and political competition, ranging from Western European democratic socialism to the more authoritarian socialisms of many third world regimes to the totalitarian excesses of Soviet-style socialism or communism.

Communism

1. Any ideology based on the communal ownership of all property and a classless social structure, with economic production and distribution to be directed and regulated by means of an authoritative economic plan that supposedly embodies the interests of the community as a whole. Karl Marx is today the most famous early theoretician of communism, but he did not invent the term or the basic social ideals, which he mostly borrowed and adapted from the less systematic theories of earlier French utopian socialists --grafting these onto a philosophical framework Marx derived from the German philosophers Hegel and Feuerbach, while adding in a number of economic theories derived from his reinterpretation of the writings of such early political economists such as Adam Smith, Thomas Malthus, and David Ricardo. In most versions of the communist utopia, everyone would be expected to cooperate enthusiastically in the process of production, but the individual citizen's equal rights of access to consumer goods would be completely unaffected by his/her own individual contribution to production --hence Karl Marx's famous slogan "From each according to his ability; to each according to his need." The Marxian and other 19th century communist utopias also were expected to dispense with such "relics of the past" as trading, money, prices, wages, profits, interest, land-rent, calculations of profit and loss, contracts, banking, insurance, lawsuits, etc. It was expected that such a radical reordering of the economic sphere of life would also more or less rapidly lead to the elimination of all other major social problems such as class conflict, political oppression, racial discrimination, the inequality of the sexes, religious bigotry, and cultural backwardness-as well as put an end to such more "psychological" forms of suffering as alienation, anomie, and feelings of powerlessness.
2. The specifically Marxist-Leninist variant of socialism which emphasizes that a truly communist society can be achieved only through the violent overthrow of capitalism and the establishment of a "dictatorship of the proletariat" that is to prepare the way for the future idealized society of communism under the authoritarian guidance of a hierarchical and disciplined Communist Party.
3. A world-wide revolutionary political movement inspired by the October Revolution (Red Oktober) in Russia in 1917 and advocating the establishment everywhere of political, economic, and social institutions and policies modeled on those of the Soviet Union (or,

in some later versions, China or Albania) as a means for eventually attaining a communist society.

Capitalism

A form of economic order characterized by private ownership of the means of production and the freedom of private owners to use, buy and sell their property or services on the market at voluntarily agreed prices and terms, with only minimal interference with such transactions by the state or other authoritative third parties.

Market

In its original meaning, a physical coming together of a sizable number of merchants and prospective customers at a pre-arranged time and place (in medieval Europe, typically once a week on the main square of the largest village in the vicinity) for the purpose of striking deals to buy and sell a variety of goods and services. Large numbers of customers came to such organized markets because they found it convenient to be able to make many of their necessary purchases on the same day in one central location (minimizing their total travel time and other travel costs) and because the presence of many merchants offering similar wares made it much more practical to comparison shop for the best deals in terms of quality and price. Merchants were often attracted from considerable distances to participate in such markets because of the opportunity to sell so many of their wares to such large numbers of potential customers in such a short time. Modern day flea markets, farmers' markets, gun shows and crafts fairs are fairly close to the original concept.

In the language of modern industrial society, and especially in the language of professional economists, the concept of a market has been generalized and abstracted far beyond the original rather concrete and localized meaning of the term. In the more modern sense of the term, a market is the generalized name tag for the whole process that gets under way whenever a sizable number of people free to buy and/or sell a particular kind of good or service are in more or less close communication with each other (either personally and directly or else through the mediation of advertising, catalogs, news reports, postal carriers, telephone systems, computer networks, etc.) so that information about the terms of recent transactions and current offers to buy or sell is generally available to a large number of interested parties at relatively low cost--regardless of the participants' physical proximity or distance. Such technological innovations of the industrial age as ever cheaper and more rapid transportation and communications over increasing distances both have dramatically increased the size of the areas from which buyers and sellers may be brought together to do business and have greatly reduced the need for them actually to meet face-to-face in one place in order to strike a bargain. The markets for many consumers' durable goods like automobiles or TVs and major agricultural and industrial commodities like oil, natural gas, wheat, beef, steel, forest products and computer chips are now literally worldwide in extent. (Of course, for many markets there do still exist central gathering places or locations that play an especially important role in the local, national or even worldwide networks of buyers and sellers --for example, the New York Stock Exchange, the Chicago Commodities

Exchange, the seasonal women's fashions shows in Paris and Milan, regional baseball card collectors conventions and so on but in nearly all such cases, it is not really necessary for an individual buyer or seller actually to travel to the relevant marketplace in order to participate in the broader markets of which these are nowadays only a part.)

Where markets exist and are allowed to function reasonably freely, there are certain predictable consequences for the way the economy will operate. Elaboration of these consequences is the primary purpose of most of the research in the theoretical subfield of microeconomics.

MARKET ECONOMY

An economy in which scarce resources are all (or nearly all) allocated by the interplay of supply and demand in free markets, largely unhampered by government rationing, price-fixing or other coercive interference. In classifying real historical economies, the level of "marketization" is not primarily an either/or issue but rather a matter of degree. The greater the proportion of the goods and services produced in the society that are allocated by market processes (rather than by government edict or the operation of unchangeable custom), the more meaningful it is to refer to its economy as a market economy --and the more useful is the abstract economic theory of the operation of markets likely to be for understanding and even predicting economic behavior within that society. Probably the most critical single distinction between "basically market" and "basically non-market" (socialist, feudal, hunter-gatherer, etc.) economies is whether or not the determinations of what is to be produced and of the corresponding allocation of producers' goods (land, raw materials, machinery, and other "capital," as well as the services of labor) are accomplished primarily through free markets rather than primarily through government command or unalterable custom.

The concept of a market presupposes the existence of certain sorts of property relations in the society involved. At least some goods and services must be legally or socially regarded as alienable property --that is, there must be ascertainable individuals (or group representatives) who are recognized as having not just the right to use particular scarce economic resources for their own purposes but also the discretionary authority permanently to transfer such rights of use to someone else in exchange for some mutually agreeable quid pro quo, such as money or other goods or services. Not all human societies have recognized any such rights to transfer ownership, and most historical human societies have forbidden or placed stringent limits on the transferability of at least certain kinds of recognized property rights. In many societies (including most of Europe during the Middle Ages), individual or family rights to the perpetual use of particular plots of land were well established and protected by law --but such rights only rarely could legally be sold to someone else because the land was socially regarded as fundamentally the inalienable property of either the local community as a whole or of the tribe or clan or church or perhaps of the reigning royal family. And even in the USA since 1865, while each person's ownership of his or her own body is well established, the law will still not allow you to make a binding contract to sell yourself into slavery or even to auction off your spare bodily organs for purposes of a surgical transplant.)

It is worth noting for clarity's sake that the concept of a market does not logically presuppose the existence of "private property in the means of production" in the sense that private individuals or family households are the owners of land and capital and thus the recipients of profits, interest, rent etc. One may at least theoretically conceive of an economy of market socialism, in which workers' collectives, consumers' cooperatives, village communes or even autonomous state agencies leased from the state or held actual title to land, mines, factories, machinery and so forth --so long as the socialist production organizations were free to buy and sell their output and the use of their assigned land or capital assets to each other at freely negotiated prices responsive to conditions of supply and demand (assuming, of course, they are allowed to keep effective control of the bulk of the proceeds). There are, of course, both theoretical and practical problems with market socialism, and the costs and benefits of capitalist markets cannot be uncritically attributed to such a system. The larger point is that socialist economies have historically included varying proportions of "remnant" market elements in their make-up, and the theoretical possibilities for additional "hybrid" forms are numerous.

PROPERTY RIGHTS

A property right is the exclusive authority to determine how and by whom a particular resource is used. More broadly, property rights may be seen as a bundle of separate and distinct rights over a particular good -including at least the right of personal use, the right to demand compensation as a prerequisite for its use by other people, and the right to transfer any or all of these rights to others (either permanently by sale or temporarily through some form of contractual arrangement). Property rights may be exercised by governments through their designated officials (public ownership or public property) as well as by private individuals and other sorts of non-governmental organizations (private property).

Private Property Rights

The basic rights of individuals (and organizations or associations of people functioning as a single conglomerate "legal person" such as corporations, partnerships, churches, non-profit foundations, etc.) to the peaceful possession, control and enjoyment of the things they own as well as their rights to make contracts to rent, sell or give away all or part of their various ownership rights over these possessions (or these possessions' services) to any other people willing to accept the owners' terms. The possessions over which a person has property rights may be tangible (like real estate, factory machinery, livestock, automobiles or a jack-knife) or intangible (like contractual obligations to provide goods or services at some time in the future, shares of common stock in a corporation, bonds, insurance policies, the right to broadcast over a designated radio frequency, patents, trademarks and copyrights). In highly specialized societies, property rights over particular resources may be "unbundled" and parcelled out among many individuals according to quite complex rules of division of authority over particular aspects or uses of the resource specified in written contracts -for example, separating mineral rights from surface rights to a parcel of land, utility easements over the same land, restrictive deed covenants and so on.

Contract

A legally binding agreement between two or more competent parties fixing the precise terms and details for a voluntary exchange of goods or services over which the contracting parties possess property rights. An agreement is a legally enforceable contract if and only if:

1. The agreement must be "mutual" (all parties have the same understanding of the meaning of their agreement --there is a "meeting of the minds");
2. The agreement must be "voluntary" (none of the parties is agreeing under the influence of violent threats or fraudulent misrepresentation of the facts);
3. There must be actual "consideration" paid (that is, each party must be achieving a benefit by giving up something he controls to get something another party controls in exchange: a simple one-sided promise to give someone else a gratuitous benefit is not a contract);
4. All parties to the agreement must be "competent" (children and the severely mentally impaired or insane are assumed by the courts to be incapable of forming a coherent intent or determining their own best interests, so the courts will not enforce the agreements they make);
5. The substance of the agreement must not be "contrary to public policy" (for example, the U.S. courts will not enforce a contract that requires one or more of the parties to commit a crime, nor will they enforce a contract by which even a legally competent adult voluntarily sells himself into life-long slavery in exchange for, say, a ten million dollar payment to his children).

Factors of Production

The scarce resources that are useful not so much for direct and immediate satisfaction of human wants as for producing other goods or services. Economists often find it useful for purposes of theoretical simplification to group the millions of different sorts of factors of production into several very broad categories and then discuss them as though all the items within each category were perfectly substitutable for each other and therefore traded on a single market. The simplest such conventional categorization of the factors of production divides them into land, labor, capital, and sometimes also entrepreneurship and/or human capital.

Derived Demand

The demand for each of the factors of production is often referred to as a "derived" demand to emphasize the fact that the relationship between the factor's price and the quantity of the factor demanded by firms employing it in production is directly dependent on consumer demand for the final product(s) the factor is used to produce. If for some reason (say, for example, a spontaneous shift in consumer tastes) the demand for men's hats increases (shifts to the right) so that more hats than before can be sold at any given price, then the "derived" demand for felt used in making hats will also increase (shift to the right) so that felt-makers will be able to sell more felt at any given price. (We would also expect the hat-makers' demand for the labor of hatters and for specialized hat-making machinery to shift to the right in a similar fashion in response to the public's greater demand for hats.) What is the mechanism by which a shift in demand for the final product is translated into a shift in demand for the factors of production used in its manufacture? The key is the change in the price of the final product brought about by the shift in demand for it. If the demand curve for hats shifts to the right and the (upwardly sloping) supply curve remains unchanged, then the equilibrium price and quantity in the hat market will now involve both a somewhat higher price for hats and a somewhat larger quantity of hats being produced and sold to the public. (Because of the price rise, the marginal revenues earned by the manufacturers per additional hat sold will be higher, so consequently their desire to maximize profits will lead them to produce additional hats until the marginal cost for the last hat rises to equal the new higher price.) But producing more hats than before will require more of the relevant factors of production than before, which they will want to purchase from their suppliers, shifting the demand curves for each of the factors to the right. (This increase in demand for the factors in turn will tend to raise the factor prices somewhat and to increase the quantity of them sold, which then affects the factor producers' demand for their own necessary inputs and brings about further price-and-quantity adjustments throughout the economy in an ever-widening ripple effect.)

Demand

The willingness and ability of the people within a market area to purchase particular amounts of a good or service at a variety of alternative prices during a specified time period. Other things being held constant, the lower the price of a good (or service), the greater the quantity of it that will be demanded by purchasers at any given time.

Demand Curve

A graphical representation of a demand schedule. Conventionally, the demand curve is usually drawn between axes with price plotted along the vertical axis and number of units of the good or service demanded plotted along the horizontal axis. Where the law of demand applies to the particular market under consideration, the demand curve will slope (either gently or steeply) downwards from left to right.

Demand Schedule

A table or listing showing the number of units of a single type of good (or service) that potential purchasers would offer to buy at each of a number of varying prices during some particular time period. Demand schedules may be drawn up to reflect the behavioral propensities of a single unique individual, household, or firm or, more frequently encountered in microeconomic analysis, composite demand schedules for the particular good may be derived by adding up all the demand schedules of the large number of individuals, households or firms that are active or potentially active as purchasers in the market under consideration.

Supply

The willingness and ability of potential sellers to offer various specific amounts of a good or service for sale at each of a variety of alternative prices during a particular time period. Other things being held constant, the higher the price of a good (or service), the larger the quantity of that good (or service) that will be offered for sale in a particular time period.

Supply Curve

A graphical representation of a supply schedule. Conventionally, the supply curve is drawn between axes with price plotted along the vertical axis and number of units of the good or service supplied plotted along the horizontal axis. Where the law of supply applies to the particular market under consideration, the supply curve will slope (either gently or steeply) upwards from left to right.

Supply Schedule

A table or listing showing the exact quantities of a single type of good (or service) that potential sellers would offer to sell at each of a number of varying prices during some particular time period. Supply schedules may be drawn up to reflect the behavioral propensities of a single unique individual, household, or firm --or, more frequently encountered in microeconomic analysis, composite supply schedules for the particular good may be derived by adding up all the supply schedules of the large number of individuals, households or firms that are active or potentially active as sellers in the market under consideration.

Law of Diminishing Returns

Sometimes also referred to as the law of variable proportions, this "law" is really a generalization economists make about the nature of technology when it is possible to combine the same factors of production in a number of different proportions to make the same product. The law states: When increasing amounts of one factor of production are employed in production along with a fixed amount of some other production factor, after some point, the resulting increases in output of product become smaller and smaller. (That is, first the marginal returns to successive small increases in the variable factor of production turn down, and then eventually the overall average returns per unit of the variable input start decreasing.) Since the law assumes that the available quantity of at least one factor of production is fixed at a given level and that technological knowledge does not change during the relevant period, the law of diminishing returns normally translates into a statement about the short-run choice of production possibilities facing a firm (since in the longer run it is virtually always possible for the firm to acquire more of the temporarily "fixed" factor --building an additional factory building, buying additional land, installing additional machines of the same kind, installing newer and more advanced machinery, and so on.)

A simple example of the workings of the law of diminishing returns comes from gardening. A particular twenty by twenty garden plot will produce a certain number of pounds of tomatoes if the gardener just puts in the recommended number of rows and plants per row, waters them appropriately and keeps the weeds pulled. If the gardener varies this approach by adding a pound of fertilizer to the topsoil, but otherwise does everything the same, he can increase the number of pounds of tomatoes the garden plot yields by quite a bit (notice the amount of land is being held fixed or constant). If he adds two pounds of fertilizer (rather than just one), probably he can get still more tomatoes per season, but the increase in tomatoes harvested by going from one pound to two pounds of fertilizer is probably smaller than the increase he gets by going from zero pounds to one (diminishing marginal returns). Applying three pounds of fertilizer may still increase the harvest, but perhaps by only a very little bit over the yields available using just two pounds. Applying four pounds of fertilizer turns out to be overdoing it --the garden yields fewer tomatoes than applying only three pounds because the plants begin to suffer damage from root-burn. And five pounds of fertilizer turns out to kill nearly all the plants before they even flower.

Another similar example of diminishing returns in an industrial setting might be a widget factory that features a certain number of square feet of work space and a certain number of machines inside it. Neither the space available nor the number of machines can be added to without a long delay for construction or installation, but it is possible to adjust the amount of labor on short notice by working more shifts and/or taking on some extra workers per shift. Adding extra man-hours of labor will increase the number of widgets produced, but only within limits. After a certain point, such things as worker fatigue, increasing difficulties in supervising the large work force, more frequent breakdowns by over-utilized machinery, or just plain inefficiency due to overcrowding of the work space begin to take their toll. The marginal returns to each successive increment of labor input get smaller and smaller and ultimately turn negative. The law of diminishing returns is significant because it is part of the basis for economists' expectations that a firm's short-run marginal cost curves will slope upward as the number of units of output increases. And this in turn is an important part of the basis for the law of supply's prediction that the number of units of product that a profit-maximizing firm will wish to sell increases as the price obtainable for that product increases.

Marginal Analysis

A concept employed constantly in microeconomic theory (and quite frequently in macroeconomic theory as well) is that of the marginal change in some economic variable (such as quantity of a good produced or consumed), or even the ratio of the marginal change in one variable to the marginal change in another variable. A marginal change is a proportionally very small addition or subtraction to the total quantity of some variable. Marginal analysis is the analysis of the relationships between such changes in related economic variables. Important ideas developed in such analysis include marginal cost, marginal revenue, marginal product, marginal rate of substitution, marginal propensity to save, and so on. In microeconomic theory, "marginal" concepts are employed primarily to explicate various forms of "optimizing" behavior. (Consumers are seen as striving to maximize their utility or satisfaction. Firms are seen as striving to maximize their profits.) The maximum value of such a variable is found by identifying a value of the independent variable such that either a marginal increase or a marginal decrease from that value causes the value of the dependent variable being maximized to fall. (The student of mathematics may recognize the opportunity to apply concepts from differential calculus here, with the various marginal concepts being special names given to first derivatives of particular functions.) The valuation of the benefits (utility) and the costs of any good is determined "at the margin." For the (individual or collective) decision maker pondering how many units of a good to consume or provide to the market, net total benefits (benefits minus costs) will always be maximized at that level of consumption (or provision to the market) where the marginal benefit derived from adding the last unit equals the marginal addition to total costs of producing or acquiring that last additional unit.

Optimum

The very "best" possible situation or state of affairs according to some explicit objective that provides a precise standard of evaluation. For example, if a business firm's objective is to make the biggest profits possible (as economists generally assume it is), then the firm's optimal level of output at any given level of sales prices and production costs is that at which its profits will be the highest possible. Most of economics is concerned with analyzing how individuals or groups of people or even whole societies may achieve optimal use of available resources, and it is normally assumed that the maximum satisfaction of people's individual wants or desires is the objective of the economy that provides the relevant standard of evaluation. (Social critics, moral philosophers, religious thinkers, and political power-seekers in their various ways have often disputed the validity of this individualistic standard of evaluation, of course.)

Efficiency

In an economic sense, the ratio or proportionality between the value of the human end achieved ("benefits" or "satisfactions") and the value of the scarce resources expended to achieve it (opportunity costs). When an economist calls a situation or a practice "inefficient," he is claiming that we could achieve exactly the same desired goals with the expenditure of fewer scarce resources, or, put another way, that the amount of resources being employed could potentially produce even more of the beneficial results intended than they do. Efficiency simply means making the most we can of the limited resources we have.

Notice that "efficiency" in the economist's sense is an inherently evaluative term, not a matter of mere technical or scientific measurement of objective physical quantities, as the term might be used in an engineering context (as for example, the "efficiency" of various kinds of steam engine in transforming heat energy to useful kinetic energy). "Value of" always requires some sort of answer to the question "value to whom." When we assess the efficiency of any process or social institution or practice, just whose evaluations of the means and the ends are we using? In a well-developed market economy, assessment of economic efficiency makes heavy use of the monetary values placed on the various inputs and the resulting outputs in the open marketplace. The valuations that count are thus the valuations of those who are willing and able to support their preferences by spending their money in the ways that seem to them most likely to maximize their own satisfactions or "utility" based on their own individual tastes and preferences. The evidence that any particular economic resource is being used efficiently is, in the end, the fact that no one finds it "worth his while" to bid up the price and pay more in order to divert it to some other use. The logical and philosophical elaboration of the idea that competitive market systems are highly efficient in a much broader sense even than this is the primary content of Adam Smith's classic work The Wealth of Nations (1776). Indeed the entire subdivision of today's economic science known as "welfare economics" specializes primarily in identifying and analyzing the necessary preconditions for voluntary market interactions to generate socially efficient outcomes (and in examining the possibilities for remedies by deliberate state economic policies where those necessary preconditions may not be fully met).

Cost

In the widest sense, the measure of the value of what has to be given up in order to achieve a particular objective. In everyday language, people most often use the term rather like an accountant does, as synonymous with the total money outlays actually paid out to achieve the objective, but this is not precisely what economists mean by the term. Economists are concerned with rational decision-making, and the rational decision-maker needs to estimate in advance the full range of consequences of each of the various alternative uses of his time and resources open to him, not just the portion of the costs accounted for by money outlays. For the economist, the true cost of any decision is the value of the next best outcome (of all the other possible outcomes) that is given up because of that decision. Unless otherwise specified, when economists say "cost," they mean opportunity cost --that is, the highest valued alternative that must be sacrificed to attain something or otherwise satisfy a want. For example, the opportunity cost of a spur-of-the-moment decision to go to the movies Tuesday afternoon instead of going in to work is not just the six dollars for the ticket plus the gasoline and wear and tear on the car to get there. It also includes (at least) the four hours' wages not earned, diminished prospects for being promoted at work, and possibly such additional consequences as future hostility from co-workers who had to take up the slack, unpleasant feelings of guilt or shame, and so on. In a more extreme vein, the opportunity cost of committing suicide is not simply the money outlay for the necessary equipment, but rather the value of the total range of future satisfactions one might otherwise be able to achieve.

Transaction Costs

The costs other than the money price that are incurred in trading goods or services. Before a particular mutually beneficial trade can take place, at least one party must figure out that there may be someone with which such a trade is potentially possible, search out one or more such possible trade partners, inform him/them of the opportunity, and negotiate the terms of the exchange. All of these activities involve opportunity costs in terms of time, energy and money. If the terms of the trade are to be more complicated than simple "cash on the barrelhead" (for example, if the agreement involves such complications as payment in installments, prepayment for future delivery, warranties or guarantees for quality, provision for future maintenance and service, options for additional future purchases at a guaranteed price, etc.), negotiations for such a detailed contract may itself be prolonged and very costly in terms of time, travel expenses, lawyers' fees, and so on. After a trade has been agreed upon, there may also be significant costs involved in monitoring or policing the other party to make sure he is honoring the terms of the agreement (and, if he is not, to take appropriate legal or other actions to make him do so). These are the main sorts of transaction costs, then: search and information costs, bargaining and decision costs, policing and enforcement costs.

Elementary versions of economic theorizing often make the simplifying assumption that information and other transaction costs are zero (and, indeed, in a generally law-abiding society with a stable money system, cheap transportation and cheap communications, they are often pretty negligible). But realism nevertheless demands that we keep in mind the fact that the benefits to the participants in an exchange have to be high enough to cover their transaction costs if the trade is to take place at all. Indeed, many otherwise mutually advantageous trades do not take place because of the very high transaction costs that would be involved. High transaction costs are very often at the root of the problems discussed under the heading of externalities, especially in those situations where the external costs or benefits accrue to very large numbers of third parties and therefore a contractual agreement to internalize the externality is extremely costly to negotiate.

Externality

A situation in which the private costs or benefits to the producers or purchasers of a good or service differs from the total social costs or benefits entailed in its production and consumption. An externality exists whenever one individual's actions affect the well-being of another individual --whether for the better or for the worse --in ways that need not be paid for according to the existing definition of property rights in the society. An "external diseconomy," "external cost" or "negative externality" results when part of the cost of producing a good or service is born by a firm or household other than the producer or purchaser. An "external economy," "external benefit," or "positive externality" results when part of the benefit of producing or consuming a good or service accrues to a firm or household other than that which produces or purchases it. Example: If one neighbor decides to repaint his house and spruce up his yard so he can get a better price when selling it, he also at the same time is slightly improving the market value of other houses in the neighborhood, creating a "positive externality" benefitting his neighbors.

On the other hand, another neighbor who is a grade-A slob and lets the external appearance of his house run down creates a "negative externality" by depressing the attractiveness and thus the market value of the whole neighborhood.

Externalities of either the "positive" or the "negative" sort create a problem for the effective functioning of the market to maximize the total utility of the society. The "external" portions of the costs and benefits of producing a good will not be factored into its supply and demand functions because rational profit-maximizing buyers and sellers do not take into account costs and benefits they do not have to bear. Hence a portion of the costs or benefits will not be reflected in determining the market equilibrium prices and quantities of the good involved. The price of the good or service producing the externality will tend toward equality with the marginal personal cost to the producer and the marginal personal utility to the purchaser, rather than toward equality with the marginal social cost of production and the marginal social utility of consumption.

Thus, normal market incentives for the buyer and seller to maximize their personal utilities will lead to the over-or under-production of the commodity in question from the point of view of society as a whole, not the socially optimal level of production. Goods involving a positive externality will be "underproduced" from the point of view of society as a whole, while goods involving a negative externality will be "overproduced" from the point of view of society as a whole. In our example above, the individual homeowner pays all the cost of sprucing up his home but realizes only part of the benefits created --so consequently each homeowner will probably not keep his house up as well as he otherwise might if his neighbors could somehow be induced or required to pay him something for their share of the benefits from his labors.

Contracts often can be worked out as a means to "internalize" potential externalities because the existence of the externality implies there is at least the potential opportunity for mutual gains if the "third party" by-standers affected can offer compensation to the buyers or sellers in exchange for adjusting production or consumption levels of the good to a more acceptableble level. For example: If each homeowner in the neighborhood will agree to be legally responsible for maintaining a high common standard of upkeep in exchange for everyone else in the neighborhood also guaranteeing to do the same, then everyone can be financially better off than they would be without the agreement which is precisely why we observe such phenomena as homeowners associations and restrictive deed covenants.

Or other homeowners in the neighborhood might even band together and agree to finance jointly the entire cost of purchasing, fixing-up, and reselling some particularly run-down homestead in the neighborhood if the expected increase in their individual property values would be greater than their share of the cost of buying out their slovenly neighbor. Unfortunately, where externalities affect very large numbers of third parties (but only to a relatively minor degree in each case), the transaction costs of negotiating such many-sided contracts among them all may often be so large as to make this contractual solution impractical. Where the transaction costs to arrive at contractual solutions to "externality" problems are prohibitively high, complex modern societies normally provide "second best" remedies to private persons through the courts. Nearly the whole area of "tort" law (including especially law suits for "nuisance" and for "negligence") deals with externality problems in one way or another. People adversely affected by other people's activities may go to court and sue them in an effort to obtain an award of financial compensation for the damages and/or a court injunction requiring their obnoxious neighbors to change their ways in the future.

Government regulations or tax policies are often justified to the public as a means of "correcting" the outcome of the market for goods involving especially sizable externalities, especially negative externalities. The government might, for example, place a special tax or licensing fee on the production (or purchase) of a good or service believed to involve significant negative externalities, with the size of the tax or fee to be determined by some estimate of the total costs being imposed on third parties. The government charges would force the sellers (or the buyers) of the good or service to begin to start taking into account these external costs along with their own and would effectively shift the supply curve (or the demand curve) to the left, resulting in somewhat smaller quantities of the good being sold at a somewhat higher price in the new equilibrium after inauguration of the tax --and thus, somewhat fewer costs will be imposed on third parties. (But note that it is the government that gets to keep the money, not the unfortunate bystanders still suffering the damage!) In the case of a good or service involving a positive externality, government might cope in an analogous fashion by offering to pay subsidies to the producers or consumers of the good or service in question in order to encourage an appropriate expansion of production, or by using government's power to compel obedience without first negotiating mutually agreeable terms of cooperation among the affected parties, government might avoid the sizable transaction costs that would be involved in achieving a contractual solution to the problem by using its law-making or regulatory powers --for example, a city ordinance requiring all householders to keep their lawns mowed and their houses painted and forbidding them to allow trash or old automobile hulks to litter their front yards.

An important problem with the tax/subsidy approach to remedying externalities problems is, of course, that it may well be impossible or prohibitively expensive for the government to determine the size of the external costs or benefits involved and hence to determine even approximately what an appropriate tax or subsidy rate would be.

More generally, there are bound to be transaction costs for all forms of government action, including regulatory or legal strategies for correcting externalities --costs of gathering information, costs of debating and making policy decisions, and costs of administration or policing once the policy has been made. It will often be the case that the costs imposed on society by government taking corrective action would be larger than the decrease in welfare to society from the externalities that the government action is supposedly designed to cure. In any given case of externality, society may well be better off by simply leaving the externality in place, unless the third-party effects of the externality are truly massive. More precisely, government policy-makers need to devote their attention to the problem of lowering total transaction costs, rather than simply focussing on "fixing" this or that externality problem regardless of costs, if their intention is to maximize social welfare.

One area in which government has a great deal of control over the size of transactions costs throughout the economy is in the design and construction of the legal system. The costs to private firms and individuals of enforcing their contracts and protecting their other property rights are largely determined by the government's arrangements for the legal system. If the legal system is costly and cumbersome and unpredictable, mutually beneficial trades may often not take place because of potentially high transactions costs involved in protecting and enforcing complex property rights and contracts once made. Moreover, negative externalities often arise because certain third party property rights have not been clearly defined or effectively enforced in some aspect of social life, and the law has mandated that social or common ownership will be imposed instead of conventional private ownership and control. Excessive air and water pollution problems are often examples of such negative externalities from flaws in property law. For example, factory owners nearly always refrain from dumping waste products on neighboring privately-owned property for fear of the massive lawsuits they would surely lose --but they can often get by with dumping noxious waste products into "the public's air" or "the public's river" or "the public's ocean" without having to pay to secure the consent of those who later will be breathing or drinking or eating these poisons (or paying extra to remove them) precisely because the victims often have had no practical legal way of purchasing or selling a fully recognized exclusive property right in the portion of the air or rivers or the oceans (and their wildlife) on which they nevertheless depend.

Tort

Legal term. A wrongful or injurious act (other than breaking a contract) for which a civil suit may be brought in court by private persons. If the suit is successful, the court may award the victims cash compensation for damages, "punitive" damages above the actual cost of the injury in order to punish the defendent, and/or a court order banning any future repetitions of the kind of behavior giving rise to the suit. For example, a householder might sue the owners of a nearby factory for creating excessive noise or pollution that interferes unreasonably with the householder's health or the peaceful enjoyment of his property. Tort law procedures are thus one of the principal mechanisms for defining and protecting property rights short of evoking criminal law and is an important governmental mechanism for trying to overcome the problem of negative externalities.

Judicial Activism

The view that the Supreme Court justices (and even other lower-ranking judges as well) can and should creatively (re)interpret the texts of the Constitution and the laws in order to serve the judges' own considered estimates of the vital needs of contemporary society when the elected "political" branches of the Federal government and/or the various state governments seem to them to be failing to meet these needs. On such a view, judges should not hesitate to go beyond their traditional role as interpreters of the Constitution and laws given to them by others in order to assume a role as independent policy makers or independent "trustees" on behalf of society.

Judicial Restraint

The view that the Supreme Court (and other lesser courts) should not read the judges' own philosophies or policy preferences into the constitution and laws and should whenever reasonably possible construe the law so as to avoid second guessing the policy decisions made by other governmental institutions such as Congress, the President and state governments within their constitutional spheres of authority. On such a view, judges have no popular mandate to act as policy makers and should defer to the decisions of the elected "political" branches of the Federal government and of the states in matters of policy making so long as these policymakers stay within the limits of their powers as defined by the US Constitution and the constitutions of the several states.

Judicial Review

The power of the federal courts to overturn or limit the enforcement of Federal or state laws or regulations that the judges determine have violated the Federal constitution. The term also covers the power of the Federal courts to overturn or limit the enforcement of state laws or regulations that the judges determine are in direct conflict with Federal laws or regulations regarding a specific subject matter where the Federal constitution gives primary jurisdiction to the Federal government. Also the power of state courts to overturn or limit the enforcement of state laws or regulations that the judges determine have violated either the Federal constitution or the constitution of their own state.

Separation of Powers

One of the most important of the basic principles that guided the framers of the US Constitution in their design for America's future governance was the idea that the root cause and essence of tyrranical government is the concentration of control over all the powers and functions of government in the hands of the same individual or narrow political faction. The corollary the Framers drew from this was the separation of powers principle: that free popular government can best be sustained by dividing the various powers and functions of government among separate and relatively independent governmental institutions whose officials would be selected at different intervals and through different procedures by somewhat different constituencies so as to make it unlikely that the same small faction could gain control of them all at the same time. Thus, in the American federal republic the Framers designed, "the power surrendered by the people is first divided between two distinct governments [the Federal government and the governments of the several states], and then the portion allotted to each subdivided among distinct and separate departments [the executive, the legislative, and the judicial]."

The idea that concentrated political power is a mortal danger to civil liberties and popular rights remains to this day one of the most persistent and characteristic features of American ideologies and popular thinking about politics. In comparison with other advanced industrial countries, the United States possesses one of the most complex governmental structures and perhaps the most broadly diffused distribution of governmental authority among independent agencies. Not only do American governmental arrangements still allocate power to separate executive, legislative and judicial branches at both the state and federal levels, but they also feature a great variety of forms of relatively autonomous and geographically overlapping governmental bodies at the local level --including not only general purpose county and municipal governments but also a wide variety of functionally specialized mini-governments such as elected district school boards, flood control district boards, water resource planning boards, transit authority boards and the like.

Autocracy

A system of government in which supreme political power to direct all the activities of the state is concentrated in the hands of one person, whose decisions are subject to neither external legal restraints nor regularized mechanisms of popular control (except perhaps for the implicit threat of coùp d'etat or mass insurrection).

Dictatorship

Government by a single person (or group) whose discretion in using the powers and resources of the state is unrestrained by any fixed legal or constitutional rules and who is (are) in no effective way held responsible to the general population or their elected representatives.

Republic

Originally, any form of government not headed by an hereditary monarch. In modern American usage, the term usually refers more specifically to a form of government (a.k.a. "representative democracy") in which ultimate political power is theoretically vested in the people but in which popular control is exercised only intermittently and indirectly through the popular election of government officials and/or delegates to a legislative assembly rather than directly through frequent mass assemblies or legislation by referendum.

Democracy

A system of government in which effective political power is vested in the people. In older usage (for example, in the writings of the classical Greek and Roman philosophers or in the Federalist Papers), the term was reserved exclusively for governmental systems in which the populace exercised this power directly through general assemblies or referenda to decide the most important questions of law or policy. In more contemporary usage, the term has been broadened to include also what the American Founding Fathers called a republic --a governmental system in which the power of the people is normally exercised only indirectly, through freely elected representatives who are supposed to make government decisions according to the popular will, or at least according to the supposed values and interests of the population.

Oligarchy

Any system of government in which virtually all political power is held by a very small number of wealthy but otherwise unmeritorious people who shape public policy primarily to benefit themselves financially through direct subsidies to their agricultural estates or business firms, lucrative government contracts, and protectionist measures aimed at damaging their economic competitors -while displaying little or no concern for the broader interests of the rest of the citizenry. "Oligarchy" is also used as a collective term to denote all the individual members of the small corrupt ruling group in such a system. The term always has a negative or derogatory connotation in both contemporary and classical usage, in contrast to aristocracy (which sometimes has a derogatory connotation in modern usage, but never in classical).

Elite (elitist) Theory

The theoretical view held by many social scientists which holds that American politics is best understood through the generalization that nearly all political power is held by a relatively small and wealthy group of people sharing similar values and interests and mostly coming from relatively similar privileged backgrounds. Most of the top leaders in all or nearly all key sectors of society are seen as recruited from this same social group, and elite theorists emphasize the degree to which interlocking corporate and foundation directorates, old school ties and frequent social interaction tend to link together and facilitate coordination between the top leaders in business, government, civic organizations, educational and cultural establishments and the mass media. This "power elite" can effectively dictate the main goals (if not always the practical means and details) for all really important government policy making (as well as dominate the activities of the major mass media and educational/cultural organizations in society) by virtue of their control over the economic resources of the major business and financial organizations in the country. Their power is seen as based most fundamentally on their personal economic resources and especially on their positions within the top management of the big corporations, and does not really depend upon their ability to garner mass support through efforts to "represent" the interests of broader social groups. Elitist theoreticians differ somewhat among themselves on such questions as how open the power elite is to "new blood," the exact degree of agreement or disagreement that usually prevails within its ranks, and the degree of genuine concern (or lack thereof) for the broader public welfare that enters into their choices of public policy goals, but all such theorists broadly share the notion that it is these few thousand "movers and shakers" who really run the country and determine the basic directions of public policy, certainly not the manipulated and powerless masses of ordinary voters choosing among candidates at election time.

Aristocracy

A privileged social class whose members possess disproportionately large shares of a society's wealth, social prestige, educational attainment and political influence, with these advantages having been acquired principally through gift or inheritance from a long line of similarly privileged and cultivated ancestors. The term refers also to a form of government in which the state is effectively controlled by the members of such a class. The term tends to have a somewhat unsavory or derogatory connotation today in the light of democratic theories, but in classical political philosophy it meant rule by "the best people" of the society, who were expected to feel a paternalistic concern for the humbler members of the society that would keep them from ruling in a purely self-seeking fashion.

Pluralist Theory

The theoretical point of view held by many social scientists which holds that American politics is best understood through the generalization that power is relatively broadly (though unequally) distributed among many more or less organized interest groups in society that compete with one another to control public policy, with some groups tending to dominate in one or two issue areas or arenas of struggle while other groups and interests tend to dominate in other issue areas or arenas of struggle. There tends to be little overlap between those leaders who participate most influentially in one policy area and those who are influential in other policy areas, and what linkage there is tends to come from popularly elected political officials (especially political executives and party leaders) who, by the nature of their jobs, must exercise leadership (or act as brokers) in a number of different policy areas. There is no single, unified "power elite", but rather there are many competing power elites with differing backgrounds, values and bases of support in the broader society. Government tends to be depicted as a mechanism for mediating and compromising a constantly shifting balance between group interests rather than as an active innovator or imposer of policies upon society.

Interest Group

A group of people who share common traits, attitudes, beliefs, and/or objectives who have formed a formal organization to serve specific common interests of the membership. Examples of interest groups would include such disparate organizations as the Auburn Chamber of Commerce, the Society for the Prevention of Cruelty to Animals, the elementary school P.T.A., the Teamsters Union, the Southern Baptist Convention, the American Numismatics Association, the National Association for the Advancement of Colored People, the Brangus Breeders Association, the American Civil Liberties Union, the Cosa Nostra, and the Benevolent Order of Elks. Interest groups typically have formal admission to membership, dues, elected officers, by-laws and regular meetings, and they often provide information and regular opportunities for communication through newsletters or magazines, sponsor recreational or educational activities, organize volunteer public service projects, make deals for group discounts or group insurance and so on. Larger interest group organizations may have full-time paid officers or professional staff to manage and to supplement the efforts of member-volunteers in furthering the work of the organization.

Many interest groups at least occasionally engage in some form of lobbying or other political activities with respect to issues that touch directly on the common interests that are the organization's reason for being --for example, the PTA may organize support for a bond issue election to pay for erecting a new school building. Some interest groups have political activity as their principal or only reason for being in the first place. Interest groups that exist primarily for exerting political influence as a means of affecting government policies or legislation are often referred to by the narrower term pressure groups. Since more and more activities have become politicized with the expansion of the scope of activities of the government in the 20th century, more and more interest groups find themselves drawn into politics to protect or promote the interests of their membership, and the distinction in usage between the terms interest group and pressure group has accordingly become less significant in ordinary language.

Political Party

An organized group that has as its fundamental aim the attainment of political power and public office for its designated leaders. Usually, a political party will advertise a common commitment by its leaders and its membership to a set of political, social, economic and/or cultural values (an "ideology") that distinguish it from other political parties and which supposedly provide the basis for the policies the party proposes to implement or maintain through its members who obtain public office. A political party differs from a pressure group in that a pressure group is primarily interested in influencing whatever government officials actually happen to be in office rather than in attaining office for its own leaders, and accordingly interest groups do not normally put forward candidates for public office under their own name (although they may sometimes endorse particular candidates put forward by party organizations). In a democracy, political parties primarily function as agencies for recruiting suitable candidates to run for elective office and for organizing and conducting election campaigns. They may also become important in selecting candidates for appointive political office when winning the election has provided the party's leaders with power to appoint new officials to the cabinet and other top policy-making positions in the government bureaucracy. Political parties may also have another function as vehicles for coordinating the day to day activities and policy decisions of their elected and appointed office-holders so as to fulfill the party's policy platform, as for example, through an organized party caucus and a full-time party leadership machinery in the parliament or other legislative assembly.

However, unless the national party organization is in a good position to reward its members for "voting the party line" after they have been elected to office or to punish them for failing to support the party platform, the party organization's preferences may often not be the most important influence on the policy decisions made by its supposed representatives. In the United States, neither the Democrat nor the Republican national convention (nor their standing national committees) have the power to deny renomination to their parties' uncooperative representatives in Congress so long as they can win renomination in local party primaries or party conventions back home in their states or districts. The national party organizations' financial contributions to the campaign expenses of Congressional candidates (and usually those of state and local party organizations as well) tend to account for only a rather small proportion of what candidates need to be re-elected, so the party leaderships' financial leverage over their parties' office holders tends to be quite limited as well. The dominant role of "seniority" in guaranteeing individual committee assignments and personal influence in the House and the Senate, as well as the fact that the House and Senate party leaderships are elected by their own House and Senate party caucuses rather than appointed by the national party organization, considerably insulate "non-conformist" representatives from retaliation by their national party organizations.

Fascism

A class of political ideologies (and historical political regimes) that takes its name from the movement led by Benito Mussolini that took power in Italy in 1922. Mussolini's ideas and practices directly and indirectly influenced political movements in Germany (especially the Nazi Party), Spain (Franco's Falange Party), France, Argentina, and many other European and non-European countries right up to the present day. The different "fascist" movements and regimes have varied considerably in their specific goals and practices, but they are usually said to be characterized by several common features:

1. Militant nationalism, proclaiming the racial and cultural superiority of the dominant ethnic group and asserting that group's inherent right to a special dominant position over other peoples in both the domestic and the international order

2. The adulation of a single charismatic national leader said to possess near superhuman abilities and to be the truest representation of the ideals of the national culture, whose will should therefore literally be law
3. Emphasis on the absolute necessity of complete national unity, which is said to require a very powerful and disciplined state organization (especially an extensive secret police and censorship apparatus), unlimited by constitutional restrictions or legal requirements and under the absolute domination of the leader and his political movement or party
4. Militant anti-Communism coupled with the belief in an extreme and imminent threat to national security from powerful and determined Communist forces both inside and outside the country
5. Contempt for democratic socialism, democratic capitalism, liberalism, and all forms of individualism as weak, degenerate, divisive and ineffective ideologies leading only to mediocrity or national suicide
6. Glorification of physical strength, fanatical personal loyalty to the leader, and general combat-readiness as the ultimate personal virtues
7. A sophisticated apparatus for systematically propagandizing the population into accepting these values and ideas through skilled manipulation of the mass media, which are totally monopolized by the regime once the movement comes to power
8. A propensity toward pursuing a militaristic and aggressive foreign policy
9. Strict regulation and control of the economy by the regime through some form of corporatist economic planning in which the legal forms of private ownership of industry are nominally preserved but in which both workers and capitalists are obliged to submit their plans and objectives to the most detailed state regulation and extensive wage and price controls, which are designed to insure the priority of the political leadership's objectives over the private economic interests of the citizenry. Therefore under fascism most of the more important markets are allowed to operate only in a non-competitive, cartelized, and governmentally "rigged" fashion.

Totalitarianism

Domination by a single, like-minded governing elite of all (or virtually all) organized political, economic, social and cultural activities in a country by means of a single-party monopoly of power, police repression not only of all forms of dissent and opposition but also of all forms of independent private organizations as such, rigorous censorship of the mass media, centralized state planning and administration of the economy, and pervasive propaganda to inculcate the principles of the obligatory official ideology. Totalitarian states differ from traditional dictatorships or despotisms primarily with respect to the broader ("total") scope of human behavior that the authorities seek to regulate in detail and with respect to their much more effective control mechanisms made possible by exploiting twentieth century breakthroughs in rapid communication and transportation, scientific psychology, pervasive mass media, surveillance technology, electronic information retrieval, and so on. The term is commonly applied both to fascist regimes and communist regimes, and occasionally by extension to other exotic cults, movements or regimes with ambitions for total control such as those led by various sorts of religious fanatics like the Rev. Jim Jones or the Ayatollah Khomeini.

Civil Rights, Civil Liberties

The rights of every citizen to freedom of thought, freedom of conscience, freedom of expression, freedom of movement, freedom to enjoy privacy and autonomy in the management of one's personal affairs, freedom of private individuals to associate voluntarily and to form organizations for pursuing common purposes, and freedom to participate politically in ways that do not infringe upon the similar rights of others. Although the two terms overlap considerably in ordinary usage (and are often difficult to distinguish in concrete instances), the term civil liberties generally refers more specifically to the protection of the individual's rights to form and express his or her own preferences or convictions and to act freely upon them in the private sphere without undue or intrusive interference by the government, while the term civil rights emphasizes more specifically the individual's rights as a citizen to participate freely and equally in politics and public affairs in order actively to promote his/her preferred public policy alternatives through lobbying policy-makers and/or through personal participation in the electoral process. Thus, civil liberties may be seen as the logical correlates of the goal of limited government, while civil rights are the logical correlates of the goal of popular or democratic government.

Liberalism

1. A 19th century political viewpoint or ideology associated with strong support for a broad interpretation of civil liberties for freedom of expression and religious toleration, for widespread popular participation in the political process, and for the repeal of protectionist legal restrictions inhibiting the operation of a capitalist free market economy.
2. In the 20th century US, the term has come to describe an ideology with similar views on civil liberties and personal freedom issues but now supporting a much stronger role for government in regulating and manipulating the private economy and providing public support for the economically and socially disadvantaged, though still stopping well short of full socialism.

In Europe, the term liberalism is still used more in its 19th century sense, and European liberals are rather more respectful of the values of the free market than their American namesakes, whose views sometimes more closely resemble those of Europeans styling themselves as social democrats.

Libertarianism

A contemporary 20th century political viewpoint or ideology derived largely from 19th century liberalism, holding that any legitimate government should be small and should play only the most minimal possible role in economic, social and cultural life, with social relationships to be regulated as much as possible by voluntary contracts and generally accepted custom and as little as possible by statute law. In other words, libertarians believe that the individual should be as free as is practically feasible from government restraint and regulation in both the economic and non-economic aspects of life. Thus, libertarians endorse stricter respect for private property rights, the establishment of a more laissez-faire laissez-faire capitalist economic system, rigorous separation of church and state, and greater respect for individual rights to freedom of expression and freedom of choice in personal lifestyles. They oppose government programs for the redistribution of income, the inculcation of "politically correct" values through government schools and propaganda outlets, all forms of government-imposed censorship, the imposition of criminal penalties for the commission of "victimless crimes," and in general all forms of social, economic or cultural "engineering" by the government.

Laissez-faire

Literally, French for "Let do." The classical liberal (and modern libertarian) doctrine that the economic affairs of society are best guided by the free and autonomous decisions of individuals in the marketplace, to the near exclusion of government interference in economic matters. That is, the doctrine that government should almost always leave people alone and let them do as they please, so long as they respect the personal and property rights of others.

Welfare State

A state whose government devotes a very large proportion of its activities and expenditures to the direct provision of personal benefits to be consumed by qualifying individuals or families (as contrasted with such more traditional and less individually divisible government activities as national defense, law enforcement, controlling the money supply, economic regulation, maintaining transportation and communications nets, administering the public lands, etc.). Welfare benefits to individuals may be in the form either of bureaucratically supplied professional services of government employees or in the form of government-issued stipends or allowances or subsidies (transfer payments) to help qualifying households pay for general subsistence or for specific categories of state-favored expenses (merit goods). Examples of such social welfare programs would include old age and disability pensions, unemployment benefits, aid to families with dependent children, income supplements for the poor, public housing and housing vouchers, health care provided in state hospitals or clinics and reimbursement for the costs of privately-provided health care, government-funded drug abuse rehabilitation programs, food stamps, public education and child care, etc.

Advocacy of extensive "welfare state" programs was at first associated mainly with socialist movements, but in most Western industrial societies today many welfare state programs are endorsed as well by non-socialist parties that nevertheless still continue to reject the socialists' traditional demands for much more extensive state ownership, state planning, and state administration of industry and commerce.

CHAPTER

3

ORGANS OF GOVERNMENT

The branch of the social sciences that is primarily concerned with analyzing and explaining the functioning of political institutions (especially governmental institutions) as well as the political behavior of individuals, groups and organizations in their efforts to influence or resist the decisions and policies of government. Whenever a group of people collectively decide about an issue the result does not only depend on the individual group members' opinions, but also, on the decision rule used. Different decision rules can thus give different results even if the group members' opinions about the issue do not vary. One aspect of this relationship, namely the purely formal one, is quite obvious. Let us, for instance, assume that 60 % of a group's members are in favor of a certain proposal.

If so, and if the group members just vote their minds, the proposal will pass if only a simple majority is required, but it will be refuted if a qualified majority of say 75 % is required. Apart from this formal aspect there is however another aspect which may be important, namely that decision rules affect more of the group members' behavior than just their voting. The rules may for instance affect the extent to which the individuals organize in various ways, their tendency to behave strategically, and so forth. The distinction made here is, by the way, the same one as made by Maurice Duverger (1964, p 224) when he discusses in particular electoral laws, namely the one between a "mechanical factor and a psychological factor". Duverger's distinction thus has a far wider application than he originally intended. Now, a democratic constitution can be considered as a decision rule, or rather as a system of such rules, and the population of a country as a decision making group. Within such a perspective the question about the constitution's impact on the resulting decisions obviously becomes pertinent. Do different kinds of constitutions, one may ask, give significantly different results, with different welfare effects and, if so, which are the differences? Is, for example, just to mention one important question, a society's public sector more likely to expand with one type of constitution than with another one? It is this kind of questions which the theory presented here deals with. When developing that theory it will obviously be important to consider not only "mechanical factors" but to a large extent also "psychological factors" in Duverger's sense.

The questions mentioned can also be phrased in a somewhat different manner. In all societies the citizens have individual opinions about various issues and some of these issues are, in fact, decided politically. The political decisions can thus be considered as aggregations of the individual opinions, but such aggregations can be related to the pattern of individual opinions in many different ways. It is therefore natural to ask about the relation between the original set of individual opinions and the emerging final political decisions, and about the constitution's impact on this relation. Questions like this have indeed been raised now and then. Quite some time ago William Niskanen (1971, p 27) thus wrote that "The relation between the population's demands and the collective organization's expressed demands in a particular institutional setting is one of the more important problems of political science -and one, incidentally, that is not well understood." Some ten years later Bingham Powell (1982, p 186) wrote in a similar vein that "From the point of view of democratic process, it is important that the government be doing what citizens desire and that it be responsive to their changes in preference.... The analysis and comparison of such policy responsiveness is an extremely difficult problem, worth several books in its own right." Melvin Hinich and Michael Munger (1994, p 102), somewhat later still, stress the same issue again when writing that "The fundamental challenge to the development of a scientifically valid theory of electoral competition in a democratic society is to link the perceptions and preferences of voters on political factors that they care about with the actions of candidates before, during, and after an election." These problems, I think, are still about as unsolved as when Niskanen, Powell and Hinich & Munger expressed their concerns. The theory presented here aims at bringing them closer to a solution.

- My main concern is thus the impact of democratic constitutions of various types on the nature of the decisions taken, and on the welfare effects of those decisions. In the following I will present a number of hypotheses about these matters.
- In addition to this I am however also interested in differences in the politics, or political life, of different countries that are attributable to constitutional differences. The main reason for this interest is my contention that it is necessary, or at least highly helpful, to start by deducing differences in the political life, as an intermediary, in order to be able to deduce differences in the resulting decisions. This, however, does not preclude that the inferences about the political life may be interesting in their own right as well. Accordingly I will also present a number of hypotheses about these relationships.

Finally I should add that I will only treat constitutions that exist or have existed. Theoretically possible constitutions are not treated if they do not exist, however interesting some such constitutions may seem.

NATURE OF THE THEORY

The theory presented here, although verbal rather than formalized, aims at being a logical, deductive system. In essence this means that a number of propositions are logically derived from a limited set of basic propositions, which thus are used as axioms. Ultimately and ideally all propositions should, of course, be empirically tested. If this leads to verification that is good so far, if not that is a problem for the theory. Here, in this context, the theory should however rather be tested for logical consistency. It is of utmost importance that propositions which are presented as logical consequences of other more basic propositions really are so. To the extent that this is not case the theory, considered as theory, is a failure. If the theory does not form a logical system in the sense described it just is not a theory. There are, I think, at least two dangerous pitfalls involved in an undertaking like this one. The first is the risk of presenting, without noticing it, circular arguments. The other is the risk of mistaking common knowledge of real matters for logical conclusions. In what follows I have, at my best, tried to be aware of these pitfalls, but I am not sure that I have succeeded in avoiding them everywhere.

At last it should be emphasized that a theory is more than an instrument for producing hypotheses. Even if it were possible, somehow, to produce hypotheses for empirical testing by other means than from a theory, the theory will still always be a necessary part of a scientific enterprise. The reason is that the logical order, and by that the predictive and explanatory power, which a theory brings to a set of empirical findings cannot be achieved in any other way. In this sense theory supports empirical results as much as empiricism supports theory. Perhaps it was something like this which the great British astronomer and physicist Arthur Stanley Eddington (1882-1944) had in mind when saying that "One should never believe any experiment until it has been confirmed by theory" (Quoted by Steven Weinberg, 1993, p 101).

LEGAL AND INFLUENTIAL POWER

In a democracy ruled by law the legally established institutions of the state, such as the legislature and the executive, have, in large and specified areas such as lawmaking, power in a very different sense than other actors in the community. That it is so is very important for a variety of reasons. In particular, in this context, it is this fact which makes possible the conception of a theory about constitutions and their effects. If legislatures and executives had not had power of a particular kind, which we may call legal power, such a theory had hardly been possible. An important characteristic of the legal power is that it is specified by legally binding rules. If, for example, the constitution says that a majority of the legislature is entitled to institute laws of a certain kind, and a majority in fact decides to institute a law of that kind, then such a law really comes into existence. In that sense, and in this case, a majority in the legislature has all the power needed for instituting laws of the kind intended. Similarly a constitution usually stipulates the decisions or actions which can be undertaken by the executive alone, by the legislature alone, by the legislature and the executive in combination, and so on. All the power needed for these decisions is thus present in the various public institutions and the exact distribution of that power is spelled out in the constitution.

This, to be sure, does not preclude that public institutions can be influenced by other actors in the society. When for example the individual members of the legislature consider whether they, in their voting, shall favor or oppose a particular law, they are likely to take the opinions of people in their constituencies, of sponsors, of lobbying groups, and so on, into account. Of course I am not denying this. What I am saying is that if a majority of the legislature, if that is what is required by the constitution, votes in favor of a proposed law, then the proposal passes, otherwise not, independently of what lobbyists, sponsors and common voters think. Or, in other words, lobbyists, etc., cannot affect things in any other way than by influencing the relevant members of the legal public power structure. All analysis of power in a community ruled by law therefore has to start with a careful delineation of the legal power as determined by the constitution. This principle of separating the legal power, and starting with it as a prerequisite for all other discussions about power, is at the same time so important and so overlooked, that it deserves a name of its own, for example the legalistic principle.

In order to clarify things further it is expedient to distinguish between different kinds of legal power. So far I have given examples of what might be called decision-making power. Actors who are explicitly mentioned in the decision rules enjoy that kind of power. In addition to this it is however also important to emphasize the importance of procedural power. Some actors may for example be authorized, formally, to make proposals to the decision-makers, and others may be entitled, again formally, to express their opinions about proposals. These kinds of rights related to the procedure do also constitute power, and since they are prescribed in the constitution they are examples of legal power. Some individuals have, of course, both decision-making power and procedural power. The positions held by individuals in a legal power structure may be called legal power positions. In democracies, at the national level, there are two types of legal power positions which are particularly important, namely the positions as legislators in the legislature, and the positions in the executive. For countries which have a constitutional court, the positions as judges in those courts should be added to the legal power positions. All of these positions are associated with decision-making power. In addition, it is also common that some persons, for example heads of executives, speakers in the legislature, and chairmen of the committees in the legislature, have a considerable amount of procedural power. The constitutional rules often warrant certain competences to the incumbents of these positions.

It is important that power basically is attached to, or linked to, positions rather than to persons. Within such a structure a person thus has power only because he or she has been appointed to a certain position, and only for the period prescribed by the rules. This contrasts sharply to systems in which persons have power because they belong to a certain family, or because they have taken it, for example by violent means, and where they may keep that power for life, unless it is taken away from them by somebody else. In such systems the power is linked to a person, or a family, rather than to a position in a legal structure. This principle of linking power to positions, rather than to persons, is obviously immensely important for the functioning of democracy and for the legal security in a society. Now, as I have already indicated, the holders of the legal power positions can, of course, be influenced, or even controlled, by outsiders such as for example unions, or big firms, or even influential individuals. Those influencing the holders of the legal power thus also have a kind of power, which we can call power of influence or influential power. Such power may be weak and partial, but it may also be complete in the sense that whenever the holder of influential power tells the holder of legal power to behave in a certain way, for example to vote in a specified manner, the holder of legal power does so. Even in this last extreme case the distinction between legal and influential power, and the existence of both, is still fundamental. This is so since the holder of influential power, according to our assumptions, can act only by influencing the holder of legal power he cannot himself do what the holder of legal power can do.

Decisive and Blocking Power

In part 2 I made a distinction between decision-making power and procedural power. Here, as a preparation for the subsequent discussion, I will continue by splitting decision-making power into the two concepts of decisive and blocking power. For illustrating I will assume, as a very simple example, that we have a single decision making group consisting of 100 persons, and that a majority of 3/4 is required for an affirmative decision. If so, any set of 75 persons, or more, can make a proposal pass. Such a set is thus decisive, and it holds decisive power. Conversely any set of 26 persons, or more, can block the passage of a proposal -such a set is consequently blocking and it possesses blocking power. The concepts can also be described by saying that a decisive set is needed for changing the status quo, while a blocking set is enough for hindering a change of the status quo.

These concepts can, of course, also be used in more elaborated situations. Here we are for instance usually considering complexes including both an executive and a legislature, the latter possibly having two houses. In such situations it is always possible to describe exactly which composition a set must have in order to be decisive, and in order to be blocking. We just have to know the decision-rules exactly.

It is often easier to form a blocking set than a decisive one. Such, for instance, was the case in the example above, where a qualified majority was stipulated: 75 persons were required for dictating a decision whereas 26 persons were enough for blocking it. The same is true in a number of situations of interest for the discussion here. It is for instance true if there are two houses in the legislature, and a proposal, in order to pass, must be affirmed in both houses, even if only with a simple majority in each house. If so a majority in either house is enough for blocking a proposal, whereas a majority in each house is required for making it pass. Another example is a presidential system in which the affirmation of both the president and the legislature is required, even if there is only one house, and even if only a simple majority in the house is required. Obviously, in such a case, the president alone, or a majority in the legislature alone, is enough for blocking a proposal, whereas the acceptance of both the president and a majority in the legislature is needed for changing the status quo.

There are, however, also situations, in which it is as difficult to form a blocking set as a decisive one. Consider for example a situation in which a simple majority in a one house legislature is enough for passing a proposal. In such a case the same kind of set, that is a simple majority, is obviously also needed for blocking the proposal. The distinction between decisive and blocking sets is, of course, commonplace in social choice theory. Now and then it also appears in texts primarily devoted to constitutional problems. One example is Shugart & Mainwaring (1997, p 41) who call the power to change the status quo proactive power, and the power to block changes of the status quo reactive power. The concepts of positive and negative power may also be used.

The Legalistic Principle Disregarded: Examples

I wrote in part 2 that the legalistic principle is often overlooked in political science, and a few examples may therefore be in order. The principle is obviously disregarded when the power of various actors, whether they belong to the legal decision-making system or not, is treated on equal terms. The first example of this kind of disregard is taken from V. O. Key, Jr. He writes as follows about the "American democratic order" (1964, p 6 f): "Actual authority tends to be dispersed and exercised not solely by governmental officials but also by private individuals and groups within the society.... On one matter the President's decision may govern; on another, the wishes of the heads of a half-dozen industrial corporations will prevail; on a third, organized labor or agriculture will win the day; and on still another, a congressionally negotiated compromise completely satisfactory to none of the contenders may settle the matter. Even the journalists may cast the deciding vote on some issues."

Another, very recent, example is taken from Peter Esaiasson and Sören Holmberg. In their book "Representation from above" about the Swedish democracy they devote a whole chapter to "Power in Society" (1996, chapter 9). There they discuss the power of 8 groups and institutions in exactly the same manner, and by using, for all groups, exactly the same terms. The groups or institutions are "The Cabinet", "Mass Media", "Trade Unions (LO)", "Parliament", "Civil Servants", "Employer Organisation (SAF)", "Private Business", and "The Electorate". This, again, constitutes a clear disregard of the legalistic principle.

ROLE OF POLITICAL PARTIES

When exemplifying influential power in part 2 I mentioned unions, firms, and individuals, but not political parties. The reason is that political parties, although they certainly have influential power, are very special, or even unique, organizations. Political parties play a fundamental role in the theory presented here. What makes the political parties special and unique is that they are directly engaged in the competition for the legal power positions, and there are several expressions of this basic contention in the political science literature. Schattschneider, for instance, wrote as follows (1942, p 35): "A political party is first of all an organized attempt to get power. Power is here defined as control of the government. That is the objective of party organization. The fact that the party aims at control of the government as a whole distingusihes it from pressure groups." A few lines later (p 36) Schattschneider adds that "Since control of a government is one of the most important things imaginable, it follows that a real party is one of the most significant organizations in society." Many years later Sartori (1976, p 63) wrote in a similar vein that "A party is any political group identified by an official label that presents at elections, and is capable of placing through elections..., candidates for public office". These conceptions of Schattschneider and Sartori correspond well to the party concept used here, and political parties are thus more directly attached to the legal power structure than any other type of organizations.

Because of this role of political parties people holding legal power positions usually belong to a party, and are thereby also controlled by that party to some extent. This control can however vary considerably from being very strong to being quite weak. This is significant since the more control a party has over its representatives in the legal decision-making bodies, the more the party as such can be considered as an actor in its own right in the political game. This also means, in other words, that strong party discipline has the important effect of reducing the number of actors in the political game considerably.

Let us consider, as a theoretical extreme, a country in which the political parties are absolutely cohesive and disciplined. In such a case the party's control of its representatives in the executive and legislature is perfect. Whenever the party wants its representatives to behave in a certain way, for example to vote in a specific manner, they will do so. Although the representatives have all the legal power they are completely in the hands of the party with its overriding influential power. In such a situation it is quite reasonable to consider the party as a unitary actor. An illustrative example, which comes close to this extreme, is given by Key (1964, p 337) when he describes the old-fashioned machine organization of political parties in US cities as follows: "The classic machine took a clearly hierarchical form, with a boss at the head of an organization of workers held together by the spoils of politics and capable of determining the party's nominations and of exerting a mighty influence in elections as well. In its most fully developed form the urban machine became the government in that many major decisions, as well as minor matters, were decided by the party functionaries who managed their puppets in public office."

The other extreme, as theoretical as the former one, is a country in which there are no political parties at all. Such a country, it should first be noted, is perfectly possible since parties, although they are defined as organizations engaged in the political competition for positions in the legal structure, are nonetheless not necessary. A situation in which individuals compete for the legal power positions by themselves, without belonging to any organization, is perfectly thinkable. In such a situation there are obviously no party actors, but rather a considerable number of individual actors. In reality we do perhaps not find any extremes like the ones just described but there are certainly cases approaching the one extreme or the other. Thus there are countries in which the parties are very well consolidated, cohesive and disciplined. There are also countries in which the parties are very loosely organized and which thus are rather close to the second extreme. There are also countries in the middle field between the two extremes. In the following I will present hypotheses about the constitutional conditions for these different patterns.

The observation that the influential power of political parties is of a special, interesting and consequential kind is certainly not new in the political science literature. In particular it has been noted that well consolidated political parties, at least to a large extent, may cancel or nullify the intended effects of constitutional rules. In his book Political Parties Maurice Duverger (1964, p 393 ff) has, for instance, a whole section on the subject where he writes, among other things, that "The degree of separation of powers is much more dependent on the party system than on the provisions of the Constitution. Thus the single party brings in its train a very close concentration of powers, even if the Constitution officially prescribes a marked separation: the party binds very closely together the various organs of government." This, of course, is a variation of the theme that the party structure is relevant for the functioning of the legal decision-making system.

The Party in the Legislature

In spite of their importance political parties are somewhat elusive and many-faced organizations. A first point to notice is that, although political parties appear and operate in all democracies, they are usually not highlighted in the constitutional texts. They may be mentioned, and their activities may also be regulated in various ways, but that is about all. Thus, according to Sartori (1976, p 33), "(e)ven today, in most countries parties remain, juridically, private associations with no constitutional recognition. Among the few notable exceptions are the Bonn Fundamental Law and the French Constitution of 1958". Another interesting exception, though negative in a sense, is the Austrian constitution in which the parties are mentioned mainly in the stipulation that the members of the constitutional court must not be party functionaries or employees (Müller, 1994, p 24). It is also interesting to quote Schlesinger (1991, p 10 f) writing that "The United States is unique among democracies in the extent to which it has sought to regulate and define party organization. ... In countries such as Great Britain or France ... parties have been free to organize as they see fit ... ".

So, usually, the constitutions do not reveal the importance of the political parties. Still, the parties are important, and, furthermore, as will be outlined in the following, various constitutional elements play important roles in shaping the parties and the party-systems, and thereby also contribute in determining the exact roles played by the parties in the political process. Another important point is that political parties, since they work in both the legal decision-making structure and in society at large, and in a sense form links between these two worlds, have several appearances. V. O. Key has (1964, p 164), for instance, made distinctions between the party-in-the-electorate, the party-in-the-legislature, and the party-in-the-government.

- Using this terminology the kind of party I am mainly interested in here is the party-in-the-legislature. Thus, when I talk about cohesion and discipline of parties, I am primarily referring to the parties-in-the-legislature, and, in particular, I think about cohesion and discipline in voting.

The Nature of the Political Party

For the theory developed here it is enough, at least for a beginning, to state that there always are political parties in a democracy; that they are important; and that their organizational structures, and thereby their ways of acting, are significantly affected by various constitutional elements. Still it may be worthwhile, at least, to ask for the reason for the omnipresence of political parties. Why do political parties always appear? A first comment to be made to this question is that parties may appear, or originate, in different contexts or arenas. Referring to the discussion in part 3.1 about the party-in-the-legislature and the party-in-the-electorate parties may, in fact, originate in the legislature or in the electorate. The distinction between these two kinds of origins is important and has been made, in particular, by Maurice Duverger (1964, p xxiii ff).

Having made that distinction we may however return to the question about why parties always appear, whether in the legislature or the electorate. This question has, in fact, considerable similarities with Ronald Coase's well-known question about firms. In his celebrated paper "The

Nature of the Firm" he asked about the basic reasons for the existence of firms. He asked why markets, on which individuals freely operate, were not enough, and why it was advantageous also to have firms, whose inner operations are hierarchical and isolated from direct influences from the market. His answer was that the firm was advantageous since, and when, it entailed savings in transaction costs. Probably there is a similar rationale for the political party. But even so the exact and detailed answers, for parties originating in the electorate as well as for those originating in the legislature, are yet not formulated. The provision of those answers thus are important tasks still waiting for their fulfillment.

It may thus be a good idea to compare firms and parties but obviously there are not only similarities. One interesting difference has been highlighted by Harold Demsetz. According to him (1990) "a political party typically holds more stubbornly to its product mix than does a business firm". The reason is that the people active within a firm usually feel quite free to adjust the product as a means towards the end of profit maximizing. In a political party, on the contrary, the products of the party, that is its political ideas and its programme, and its candidates, are valuable in themselves for those working in the party, and therefore not likely to be basically changed in the efforts to get more votes. The products are, in Demsetz' words, laden with "amenity potential".

THE MAIN ACTOR CONCEPT

The theory presented here is strongly actor oriented. In particular the concept of main actor is important. A main actor is an actor operating in the legal system. An individual legislator may thus be a main actor, whereas a lobby group is just an actor. Things are however more complicated than this since a legislator is not necessarily a main actor, and also since a political party may be a main actor. An individual holder of a legal power position is a main actor if he or she enjoys a significant amount of freedom in relation to his or her party. Such a person obviously has a capacity to act, in a real sense, on its own. It is for this reason, and since the person holds a legal power position, that I call such a person a main actor. Even political parties may however be main actors. If, for example, a party controls all its representatives in the legal structure, that party is a main actor (and the representatives are not main actors). The reason is that the party, in contrast to its representatives, enjoys a real freedom of its own. Obviously, however, a party need not necessarily control all its representatives, or none. Other patterns are quite conceivable. A party may, for instance, control some of its representatives, while some other ones may enjoy a considerable freedom. If so these latter representatives are main actors. As long as a party controls at least some of its representatives, to some extent, the party is however also a main actor, as the concept is used here.

- We thus have two types of main actors. An individual main actor is an individual who holds a legal power position and who, in that capacity, enjoys a substantial amount of individual freedom. A party main actor is a political party which is represented in the legal decision-making system, and which deprives at least one of its representatives there of a substantial amount of personal freedom and thus, to that extent, controls that individual.

A first obvious implication of this definition is that there is no rule saying "one main actor -one vote". A big party which controls all its representatives is for example a main actor with a lot of votes. Another implication is that the number of main actors will be big if the parties are weak and undisciplined, whereas the number will be small if the parties are cohesive and embracing in the sense of controlling all, or at least most, of their representatives. A third implication is that the voting result is known when the positions of all main actors on a particular issue, together with the decision rule, is known. Finally it should perhaps be said that a particular main actor may regularly happen to be a member of defeated minorities. A main actor is therefore not necessarily a powerful actor in this sense.

MAIN TYPES OF CONSTITUTIONS

In the preceding parts I have argued that a legal decision-making system's way of functioning to a large extent depends on its constellation of main actors, which in turn depends on the properties of the political parties. In the following I will furthermore show that some constitutional traits are important determinants of these properties. Thus we will see that it matters how the executive is appointed, and how the legislators are appointed.

There are two main methods for appointing the executive, the one used in parliamentary systems, the other one in presidential systems. According to the parliamentary method the people first elects the legislature, which, in turn, appoints the executive. In a pure parliamentary system the executive, furthermore, can remain in office only as long as it enjoys the support, or confidence, of a majority in the legislature. This requirement is often referred to as the parliamentary principle. According to the presidential method separate popular elections are held for appointing a president and, thereby, the rest of the executive. In a presidential country, there are thus two main types of popular elections, those for electing the executive and those for electing the legislature. As for methods for appointing the members of the legislature there are, again, essentially two types of methods. First there are the majoritarian methods using single-member constituencies and giving, in each constituency, the mandate to the candidate who, according to some set of rules, gets most votes. Second there are the proportional methods which use multi-member constituencies and distributes the mandates to the parties in proportion to their votes.

Now, by combining the methods for appointing the executive, and the legislators, we get the following four types of constitutions.

- Parliamentary constitutions with proportional elections.
- Parliamentary constitutions with majoritarian elections.
- Presidential constitutions with proportional elections.
- Presidential constitutions with majoritarian elections.

This fourfold classification includes the main types of democratic constitutions dealt with in the theory presented here. The classification is thus of fundamental importance, and a few comments on it are in order. First, the actual distribution of the different types of constitutions exhibits a discernible pattern. The main examples of parliamentary constitutions with proportionalism are found in Western Europe; parliamentarism combined with majoritarianism is characteristic for the United Kingdom and some other countries in the Commonwealth; presidentialism combined with proportionalism is mainly met with in Latin America; and finally, the main example of presidentialism combined with majoritarianism is the US.

Second, the classification is not completely exhaustive. In particular constitutions which simultaneously have elements of presidentialism and parliamentarism, as for example the French constitution, are not represented -although they are gaining popularity. I do however hope, and believe, that the classification is fruitful in spite of this deficiency. The reason is my contention that it is expedient to analyze the simple and clear-cut cases before turning to the more complex, mixed forms. Third, the fourfold classification of constitutions presented here is not totally absent in the political science literature. It is thus clearly indicated in for example Powell (1982) and Sartori (1994), and it is explicitly emphasized in Lijphart (1991). None of these authors do, however, stress the importance of the classification for the shaping of parties and party systems.

Majoritarian Elections

The plurality method, also called the first-past-the-post method, is used when the problem is to elect one member from each constituency, and it is the simplest method serving that purpose. The candidate which gets most votes, that is a plurality, wins. If for example candidate A gets 20 000 votes, candidate B 15 000 votes, candidate C 15 000 votes and candidate D 25 000 votes, then candidate D wins. The method has been criticized on the ground that a candidate who in reality enjoys only quite a weak support may be elected. Suppose, for instance, that all people who support A, or B, or C in the example above prefer anyone of these candidates to D. If so A, or B, or C would get 50 000 votes if put alone in a contest against D, who still would get just 25 0000 votes. D:s winning in the original example is thus, in a sense, due to the opposition's division.

Several methods have been designed in order to mitigate this problem and the double ballot method is one of them. As the name indicates the method stipulates the use of two ballots separated by some time, for example a week. If some candidate gets an absolute majority in the first ballot, then that candidate is elected. Otherwise there will be a second ballot, and in that second ballot plurality is enough for winning.

Illustrating with the same example as above, and assuming that the figures represent the result of the first ballot, we see that none of the four candidates A, B, C and D has an absolute majority. Therefore there will be a second ballot. What happens there is, however, impossible to predict without further assumptions. We may for example assume that the candidates B and C are politically rather close to each other, that both are somewhat distant from A, and that both are very hostile towards D. If so B and C may make the agreement that C shall withdraw from the second ballot and urge its supporters in the first ballot to vote for B in the second ballot. If they succeed with that A will get 20 000 votes in the second ballot, B 30 000 votes and D 25 000 votes. B thus gets a plurality and wins. There is a variant of the method, it should be mentioned, in which the second ballot is restricted to the two candidates with the highest number of votes in the first ballot, and thus it is ensured that the final winner gets an absolute majority of the votes.

It is important to note that neither the plurality method, nor the double ballot method, presupposes any political parties. The candidates may be supported by, or even appointed by, parties, but they may, also, be free, independent individuals who, on their own, decide to compete. The methods work perfectly well in both cases.

Proportional Elections

Proportional methods are used when several representatives from each constituency are to be elected. They are motivated by a quest for proportional representation of existing political opinions, or fair representation as some would say. If, for example, there are 70 % socialists among the constituency's voters, and 30 % liberals, then the ambition is to elect representatives in the same proportions. Exact proportionality is not always possible but the larger the number of representatives from the constituency is, the easier it is, of course, to come close to that goal. From this point of view large, and consequently few, constituencies, is desirable. In the extreme the whole country may form one single constituency.

In principle the proportional methods are quite simple. Let us start by considering a method according to which the political parties, in each constituency, present lists with their candidates in sequence. Thus, on each party's list, there is a first candidate, a second candidate, and so on. The voters cast their votes on the parties, each voter voting for his or her favored party. The election result is thus, primarily, a distribution of votes on parties. Representatives are then, according to this method, taken from the parties' lists, in proportion to the number of votes they have got, starting, for each party, with its first candidate, and so on. Elections of this kind are usually called list elections. This general method may be varied, or complemented, in various of ways. In countries where the ideal is a very exact proportionalism it may thus be considered important to "correct", nation-wide, the perhaps somewhat erratic combined result of all the individual constituencies. Such a correction can be achieved by distributing a number of additional mandates in a proper way. In other countries it may, on the contrary, be considered desirable to make big parties' shares of the representatives somewhat bigger than their shares of the votes. This purpose may be achieved by using an appropriate formula, designed for the purpose, for the distribution of the mandates. In some countries it may also be considered expedient to discourage very small parties, which can be done by means of a threshold-rule of some kind.

Furthermore, it is sometimes considered desirable to give the voters a chance to express their feelings about particular candidates, for example by adding, or by erasing, names on the list of the party they are voting for. A candidate added, or erased, by a sufficient number of voters, may thus win, or lose, a place in the legislature in spite of the original list. Electoral systems like this may in fact be made completely independent of ordered lists of candidates. In Finland, for instance, the parties just nominate their candidates, without ordering them, and the voter then writes the name of one single candidate on his or her voting paper, which is blank from the beginning. Each vote thus becomes a vote both for a party and for a candidate. Within each party the candidates are then ordered according to the number of votes they have got, and each party becomes represented, from the top of the list determined by the voters and downwards, according to the number of votes it has got. This system thus gives the voters a very substantial influence over the composition, in terms of individuals, of the legislature.

But even if the proportional methods, as we have seen, can be varied in many ways, they all have one very important property in common, namely that they presuppose political parties. First the parties are needed for making the lists of candidates, or at least for nominating candidates. Second, and more basic, the very idea of proportionalism presupposes that there is something in the electorate, which can be proportionally represented in the legislature. It is the political parties which constitute that something. Proportional methods are therefore unthinkable without political parties.

Having said that it should however also be noted that there are electoral methods, which may be used in multi-member constituencies, and which do not presuppose parties. The single transferable vote method is an example. Certainly such methods are sometimes called proportional but, since there is nothing that is represented proportionally, that terminology is hardly appropriate.

Parliamentarism

The parliamentary principle, requiring that the executive enjoys a continous confidence from the legislature, may take slightly different forms. First there is a distinction between positive and negative parliamentarism, the former meaning that the executive must be actively supported by a majority of the legislature, the latter that it is enough for the executive not to be actively opposed by a majority of legislators. It may also be stipulated that the incumbent executive cannot be dismissed without the simultaneous appointment of a new one. This is usually referred to as a constructive vote of no confidence. The parliamentary principle can thus be varied within certain limits. For all of these varieties it is, however, for their proper functioning, of crucial importance that the political partygroups in the legislature are stable, centralised and cohesive.

This condition is, as far as I know, universally acknowledged. Some authors express it quite distinctly and I am not aware of anyone who objects. Sartori says (1994, p 94, his italics), for example, that "... parliamentary democracy cannot perform -in any of its varieties -unless it is served by parliamentary fit parties, that is to say, parties that have been socialized (by failure, duration, and appropriate incentives) into being relatively cohesive and/or disciplined bodies.... indeed, disciplined parties are a necessary condition for the 'working' of parliamentary systems."

But even if this is so it is hardly obvious why. The basic reason for the necessity of stable, disciplined, parties, is, I think, that the parliamentary confidence, in order to be reliable and lasting, cannot be anonymous. The confidence has to be expressed by a few stable and identifiable actors, which, in effect, means political parties. In such a case there are also substantial organisational links between the part of the legislature supporting the executive and the executive itself, which, of course, facilitates, the confidence problem. The relevant part of the legislature may even to some extent control the executive, should the need appear. All of this is, in fact, implicit in the concept fusion of power, which was introduced by Walter Bagehot (1826-77).

If, on the other hand, no political parties are present things become quite different. If, under such conditions, an executive gets a declaration of confidence from a majority of the assembly, that majority will necessarily be an ad hoc-majority which may perish at any moment, and because of any kind of dissatisfaction with the executive. This, in fact, means that the country really does not have an executive at all. Rather, the executive's functions are, in a sense, performed by ad hoc-majorities in the assembly, which is hardly in accordance with the ideas of parliamentarism.

In a parliamentary democracy it is thus important that political parties exist, and that they are stable, cohesive and disciplined enough, since otherwise a stable executive cannot be formed, and the system will not function as intended. This, by itself, does however not imply that such parties are likely to exist. There is no guarantee that a system, such as a parliamentarian one, automatically will function as intended. A system may obviously fail to work. What seems to be required therefore is that the properties which the parties acquire, when their functionaries and other supporters try to fulfil their ambitions, coincide with the properties required for the system's functioning. This may or may not be the case. I will return to this important topic in the following.

Here I will just finish by saying that the distinction between what parliamentarism requires for its functioning, and what in fact it brings about, is often disregarded. Peter Esaiasson, for instance, says (2000, p 51) that legislators in a parliamentary system may be looked upon "as more or less anonymous members of a cohesive party collective, and thus best analyzed as a group", and that the "main argument" for this position "of course, is that parliamentary systems require cohesive parties in order to function." Here, what is, and what is needed, is obvioulsy treated as one and the same thing. But there are also authors who honor the distinction. Michael Laver and Kenneth Shepsle thus write (1996, p 29 f, my italics) that "The effective operation of parliamentary democracy, in short, both depends upon and encourages disciplined behavior by political parties in the government formation process."

Presidentialism

Presidents can be appointed in popular elections in different ways. In essence, however, the whole country may, in a presidential election, be considered as one single-member constituency. The methods used are therefore usually variants of the plurality method or the double ballot method. When those methods are used there is, as we saw in part 5.1, and just considering the character of the method, no need for political parties at all, but still parties usually do play important roles.

In part 5.3 we saw that parliamentary systems depend, for their proper functioning, on cohesive and disciplined parties. With presidential systems it is the other way round. There stable, cohesive parties, rather, are a problem since they may impede or block the proper decision-making. Such mechanisms will be further discussed when we come to the presidential systems in the following. The mechanisms, it should be noted, are observed by some political scientists. Sartori, for instance, remarks (1994, p 94, my italics) that in a presidential system "under conditions of divided government stalemate is avoided precisely by party indiscipline".

SIX HYPOTHESES ABOUT THE SHAPING OF PARTIES

In the preceding parts I have said that the constellation of main actors is dependent on the number of political parties, and their discipline and cohesion, in particular as manifested by the voting patterns in the legislature. Accordingly it is important to consider mechanisms which shape parties and party systems in these respects. In particular mechanisms with a constitutional basis, if there are any, are relevant in this context. Here, I shall present six hypotheses about such mechanisms -the first five are related to the constitutional traits identified. Then, I will discuss the hypotheses in more detail. This discussion will however be confined to the hypotheses' logical foundations, and their places in the logical structure, or theory, developed here. The issue about the hypotheses' empirical truth will, on the whole, not be dealt with.

- The first hypothesis says that majoritarian elections tend to reduce the number of parties. Or, in other words, a democracy with majoritarian elections should, under otherwise equivalent conditions, have fewer parties than one with proportional elections.

This hypothesis is often referred to as Duverger's law. The French political scientist Maurice Duverger was certainly not the first one to entertain the idea, but he was the first to give it a sharp formulation and, simultaneously, to maintain its status as a scientifically valid generalisation, and he also collected and systematically arranged a lot of empirical information in order to prove its truth (Riker, 1986, p 26). The hypothesis has been, and continues to be, extensively and explicitly discussed in political science, and it remains controversial.

- The second hypothesis (part 6.2) says that parliamentarism, in particular in combination with proportional elections, gives the political parties strong incentives for discipline and cohesion. In a presidential system there is no corresponding incentive-creating mchanism.
- The third hypothesis (part 6.3) says that proportional elections put strong means of discipline in the hands of the leaderships of political parties. Under otherwise equivalent conditions these means are thus more efficient than those in a system with majoritarian elections.
- The fourth hypothesis (part 6.4) says that parliamentarism, in contrast to presidentialism, also gives some means of discipline to the leaderships of the political parties.

These three last hypotheses, as we see, deal with the discipline of political parties -and, again, it is in particular the discipline in legislative voting which is at issue. These hypotheses are not at all discussed in the same systematic way as Duverger's law. Rather, there are just occasional references, in passing as it were, to the hypotheses or similar ideas. Furthermore the distinction made here between means and incentives is never, to my knowledge, done explicitly. Sometimes the distinction is not even made implicitly and the idea expressed is rather that parliamentarism leads to discipline, or something like that. A few examples may illustrate this.

Lipset, for instance, quoting a paper of his own from 1976, talks about "the tight national party discipline imposed by a parliamentary as compared with a presidential system" (1990, p 199). Some authors also hold that the cohesion of the parties in a parliamentary system is, indeed, so strong that the parties can be treated as individual, or unitary, actors. In a discussion mainly devoted to other matters Hinich & Munger (1994, p 134) thus suddenly claim that "The same model holds for parliamentary systems, where parties, rather than individual candidates, are the main actors in elections." Similarly Laver & Shepsle (1994), although they admit (p 309) that they "have not gone into the mechanisms of party discipline" emphasize (p 301) "the role of the parliamentary-party machine in enforcing party discipline, and hence in enhancing the party to function as a single monolithic actor."

But even if most of the authors, who talk about the matter at all, thus seem to agree that parliamentarism enhances party discipline, there are also exceptions. Sartori, for instance, bluntly states (1994, p 95, his italics) that "... party solidification and discipline (in parliamentary voting) has never been a feedback of parliamentary government. If a system is assembly-based, atomized, unruly, magmatic, on its own intertia it will remain as it is. I cannot think of any party system that has evolved into a veritable 'system' made of strong, organization-based mass parties on the basis of internal parliamentary learning."

I do take side with those who claim that parliamentarism encourages discipline. In order to get deeper into the relevant mechanisms I have however found it productive to make a distinction between the incentives for discipline, and the means for enforcing it. Within this perspective discipline does not come about unless both incentives are present, and means available. The incentives are the subject matter of the second hypothesis, and the means are dealt with in the third and fourth hypotheses.

The two last hypotheses, number five and six, deal, without making the distinction between incentives and means, with mechanisms impeding party discipline.

- The fifth hypothesis (part 6.5) says that presidentialism is likely to impede party discipline somewhat.
- The sixth hypothesis (part 6.6) says that some popular democratic techniques are likely to impede party discipline.

The Number of Parties

When stating his law Duverger wrote (1964, p 217, his italics) that "Only individual investigation of the circumstances in each country can determine the real origins of the two-party system. The influence of such national factors is certainly very considerable; but we must not in their favour underestimate the importance of one general factor of a technical kind, the electoral system. Its effect can be expressed in the following formula: the simple-majority single-ballot system favours the two-party system. Of all the hypotheses that have been defined in this book, this approaches the most nearly perhaps to a true sociological law."

Part of the controversies about Duverger's law are, I think, a consequence of his formulation that majoritarianism "favours" a two-party system. Since a law should be law this has been interpreted as a claim that majoritarianism leads to a two-party system. After that, since it is easy to find exceptions such as India and Canada, it is also easy to conclude that Duverger is just wrong. But that is hardly sensible. What can be claimed is that majoritarianism, in contrast to proportionalism, involves strong forces tending to reduce the number of political parties. From this, by thinking in terms of equilibrium processes and taking countervailing forces into account, it is perfectly reasonable to conclude that, on the whole, we should expect fewer parties in countries with majoritarian elections than in those with proportional elections. This is a strong and important statement, which is perfectly compatible with Duverger's text, and it is this statement which I here call Duverger's law.

Our main interest here concerns the mechanisms behind Duverger's law. Why, other things being equal, should we expect fewer parties in a majoritarian system than in a proportional one? Duverger himself answered this question by referring (p 224) to "a mechanical factor and a psychological factor". The first one consists in the pure mathematical effects of the application of the electoral rule -essentially the suppression of all parties but the biggest in each constituency. The second factor consists in the parties' and voters' reactions, and adaptations, to this suppression.

Duverger's idea about a mechanical and a psychological factor is of course perfectly reasonable even if the mechanisms behind the law can be described in a more detailed manner. In particular it is important to distinguish between the constituency level, where the important mechanisms work, and the national level where the result we are interested in is manifested. Duverger himself was well aware of this and wrote (1964, p 223) that "the true effect of the simple-majority system is limited to local bipartism."

Starting at the constituency level we can assume, as an example, that we have a constituency with five candidates representing the parties P1-P5. Let us furthermore assume that these parties, in an imagined first election, get 30, 25, 20, 15, and 10 % of the votes respectively. We shall also assume that these votes reflect the real preferences of the voters, and that these preferences remain constant over time.

P1	P2	P3	P4	P5
30 %	25 %	20 %	15 %	10 %

In the first election P1 thus gets a plurality and its candidate will consequently represent the constituency in the legislature. That result may make P1 and its voters happy, but the other parties, and their voters, are hardly likely to repeat their behavior exactly in the ensuing elections. Various adaptations are likely to take place.

Thus at least some of the voters, who are not satisfied by merely expressing their opinion, but really want to affect things, may change their votes from the most preferred party to their second or even third preference, if that party is considered better than the incumbent P1 and is also judged to stand a better chance than their first preference to beat P1. As the years pass, and the number of effectuated elections increases, this means that some parties, perhaps the initially smallest ones, will become still smaller, while a few, perhaps just two, main combatants will increase their vote support. In the long run the voters themselves, by departing from their initial first preferences, are thus likely to concentrate their votes on a few main combatants having real chances to win. As for the parties and their candidates, assuming that they really want to take part in decision-making and thus are not content with just manifesting their existence, a corresponding behavior is likely. The parties, which remain small, and perhaps even decrease, as the years pass, are thus likely to withdraw from the competition altogether.

The combined behavior of the voters, and the parties, is thus likely to bring about a long term equilibrium with just a few parties, say two or three. If, at some time, there are considerably more parties than that, some of them are consequently likely to be eliminated in the long run.

After this the consequences at the national level may be considered. Let us assume that we have a country in which, initially, there are 10 parties. We shall also assume that all constituencies in important respects have the same properties. They thus have the same size, and the same patterns of political opinions. Initially all ten parties are thus represented in each constituency. After this we should thus expect, over the years and in each constituency, an equilibrium process of the kind. Since the constituencies have the same properties the process will be the same everywhere. Therefore, if it ends with for instance two parties in one constituency, it will end with the same two parties in each constituency, and thus also nationwide. In this case therefore, and due to the assumptions made, what happens in one constituency happens in the same way in the other ones, and consequently nationwide as well. Everywhere there is a reduction from 10 to two parties.

Things may however be different. Let us change the assumption that the constituencies have similar properties into its opposite, namely that all constituencies, due to important regional differences, are very different from each other. Let us also specify that there are five constituencies altogether. As for the rest everything is as before. From the beginning there are thus ten parties, which we may call p1-p10, all of which are represented in each constituency. Now, as in example above, and as the years pass, the number of parties will be reduced in each constituency. Since the constituencies are different in this example the reduction will however affect different parties in the different constituencies. We may for instance assume that, in the end, there will only be two parties in each constituency, and that these remaining parties are p1 and p2 in the first constituency, p3 and p4 in the second, p5 and p6 in the third, p7 and p8 in the fourth, and p9 and p10 in the final and fifth constituency. In this example therefore, and although the number of parties in each constituency has again been reduced from 10 to two, there is no reduction at all on the national level.

These two examples are, of course, extremes. What they have in common is that the number reducing process in the individual constituencies is the same in both cases, and the same as in the description of the mechanisms at the constituency level above. The difference is that in the first example, where all constituencies have the same properties, the national number of parties is reduced as much as the number in each constituency, whereas in the other example, where the constituencies are utterly dissimilar, the national number of parties is not reduced at all. In real situations, where there are some differences between different constituencies, but also a lot of similarities, the result is likely to be something in between. When the mechanisms operating in the constituencies reduce the number of parties there, the national number of parties is also likely to be reduced, but not as much as in the individual constituencies.

The discussion about the effects on the national level has, so far, only considered the logical effects of similarities, or differences, between constituencies. No further mechanisms other than the ones operating at the constituency level have been introduced. Mechanisms operating at the national level are, however, also imaginable. Economies of scale may for instance be important. The formation of parties, and of party opinions and positions, are thus likely to be demanding tasks requiring considerable basic investments which are independent of the number of constituencies involved. Therefore, and in order to make these investments pay off, a certain minimum number of constituencies may be required. If so, we have a mechanism which is likely to reduce the number of parties nationally as well. This mechanism, however, is as relevant for proportional as for majoritarian elections, and therefore we need not consider it further here.

Summing up we may say that the numbers of parties is likely to be smaller in a majoritarian system than in a proportional one, other things being equal. The basic mechanisms leading to this result operate at the constituency level. The result will however, even if attenuated, remain at the national level, provided that differences between the constituencies are not too many and too great.

A Corollary

Presidents, as we saw in part 5.4, are usually appointed by some kind of majoritarian method. In presidential elections there are therefore forces operating which tend to reduce the number of parties. Now, since the same political parties usually appear in presidential elections and in elections for the legislature, the forces affecting the parties in presidential elections are likely to be relevant for the elections to the legislature as well. Presidentialism will thus have some tendency to reduce the number of parties generally.

Incentives for Party Discipline

The second hypothesis, that parliamentarism gives political parties strong incentives for cohesion and discipline, has not, to my knowledge been systematically discussed anywhere. I will therefore start from scratch with the logical foundations of the hypothesis as I see them.

Using the concepts of decisive and blocking sets it seems natural that legislators in general are trying to form, or become members of, decisive sets in favor of their own ideas or positions. If they do not succeed with that they will at least try to bring about sets which are able to block proposals they are against.

Now, it is an important property of a parliamentary system that most decisive constellations necessarily consist of the executive, or at least has the executive as a constituent part. It is thus not possible that the executive is excluded from most decision-making constellations since that would be tantamount to regular no-confidence votes, and thus against the parliamentarian principle. The legislators thus have incentives to make the system work, and therefore, since stable, cohesive and disciplined parties according to part 5.3 is a prerequisite for that, to form such parties.

The incentives may however be stronger in a proportional parliamentary system than in a majoritarian one, in particular if the majoritarian system (because of the operation of Duverger's law) comes close to being a two party-system. This is so because the majority, in a two party situation and for statistical reasons, often is considerably bigger than the minority. The majority which supports the executive therefore can afford some defectors and still deliver the necessary confidence. In proportional systems, on the contrary, where coalition executives are the rule the executive's marginals are usually much narrower and discipline therefore more important. (The nature of these reasons, both the statistical mechanisms in the majoritarian case, and the mechanisms behind the narrow margins in the proportional case, will be treated in more detail later on.)

Anyway, the existence of incentives among the legislators is not enough for cohesive and disciplined parties to appear. Without some further mechanism, such as reasonably effective means for enforcing discipline at the party leaderships' disposal, the parties are likely to remain rather loose and unconsolidated organizations. This is so since the parties, in spite of being parties, are likely to harbor, within themselves, considerable differences of opinions, which it is difficult to erase. The establishment of common clear-cut party positions is likely to require some kind of organizational power.

MEANS OF DISCIPLINE RELATED TO PROPORTIONALISM

There is, to my knowledge, no systematic discussion about the third hypothesis that proportionalism gives strong means of discipline to the party leaderships. Rather there are just occasional assertions of the hypothesis, or similar ideas. Duverger (1964, p 183), for instance, writes that "proportional representation with fixed lists and the ranking of candidates in strict order naturally makes parliamentary representatives dependent on the leaders within the party who prepare the lists and determine the order of the names." Similarly Matthew Shugart and John Carey (1992, s 173) write about "mechanisms, such as a closed party list, by which party leaders exert discipline over their rank and file." But even if the references to the hypothesis are scattered and few, they all seem to go in the same direction. I have not come across any denials of the hypothesis, and it is thus, as it seems, uncontroversial.

Still, the mechanisms behind the hypothesis can hardly be as simple as indicated in the quotations above, namely that those deciding about the lists easily can eliminate obstinate candidates. This argument applies equally well to the majoritarian case, since also there those responsible for the nominations obviously can exclude those who do not follow the group. We have to look for more fundamental mechanisms.

The main point seems to be that the incentives for campaigning are very different in the two types of systems. In a majoritarian system the efforts of the local party organization in the constituency, as well as the efforts, and the personality, of the individual candidate, are of great importance for the result. The campaigning efforts of a candidate in a single-member constituency will to a very large extent favor the candidate himself. If the candidate campaigns successfully the voters will vote for just him. Therefore, to a considerable extent, a legislator in a majoritarian context is the architect of his or her own fortune.

When considering the corresponding mechanisms in proportinal systems I will start with list systems. In such a system an imagined campaigning candidate in a constituency -which always is a multimember one -does not work for himself but rather, and necessarily, produces a collective good. The obvious reason is that the voters cannot reward an appreciated campaigner individually -they have to vote for his party rather than for the candidate himself. Things being like that it is interesting to ask more exactly about the nature of the collective good produced by the imagined local candidate.

At first it may then be stated that he works for his party rather than for himself. Furthermore, and to the extent that his constituency party organization is not a meaningful unit for the voters, he will be working for the national party rather than for the constituency organization. For that kind of work he is, however, because of his local, low level, position, probably most unfit. The amount of the collective good produced by his campaigning will therefore be quite small, and it will also be diffusely spread out, to a considerable extent beyond the borders of his own constituency. Thus, from the imagined candidate's own point of view, his efforts will in all likelihood seem wasted. The conclusion is that the imagined candidate will remain imagined. There will not be much local campaigning at all. This, incidentally, is exactly what the theory of collective action (Mancur Olson, 1965) tells us: the incentives for producing collective goods are notoriously weak.

At the summits of the parties in a proportional list system things are however different. For the party leaderships residing there campaigning may very well be profitable. Their campaigning is at first relatively effective since they are in the proper positions for that kind of work. Furthermore, on the whole, they will reap the fruits of their own efforts. True, it may be argued that a party's candidates in all constituencies benefit from what the leadership is doing, but even so the leadership itself also benefits more the more candidates it really gets into the legislature. It is usually better to belong to the leadership of a big party than to that of a small one. It is this necessary dominance of the party leaderships in campaigning in proportional list systems, I would argue, which also supplies the leaderships with power over their legislators. If the leadership of a party wants control a certain legislator or candidate, by sticks or by carrots, the latter usually has no personal resources of his own, such as for instance popularity among voters, to mobilize for resistance. This argument applies however, as I have said, primarily to pure list elections. In other kinds of proportional systems, in which the candidates' individual campaigns matter to some extent, for instance because the voters can add or erase names on the lists, or because (as in the Finish case as described in part 5.2) there are no lists at all, the effects described are more or less attenuated. Or, in other words, the means of discipline become weaker and more similar to those in majoritarian systems.

Means of Discipline Related to Parliamentarism

According to the fourth hypothesis there is also another mechanism of discipline, which is related to parliamentarism rather than to proportionalism. This mechanism has been discussed now and then since long.

Gary Cox (1987, p 80 ff) thus gives an account of an interesting discussion in which Walter Bagehot (1826-77) notices and explains the discipline of the British parties. According to Bagehot the legislators were afraid of voting against the executive, since thereby, through the dissolution of the Parliament, they might lose their places there. This explanation was however refuted in the discussion on the ground that it did not explain the cohesion of the opposition party. Duverger gives a slightly different version of the same argument when he asserts (1964, p 404) that the British government often uses the vote of confidence, and thereby the threat of dissolution, and a new election, as a disciplinary weapon within its own party. Later still Shugart & Carey write (1992, p 173) that "Where parliamentary systems have become fully developed, the existence of the institution of the vote of no-confidence has mandated an imposition of discipline. This party discipline in an archetypal parliamentary system (such as the United Kingdom, New Zealand, or Norway, for example) is sure to be far stronger than in a typical presidential system's assembly... ". Obviously there may be a mechanism like this, even if it also seems correct that it does not explain the discipline of opposition parties. But perhaps the discipline of the opposition, in parliamentarian and majoritarian systems, really is lower than that of the party, or parties, in power.

Anyway, there is an interesting and important difference between the means of discipline discussed here and those related to proportionalism treated in part 6.3. The difference is that the latter are discriminating in the sense that they could be used against a single legislator or candidate, whereas those discussed here are non-discriminating and usable only against the governing party's parliamentary group as a whole.

A Mechanism Impeding Party Discipline Related to Presidentialism

Presidential elections may affect the inner structures of the parties. Since presidential candidates usually have to win a majority of the votes in order to be elected they may, one could suspect, modify or attenuate their parties' programs considerably in order to get more votes. This may lead to tensions within the parties, and to a degradation of the party programs.

Mechanisms Impeding Party Discipline Related to Primaries, Referendums and Initiatives

Some democratic techniques or institutions, such as primaries, referendums and initiatives, give additional power to the ordinary voter. For this reason these institutions also may impede party discipline. Popular primary elections, by which candidates for political posts are nominated, obviously deprive party leaderships of important power and thereby impede party cohesion and discipline. The relation between referendums and party cohesion is a somewhat more complicated issue since referendums sometimes can be used in the service of party cohesion. Imagine for example that in a parliamentary country, in which party cohesion is essential, an important issue which divides the parties appears. If, in such a case, the referendum institute is used for the decision making, rather than the regular machinery, a potential threat to party cohesion is bypassed, which serves the system's functioning.

Referendums may however also be used frequently and regularly with the main purpose of reaching decisions, without any regards for party cohesion. If so the popular initiative is also an interesting institute, which may be made available for the citizens. Now, if referendums and initiatives are used without any regard for the parties, it is still interesting to ask whether, in fact, they are likely to affect the parties in any substantial way. I think they are, and the hypotheses is that the parties' consolidation and cohesion is likey to be undermined. The reason is that the parties, in order to be consolidated and cohesive also must have some importance, which means that they must be allowed to handle as many issues as possible. If a lot of issues are taken away from the parties' dominating influence, and are given away to people's direct initiatives and decisions, the parties will, I think, disintegrate.

FOUR MAIN ACTOR CONSTELLATIONS

Using the hypotheses about party-shaping mechanisms it is now possible to derive conclusions, also hypothetical, about the constellations of main actors in the four constitutional systems.

The upper, left part of the figure illustrates the main actor constellation in parliamentary systems with proportional elections. Here, there is no strong constitutional mechanism reducing the number of parties, and hence we are likely to find considerably more than two parties, perhaps five to ten. Furthermore the incentives for upholding party discipline are strong, since the system is parliamentarian, and effective means towards that end are also available, due to the proportional elections. The parties are thus likely to be disciplined and cohesive. Looked at from outside they may be considered as unitary actors. This is the reason why the party-actors are indicated by solid circles in the figure.

In the upper, right part of the figure we have parliamentary systems with majoritarian elections. The number of parties shall, on the average, and because of the number-reducing tendency of the majoritarian elections, be smaller than in the former group of constitutions. The figure shows a case for which the reduction has been very effective, and where, as a result, there are only two parties. Obviously, and even with the number-reducing mechanism operating, there may however be more than two parties. Anyway, the parties are likely to be less disciplined than in the former case. One reason is that the incentives given by parliamentarism, according to the hypothesis in the preceding part, are weaker than in case of proportionalism. Another reason is that the means for enforcing discipline are weaker than in a proportional system. Since the discipline is less than perfect the party actors are indicated by broken circles in the figure.

Turning then to the lower parts of the figure, which show presidential systems, it may at first be noted that the actors are placed in two levels rather than one. The presidential executive is placed at an upper level, whereas the actors in the legislature are indicated at a lower level. The basic reason for placing the president at a separate level is that the rules regulating his or her actions usually differ in important respects from the rules for the legislative actors -particularly by giving the president much more power. Furthermore, as will be developed in the following, the president's general incentives may differ considerably from those of the legislative actors.

The president may, for instance, sometimes be endowed with incentives for favoring the common good rather than partisan interests. Now, the lower, left part of the figure, shows the constellation of actors in presidential systems with proportionalism. Here, in the elections for the legislature, there are no strong constitutional forces reducing the number of parties, and consequently we may expect quite a lot of them, as indicated. As for incentives for discipline, there are obviously no ones of the same nature as those in a parliamentary system, but perhaps there are other ones. Anyway, the means for discipline are there, since we are dealing with a proportional system. The parties may thus be disciplined and cohesive, but it may also be the other way round. In order to settle this issue additional assumptions about the incentives for discipline are required. So far, I have however not introduced any such assumptions, and the resulting ambivalence is illustrated in the figure by some broken, and some solid, circles.

THE MAIN ACTORS' INTERACTIONS

Having put the main actors on the stage it is now time to consider their actions, and the results of those actions. In this part, and the next two ones, I will introduce three topics related to these actions. These topics will then be treated in detail in the discussions about each one of the four main types of constitutions.

- The topic introduced in this part concerns the main actors' interactions. How do the main actors relate to each other? What kinds of decision-making patterns will they form? And by which mechanisms or processes? And why? These are typical questions related to this topic. The answers to the questions, as we will see in the following, will to a large extent depend on the type of constitution considered.

In part 2.1 the concepts of decisive and blocking sets were introduced. Those concepts may, of course, be used for main actors as conceived here. Doing so it is now possible to state that a very important aspect of the political competition in a democratic society consists in the main actors' efforts, by positioning and bargaining and so forth, to form and enter, depending on the circumstances, decisive or blocking sets, and thereby further their ambitions.

The possibilities to act like this vary however considerably from case to case, depending among other things on the constitutional setting. For the discussion of these matters, which largely are of a behavioral nature, it may be useful to consider the degree of coordination among the main actors. Imagine, as an extreme example, a decision-making assembly which has so many main actors, and takes new decisions so often, that it is virtually impossible for the actors communicate with each other about what is going on. When a proposal is presented for such an assembly each actor thus have to vote for or against the proposal without any prior discussions with its fellow-actors. This voting behavior is thus completely uncoordinated. In the opposite extreme the number of main actors is so small, and other factors enhancing cooperation so favorable, that it easy for the actors to communicate extensively, and negotiate, about all proposals, and about the votes for the proposals. In such a case we should thus expect a very coordinated main actor behavior. When the conditions for coordination are favorable the coordination, it may be noted, is not necessarily limited to a single decision, or a few related decisions. If the interests of the actors concerned so dictate, the coordination may very well be extended over a considerable time period such as, for instance, a complete election period. The topic of coordination will be further discussed "Two kinds of compromises".

Two Kinds of Compromises

In previous part I said that the actors' behavior was uncoordinated when they just voted their minds, whereas coordination involved discussion and negotiations between the actors. When coordinating, the actors are thus likely to adjust their positions and behavior in various ways in order to achieve benefits, for instance by forming and entering favorable decisive constellations, or at least blocking ones. That of course requires compromises, but political compromises may be of different kinds and the differences are of considerable interest. Here I will describe two kinds of compromises. Imagine two actors, A and B, which respectively have the opinions, or take the positions, a1-am and b1-bn. Now, for any pair of positions with one position from each actor, it is interesting to ask whether the positions are compatible or not. Each cell in the figure below represents one such comparison, and a few answers are also inserted as illustrations. Thus the positions a2 and bn, and a3 and b2, are compatible, whereas the positions a1 and b1, and am and b2, are not compatible. Now, in politics, both compatibility and non-compatibility are common. In principle the issue of compatibility has to be judged in each individual case, but two general rules, with possible exceptions, may however be hypothesized.

- Different ideological positions are likely to be in conflict with each other, and thus not compatible. A society can, for instance, not be built in accordance with both socialistic and capitalistic principles. It has to be the one way or the other. Socialism and capitalism are not compatible. Or, to take another example, a position on a spatial left-right scale is not compatible with another position on the same scale. Thus, an actor cannot adopt several positions on such a scale, it has to be just one.
- Positions about interests may, on the contrary, very well be compatible. The position that a certain group in society, say small farmers, should be supported is thus perfectly compatible with the position that another group, say widows with small means, should also be supported. There is no problem in adopting the two positions simultaneously.

Now compromises between political actors about political positions may be of two types.

- The first type of compromise consists in agreeing about a common program involving compatible positions from the actors concerned. Using the example in the figure the actors A and B may for example compromise about a program involving A's positions a2 and a3 and B's positions b2 and bn. The common policy or program thus is a2 + a3 + b2 + bn +.... Such a compromise is likely to be quite easy to reach, since no adjustments of original positions are needed. It is only required that all actors feel that a fair amount of their original positions are included in the final common policy.
- The second type of compromise, which in the general case should be much more difficult to reach, requires adjustments of positions which originally are incompatible. An example would be a compromise between A and B in the figure about the positions a1 and b1. If both actors adjust their positions they may finally become compatible, or perhaps even identical, and thus represent a possible compromise. a1 and b1 may for instance be two different positions on a spatial left-right scale, and the actors may agree to settle for a

specific position between a1 and b1. This is however likely to be difficult since it requires that both actors change their original positions in favor of a new one.

A conclusion to be drawn from the reasoning here thus is that political compromises about interests are likely to be easier than compromises about ideological matters.

THE MAIN ACTORS AND THE VOTERS

In the preceding part I said that the main actor interaction constituted an important aspect of the political competition in democratic societies.

- Another equally important aspect of this competition is the fight for votes.

The voters obviously are of crucial importance for the main actors. A main actor without electoral support is unthinkable. Each main actor is supported by voters, and without that support the main actor would not be a main actor. For this reason electoral support can never be substituted completely by, or traded for, other goods appreciated by the main actor such as, for instance, beneficial relations with lobbyists or extensive and favorable publicity in media. Such goods are subordinated to votes, even if they may be used in the hunt for votes. Ultimately, and in the final count, a main actor depends on its electoral support.

- The topic introduced in this part concerns the relationships between the main actors and the voters. What will individuals and parties aspiring to get into the legal decision-making system, and thus to become main actors, do in order to get the necessary votes? What will the incumbent main actors do in order to keep their electoral support, and thereby their positions? How will the voters react to messages from campaigning individuals or parties, and choose between them? These are typical questions within this topic, and again we will see that the answers to a considerable extent will vary with the constitutional type considered.

Trying to attract voters a campaigning actor may use various ideological arguments, support various interests, or, if we are dealing with an individual actor, emphasize its own personal qualities. Furthermore, the actor may address the electorate at large, or, perhaps, particular target groups within the electorate. In these activities, however, the actor obviously also runs the risk of repelling voters, and it is therefore important to keep the net result positive. A good strategy attracts more voters than it repels.

As for the voter, the decision about which actor to vote for may be quite complex. The voter may consider the actors' positions on various ideological or interest-related issues, or the actors' personalities when the actors are individuals. The voter may also entertain ideas about the relative importance of these different aspects, and so forth. By weighing all this together the voter reaches a decision about how to vote. We may call this kind of voting compound voting. The contrast is voting on a single issue, for example in a referendum. In such a case the voting is straightforward rather than compound. The citizen just votes its position on the issue to be decided, and that is all. Voting, which aims at appointing main actors, is however usually compound.

In order to bring the analysis further ahead it is necessary to be more detailed about the relations between voters and politicians. In politics, and political analysis, it is common to talk about mandates from voters to politicians. Using another, and perhaps more modern terminology, it may also be said that the relationship between voters and politicians is a principal-agent relation, the voters being the principals and the politicians the agents (for an introduction to this terminology see, for instance, Milgrom & Roberts). The relation can take different forms. It is convenient to distinguish between two main types of such forms, namely delegation and instruction.

Delegation is, in a way, the simpler of the two relationships and many people have experience of it from everyday life. When people in typical voluntary associations like the local sports club or charity association elect presidents, cashiers, secretaries, and so on, they usually do not require more than having confidence in the persons elected. They just want to be able to rely on them to act in a way that is in accordance with common sense and the purposes of the club. Feeling such confidence they delegate the decision-making to the people elected. This rather simple kind of relationship is present not only in clubs and the like, but to a considerable extent also in politics.

Instruction, on the other hand, prevails when the voters do not limit themselves to a simple confidence in the ones elected but rather require that they shall execute a certain program, which may be worked out in a rather detailed way. Therefore, at the same time as people are elected, a program, or an instruction, which the ones elected shall realize, is adopted. It should be noted that the program may very well be, and often is, formulated by the people who wants to get elected. Different candidates for political positions thus offer voters to carry through different programs if elected. Even so, however, and as soon as a candidate is elected, the program can, from a formal point of view, be considered an instruction from the voters to the elected.

Here delegation and instruction have been presented as two rather pure, or archetypal, relationships. In reality, however, it is easy to see that mixtures of the two types often appear. Sometimes the element of delegation may dominate, sometimes the element of instruction, and it is interesting to ask about the reasons why. Before taking up that issue it should however be noted that instructions may be of different kinds. They may be specific or general. This distinction is closely is related to the one between generality and particularity made by Buchanan (1993).

General instructions may be based on ideological ideas about the ideal character or construction of society, or they may be derived from ideas about the common, or public, or general, interest. Often general instructions are about new rules or laws, and those supporting such new laws tend to emphasize the incentives created by the laws. The likely ambition is to create incentives which enhance the societal development, and people's general welfare, in the long run.

Specific instructions, on the other hand, are independent of notions about ideal societies, or about the common good. If general instructions often deal explicitly with rules and incentives, specific instructions are, rather, interventionistic. Their implementation usually means that some people, on purpose, satisfy their special interests at the expense of others. In these cases, therefore, the incentives created are not a main concern of those favoring the interests, and there is usually not much talk about incentives. But obviously some incentives will be affected, or created, as unintended side-effects of the instructions, and those incentives are worth investigating. They may very well be destructive.

Now, in their campaigning, the political actors may try to establish relationships of delegation, or instruction, or some mixture of the two. When considering what they are likely to do it is important to realize that the possibilities to effectuate instructions, that is to deliver, to a large extent depend on the constitutional setting. These matters will be dealt with in detail in the following parts, but generally speaking it may be said the possibilities to deliver are, on the whole, greater when the conditions for coordination are good than when they are not. Furthermore, if the possibilities to deliver are slim, it is likely to be more prudent for the actor to strive for a relationship of delegation rather than instruction. From this point of view we should therefore expect delegation, at least to a large extent, to be associated with individual main actors and instruction with party main actors. In addition to this there is another argument which points in the same direction. The argument is that a consolidated party, with a recognizable identity over a considerable time span, has great, and perhaps even crucial, advantages in relation to individuals for developing and "marketing" instructions, and in particular such a bundle of instructions which constitute a political program.

- We should thus, on the whole, expect party main actors to rely on instructions, and individual main actors to strive for delegation.

THE MAIN ACTORS AND THE LOBBYISTS

It is commonplace in politics that various actors which do not belong to the legal decision-making system, and which in that sense are external, try to enhance their goals by influencing the main actors. Such actors are called lobbyists, and their activity is known as lobbying.

- The topic introduced in this part concerns the activities of the lobbyists, and the relationships between them and the main actors. Who are the lobbyists? How do they work in order to become effective and influential? Why do the main actors yield to their demands when they do so? These are typical questions within this topic, and the answers depend on the constitutional setting.

The actors engaged in lobbying may be of many different kinds. They may be single individuals, business firms, unions, interest groups or many other kinds of organizations (other than, by definition, political parties). The targets of lobbying are actors which have a potential for influencing the outputs of the legal decision-making system. This means, as I have already taken for granted in a few formulations above, that the lobbyist are likely to approach the main actors, which may be individuals or parties.

Furthermore the lobbyists may either try to influence incumbents, or to affect the appointment of new main actors. Both activities are important and common. In the latter case the lobbyists may for example, because of sympathy with their policies, add to their campaign efforts. There are also mixtures between these two activities. A lobbyist may thus, while supporting an actor's campaign, at the same time try influence the actor's future behavior.

The lobbyists, since they are not political parties, are likely to pursue interests rather ideologies or other general issues. Furthermore, within this general kind of ambition, the lobbyists are likely to limit their efforts to what can reasonably be achieved. If, for instance, it seems possible to influence decisive constellations of main actors, or to stimulate the creation of such constellations, and thus to change the status quo, the lobbyists are likely to do so. But if that is not within reach the lobbyists may confine themselves to stimulating the creation of blocking constellations, and thus to impede changes of the status quo.

It is interesting to note that, in constitutional settings where lobbyists are unlikely to be able to bring about changes of the status quo, and thus are restricted to blocking strategies, laws favoring various interests are likely to stimulate the creation of, and thus to precede, organizations defending them. In a setting where the lobbyists realistically may hope to change the status quo organizations are, on the contrary, likely to be created in order to bring such changes about, and thus to precede the changes.

It may also be noted that lobbying organizations sometimes may find it advantageous to form close relations, even in an organizational sense, with main actors. An obvious prerequisite for this is that we are dealing with party main actors rather than individual main actors, but this is not enough. It is also required, at least for organizational ties to develop, that the political parties themselves have enough of organizational structure, or, in other words, that they are cohesive and consolidated enough. It is difficult to imagine a close relationship between a well organized interest group and a party which is just a very loose conglomerate.

Sometimes lobbying organizations are called "pressure groups". This, I think, is a highly misleading term. It gives the impression that the organization uses some kind of almost physical force for driving the resisting main actor backwards, which is, I submit, a completely wrong idea about the nature of the relationship between the two parties. The lobbyists just do not have any power like that. When a main actor yields to a lobbyist's demand it does so rather because it finds its own interests enhanced thereby -if it were not for that it would not yield at all. We thus have to think about the two parties as reaching a mutually beneficial agreement. The understanding of lobbying is tantamount to knowledge about the relation between the two parties, which has to be analyzed in as detailed a way as is done, for instance, with sellers and buyers on a market in economic theory. Each party gives something away, gets something else in return, and comes out in a better state.

The benefits of the lobbyist always consist in favorable public decisions. The costs, on the contrary, may be of different kinds. One type of costs occur if the lobbyist, which in this case may be an organization, exercises its influence over its members to vote for the lobbied main actor. If so the costs do not only consist in the efforts made to get the members to change their votes, but also, for the members themselves, in the benefits foregone by not voting in the way they had originally intended to do. Another type of costs occur if the lobbyist provides money in cash in order to support the lobbied actor's election campaign. That, of course, is also a way of furnishing votes, albeit an indirect one. The lobbyist thus can fulfil his part of a bargain either by exercising influence over voters, or by supplying money, and it is, of course, of great interest to find out when and why the one or the other possibility is used. Finally it should be said that the lobbyist obviously also may supply money, or other valuables, for the lobbied actor's private use. Such manners, however, are obviously corrupt.

Within the perspective applied here the widely spread idea, which is given support by the term pressure group, that an organization is necessarily more effective the bigger, and the better organized, it is, seems dubious. Big and well administered organizations could quite conceivably lack influence, for example if the political counterpart does not see any benefits, such as votes, to result from yielding. On the other hand even a very weak organization may get influence simply by informing legislators about its position, and thereby about ways to get votes. In fact, it seems quite possible for groups of citizens, for example marginal voters, to be influential without being organised at all, and one might therefore even speak about implicit organizations or lobbyists. So far I have just taken for granted that both political parties, and interest organizations, usually exist in a democratic system. Still it is important to ask why this is so. Which is the division of labor between political parties and interest organizations?

The Division of Labor Between Political Parties and Lobbying Organizations

Why, one may ask, are both lobbying organizations and political parties always present in a democratic political system? Why is it not enough with the organizations working close to the legal structure, that is the political parties? Why are there, in addition to that, interest groups? Which functions do the latter have which cannot, at least not conveniently, be fulfilled by the parties? Which is the division of labor between them? The answers to these questions are, again, dependent on the constitutional setting and therefore not fit for a detailed treatment in this chapter. Two general points may, however, be made. First, while political parties usually have at least some ideological inclination, although it may be weak, lobbying organizations focus strongly on interests. This point is emphasized by the fact that the majority rule, which is important in all democracies, makes it possible to further special interests of various kinds. In a context dominated by the unanimity rule interests would, on the contrary, usually be defeated, and there would thus not be any room for lobbying organizations. Second, while political parties come and go from incumbency to opposition, lobbying organizations, by being free from the parties, can always direct their demands towards the incumbents.

PARLIAMENTARY CONSTITUTIONS WITH PROPORTIONAL ELECTIONS

In this constitutional setting the main actors are, as we have seen, likely to be cohesive and disciplined political parties. Some of these actors or parties are furthermore likely to form an executive, and they are also likely, to rely to a considerable extent on instructions, and bundles of instructions or programs, in their efforts to get votes.

Now, when discussing the formation of an executive it is essential that the number of main actors, although they are few, most likely are more than two. Each party therefore knows that in all likelihood it will have to make deals with other parties. Thus, the main actors must adopt strategies which are instrumental in bringing them into coalitions, and in affecting the policies of those coalitions. What kind of strategies are these? What kind of matters are the parties to a coalition likely to agree about? In part 9 we concluded tentatively that the parties to a large extent will rely on instructions in their electoral strategies. This topic will finally be discussed in part 12, but assuming so far that the tentative conclusion is correct, the coalition agreements are likely to be about instructions as well. But what kind of instructions?

A first point is that specific instructions, rather than general, are likely to be particularly important in these agreements. There are two reasons for this contention. The first one is that it is easier for political parties to make deals about specific instructions than about general ones. If, for instance, one party is committed to a particular specific instruction, and another party to another one, they can easily agree about supporting each other -if you support my instruction, I support yours. General instructions, on the contrary, are often in conflict with each other and, if so, not easily reconciled. This first reason is thus related to the compatibility of various political positions as such.

The second reason, on the other hand, has to do with the acceptability for those concerned of a reconciliation. This problem, as it happens, is the subject matter of a theorem saying that a coalition executive cannot have a purely ideological foundation (Moberg, 2000). Following the terminology used here it may also be said that a reconciliation of two general instructions, even if such a reconciliation, in spite of the technical difficulties, is reached, is not likely to be accepted by the parties concerned.

But even if compromises based only on general instructions from the different parties are unlikely, there may be deals in which a general instruction of one party is knit together with a specific instruction of another party. They may agree that the first party supports the second party's specific instruction, if the second party supports, or perhaps just tolerates, the first party's general instruction. This, however, requires that the general instruction involved is not too offensive but rather attenuated or pragmatic enough. It may also be argued that general instructions, which give a prominent and far-reaching role to the state, are more easily reconciled with specific instructions than those giving a limited role to the state. The reason is that specific instructions often are natural parts of state interventionism. From these general arguments we can now infer the following hypotheses about the parties' programs:

- Specific instructions are likely to be frequent in all parties' programs.
- All parties do not necessarily have general instructions in their programs, and when such instructions appear they are likely to be pragmatic or attenuated.

We also get these hypotheses about the executive coalitions likely to emerge, and about their governmental programs:

- A governmental program containing only specific instructions is perfectly possible.
- A small party may be committed to some general instructions, but it is not likely to get them included in a governing coalition's program.

- If a governmental program contains general instructions, and in that sense has an ideological inclination, those instructions are likely to have come directly from a big, dominating party's program. Either that party has been able to form an executive of its own, or it is the main participant in an executive involving one or a few small extra coalition members. In this latter case there may be a deal saying that the dominating party will support some specific instructions of the smaller parties, if they support, or tolerate, the dominating party's general instructions.
- Parties with articulated (in contrast to pragmatic or attenuated) and conflicting general instructions on their programs are not likely to be able to make deals about specific instructions with each other. The freedom of such parties is thus somewhat restricted.
- A party not having any general instruction in its program is completely free in choosing its partners, irrespective of their general instructions. Such a party is often able to play a pivotal role in coalition building processes. It can, for example, credibly threaten to leave, and thereby destroy, a coalition to which it presently belongs in order to join another one. Such threats can be used for enforcing concessions from the other members of the first coalition, or from the members of the second potential coalition, and thus for giving favors to the supporters of the party itself. For operating in that way a party need not be very big -in fact a moderate size may by an advantage since the party, thereby, fits into more places and thus gets more opportunities to have its specific instructions implemented.
- A party with strongly held, articulated and controversial general instructions in its program, for example a party with an extreme ideological inclination, may affront most other parties. If so the party may be excluded from all possible coalitions, and thus from all influence.

The purpose of the negotiating parties is, as I have mentioned above, to form a durable executive. This means that, in this constitutional setting, the main actor interaction, and thereby also the real decision making, to a large extent occurs in the government formation process. After that the executive will just go on presenting its agreed upon program, bit by bit, for the legislature. The real decision making is thus a batch process rather than a continuous process. The interval between the batches may be as long as the whole election period. This obviously also means that the majorities are fairly constant over the same long time periods. There is no constant recomposition of decisive majorities. Matters may, however, turn out somewhat differently if a minority executive, rather than a majority executive, is formed. Even such an executive depends, for its existence, on the support of a majority, but that majority, by definition, will contain parties which do not belong to the executive proper, and therefore the membership of that majority may shift to some extent, for example from decision to decision in the legislature, or from time to time. This means that the decision-making will become somewhat more of a continuous process, and also that the composition of the majorities may change to some extent.

Another conclusion is that a big party may dominate the politics of its country for a long period even if it suffers occasional electoral recessions and, indeed, even if it never has a majority of its own. The party can stay in the executive all the time just by making deals about some specific instructions favored by one or two small parties, and then govern together with them. Most likely such a party continuously appoints the prime minister and the heads of a number of key ministries. This possibility for ideological influence may, in fact, be an important driving force for big parties to suppress internal divisions, or to live with them in one way or another, in order to remain big. If so we should expect to find an important ideological component in the programs of big parties like that.

We may also conclude that an organized opposition, in the form of for instance a shadow cabinet, is unlikely. The reason is that a new governing coalition, since the parties can combine in many ways, not necessarily consists exclusively of the former outsiders. Rather, some former outsiders may join some former incumbents in a new executive. In order not to jeopardize any such possibilities the present outsiders are therefore not likely to form an organized group and thereby link their destinies. For a party aiming to develop and keep a pivotal position this consideration is particularly important. Finally it may be concluded that the executive coalitions formed are likely to be minimal winning in William Riker's sense (Riker, 1962). The reason is the important roles played by interests and specific instructions in the coalition agreements. Thus, and in other words, the executive coalitions are likely to exploit their outside minorities.

Some Conditions for the System's Proper Functioning

A parliamentary system depends, for its proper functioning on cohesive, disciplined political parties. Therefore some constitutional elements or constructions, which from a logical point may seem possible are, nevertheless, destructive in real politics.

First, it is important that the proportional technique used for appointing the legislators is of a pure list character, or at least rather close to that. A system without any lists at all -such as the Finish system is hardly useful in a purely parliamentary setting. The reason, of course, is that it may be difficult for the party leaderships to maintain party discipline within such a system..

Second, it is important that the popular techniques of primaries, referendums and initiatives are not frequently used. The reason is that these techniques, as explained in part 6.6, are detrimental to party discipline. Still, and in some particular and rare cases, referendums may be used for upholding party discipline, as is also mentioned in part 6.6.

The Impossibility of a Coalition with a Purely Ideological Foundation

In previous part I said that a coalition executive cannot have a purely ideological foundation. This, in fact, is a theorem which says that it is impossible to account for the formation of the executive only in terms of a simple a left-right scale, or, in somewhat more technical terms, that it is impossible to account for the formation of the executive within the framework of the spatial model, at least in its one-dimensional version.

In the figure below we see a situation which can be used for proving the theorem. The figure represents a legislature with six political parties, P1-P6, each one with a certain position on the left-right scale and with a certain number of representatives in the assembly with altogether 300 members. Now, we may at first assume that there is no executive at all. If so the decisions taken by the legislature will be determined by the median voter theorem. This means that the decisions will become m, which is the ideological position of the party P3 and also the median position.

For proving the theorem we may compare this situation with one in which there is an executive. Clearly, if the executive is to make any difference at all, and thus to be of any interest for its members, its policy must diverge somewhat from m. We may for example think about an executive which has the policy indicated by l, and thus a leftist inclination, and which is supported by the majority composed of P2 and P3.

Now, it is easy to see that l is worse than m for P3. P3 is therefore in fact disfavored by belonging to the executive. Therefore, contrary to our assumption, P3 will not be member of the executive or support it. Our assumption that P3 belongs to the executive, since it is advantageous to do so, thus leads to a contradiction. This kind of argument is usually called a reductio ad absurdum. If it is possible to show that an assumption leads to a contradiction, then it is also fair to conclude that the assumption is unreasonable or absurd.

So far I have only dealt with the particular example in the particular figure above. Obviously we have to ask if other examples, with other possible party constellations in the legislature, also lead to contradictions for the same reasons. The answer is in the affirmative since the examples, however they are varied, will always have two crucial properties. First, the executive's policy must always diverge from m since otherwise the executive would not matter at all and, consequently, it would not be important to be a member of it. Second, since the constellation supporting the executive has to be a majority, it necessarily includes the median member of the assembly. (This, of course, presupposes that the coalition supporting the executive is connected, but departing from this assumption does hardly add anything of interest.) Thus, contrary to our assumptions, the executive will always include at least one party member for whom the membership is a unfavorable. We are thus entitled to draw the general conclusion that it is impossible to account for the formation of the executive within the framework of a simple, one-dimensional ideological model. As a contrast, it is easy to account for a coalition executive in terms of interests. Thus, the parties belonging to an executive can, for instance, agree to tax those outside the coalition and share the spoils between themselves.

Let us consider the following scenario. A party A tries, in an election campaign, to attract a particular group of voters by offering them some advantages at the expense of other voters. This offer, or proposal, which we can call P, is thus a specific instruction. Then some members of the target group, who appreciate the proposal, vote for A, which thereby becomes somewhat bigger than it otherwise would be. After the election A will be considered a possible executive member and, in the negotiations preceding the formation of the executive, A promises to support important points in the other prospective member parties' programs in return for their support of P. The parties reach an agreement along these lines and form an executive. P thus becomes part of the executive's program and will, accordingly, become implemented. Is this kind of scenario, we may ask, likely, or even typical, of a parliamentary democracy with proportionalism?

My answer is in the affirmative. A first prerequisite for this answer is that the parties are able to deliver in the way described, and this condition, as we have seen, is fulfilled. This, however, does not settle the issue. It is obviously not sufficient for the parties to be able to act in the way described -they must also find it expedient to do so, it must pay in terms of votes. More exactly, the behavior must be expected to result in a net gain in votes -the number of voters attracted from other parties must be greater than the number of voters repelled.

In principle this is quite possible. The negative effects may for example be spread out so thinly, and over so many people, that those hit hardly notice. With some shrewd maneuvering it may even be possible to allocate the negative effects mainly on voters who would not have voted for the party anyway. This is so since the campaigning politicians, in a setting in which specific interests are important, are likely to be able to recognize "their own people" to a considerable extent. In a presidential setting with plurality, on the contrary, and as I will later argue, such a behavior is hardly imaginable. There, as we will see, it is imperative for all campaigners not to hurt anybody. In addition to these problems about the management of the negative effects it is, however, also necessary to consider the reactions of those favored by the proposal. Are they really likely to feel attracted and thus to change their minds in favor of the proposing party? Some may perhaps do so immediately, but there may also be those in the target group who, although favored by the particular proposal, generally dislike the system of politically distributed goods and clientelism, and therefore want to change the system rather than to use it. Such a voter, according to the terminology used here, favors some general instruction rather than the specific instruction at issue. But perhaps there is no party committed to the general instruction which the voter endorses, or if there is such a party its chances of becoming big enough for getting the instruction into a governmental program may be slim. Such dilemmas are, in fact, as we saw in part 11, quite likely. Our voter may thus find it best to play safe and vote for the party offering the favors. Voting for the second best may, after all, seem more prudent since it may give a payoff even if the favored party, after the election, still is quite small.

- The conclusion thus is that electoral strategies including specific instructions about favors to particular target groups may be quite profitable in the parliamentary, proportional setting.

From a methodological point of view it is, I think, important to note that I have not assumed any kind of rational ignorance among the voters in order to reach this conclusion. Rational ignorance, we remember, is the kind of ignorance that ordinary citizens have about public matters, since it does not pay to keep informed. The likelihood that a particular citizen voter will become pivotal in a general election is infinitesimal, and therefore the efforts needed for finding out about the campaigners programs are not worthwhile. The idea put forward here, that small target groups of voters may be favored at the expense of others, may thus be supported by the assumption that these others are rationally ignorant, and that, in fact, is often done. That assumption is however not necessary. The redistribution can, in fact, as I have shown, be explained as a consequence of perfectly enlightened and rational voter behavior within the institutional structures present. Such an explanation tells as much more about the situation than one relying on rational ignorance, and is therefore much more interesting. It is therefore, I would say, a good research strategy to avoid assumptions about rational ignorance as long as possible. In addition to this I would like to argue that ignorance, in the situation described, with several parties and a lot of interests involved, is more limited than usually assumed. People, in particular since they are not only voters but often also rent-seekers, are likely to know quite a lot about the favors offered by the political system. Another interesting point is that relations between voters and campaigners in the particular setting discussed here have important similarities with a market type contract relation.

Having said this it is however also important to emphasize, since we are dealing with compound voting, that other approaches to the voters than the one illustrated are by no means excluded. The campaigning parties may, for instance, try to attract ideologically committed voters with various ideological arguments, they may support various general instructions, or they may just refer to their achievements in the past hoping to get the voters confidence.

But even if various strategies thus may be useful, they can usually not be used without due regards. A party may for example be hurt if its various messages and promises do not form a reasonably coherent totality. If, for instance, some promise given to a group of marginal voters is to strikingly at odds with the party's ideology, some voters belonging to the party's core may leave the party. This importance of coherence has been emphasized by, among others, Downs (1957, pp 109 ff).

The Quasi Contractual Relations between Parties and Voters

In the constitutional setting discussed here, the parties have a considerable capacity for delivering. It may also be said that they have a considerable capacity for credible commitment towards the voters, and from there it is not long to think about tacit deals, or quasi contracts, between the parties and their voters in various target groups. In a real deal, or a contract, as we know, each of the parties undertakes to do something in return for the undertakings of the other parties. Here we may think of a contract like this: The party says that it will give favors to the members of the target group in return for their votes, and the members of the target group say that they will vote for the party in return for the favors. Obviously there is no contract like this, but there is something that may be considered as an approximation, and it is interesting to see how this approximation differs from the imagined real contract.

In the imagined real contract situation the party would not go ahead fulfilling its promises without making sure that the voters had fulfilled theirs. In the political situation there is obviously no such possibility -voting is anonymous and the party has no way of controlling the voters. A main rationale for anonymity, in fact, is to prevent parties and voters from bargaining. Joseph Schlesinger, for instance, writes (1991, p 146) that "... benefit seekers need some mechanisms to assert their claims.... One of the principal arguments for the secret ballot is that it makes it difficult for benefit seekers to prove their support and be paid for their vote". But even if anonymity certainly makes real contracts impossible it cannot prevent quasi contracts universally. In such a quasi contract situation the party, in its own interest, is likely to go ahead in good faith once it has made its commitment. It will try to get into the executive, and it will try to get the promise incorporated in the executive's program. Or, in short, it will behave as in a real contract situation and thereby, for future needs, enhance its own credibility. The voters, in contrast to the party, have not even made a public commitment, but just listened to the party. Still, even they, to the extent they are attracted by the offer, are likely to behave as in a real contract situation, and thus vote for the party. True, a voter might speculate that she will get the favor anyway, and therefore use her vote for some other purpose. But that means taking a risk and if the voter really wants to add the party in its efforts to fulfil its part of the deal, the best the voter can do is to vote for the party and thereby contribute to its chances of becoming a member of the executive, and to get the proposal included in the governmental program.

Obviously there is no real contract in the situation described. There is no formal agreement, no control, and no enforcement. Still the parts are likely to behave as if they were parts to a real contract, and it is therefore quite reasonable to talk about a quasi contract between the party and the attracted voters in the target group. The factor which mainly accounts for the possibility of such a quasi contract is the party's capacity for delivering, or for credible commitment. That capacity is linked to the particular constitutional setting dealt with here.

According to the discussion the main actors are the likely targets for lobbying. In this constitutional setting, it is thus the political parties, which essentially means the party leaderships at the summits of the party hierarchies, which will be approached by the lobbyists. Since these targets are few and powerful the lobbying will become a very concentrated, and possibly closed, activity. Furthermore, and since this constitutional setting to such a large extent is tuned towards interest politics, it should be a very fertile ground for lobbying activities. The lobbying is thus also likely to very effective.

- Our first conclusion thus is that the lobbying activities are likely to be concentrated, possibly closed, and very effective.

I argued that the lobbyists are likely to demand what they can reasonably get. Here, since that is possible, the lobbyists are likely to ask for changes of status quo -they will not be confined to merely blocking.

- From this -and following the argument in part 10 -it may be concluded that the interest organizations are likely to be long lasting and formed before the laws, which support their interests, are created.

One interesting possibility is that trade unions, which are formed for negotiating with their counterparts about wages and other conditions of labor, are likely to become important lobbyists as well. Since the unions are likely to be able to influence the voting behavior of their members to some extent, they may even, by playing a mediating role, enforce the contract character of the relation between parties and voters.

- Another conclusion, which follows form the fact that the prerequisites for organizational ties between parties and organizations as stated in part 10 are fulfilled, is that such ties are quite possible -and perhaps even likely.

This conclusion, it should be noted, is further supported by the fact that politics in the constitutional setting at issue here is likely to be strongly interest oriented. Thus not only the organizational prerequisites for alliances between parties and interest organizations are present, but also strong positive incentives for that kind of collaboration.

Parliamentary Constitutions with Proportional Elections: In this constitutional setting we are likely to get several political parties since the elections for the legislature are proportional. Furthermore it is important for the parties to get into the executive, since in a parliamentarian system most decisive constellations include the executive. Since there are numerous parties the executive is likely to be a coalition.

A party aspiring for a place in a coalition executive is greatly helped by being cohesive and disciplined, and therefore the parties will be so, if effective means for discipline are available. In a proportional system that is the case, and thus the parties are likely to become cohesive and disciplined. The main actors will consequently be party main actors.

As for their policies the basic important fact is that the parties are capable of delivering, or, in other words, have a capacity for credible commitment towards the voters. In their relations to the voters they are therefore likely to strive for instruction rather than delegation. Furthermore, and since it is much easier to agree about specific instructions than about general ones when forming a coalition executive, specific instructions are likely to be particularly important components of policies. Politics will to a large extent be interest politics. Since lobbyists are expected to approach the main actors they will, in this constitutional setting, turn to the leaderships of the cohesive political parties.

The lobbying activities will thus be very concentrated, and to some extent perhaps also closed or secret. Since politics to such a large extent is tuned towards interests, lobbying is also likely to be quite effective. The interest organizations, which may have organizational ties with the parties, are likely to get interests satisfied in exchange for votes from their members. This, so far, is a short summary of some earlier main points. In addition to this a few further conclusions may be added. I will start from the contention that the main actors, in this constitutional setting, are political parties, and that politics therefore, on the whole, is party politics. It may also be said that we are dealing with a partyocracy.

- Now, since the parties are just parties, this means that there is no democratically appointed main actor with a responsibility for the common good. All actors represent primarily, and basically, their own interests.
- Another related conclusion is that all proposals for decisions are made by those directly interested in them. The making of proposals, and of decisions, are in a sense inseparable aspects of one and the same process. Almost everything is done when the executive is formed, and by the parties taking part in that process.

The fact that the main actors are parties, does not, of course, mean that individuals are unimportant. The parties do obviously consist of individual human beings and this fact should certainly, and in accordance with methodological individualism, be recognized. The individuals do however almost exclusively play their roles within, or on behalf of, the parties. Thus, and when it comes to dealings with actors outside the party, for example with other parties, or with the electorate in campaigns, or with lobbyists, it is usually the individuals belonging to the party leaderships which acts on behalf of their parties. Party positions on political issues are of course also determined by the individuals who belong to the party, usually with more influence the higher up in the party hierarchy they are:

- An important conclusion of this, since the individuals essentially play their roles within, or on behalf of, the parties, is that political careers, in this type of system, always are party careers.

Since the parties are likely to be well developed organizations, and to have an easily recognized identity over time, they will be able to develop successively, and to harbor, more and more elaborated, and more and more comprehensive, party programs.

- Furthermore, since the programs are likely to favour the interests of particular groups of voters, long-lasting, mutually supportive relations between parties and voters tend to develop. The party leaderships will thus to a large extent be able to recognise their own people in the electorate.

I have already said several times that politics in this constitutional setting tends to be focused on special interests.

- Another formulation of this conclusion, which alludes to the well known Gresham's law in economics ("cheap money drives out good"), is that specific instructions drive out general ones.

This does not mean that general instructions are altogether eradicated -we have for example seen that general instructions in a big party's program may prevail. Specific instructions are, however, much less threatened, and even encouraged by the system. Most parties, as it seems, will have to deal extensively with specific instructions in order to survive. Specific instructions are thus, in a sense, forced upon politics. This may also impede the voters from favouring ideological positions, and reduce them to interest seekers. All of this, it may be noted, is to a large extent in agreement with Buchanan's contention (1993) that "Political players who might seek to further some conception of an all-encompassing general, or public, interest cannot survive". Buchanan is however discussing democratic constitutions in general, whereas the focus here is on parliamentary constitutions with proportional elections.

- One implication of this focussing on special interests is that the turnout in elections is likely to be high. Since people are stimulated to pursue their own private or personal interests by political means, the turnout is likely to be greater than in other types of democratic systems.
- Another implication is that the system is likely to exhibit the kind of properties which are usually associated with the so called "tragedy of the commons". There, we remember, the single farmer, since he is unable to affect the general handling of the common pasture, will have to put his cow on the pasture as quickly as possible if it shall get any grass

at all. Consequently, and since all farmers are driven to behave in the same way, the pasture will be destroyed. In the political system discussed here the incentives of politicians and voters will bring them to treat common societal resources in a similar destructive way.

PARLIAMENTARY CONSTITUTIONS WITH MAJORITARIAN ELECTIONS

As I mentioned in previous part, there may also be more than two parties. Here, in this part, and in the following parts, I will however concentrate on the two-party case. The reason is that this case has important unique properties, since there will not be any coalition building. If, on the contrary, there are more than two parties we are likely to get coalition politics, and the analysis, although different in some respects, will also have important similarities with the analysis of proportional, parliamentary systems.

The most important fact in the two-party case is that there is normally no interaction at all between the main actors. The biggest party, that is the party which won the last general election, is likely have a safe majority of its own. That party will thus form the executive single-handedly. There will not be any need for the party to cooperate with the other party. The governing party will act alone. In this respect the system differs starkly from the three other main types of constitutional systems we are considering here.

There may, however, be exceptions to this general rule. Thus, if the biggest party's majority is narrow, relatively strong and independent, individual legislators of the governing party may be able to challenge the party leadership. Such legislators may for example force the party leadership to change some proposal in some way, or to deliver some other kind of favor, for example for the legislators' local constituencies. In these situations individual main actors thus become important, and the governing party main actor will have to deal with them. This, of course, is tantamount to main actor interaction.

Here, after having said what there is to say about main actor interaction in a narrow sense, I could end this part. It does, however, seem fitting to add a few consequences of the general rule of no main actor interaction at all, since they constitute contrasts to the preceding proportional variety of parliamentarism. Here are two consequences of that kind.

- First, the governmental process may be more continuous, and less of a batch process, than in the proportional variety of parliamentarism. The reason is that the proposals, which are presented for the legislature, are prepared by the governing party alone. The governmental program may therefore develop gradually during the electoral period.
- Second, in this system, there is always a clear-cut opposition. The party which does not govern is the opposition. There is no ambiguity in that sense, and there is nothing to be lost, such as valuable pivotal positions, by organizing the opposition. The establishment of a shadow cabinet should therefore cause no surprise.

The Cube Rule

In a majoritarian system the party getting most votes usually becomes over-represented in the legislature to a very considerable extent, and the party getting least votes is usually, and consequently, largely under-represented. The so called cube rule is the result of efforts to find a simple relationship, in a majoritarian system, between the quantities involved here. Originally it was formulated in 1909 by J. P. Smith in a report to the British Royal Commission on electoral systems. Let us assume that there are two parties which get V1 and V2 votes in an election, counted nationwide, and after that, using the plurality method, get M1 and M2 mandates respectively in the legislature. Then, according to the cube rule, (M1/M2) = (V1/V2)3. This rule has given a fairly good picture of the development in England during certain periods.

Some Conditions for the System's Proper Functioning

We saw that a parliamentary system, for its proper functioning, depends on disciplined and cohesive parties. This requirement is however probably more important in a proportional system than in a majoritarian one. The reason is that the dominating party in a two-party system usually represents a considerably greater majority in the legislature than a governing coalition in a multiparty-system. The somewhat lesser discipline which is likely in a majoritarian system may therefore be compensated for the smaller number of parties.

It therefore seems reasonable to assume that both proportional and majoritarian electoral systems can sustain a parliamentary regime, but the requirement is that the electoral system is of an appropriate variety. We saw that a proportional system, when that is used, basically has to be of the list kind. Here, a similar condition is that the majoritarian method used probably has to be of the first-past-the-post type, whereas the double ballot method probably is unsuitable. The reason is that this latter method is likely to give a considerable number of parties with rather low discipline. The number of parties is thus likely to be greater than if the first-past-the-post method is used, and their discipline is likely to be considerably less than in the case of proportional list elections. A parliamentary system using the double-ballot method is thus likely to fail.

Furthermore, and for the same reasons as in the proportional, parliamentary setting, the popular techniques of primaries, referendums and initiatives are alien to the system and thus not likely to be used. Indeed, even the possibility of using referendums occasionally for saving the parties from dealing with potentially splitting issues, which was real in the proportional context. The reason is that, in this majoritarian context, it is important for the parties, in order to demonstrate a capacity for governing, to have a complete governmental program.

THE POSSIBILITY OF PURELY IDEOLOGICAL SINGLE PARTY EXECUTIVES

As we saw it is impossible to account for the appearance of a coalition executive within the framework of an one-dimensional spatial model. If there are just two parties in the legislature, as we are now assuming (or if one party has a majority of its own), the executive may very well have an ideological foundation. Consider, for example, the situation. There P2 can easily, by itself, form an executive, and that executive is obviously able to pursue a policy equivalent to P2's position on the ideological scale. In a parliamentary-majoritarian context with two main parties it is thus perfectly possible to account for the executive formation in purely ideological terms. Here, as always when we are talking about general elections in democracies, we have to do with compound voting. The parties may thus mix various specific or general instructions in their programs, and they may try to obtain some elements of delegation in the relations to the voters, and each individual voter will have to react to all this in his or her personal way. So far everything is the same as in the parliamentary, proportional.

Since we are dealing with parliamentary systems, with fairly cohesive and disciplined parties, it also seems reasonable to conclude that the parties, as in the proportional setting, have a clear capacity for credible commitment towards the voters in general, or towards particular segments of the electorate. A main problem, however, concerns the extent to which they are likely to make use of this latter capacity, the one related to specified target groups.

In the parliamentary, proportional setting, the voters, we remember, could be deterred from voting for general instructions, for example ideological ones, since such votes were easily wasted. In many situations the voters would rather settle for the second best and vote for some specific instruction. Here, these mechanisms are clearly different. Since we are dealing with one-party executives rather than coalition executives, the winning party will have no difficulty in implementing its general instructions, and therefore a voter, who likes a party's general principles, is not deterred from voting for it. The conclusion drawn in the previous chapter, that specific instructions tend to drive out general instructions, is thus not valid here. General instructions will obviously have a place in the election campaigns.

After that conclusion it is tempting to continue by asking whether, in fact, general instructions even tend to drive out specific instructions. I believe that there will be, at least, some such tendency. The reason is that the two parties in this setting, since either of them is going to form the executive single-handedly, must show some fitness for being able to govern, for statesmanship, or, in other words, for caring about general things, in order to get votes. The voters know that they are voting, directly, for a government. In the proportional setting that is not so. There the formation of the executive is, exclusively, a matter for the parties. The voters are devoid of means of influence in that respect, and to a large extent restricted to expressing their interests. Thus, in this situation, where the voters are, in fact, voting for a government, they are likely to be interested in, and to respond to, ideological signals from the campaigning parties.

Ideology may thus be important and politics may therefore be quite well represented by models such as the one in the figure in part 15.3. The implication is that politics is mainly about ideological matters, and that the ideologies represented by the two parties are fairly close to each other, and also close to the median position on a single scale, which may be a left-right scale. The ideologies are thus not extreme. This kind of politics could be called median voter ideological politics.

This leads to some important conclusions. A first one is that phrases such as "the winner takes all", or "majoritarian politics", which are sometimes used for describing the parliamentarian, majoritarian setting, are wrong, at least to the extent that we are dealing with median voter ideological politics. Rather, and since all voters in a sense contribute to determining the median position, it may be appropriate to talk about ideological consensus. Another conclusion is that we should not necessarily expect very narrow, or minimal, majorities in the legislature. Broad majorities, if they occur, should not be a surprise.

For countries characterized by median voter ideological politics we may, furthermore, conclude that a regular change of the governing party is likely to occur. The reason is that the parties take positions close to the median position and there will always, ex ante, be a considerable uncertainty about the electoral payoff of the positioning. In addition to that the mechanisms illustrated by the cube rule will usually make sure that small differences in electoral payoff are transformed into big differences in the legislature. The possibilities for a big party to dominate a country's politics for long periods, as in the parliamentary, proportional case, are consequently slim.

So far I have only talked about the parties' efforts to win elections but it is, since we are dealing with single member constituencies, and as I have already mentioned several times, also necessary to consider the individual candidates' efforts. These candidates, to the extent that they engage in campaigns of their own, will, as it seems, have to rely on emphasizing their own personalities in various ways. Consequently we shall expect, in this system, beside instructions, a certain amount of delegation as well.

Parliamentary Constitutions with Majoritarian Elections

Since we are dealing with a parliamentary system lobbying will, on the whole, occur at the summits of the party hierarchies. It is however likely to be less influential than in the parliamentary-proportional case, because interests plays a less important role in the politics of this system. In particular, since the governing party is likely to change, and since the programs of both parties are likely to be close to the median, and thus quite similar, fusions of interest organizations and parties are not likely to occur. In this constitutional setting we are likely to get fewer parties than in the parliamentary, proportional setting. In the extreme case we will get just two dominating parties and that is the case I am dealing with here.

Since we are dealing with a parliamentary system it is important for the parties to be cohesive and disciplined. The requirements in this respect are, however, less far-reaching than in the parliamentary, proportional setting, since the bigger party usually, is considerably bigger than the smaller party in the legislature. Therefore it should not be a problem that the means of discipline are somewhat weaker than in the proportional case. Furthermore, and since there are just two parties, the one or the other will single-handedly form the executive and we will thus not get any coalition politics. This is likely to be quite consequential since it opens the door for ideological politics concerned with general instructions rather than interest politics concerned with specific instructions. We are likely to get median voter ideological politics.

The fact that the parties try to occupy positions close to the median voter's position, in combination with the tendency for the bigger party to become grossly over-represented in the legislature, is also likely to lead to frequent changes of power. The mechanisms in the parliamentary, proportional setting which allow a party to dominate its country's politics over extended periods are not operating here. Since there are just two parties, the one forming the executive and the other the opposition, we are also likely to get a shadow cabinet. This, again, is in contrast to the situation in the parliamentary, proportional context, where some parties' wish to obtain pivotal positions was likely to prevent the emergence of a shadow cabinet. Here, as in the proportional context, the lobbying organizations are likely to approach the party leadership's with their demands. Since the politics is less likely to be tuned towards interests, the politicians in the parties are, however, likely to be less inclined to listen to the lobbyists and make deals with them.

PRESIDENTIAL CONSTITUTIONS WITH PROPORTIONAL ELECTIONS

Here, as in the other systems we are studying, the main actors will try to further their ambitions by forming, or by just supporting, various decisive or blocking sets. In the presidential systems -this one as well as the majoritarian variety -the president has a particularly important role in these interactions. This is due to the following three aspects of the presidential power.

1. The inclusion of the president is often required for making a set decisive. Sometimes that requirement is dropped, but if so the requirements for a decisive set composed only of legislators is usually sharper. Some kind of qualified majority of legislators may for example be required.
2. The president is usually equipped with special, legal procedural power for making proposals.
3. The president may command resources of various kinds which may be used for giving favors, or compensations, to legislators in order to make them support a presidential proposal.

In the presidential, proportional system discussed here there may, as I have already mentioned, be some party main actors. Even so, however, there will also in all likelihood be quite a number individual main actors. The total number of main actors will therefore be rather great, and the conditions for coordination are consequently not the best. The main actor interaction is therefore likely to be characterized by a lot of uncoordinated behavior. Furthermore, and from the legislators' point of view, coordination, to the extent that it is possible at all, will be considerably easier when it aims at creating blocking sets rather than decisive sets. In particular this is so if there are two houses in the legislature. Now, taking all of this, into account, the following hypothetical conclusions can be drawn about the main actor interaction in proportional, presidential systems:

- The reactions to the proposals presented, whether they come from the president or the legislature, will to a large extent be uncoordinated. This means that the voting pattern, at least to a considerable extent, will vary from decision to decision. It also means that occasional majorities which are considerable larger than minimal winning should cause no surprise. It furthermore means that the political process will be continuous, rather than of the batch type. It also means that an organized opposition is unlikely.
- Proposals for new legislation require, in order to pass, the creation of decisive sets, and they will therefore, in fact, often come from the president. This is a consequence of the aspects 1 and 2 above. The president has an advantage in creating decisive sets.

- But even if it is difficult for the legislators to initiate new legislation, they may be successful in the much easier task of creating blocking sets. This is particularly so in this proportional setting, where some party groups in the legislature may be quite consolidated. The purpose may be to bring abqut some wanted changes in the proposal blocked. The purpose may however also be obstructive -the proposal may be blocked even by legislators symphatizing with the proposal. If so the idea of the blocking legislators may be to blackmail the president -to force him to give favors to themselves, or to their constituencies, in exchange for an end to the blocking. What makes this kind of blackmail possible, and attractive, is, of course, the fact indicated in point 3 above that the president controls resources of various kinds. Thus, and since the legislature does not dispose of any resources of the kind mentioned, we will never see any blackmailing in the opposite direction -the president will not try to blackmail the legislature.

Some Conditions for the System's Proper Functioning

For the other three main types of constitutional systems treated in this theory it seems possible to consider some kind of functioning as the proper functioning, and therefore also to talk about the conditions for this proper functioning. In this case it is, however, not so clearly like that. I am rather inclined to say that this constitutional system, inherently, is inept and unlikely to function properly. The reason is that presidentialism, which requires party indiscipline is combined with proportional elections, which, at least if we are considering list elections, provide means for enforcing party discipline. Blocking and obstruction are thus likely to be frequent. Pure list elections thus seem to be incompatible with the systems proper functioning, but perhaps it may work in combination with other kinds of proportional systems, which give the voters influence on the fate of individual candidates. The Finnish system is an example. The use of primaries may also, take power away from the party leaderships, and thus enhance the functioning of the system. Frequent use of initiatives and referendums may also have similar effects.

The upshot of all this is that presidential systems with proportional elections contain a kind of tension, or balance on a very thin edge. As we saw that proportional elections require that political parties of some kind exist. Still, and according to the argument just presented, the constitutional system treated here requires, for its proper functioning, that the parties are not too homogenous, or too disciplined, or, in other words, that they are not too much of parties.

Presidential Constitutions with Proportional Elections: When discussing the relation between the main actors and the voters in this case it is, at first, necessary to distinguish between the presidential elections and the elections for the legislature.

The position for which presidential candidates are striving is, of course, even if the candidates belong to political parties, an individual main actor position. According to the final conclusion we should therefore expect the presidential candidates to strive for a relation of delegation, rather than instruction, with the voters. In their campaigns they will therefore concentrate on their own personalities and personal qualities rather on detailed political programs. Furthermore, since a candidate in order to win has to win a majority of the votes, or, depending on the circumstances and the exact rules, at least almost a majority, he or she has to treat all members of the electorate as potential supporters. The campaign messages are thus not likely to offend any voters, for instance by attacking their interests. The nature of the election campaigns for the legislature will depend on whether we are dealing with pure list elections or not. In the case of list elections, the party leaderships are likely to do a main part of the campaign work. Furthermore, the campaigning will mainly be about instructions or political programs. These conclusions are valid, I think, independently of the extent to which the party leaderships choose to discipline their "troops" in the legislature. Thus, if we have pure list elections, the party leaderships will dominate the campaigns, and the message will be about instructions and programs, even if, after that, the party leaderships give the individual legislators a considerable amount of freedom in their activities in the legislature. If, however, we are not dealing with pure list elections, but with some other proportional method which makes it possible for the voter to choose, to some extent, among individual candidates, things become different. If so we will also see some individual campaigning and consequently, also, more of delegation and less of instruction. Taking everything into account we are thus likely to see, side by side, very different kinds of campaigning in this constitutional setting, in particular if pure list elections are used for legislature. If so the presidential campaigns will emphasize delegation and personal qualities, whereas the campaigns for the legislature will emphasize instruction and party programs.

PRESIDENTIAL CONSTITUTIONS WITH PROPORTIONAL ELECTIONS

In this constitutional setting, as well as in the other ones, the lobbyists are likely to approach the main actors. Furthermore, the purposes of the lobbyists may either be to get new legislation into being, or to prevent the removal of existing legislation. In the former case, since the problem is to bring about a decisive constellation, the lobbyist may find it best to approach the president. In the latter case, which is easier since the creation of a blocking constellation is enough, the lobbyist may however also find it worthwhile to approach party main actors in the legislature. Lobbyists approaching individual main actors in the legislature is, however, likely to be an infrequent phenomenon. At least this is so if there are any suitable party main actors in the legislature. Since the lobbyists thus may either try to initiate new legislation, or to prevent the removal existing legislation, we may, se both lobbying organizations, which are formed in order to bring changes about, and thus prior to any such changes, and organizations which are formed after some beneficial legislation, in order to prevent its removal. Finally, and since some of the parties may be well consolidated, organizational ties between such parties and lobbying organizations should not be excluded.The main characteristic of this constitutional system is that its two main components -that is the president or the presidency on one side, and the legislature on the other -are likely to be ill-matched. The politics of the legislature is likely to be party politics to a large extent. This means that party main actors are likely to play dominant roles. It also means that all legislators, in all likelihood, are people making party careers.

Candidates aspiring for the presidency do not, however, necessarily have to belong to a political party. Their careers are not necessarily party careers. Still, of course, an elected president does have a personal mandate of some kind of his or her own. The important main implication of this incongruous pattern is that clashes between the president and the legislature are likely and, in particular, that main actors in the legislature may try to blackmail the president. In this system all main actors are likely to be individuals -we are not likely to find any party main actors. Therefore, although there are some similarities with the presidential, proportional system, there are also some differences. The president's role is important for the same reasons as in the presidential, proportional setting, but it is considerably more difficult for the main actors in the legislature to co-ordinate their behavior. The reason, of course, is that individual main actors dominate in this system. This means that the first two conclusions for presidential, proportional systems, as presented in part 19, will be the same here. Thus:

- The reactions to the proposals presented, whether they come from the president or the legislature, will to a large extent be uncoordinated. This means that the voting pattern, at least to a considerable extent, will vary from decision to decision. It also means that occasional majorities which are considerable larger than minimal winning should cause no surprise. It furthermore means that the political process will be continuous, rather than of the batch type. It also means that an organized opposition is unlikely.
- Proposals for new legislation require, in order to pass, the creation of decisive sets, and they will therefore, in fact, often come from the president. The president has an advantage in creating decisive sets.

The main difference concerns the third conclusion in part 19. Here -in contrast to the situation there -organized blocking, fund thus obstruction, will be less frequent.

Some Conditions for the System's Proper Functioning

Since the main actors in the legislature are likely to be individual main actors the threats to the system's functioning, in the form of clashes between the legislature and the president, that is blocking and obstructive behavior in the legislature, are much smaller here than in the presidential, proportional setting. Still some such threats may exist. If so, the likely reason is that the legislators for some reason are dependent on political parties, and that the party leaderships somehow manage to discipline their troops. A corrective may be the introduction of primaries, and perhaps also of referendums and initiatives.

Imagine a person running for the presidency, or for a seat in the legislature. In both cases everybody knows that the person, after the election, and however great the electoral success, will not, without anything further, be in a position to implement his or her delivered campaign proposals, since she also has to deal with the heterogeneous legislature. Exactly for that reason it would not be particularly clever, and perhaps even somewhat ridiculous, to let detailed proposals dominate the campaign. It seems more expedient for the candidate to emphasize his or her own personal very general political inclinations, and personal qualities, thereby indicating a capacity for prudent action in various future situations which, at the moment of the election, are impossible to foresee. The candidate's capacity for credible commitment towards the voters is very limited indeed. The relation between voters and politicians will thus be more of delegation than of instruction. Furthermore, in this system, with no clear opposition, and without elaborated party programs, it is difficult, or impossible, for the politicians to distinguish between their own voters and the other ones. All citizens are potential supporters and it is therefore important to avoid repelling any voters. All policies which are distinctly harmful for specific groups of voters must be avoided. For this reason a politician may be ill advised to propose the canceling of favors which already happen to exist. In contrast to the situation in parliamentary systems there is a very large number of targets for lobbying in this setting. The president is obviously a main target. There may also be key persons in the legislature with a lot of procedural power, for example chairmen of committees, which are likely to be approached. In addition to this all individual members of the legislature are also interesting targets. The lobbying activities are thus likely to be spread out, rather than concentrated, and therefore they are also likely to be very costly, or inefficient. If a lobbying organization, for instance, strives for getting a decisive constellation behind a proposal it favors, it will have to approach a great number of different individuals, one by one, rather than one or a few consolidated parties as in a parliamentary system.

This, in turn, may mean that it is considerably easier to lobby for blocking, than to lobby for changes of the status quo. The reason is not only that the constellations needed for blocking usually are smaller than the ones needed for a positive decision. In addition, as we saw in the preceding section, the politicians must be careful not to offend any voters. That should make it wise to abstain from supporting a proposal which a lobbyist wants to see defeated. Lobbying for change of status quo may preferably be directed towards the president.

Since the parties, considered as organizations, are too loose to be able to be parts in joint organizations, the lobbyists are likely to be free in relation to them. In contrast to the case in the parliamentary, proportional setting we will thus not see any fusions between political parties and interest organizations. There is also, a possibility that lobbyists form after reforms are implemented, rather than the other way round.

In this system political parties are significantly less important than in the other three system types. Political parties are not even necessary for the system's functioning since all elections, the presidential ones as well as those for the legislature, are majoritarian. Even so, parties may appear. The system's functioning is however not hampered, and it may indeed be improved, if the parties activities are constrained by for instance primaries.

An important consequence of this restricted role for political parties is that political careers do not have to be party careers, and that individual main actors are more important than in any other constitutional setting. It may, in fact, be argued that this constitutional type, more than any other type, resembles an ordinary association, say a sports club or a charity association. In such an association, as we know, there are usually no parties. The main decision-makers, or decisions-making bodies, of such an association may be a president, a board, and a general congress. These entities, and their workings, may correspond quite closely to the president with his executive, and the legislature, in this constitutional setting.

CHAPTER

4

POLITICAL CULTURE

Politics is the process by which groups make decisions. Although the term is generally applied to behavior within governments, politics is observed in all human (and many non-human) group interactions, including corporate, academic, and religious institutions. In general, politics can be considered the art of navigating through tensions among multiple "I"s and the "we" to achieve collectively desired ends.

The study of politics originated in Greek political philosophy. For the Greek philosophers, politics was the means by which philosophy came into practicality. Political philosophy concerned the life of man in the polis (Greek roughly meaning "city").

Today, Political Philosophy is the study of what politics is and what the best regime is. Political science (also political studies) is the study of political behavior and examines the acquisition and application of power. Government may refer to the study of particular political regimes and practices, though "government" is sometimes used as a synonym for political science. In practice, political philosophy, politics as a social science and/or practical concerns may be integrated in various kinds of political studies.

A NATURAL STATE

There are many debates as to who was the first person to study politics, many credit Socrates with the first study of politics, while others credit Aristotle. One of the first works concerning politics was Plato's. In Plato's concept, the polis was the way in which man became virtuous. His student and successor Aristotle went on to right the Politics (book) Politics, where he asserts that the city is, by nature, and that man is, by nature, a political animal. Though he does not define it in this manner, Aristotle's assertions point to the natural state of man as being in the city. Only through the city can man become totally self sufficient and thus truly human. These two positions held supreme until the dawn of Modernity (a reaction to the Classical and Scholastic view of philosophy). Machiavelli was among the first political philosophers of Modernity. His most famous work was the Prince (book) Princewhere he discusses the nature of principalities. The idea of "ends justify the means" came from this book, along with the idea of harsh politics. Many people misunderstand Machiavelli's most well known work, believing him to be a fan of strong princes with absolute control. In fact, Machiavelli was a well known republican (one who believes in republican government) and praises it in his Discourses on Livy (book) Discourses on Livy. Modernity thinkers (Enlightenment thinkers), believed that man by nature was not born into a polis, separating from the classical view of Plato and Aristotle. The idea of politics changed from what can the state do for you to what can you do for the state. It became man's job to perfect nature. In 1651, Thomas Hobbes published his most famous work, Leviathan, in which he proposed a model of early human development to justify the creation of a government.

Hobbes described an ideal state of nature wherein every person had equal right to every resource in nature and was free to use any means to acquire those resources. He claimed that such an arrangement created a "war of all against all" (bellum omnium contra omnes). Further, he noted that men would enter into a social contract and would give up absolute rights in exchange for certain protections. Hobbes' During the latter half of the 1600's and into the 1700's an Englishman named John Locke wrote his first and second Treatises on Government (book) first and second Treatises on Government.

In the first, Locke argues against the idea of divine right monarchy. He goes to great lengths to prove that no man is by nature placed over another man. In the second treatise (much more well known), Locke asserts that the state of nature consists of every man being equal to every other and all of nature was in common for every one else. Unlike Hobbes, this state of nature did not mean a state of war. Locke believed that man by nature possesses reason (which he calls the Law of Nature) and only when he separates from that reason does he enter a state of war. Man leaves the state of nature, according to Locke, because in nature there are no general laws, no common judge, and no one to enforce the laws. By the end of the 1700's the Enlightenment was ending and on the cusp of Post-Modernity sat Jean-Jacque Rousseau. Rousseau asserted that man by nature was utterly free to do what he wished, and is not a social animal. When man leaves the state of nature and enters civil society he becomes sort of a slave to the state. While each era of political thought changed the state of nature, man must leave nature and enter into societies. Politics then is the study of how humans interact with each other and cooperate to become self sufficient.

DEFINITIONS

- Power Max Weber defined power as the ability to impose one's will upon another, while Hannah Arendt states that "political power corresponds to the human ability not just to act but to act in concert."
- Authority is the ability to enforce laws, to exact obedience, to command, to determine, or to judge.
- A government is the body that has the authority to make and enforce rules or laws.
- Legitimacy is an attribute of government gained through the acquisition and application of power in accordance with recognized or accepted standards or principles.
- Sovereignty is the ability of a government to exert control over its territory free from outside influence.

CLASSIFICATION OF POLITICAL IDEOLOGIES

PRAGMATIC VIEW OF POWER

Samuel Gompers' maxim, often paraphrased as,"Reward your friends and punish your enemies," hints at two of the five types of power recognized by social psychologists: incentive power (the power to reward) and coercive power (the power to punish). Arguably the other three grow out of these two. Legitimate power, the power of the policeman or the referee, is the power given to an individual by a recognized authority to enforce standards of behavior. Legitimate power is similar to coercive power in that unacceptable behavior is punished by fine or penalty. Referent power is bestowed upon individuals by virtue of accomplishment or attitude. Fulfillment of the desire to feel similar to a celebrity or a hero is the reward for obedience. Expert power springs from education or experience. Following the lead of an experienced coach is often rewarded with success. Expert power is conditional to the circumstances. A brain surgeon is no help when your pipes are leaking.

GOVERNMENT

A government is a body that has the authority to make and the power to enforce laws within a civil, corporate, religious, academic, or other organization or group. In its broadest sense, "to govern" means to administer or supervise, whether over a state, a set group of people, or a collection of assets. The word government is ultimately derived from the Greek kybernan, which means "to steer" or "to control". Typically, "the government" refers to the executive function of the state. In many countries (particularly those having parliamentary systems), the government refers to the executive branch of government or a specifically named executive, such as the Blair government (compare to the administration as in the Bush administration in U.S. usage). In countries using the Westminster system, the party in government will also usually control the legislature.

FORMS OF GOVERNMENT

Governments are often classified according to the number of people who hold political power.

- In Autocracies one individual holds all the power. This category includes absolute monarchies as well as dictatorships with an all-powerful president or other central figure.
- In Oligarchies political power is held by a small group of individuals who share interests. For example a plutocracy is composed of the wealthiest members of society.
- Democracies are governments where the people as a whole hold political power. It may be exercised by them (direct democracy), or through representatives chosen by them (representative democracy).

The lines between some of the above forms of government can sometimes be ambiguous. For example, during the 19th century, most self-proclaimed "democracies" restricted voting rights to a minority of the population (e.g. property-owning males). This could qualify them as oligarchies rather than democracies. On the other hand, the voting minority was often quite large (20-30% of the population) and its members did not form the compact group with common interests that is the hallmark of most oligarchies. Thus, this form of government occupied a space between democracy and oligarchy as they are understood today.

Ideas about the Origin of Government

There are a wide range of theories about the reasons for establishing governments. The four major ones are briefly described below. Note that they do not always fully oppose each other -it is possible for a person to subscribe to a combination of ideas from two or more of these theories.

Force Theory

Many political philosophies that are opposed to the existence of a government (such as Anarchism, Nihilism, and to a lesser extent Marxism), as well as others, emphasize the historical roots of governments -the fact that governments, along with private property, originated from the authority of warlords and petty despots who took, by force, certain patches of land as their own (and began exercising authority over the people living on that land). Thus, it is argued that governments exist to enforce the will of the strong and oppress the weak, maintaining and protecting the privilege of a ruling class. It states that the government emerged when all the people of an area were brought under the authority of one person or group!

Order and Tradition

The various forms of conservatism, by contrast, generally see the government as a positive force that brings order out of chaos, establishes laws to end the "war of all against all", encourages moral virtue while punishing vice, and respects tradition. Sometimes, in this view, the government is seen as something ordained by a higher power, as in the divine right of kings, which human beings have a duty to obey.

Natural Rights

Natural rights are the basis for the theory of government shared by most branches of liberalism (including libertarianism). In this view, human beings are born with certain natural rights, and governments are established strictly for the purpose of protecting those rights. What the natural rights actually are is a matter of dispute among liberals; indeed, each branch of liberalism has its own set of rights that it considers to be natural, and these rights are sometimes mutually exclusive with the rights supported by other liberals. As a result, there is some debate between natural rights theorists, ranging from modern writers such as Tibor Machan to Enlightenment thinkers such as Locke, Kant, or Jefferson.

Social Contract

One of the most influential theories of government in the past two hundred years has been the social contract, on which modern democracy and most forms of socialism are founded. The social contract theory holds that governments are created by the people in order to provide for collective needs (such as safety from crime, poverty, illiteracy) that cannot be properly satisfied using purely individual means. Governments thus exist for the purpose of serving the needs and wishes of the people, and their relationship with the people is clearly stipulated in a "social contract" (a constitution and a set of laws) which both the government and the people must abide by. If a majority is unhappy, it may change the social contract. If a minority is unhappy, it may persuade the majority to change the contract, or it may opt out of it by emigration or secession. This theory is based on the idea that all men live in a state of nature which is not ideal to perfect harmony. It is also an agreement among the members of an organized society or between the governed and the government defining and limiting the rights and duties of each. Thomas Hobbes, John Locke, Jean-Jacques Rousseau are three of the most famous philosophers of contractarianism. Today, natural rights are the basis for many issues involving the constitution and ones right to privacy under the government.

Governmental Operations

Governments concern themselves with regulating and administering many areas of human activity, such as trade, education, or medicine. Governments also employ different methods to maintain the established order, such as secrecy, censorship, police and military forces (particularly under despotism, see also police state), making agreements with other states, and maintaining support within the state.

Typical methods of maintaining support and legitimacy include providing the infrastructure for administration, justice, transport, communication, social welfare, etc.; claiming support from deities; providing benefits to elites; providing shops for important posts within the state; limiting the power of the state through laws and constitutions; and appealing to nationalism. Different political ideologies hold different ideas on what the government should or should not do.

The modern standard unit of territory is a country. In addition to the meaning used above, the word state can refer either to a government or to its territory. Within a territory, subnational entities may have local governments which do not have the full power of a national government (for example, they will generally lack the authority to declare war or carry out diplomacy).

Size of Government

The scale to which government should exist and operate in the world is a matter of debate. Government spending in developed countries varies considerably but generally makes up between about 30% and 70% of their GDP. One major exception is the United States, where central government spending takes up less than 20% of GDP.

World Government

Some speculate that technological changes such as the Internet and the global English language would bring a World Government into existence. Some consider some governments such as the European Commission as trends towards such a system; however, others do not see this as possible.

CONSTITUTION

A constitution is a system, often codified as a written document, that establishes the rules and principles whereby an organization or political entity is governed. In the case of countries, this term refers specifically to a national constitution defining the fundamental political principles, and establishing the power and duties, of each government. Most national constitutions also guarantee certain rights to the people. Historically, before the evolution of modern-style, codified national constitutions, the term constitution could be applied to any important law that governed the functioning of a government. Constitutions are found in many organizations. They are found extensively in government, at supranational (e.g. United Nations Charter), national (e.g. Constitution of Japan), and sub-national or provincial (e.g. Constitution of Maryland) levels. They are found in many political groups, such as political parties and pressure groups, including trade unions (labour unions). There are many non-political groups and entities that may have constitutions of a sort such as companies and voluntary organisations.

Etymology

The term constitution comes from Latin, referring to issuing any important law, usually by the Roman emperor. Later, the term was widely used in canon law to indicate certain relevant decisions, mainly from the pope.

General Features

Generally, all constitutions confer specific powers to an organization on the condition that it abides by this constitution or charter limitation. The Latin term ultra vires describes activities that fall outside an organisation's or legislative body's legal or constitutional authority.

For example, a students' union may be prohibited as an organization from engaging in activities not concerning students; if the union becomes involved in non-student activities these activities are considered ultra vires of the union's charter. An example from the constitutional law of nation-states would be a provincial government in a federal state trying to legislate in an area exclusively enumerated to the federal government in the constitution.

For example, in the United States, any attempt by a state legislature to ratify a treaty with a foreign nation would be considered ultra vires of Congress' constitutional authority, being contrary to the constitution. In both cases, "ultra vires" gives a legal justification for the forced cessation of such action, which would be enforced by the judiciary in government.

Governmental Constitutions

Most commonly, the term constitution refers to a set of rules and principles that define the nature and extent of government. Most constitutions seek to regulate the relationship between institutions of the state, in a basic sense the relationship between the executive, legislature and the judiciary, but also the relationship of institutions within those branches.

For example, executive branches can be divided into a head of government, government departments/ministries, executive agencies and a civil service/bureaucracy. Most constitutions also attempt to define the relationship between individuals and the state, and to establish the broad rights of individual citizens. It is thus the most basic law of a territory from which all the other laws and rules are hierarchically derived; in some territories it is in fact called "Basic Law".

KEY FEATURES

The following are features of democratic constitutions which have been identified by political scientists to exist, in one form or another, in virtually all national constitutions.

Codification

A fundamental classification is codification or lack of codification. A codified constitution is one that is contained in a single document, which is the single source of constitutional law in a state. The classic example of this is the Constitution of the United States. An uncodified constitution is one that is not contained in a single document, consisting of several different sources, which may be written or unwritten. The Constitution of Australia is an example of a constitution in which constitutional law mainly derives from a single written document, but other written documents are also considered part of the constitution. The Constitution of the United Kingdom is an example of an uncodified constitution which consists of both written and unwritten sources and has no single written fundamental document.

The term written constitution is used to describe a constitution that is entirely written, which by definition includes every codified constitution. However, some constitutions are entirely written but, strictly speaking, not entirely codified. For example, in the Constitution of Australia, most of its fundamental political principles and regulations concerning the relationship between branches of government, and concerning the government and the individual are codified in a single document, the Constitution of the Commonwealth of Australia. However, the presence of statutes with constitutional significance, namely the Statute of Westminster, as adopted by the Commonwealth in the Statute of Westminster Adoption Act 1942, and the Australia Act 1986 means that Australia's constitution is not contained in a single constitutional document. The Constitution of Canada, which evolved from the British North America Acts until severed from nominal British control by the Canada Act 1982 (analogous to the Australia Act 1986), is a similar example. The term written constitution is often used interchangeably with codified constitution, and similarly unwritten constitution is used interchangeably with uncodified constitution. As shown above, this usage with respect to written and codified constitutions can be inaccurate. Strictly speaking, unwritten constitution is never an accurate synonym for uncodified constitution, because all modern democratic constitutions consist of some written sources, even if they have no different technical status than ordinary statutes. Another term used is formal (written) constitution, for example in the following context: "The United Kingdom has no formal constitution". This usage is correct, but it should be construed to mean that the United Kingdom does not have a written constitution, not that the UK has no constitution of any kind, which would not be correct.

Codified Constitution

Most states in the world have a codified constitution. Only three nations, Israel, New Zealand and the United Kingdom, have uncodified constitutions as of October 2006. Codified constitutions -unlike uncodified constitutions, which are the product of an "evolution" of laws and conventions over centuries -are usually the product of dramatic political change, such as a revolution. For example, the US constitution was written and subsequently ratified less than 25 years after the American Revolution. The process by which a country adopts a constitution is closely tied to the historical and political context driving this fundamental change. This becomes evident when one compares the elaborate convention method adopted in the United States with the MacArthur inspired post war constitution foisted on Japan. Arguably the legitimacy (and often the longevity) of codified constitutions are tied to the process by which they are initially adopted. The most obvious advantage of a codified constitution is the coherent and easily understood body of rules. A codified constitution at the least is simple to read, being a single document. Although (entrenched) codified constitutions are relatively rigid, codified constitutions still yield a potentially wide range of interpretations by constitutional courts.

States that have codified constitutions normally give them supremacy over ordinary statute law. That is, if there is a conflict between a legal statute and the codified constitution, all or part of the statute can be declared ultra vires by a court and struck down as unconstitutional. Second, an extraordinary procedure is required for constitutional amendments that may involve obtaining ? majorities in the national legislature, the consent of regional legislatures, a referendum process or some other procedure that makes obtaining a constitutional amendment more difficult than passing a simple law.

Uncodified Constitution

By contrast, in the Westminster tradition which originated in England, uncodified constitutions include written sources: e.g. constitutional statutes enacted by the Parliament (House of Commons Disqualification Act 1975, Northern Ireland Act 1998, Scotland Act 1998, Government of Wales Act 1998, European Communities Act 1972 and Human Rights Act 1998); and also unwritten sources: constitutional conventions, observation of precedents, royal prerogatives, custom and tradition, such as always holding the General Election on Thursdays; together these constitute the British constitutional law. In the days of the British Empire, the Judicial Committee of the Privy Council acted as the constitutional court for many of the British colonies such as Canada and Australia which had federal constitutions.

In states using uncodified constitutions, the difference between constitutional law and statutory law (i.e. law applying to any area of governance) in legal terms is nil. Both can be altered or repealed by a simple majority in Parliament. In practice, democratic governments do not use this opportunity to abolish all civil rights, which in theory they could do, but the distinction between regular and constitutional law is still somewhat arbitrary, usually depending on the traditional devotion of popular opinion to historical principles embodied in important past legislation. For example, several Acts of Parliament such as the Bill of Rights, Human Rights

Act and, prior to the creation of Parliament, Magna Carta are regarded as granting fundamental rights and principles which are treated as almost constitutional.

Entrenchment

The presence or lack of entrenchment is a fundamental feature of constitutions. Entrenchment refers to whether the constitution is legally protected from modification without a procedure of constitutional amendment. Entrenchment is an inherent feature in most written constitutions. The US constitution is an example of an entrenched constitution, and the UK constitution is an example of a constitution that is not entrenched. The procedure for modifying a constitution is often called amending. Amending an entrenched constitution requires more than the approval of the national legislature, it requires wider acceptance. Sometimes, the reason for this is that the constitution is considered supreme law, such as according to the supremacy clause in the US constitution. Regardless of whether a constitution has this technical status, all states with an entrenched constitution recognise the difference between constitutional law and ordinary statutory law. Procedures for ratification of constitutional amendments vary between states. In a federal system of government, the approval of a majority of state/provincial legislatures may be required. Alternatively, a national referendum may be required in some states, such as in Australia. In constitutions that are not entrenched, no special procedure is required for modification. In the small number of countries with un-entrenched constitutions, the lack of entrenchment is because the constitution is not recognised with any higher legal status than ordinary statutes. In the UK, for example, passing laws which modify sources of the constitution, whether they are written or unwritten, are passed on a simple majority in Parliament. The concept of "amendment" does not apply, as the constitution can be altered as easily in terms of procedure as any national law.

Distribution of Sovereignty

Constitutions also establish where sovereignty is located in the state. There are three basic types of distribution of sovereignty: federal, unitary and confederal. A federal system of government will inevitably have a constitution that recognizes the division of sovereignty between the centre and peripheral/provincial regions of the state. The Canadian Constitution is an example of this, dividing power between the federal government and the provinces. A unitary constitution recognises that sovereignty resides only in the centre of the state. In the UK, the constitutional doctrine of Parliamentary sovereignty dictates than sovereignty is ultimately contained at the centre. Confederal constitutions are rare, and there is often dispute to whether so-called "confederal" states are actually federal. In a confederacy, sovereignty is located in peripheral regions/provinces and only limited power is granted to the centre. A historical example of a confederal constitution is the Swiss Federal Constitution.

Separation of Powers

Constitutions vary extensively as to the degree of separation of powers, usually meaning the constitutional separation of the executive, legislative and judicial branches of government. The United States constitution has a full separation of powers, with each branch having particular enumerated powers. For instance, Congress, the US legislature, has the power of impeachment, which cannot be exercised by another branch.

Lines of Accountability

Lines of accountability are a common feature in all democratic constitutions. In presidential systems of government, such as the United States, and semi-presidential systems, such as France, department secretaries/ministers are accountable to the president, who has patronage powers to appoint and dismiss ministers. The president is accountable to the people in an election. In parliamentary systems, such as the United Kingdom and Australia, ministers are accountable to Parliament, but it is the prime minister who appoints and dismisses them (in Westminster systems this power derives from the monarch, a component of Parliament). There is the concept of a vote of no confidence in many countries with parliamentary systems, which means that if a majority of the legislature vote for a no confidence motion, then the government must resign, and a new one will be formed, or parliament will be dissolved and a general election called.

Facade Constitutions

Italian political theorist Giovanni Sartori noted the existence of national constitutions which are a façade for authoritarian sources of power. While such documents may express respect for human rights or establish an independent judiciary, they may be ignored when the government feels threatened or entirely dishonoured in practice. An extreme example was the Constitution of the Soviet Union that on paper supported freedom of assembly or freedom of speech; however, citizens who acted accordingly were summarily imprisoned. The example demonstrates that the protections and benefits of a constitution are provided less through its written terms, but more through deference by government and society to its principles.

Constitutional Courts

The constitution is often protected by a certain legal body in each country with various names, such as supreme, constitutional or high court. This court judges the compatibility of legislation with the provisions and principles of the constitution, which is termed "constitutionality". Especially important is the court's responsibility to protect constitutionally established rights and freedoms. In constitutions without the concept of supreme law, such as the United Kingdom constitution, the concept of "constitutionality" has little meaning, and constitutional courts do not exist.

A "constitutional violation" is an action or legislative act that is judged by a constitutional court to be contrary to the constitution, that is, "unconstitutional". An example of constitutional violation by the executive could be a politician who abuses the powers of his constitutionally-established office. An example of constitutional violation by the legislature is an attempt to pass a law that would contradict the constitution, without first going through the proper constitutional amendment process.

A constitutional court is normally the court of last resort, the highest judicial body in the government. The process of judicial review is then integrated into the system of courts of appeal.

This is the case, for example, with the Supreme Court of the United States. Cases must normally be heard in lower courts before being brought before the Supreme Court, except cases for which the Supreme Court has original jurisdiction. Some other countries dedicate a special court solely to the protection of the constitution, as with the German Constitutional Court.

Most constitutional courts are powerful instruments of judicial review, with the power to declare laws "unconstitutional", that is, incompatible with the constitution. The effect of this ruling varies between governments, but it is common for the courts' action to rule a law unenforceable, as is the case in the United States. However, many courts have the problem of relying on the legislative and executive branches' cooperation to properly enforce their decisions.

For example, in the United States, the Supreme Court's ruling overturning the "separate but equal" doctrine in the 1950s depended on individual states cooperation to enforce. Some failed to do so, prompting the federal government to intervene. Other countries, such as France, have a Constitutional Council of France which may only judge the constitutionality of laws before the ratification process. Some countries, mainly those with uncodified constitutions, have no such courts at all -for example, as the United Kingdom traditionally functions under the principle of parliamentary sovereignty: the legislature has the power to enact any law it wishes.

However, through its membership in the European Union, the UK is now subject to the jurisdiction of European Community law and the European Court of Justice; similarly, by acceding to the Council of Europe's European Convention on Human Rights, it is subject to the European Court of Human Rights. In effect, these bodies are constitutional courts that can invalidate or interpret UK legislation, first established as a principle by the Factortame case.

History and Development

Excavations in modern-day Iraq by Ernest de Sarzec in 1877 found evidence of the earliest known code of justice, issued by the Sumerian king Urukagina of Lagash ca. 2300 BC. Perhaps the earliest prototype for a law of government, this document itself has not yet been discovered; however it is known that it allowed some rights to his citizens. For example, it is known that it relieved tax for widows and orphans, and protected the poor from the usury of the rich. After that, many governments ruled by special codes of written laws. The oldest such document still known to exist seems to be that of Ur-Nammu of Ur (ca. 2050 BC). Some of the more well known among these include the code of Hammurabi of Babylonia, the Hittite code, the Assyrian code, Mosaic law, and likewise the commandments of Cyrus the Great of Persia.

In 621 BC, a scribe named Draco wrote the laws of the city-state of Athens; and being quite cruel, this code prescribed the death penalty for any offense. In 594 BC, Solon, the ruler of Athens, created the new Solonian Constitution. It eased the burden of the workers, however it made the ruling class to be determined by wealth, rather than by birth. Cleisthenes again reformed the Athenian constitution and set it on a democratic footing in 508 BC.

Aristotle (c. 350 BC) was one of the first in recorded history to make a formal distinction between law and constitutional law, establishing ideas of constitution and constitutionalism, and attempting to classify different forms of constitutional government. The most basic definition he used to describe a constitution in general terms was "the arrangement of the offices in a state".

In his works Constitution of Athens, Politics, and Nicomachean Ethics he explored different forms of constitutions. He classified both what he regarded as good and bad constitutions, and came to the conclusion that the best constitution was a mixed system, including monarchic, aristocratic, and democratic elements. He also distinguished between citizens, who had the exclusive opportunity to participate in the state, and non-citizens and slaves who did not. The Romans first codified their constitution in 449 BC as the Twelve Tables. They operated under a series of laws that were added from time to time, but Roman law was never reorganised into a single code until the Codex Theodosianus (AD 438); later, in the Eastern Empire the Codex Justinianus (534) was highly influential throughout Europe. This was followed in the east by the Ecloga of Leo III the Isaurian (740) and the Basilica of Basil I (878). Many of the Germanic peoples that filled the power vacuum left by the Western Roman Empire in the Early Middle Ages codified their laws. One of the first of these Germanic law codes to be written was the Visigothic Code of Euric (471).

This was followed by the Lex Burgundionum, applying separate codes for Germans and for Romans; the Pactus Alamannorum; and the Salic Law of the Franks, all written soon after 500. In 506, the Breviarum or "Lex Romana" of Alaric II, king of the Visigoths, adopted and consolidated the Codex Theodosianus together with assorted earlier Roman laws. Systems that appeared somewhat later include the Edictum Rothari of the Lombards (643), the Lex Visigothorum (654), the Lex Alamannorum (730) and the Lex Frisionum (c. 785). Japan's Seventeen-article constitution written in 604, reportedly by Prince Shotoku, is an early example of a constitution in Asian political history. Influenced by Buddhist teachings, the document focuses more on social morality than institutions of government per se and remains a notable early attempt at a government constitution. Another is the Constitution of Medina, drafted by the prophet of Islam, Muhammad, in 622. The Gayanashagowa, or 'oral' constitution of the Iroquois nation, has been estimated to date from between 1090 and 1150, and is also thought by some to have provided a partial inspiration for the US Constitution.

In England, King Henry I's proclamation of the Charter of Liberties in 1100 bound the king for the first time in his treatment of the clergy and the nobility. This idea was extended and refined by the English barony when they forced John to sign the Magna Carta in 1215. The most important single article of the Magna Carta, related to "habeas corpus", provided that the king was not permitted to imprison, outlaw, exile or kill anyone at a whim --there must be due process of law first. This article, Article 39, of the Magna Carta read:

No free man shall be arrested, or imprisoned, or deprived of his property, or outlawed, or exiled, or in any way destroyed, nor shall we go against him or send against him, unless by legal judgement of his peers, or by the law of the land.

This provision became the cornerstone of English liberty after that point. The social contract in the original case was between the king and the nobility, but was gradually extended to all of the people. It led to the system of Constitutional Monarchy, with further reforms shifting the balance of power from the monarchy and nobility to the House of Commons.

Between 1220 and 1230, a Saxon administrator, Eike von Repgow, composed the Sachsenspiegel, which became the supreme law used in parts of Germany as late as 1900.

In 1236, Sundiata Keita presented an oral constitution federating the Mali Empire, called the Kouroukan Fouga.

Meanwhile, around 1240, the Coptic Egyptian Christian writer, 'Abul Fada'il Ibn al-'Assal, wrote the Fetha Negest in Arabic. 'Ibn al-Assal took his laws partly from apostolic writings and Mosaic law, and partly from the former Byzantine codes. There are a few historical records claiming that this law code was translated into Ge'ez and entered Ethiopia around 1450 in the reign of Zara Yaqob.

Even so, its first recorded use in the function of a constitution (supreme law of the land) is with Sarsa Dengel beginning in 1563. The Fetha Negest remained the supreme law in Ethiopia until 1931, when a modern-style Constitution was first granted by Emperor Haile Selassie I.

The earliest written constitution still governing a sovereign nation today may be that of San Marino. The Leges Statutae Republicae Sancti Marini was written in Latin and consists of six books. The first book, with 62 articles, establishes councils, courts, various executive officers and the powers assigned to them. The remaining books cover criminal and civil law, judicial procedures and remedies. Written in 1600, the document was based upon the Statuti Comunali (Town Statute) of 1300, itself influenced by the Codex Justinianus, and it remains in force today.

In 1639, the Colony of Connecticut adopted the Fundamental Orders, which is considered the first North American constitution, and is the basis for every new Connecticut constitution since, and is also the reason for Connecticut's nickname, the Constitution State.

The Commonwealth of Massachusetts adopted its constitution in 1780, before the ratification of the Articles of Confederation and the United States Constitution. It is probably the oldest still-functioning nominal constitution, that is, where the document specifically declares itself to be a constitution. The United States Constitution, ratified 1789, was influenced by the British constitutional system and the political system of the United Provinces, plus the writings of Polybius, Locke, Montesquieu, and others. The document became a benchmark for republican and codified constitutions written thereafter and is commonly believed to be the oldest modern, national, codified constitution in the world.

CHAPTER

5 POWER, AUTHORITY AND LEGITIMACY

DIVISION OF POWERS

In a federation, the division of power between federal and regional governments is usually outlined in the constitution. It is in this way that the right to self-government of the component states is usually constitutionally entrenched. Component states often also possess their own constitutions which they may amend as they see fit, although in the event of conflict the federal constitution usually takes precedence.

In almost all federations the central government enjoys the powers of foreign policy and national defence. Were this not the case a federation would not be a single sovereign state. Beyond this the precise division of power varies from one nation to another. The United States Constitution provides that all powers not specifically granted to the federal government are retained by the states. The Constitution of Canada, on the other hand, provides the opposite: that powers not explicitly granted to the provincial governments are retained by the centre. In Germany, the division of powers is less one of content than of administration: the federal government often merely issues broad directives to the Länder (self-governing regions), which then have broad discretion as to how to implement them. In the People's Republic of China, regarded by some as a de facto although not de jure federation, the central government sets up general economic policy and goals, and leaves the implementation to provincial governments. Much like the Canadian system, the Australian Division of Powers serperates some powers which were considered too difficult for the states to manage so that the Federal Government takes on that responsibility.

Where every component state of a federation possesses the same powers, we are said to find 'symmetric federalism'. Asymmetric federalism exists where states are granted different powers, or some possess greater autonomy than others do. This is often done in recognition of the existence of a distinct culture in a particular region or regions. In Spain, "historical communities" such as Navarre, Galicia, Catalonia, and the Basque Country have more powers than other autonomous communities, partly to deal with their distinctness and to appease nationalist leanings, partly out of respect of privileges granted earlier in history.

It is common that during the historical evolution of a federation there is a gradual movement of power from the component states to the centre, as the federal government acquires additional powers, sometimes to deal with unforeseen circumstances. The acquisition of new powers by a federal government may occur through formal constitutional amendment or simply through a broadening of the interpretation of a government's existing constitutional powers given by the courts.

Usually, a federation is formed at two levels: the central government and the regions (states, provinces, territories). Brazil is an exception, because the 1988's Constitution has included the municipalities as autonomous political entities making the federation tripartite: encompassing the Union, the States, and the municipalities. Each state is divided into municipalities (municípios) with their own legislative council (câmara de vereadores) and a mayor (prefeito), which are autonomous and hierarchically independent from both Federal and State Government. Each municipality has a "little constitution", called "organic law" (lei orgânica).

Federations often employ the paradox of being a union of states, while still being states (or having aspects of statehood) in themselves. For example, James Madison (author of the US Constitution) wrote in Federalist Paper No. 39 that the US Constitution "is in strictness neither a national nor a federal constitution; but a composition of both. In its foundation, it is federal, not national; in the sources from which the ordinary powers of the Government are drawn, it is partly federal, and partly national...." This paradox stems from the fact that states in a federation maintain all sovereignty that they do not yield to the federation by their own consent. The sharing of sovereignty between a federation and its constituent states sometimes makes it difficult to differentiate between a sovereign state and a non-sovereign state.

ORGANS OF GOVERNMENT

The structures of most federal governments incorporate mechanisms to protect the rights of component states. One method, known as 'intrastate federalism', is to directly represent the governments of component states in federal political institutions. Where a federation has a bicameral legislature the upper house is often used to represent the component states while the lower house represents the people of the nation as a whole. A federal upper house may be based on a special scheme of apportionment, as is the case in the senates of the United States and Australia, where each state is represented by an equal number of senators irrespective of the size of its population.

Alternatively, or in addition to this practice, the members of an upper house may be indirectly elected by the government or legislature of the component states, as occurred in the United States prior to 1913, or be actual members or delegates of the state governments, as, for example, is the case in the German Bundesrat. The lower house of a federal legislature is usually directly elected, with apportionment in proportion to population, although states may sometimes still be guaranteed a certain minimum number of seats.

In Canada, the provincial governments represent regional interests and negotiate directly with the central government. A First Ministers conference of the prime minister and the provincial premiers is the de facto highest political forum in the land, although it is not mentioned in the constitution.

Federations often have special procedures for amendment of the federal constitution. As well as reflecting the federal structure of the state this may guarantee that the self-governing status of the component states cannot be abolished without their consent. An amendment to the constitution of the United States must be ratified by three-quarters of either the state legislatures, or of constitutional conventions specially elected in each of the states, before it can come into effect. In referenda to amend the constitutions of Australia and Switzerland it is required that a proposal be endorsed not just by an overall majority of the electorate in the nation as a whole, but also by separate majorities in each of a majority of the states or cantons. In Australia, this latter requirement is known as a double majority.

Some federal constitutions also provide that certain constitutional amendments cannot occur without the unanimous consent of all states or of a particular state. The US constitution provides that no state may be deprived of equal representation in the senate without its consent. In Australia, if a proposed amendment will specifically impact one or more states than it must be endorsed in the referendum held in each of those states. Any amendment to the Canadian constitution that would modify the role of the monarchy would require unanimous consent of the provinces. The German Basic Law provides that no amendment is admissible at all that would completely abolish the federal system.

OTHER TECHNICAL TERMS

- Fiscal federalism -federalism involving the transfer of funds between different levels of government.
- Formal federalism (or 'constitutional federalism') -the delineation of powers is specified in a written constitution.
- Executive federalism (also known as 'administrative federalism').

Federalism as a Political Philosophy

The meaning of federalism, as a political movement, and of what constitutes a 'federalist', varies with country and historical context. Movements associated with the establishment or development of federations can be either centralising or decentralising. For example, at the time those nations were being established, 'federalists' in the United States and Australia were those who advocated the creation of strong central government. Similarly, in European Union politics, federalists are mostly those who seek greater EU integration. In contrast, in Spain and post-war Germany, federal movements have sought decentralisation: the transfer of power from central authorities to local units. In Canada, where Quebec separatism has been a political force for several decades, the 'federalist' force is dedicated to keeping the federation intact and adapting the federal structure to better suit Quebec interests.

Internal Controversy and Conflict

Certain forms of political and constitutional dispute are common to federations. One issue is that the exact division of power and responsibility between federal and regional governments is often a source of controversy. Often, as is the case with the United States, such conflicts are resolved through the judicial system, which delimits the powers of federal and local governments. The relationship between federal and local courts varies from nation to nation and can be a controversial and complex issue in itself.

Another common issue in federal systems is the conflict between regional and national interests, or between the interests and aspirations of different ethnic groups. In some federations the entire jurisdiction is relatively homogeneous and each constituent state resembles a miniature version of the whole; this is known as 'congruent federalism'. On the other hand, incongruent federalism exists where different states or regions possess distinct ethnic groups. The ability of a federal government to create national institutions that can mediate differences that arise because of linguistic, ethnic, religious, or other regional differences is an important challenge. The inability to meet this challenge may lead to the secession of parts of a federation or to civil war, as occurred in United States and Switzerland. In case of Malaysia, Singapore was expelled from the federation because of rising racial tension. In some cases internal conflict may lead a federation to collapse entirely, as occurred in Nigeria, the Federation of Rhodesia and Nyasaland, the United Provinces of Central America and the West Indies Federation.

POLITICAL POWER

Political power (imperium in Latin) is a type of power held by a person or group in a society. There are many ways to hold such power. Officially, political power is held by the holders of the sovereignty. Political powers are not limited to heads of states, however, and the extent to which a person or group holds such power is related to the amount of societal influence they can wield, formally or informally. In many cases this influence is not contained within a single state and it refers to international power.

Political scientists have frequently defined power as "the ability to influence the behaviour of others" with or without resistance.

For analytical reasons, MacMillan separates the concepts power

Power is the capacity to restructure actual situations. —I.C. Macmillan

and influence

Influence is the capacity to control and modify the perceptions of others.

—I.C. Macmillan

Abuse of Power

Throughout history there have been many examples of the destructive or senseless use of political power. This has happened most frequently when too much power has been concentrated in too few hands, without enough room for political debate, public criticism, and other types of correctives. Examples of such regimes are despotism, tyranny, and dictatorship. To counter these potential problems, people have devised and practised different solutions, most of them related to the sharing of power (as in democracy), the placing of limitations on the extent of power one individual or group can have, and the creation of protective rights for individuals through legislation or charters (such as human rights).

Separation of Powers

Charles de Montesquieu claimed that without following a principle of containing and balancing legislative, executive and judiciary powers, there is no freedom and no protection against abuse of power. This is the separation of powers principle.

Division of Power

A similar concept, termed Division of Power, also consists of differentiated legislative, executive and judiciary powers. However, while Separation of Power prohibits one branch from interfering with another, Division of Power permits such interference. For example, in Indonesia, the President (who wields executive power) can introduce a new bill, but the People's Consultative Assembly (holding legislative power) chooses to either legalize or reject the bill.

POLITICAL SCIENCE PERSPECTIVES

Within normative political analysis, there are also various levels of power as described by academics that add depth into the understanding of the notion of power and its political implications. Robert Dahl, a prominent American political scientist, first ascribed to political power the trait of decision-making as the source and main indicator of power. Later, two other political scientists, Peter Bachrach and Morton Baratz, decided that simply ascribing decision-making as the basis of power was too simplistic and they added what they termed a 2nd dimension of power, agenda-setting by elites who worked in the backrooms and away from public scrutiny in order to exert their power upon society. Lastly, British academic Steven Lukes added a 3rd dimension of power, preference-shaping, which he claimed was another important aspect of normative power in politics which entails theoretical views similar to notions of cultural hegemony. These 3 dimensions of power are today often considered defining aspects of political power by political researchers.

A radical alternative view of the source of political power follows the formula: information plus authority permits the exercise of power. Political power is intimately related to information. Sir Francis Bacon's statement: "Nam et ipsa scientia potestas est" for knowledge itself is power, assumed authority as given. Many will know that unless someone with authority listens and acts, there is no political power. It is said democracy is the best method of informing those entrusted with authority. They are best able to use authority without ignorance to maximize political power. Those who exercise authority in ignorance are not powerful, because they do not realize their intentions and have little control over the effects of using their authority.

Post-modernism has debated over how to define political power. Perhaps, the best known definition comes from the late Michel Foucault, whose work in Discipline and Punish (and other writings) conveys a view of power that is organic within society. This view holds that political power is more subtle and is part of a series of societal controls and 'normalizing' influences through historical institutions and definitions of normal vs. abnormal. Foucault once characterized power as "an action over actions" (une action sur des actions), arguing that power was essentially a relation between several dots, in continuous transformation as in Nietzsche's philosophy. His view of power lent credence to the view that power in human society was part of a training process in which everyone, from a Prime Minister to a homeless person, played their role within the power structure of society. Jürgen Habermas opposed himself to Foucault's conception of discourse as a battlefield for power relations, arguing that it should be possible to achieve consensus on the fundamentals rules of discourse, in order to establish a transparent and democratic dialogue. Thenceforth, he argued against Foucault and Althusser that power was not immanent to discourse, and that philosophy could be completely distinguished from ideology. More recently, there has been a move among academics to differentiate power from a new concept of luck. Under some conditions (particularly the when examining the third dimension of power) it becomes necessary to determine who obtains a favourable result through the wielding of genuine power and who is simply "lucky". An example might be an ethnic minority who receive favourable treatment while not intentionally seeking it. A person promoted through positive discrimination would be considered "lucky" rather than "powerful". The eventual aim of such discrimination would be to eventually convert some (or all) of that luck into power. Some groups remain serially lucky without ever obtaining power.

ANARCHY IN INTERNATIONAL RELATIONS

Anarchy in international relations posits that the world system is leaderless: there is no universal sovereign or worldwide government. There is thus no hierarchically superior, coercive power that can resolve disputes or order the system. Political scientists do not use the term "anarchy" to signify a world in chaos, in disorder, or in conflict. It simply reflects the order of the international system: independent states with no central authority above them. The concept of anarchy is the foundation for realist, liberal, neorealist, and neoliberal international relations theories. Constructivist theory disputes that anarchy is a fundamental condition of the international system, saying that "anarchy is what states make of it" (Alexander Wendt).

REALISM AND INTERNATIONAL RELATIONS

Realism, also known as political realism, in the context of international relations, encompasses a variety of theories and approaches, all of which share a belief that states are primarily motivated by the desire for military and economic power or security, rather than ideals or ethics. This term is often synonymous with power politics. The term realism can, instead of referring to the broad family of realist theories, refer specifically to classical realism, the common ancestor and original form of realism.

Common Assumptions

Realist theories share the following key assumptions:

- The international system is anarchic. There is no authority above states capable of regulating their interactions; states must arrive at relations with other states on their own, rather than it being dictated to them by some higher controlling entity (that is, no true authoritative world government exists).

- Sovereign states are the principal actors in the international system. International institutions, non-governmental organizations, multinational corporations and other sub-state or trans-state actors are viewed as having little independent influence.
- States are rational unitary actors each moving towards their own national interest. There is a general distrust of long-term cooperation or alliance.
- The overriding 'national interest' of each state is its national security and survival.
- In pursuit of national security, states strive to amass resources.
- Relations between states are determined by their comparative level of power derived primarily from their military and economic capabilities.

In summary, realists believe that mankind is not inherently benevolent but rather self-centered and competitive. This Hobbesian perspective contrasts with the liberalism approach to international relations which views human nature as selfish and conflictual unless given appropriate conditions under which to cooperate. Further, they believe that states are inherently aggressive (offensive realism) and/or obsessed with security (defensive realism); and that territorial expansion is only constrained by opposing power(s). This aggressive build-up, however, leads to a security dilemma where increasing one's own security can bring along greater instability as the opponent(s) builds up its own arms. Thus, security is a zero-sum game where only relative gains can be made.

HISTORY AND BRANCHES

Historic Antecedents

While Realism as a formal discipline in international relations didn't arrive until World War II, its primary assumptions have been expressed in earlier writings:

- Sun Tzu (or Sunzi), an ancient Chinese military strategist who wrote the Art of War.
- Chanakya early Indian statesman, and writer on the Arthashastra.
- Thucydides, an ancient Greek historian who wrote the History of the Peloponnesian War and is also cited as an intellectual forebearer of realpolitik.
- Hanfeizi, Chinese scholar who theorised Legalism (or Legism) and who served in the court of the King of Qin -later unifier of China ending the Warring States Period. His writings include The Two Handles (about punishments and rewards as tools of governance). He theorised about a neutral, manipulative ruler who would act as Head of State while secretly controlling the executive through his ministers -the ones to take real responsibility for any policy.
- Niccolò Machiavelli, a Florentine political philosopher, who wrote II Principe (The Prince) in which he held that the sole aim of a prince (politician) was to seek power, regardless of religious or ethical considerations.

- Thomas Hobbes, an English philosopher who wrote Leviathan in which he stated that in anarchy there is a "war of all against all".
- Otto von Bismarck, a Prussian statesman coined the term balance of power. Balancing power meant keeping the peace and careful realpolitik practitioners tried to avoid arms races.
- Carl von Clausewitz was a 19th century Prussian general and military theorist who wrote Vom Kriege (On War).

"Classical Realism"

Modern realism began as a serious field of research in the United States during and after World War II. This evolution was partly fueled by European war migrants like Hans Morgenthau who had a negative view of human nature, thought by some to be due to their experiences in war. Prominent classical realists:

- George F. Kennan -Containment
- Nicholas Spykman -Geostrategy, Containment
- Herman Kahn -Nuclear strategy
- E. H. Carr
- Reinhold Niebuhr
- Hans Morgenthau
- Arnold Wolfers
- Charles Beard
- Walter Lippmann

"Liberal Realism" or the "English School" or "Rationalism"

The English School holds that while the international system is anarchical, order can be promoted through diplomacy, international law and society. This school thus gives credence to establishing IGOs such as the United Nations.

Prominent liberal realists:

- Hedley Bull -Liberal realism (sometimes called the "English School" or "Rationalism")

Hedley Bull argued for both the existence of international society of states and its perseverance even in times of great systemic upheaval, meaning regional or so-called "world wars."

- Martin Wight : This section is a stub. You can help by expanding it.

"Neorealism" or "Structural Realism"

Neorealism derives from classical realism except that instead of human nature, its focus is predominantly on the international system. While states remain the principal actors, greater attention is given to the forces above and below the states through a levels of analysis or structure-agency debate. The international system is seen as a structure acting on the state with individuals below the level of the state acting as agency on the state as a whole. While neorealism shares a focus on the international system with the English School, neorealism differs in the emphasis it places on the permanence of conflict. To ensure state security, states must be on constant preparation for conflict through economic and military build-up.

Prominent neorealists:

- Robert Jervis -Defensive realism
- Kenneth Waltz -Defensive realism
- Stephen Walt -Defensive realism
- John Mearsheimer -Offensive realism
- Robert Gilpin -Hegemonic theory

"Neoclassical Realism"

Neoclassical Realism can be seen as the third generation of realism, coming after the classical authors of the first wave (Thucydides, Machiavelli, Hobbes, Morgenthau), and the neorealists (esp. Kenneth Waltz). Its designation of "neoclassical", then, has a double meaning: 1) It offers the classics a renaissance; 2) It is a synthesis of the neorealist and the classical realist approaches.

Gideon Rose is responsible for coining the term in a book review he wrote.

The primarily motivation underlying the development of neoclassical realism was the fact that neorealism was only useful to explain political outcomes (classified as being 'theories of international politics'), but had nothing to offer about particular states' behavior (or 'theories of foreign policy'). The basic approach, then, was for these authors to "refine, not refute, Kenneth Waltz", by adding domestic intervening variables between systemic incentives and a state's foreign policy decision. Thus, the basic theoretical architecture of Neoclassical Realism is:

Distribution of power in the international system (Independent Variable) >>> Domestic perception of the system and/or domestic incentives (Intervening Variable) >>> Foreign Policy decision (Dependent Variable) While neoclassical realism has only been used for theories of foreign policy so far, Randall Schweller notes that it could be useful to explain certain types of political outcomes as well..

Neoclassical realism is particularly appealing from a research standpoint because it still retains a lot of the theoretical rigor that Waltz has brought to realism, but at the same time can easily incorporate a content-rich analysis, since its main method for testing theories is the process-tracing of case studies.

NEOREALISM

Neorealism or structural realism is a theory of international relations, outlined by Kenneth Waltz in his 1979 book, Theory of International Politics. Waltz argues in favor of a systemic approach: the international structure acts as a constraint on state behavior, so that different states behave in a similar rational manner, and outcomes fall within an expected range. Neorealism, developed largely within the American political science tradition, seeks to reformulate the classical realism tradition of E.H. Carr, Hans Morgenthau, and Reinhold Niebuhr into a rigorous and positivistic social science.

Theory

Neorealism shuns classical realism's use of often essentialist concepts such as "human nature" to explain international politics. Instead, neorealist thinkers developed a theory that privileges structural constraints over agents' strategies and motivations.

Neorealism holds that the international structure is defined by its ordering principle, anarchy, and by the distribution of capabilities, measured by the number of great powers within the international system. The anarchic ordering principle of the international structure is decentralized, having no formal central authority, and is composed of formally equal sovereign states. These states act according to the logic of self-help--states seek their own interest and will not subordinate their interest to another's.

States are assumed at a minimum to want to ensure their own survival as this is a prerequisite to pursue other goals. This driving force of survival is the primary factor influencing their behaviour and in turn ensures states develop offensive military capabilities, as a means to increase their relative power. Because states can never be certain of other states' future intentions, there is a lack of trust between states which requires states to be on guard against relative losses of power which could enable other states to threaten their survival. This lack of trust, based on uncertainty, is called the security dilemma.

States are deemed similar in terms of needs but not in capabilities for achieving them. The positional placement of states in terms of abilities determines the distribution of capabilities. The structural distribution of capabilities then limits cooperation among states through fears of relative gains made by other states, and the possibility of dependence on other states.

The desire and relative abilities of each state to maximize relative power constrain each other, resulting in a 'balance of power', which shapes international relations. It also gives rise to the 'security dilemma' that all nations face. There are two ways in which states balance power: internal balancing and external balancing. Internal balancing occurs as states grow their own capabilities by increasing economic growth and/or increasing military spending. External balancing occurs as states enter into alliances to check the power of more powerful states or alliances.

Neorealists contend that there are essentially three possible systems according to changes in the distribution of capabilities, defined by the number of great powers within the international system. A unipolar system contains only one great power (this is often referred to as hegemony), a bipolar system contains two great powers, and a multipolar system contains more than two great powers. Neorealists conclude that a bipolar system is more stable (less prone to great power war and systemic change) than a unipolar system because balancing can only occur through internal balancing as there are no extra great powers with which to form alliances. Because there is only internal balancing in a bipolar system, rather than external balancing and internal balancing, there is less opportunity for miscalculations and therefore less chance of great power war.

Neorealists conclude that because war is an effect of the anarchic structure of the international system, it is likely to continue in the future. Indeed, neorealists often argue that the ordering principle of the international system has not fundamentally changed from the time of Thucydides to the advent of nuclear warfare.

The view that long-lasting peace is not likely to be achieved is described by other theorists as a largely pessimistic view of international relations. One of the main challenges to neorealist theory is the democratic peace theory and supporting research such as the book Never at War. Neorealists answer this challenge by arguing that democratic peace theorists tend to pick and choose the definition of democracy to get the wanted empirical result. For example, Germany of Kaiser Wilhem II, the Dominican Republic of Juan Bosch, or Chile of Salvador Allende are not considered to be democratic or the conflicts do not qualify as wars according to these theorists. Furthermore they claim several wars between democratic states have been averted only by causes other than ones covered by democratic peace theory.

Criticism

Neorealism has been criticized from the point of view of the philosophy of science. John Vasquez uses the Lakatosian criteria of the Methodology of Scientific Research Programs in an attempt to prove the degenerative nature of the neorealist research program. Thus, Waltz's theory of neorealism explains international behaviour through the balance-of-power concept, according to which states in almost all cases balance each other in order to survive. Stephen Walt, on the other hand, argues that states do not balance power, but there is a so-called balance-of-threat, thus always balancing states which seem to be the most threatening, not necessarily the most powerful. Randall Schweller introduces the concept of balance-of-interests, better known as bandwagoning. Thomas J. Christensen and Jack Snyder try to correct gaps in Waltz's original theory by using the concepts of buck-passing and chain-ganging. However these similar theories contradict each other, at least partially: for example balancing versus bandwagoning. Vasquez considers them as theory shifts which explain away discrepant evidence. These contradictory hypotheses increase the probability that at least one passes an empirical test, thus the whole neorealist research program showing signs of degeneration.

IDEALISM AND INTERNATIONAL RELATIONS

Idealism in international relations usually refers to the school of thought personified in American diplomatic history by Woodrow Wilson, such that it is sometimes referred to as Wilsonianism. Idealism holds that a state should make its internal political philosophy the goal of its foreign policy. For example, an idealist might believe that ending poverty at home should be coupled with tackling poverty abroad. Wilson's idealism was a precursor to liberal international relations theory, which would arise amongst the "institution-builders" after World War II.

Idealism is also marked by the prominent role played by international law and international organizations in its conception of policy formation. One of the most well-known tenets of modern idealist thinking is democratic peace theory, which holds that states with similar modes of democratic governance do not fight one another. Wilson's idealistic thought was embodied in his Fourteen points speech, and in the creation of the League of Nations.

Idealism transcends the left-right political spectrum. Idealists can include both human rights campaigners (traditionally, but not always, associated with the left) and American neoconservatism which is usually associated with the right. Idealism may find itself in opposition to Realism, a worldview which argues that a nation's national interest is more important than ethical or moral considerations; however, there need be no conflict between the two. Realist thinkers include Hans Morgenthau, Niccolò Machiavelli, Otto von Bismarck, George F. Kennan and others.

Descendant Theories

Idealism proper was a relatively short lived school of thought, and suffered a crisis of confidence following the failure of the League of Nations and the outbreak of World War II. However, subsequent theories of international relations would draw elements from Wilsonian Idealism when constructing their world views.

Liberalism

Liberalism manifested a tempered version of Wilson's idealism in the wake of World War II. Cognizant of the failures of Idealism to prevent renewed isolationism following World War I, and its inability to manage the balance of power in Europe to prevent the outbreak of a new war, liberal thinkers devised a set of international institutions based on rule of law and regularized interaction. These international regimes, such as the United Nations, NATO, the Bretton Woods system, and the GATT, were calculated both to maintain a balance of power as well as regularize cooperation between nations.

Neoconservatism

Neoconservatism drew from Liberalism its intense focus on the promotion of "universal values", in this case democracy, human rights, free trade, women's rights and minority protections. However, it differs in that instead of building institutions or negotiating treaties, neoconservatism is less wedded to the importance of preserving international institutions and treaties while pursuing assertive or aggressive stances which it deems morally worthy, and is willing to use force or the threat of force, unilaterally if necessary, to push for its goals.

IDEALISM

Idealism is a class of positions in ontology and epistemology. Idealism as an epistemological position asserts that everything we experience is of a mental nature. That is, we can only have direct, immediate knowledge of the contents of our mind. We can never directly know or experience an external object itself. As an ontological position Idealism asserts either that only minds and the objects of mind exist, or that everything is composed of mental realities (e.g., thoughts, feelings, perceptions, ideas, or will). As a foundation for cosmology, or an approach to understanding the nature of existence, idealism is often contrasted with materialism, both belonging to the class of monist as opposed to dualist or pluralist ontologies. (Note that this contrast bètween idealism and materialism is approximately as to whether the substance of the world is at base mental or physical -it has nothing to do with thinking that things should be idealized, or with coveting goods.) Subjective Idealists and Phenomenalists (such as George Berkeley) hold that minds and their experiences constitute existence. Objective Idealists hold either that all of reality is included in a Universal Thought or Experience (Absolute Idealism), or hold that the world is composed of mental realities. Panpsychists (such as Leibniz) hold that all objects of experience are also subjects. That is, plants and minerals have subjective experiences--though very different from the consciousness of animals. Most Idealists tend to reject representationalist views of experience and instead hold that the world of experience is the same as the world of reality. The approach to idealism by Western philosophers has been different from that of Eastern thinkers. In much of Western thought (though not in such major Western thinkers as Plato and Hegel) the ideal relates to direct knowledge of subjective mental ideas, or images. It is then usually juxtaposed with realism in which the real is said to have absolute existence prior to and independent of our knowledge. Epistemological idealists (such as Kant) might insist that the only things which can be directly known for certain are ideas. In Eastern thought, as reflected in Hindu idealism, the concept of idealism takes on the meaning of consciousness, essentially the living consciousness of an all-pervading God, as the basis of all phenomena. A type of Asian idealism is Buddhist idealism.

History

Idealism names a number of philosophical positions with quite different tendencies and implications.

Idealism in the East

Several Hindu traditions and schools of Buddhism can be accurately characterized as idealist. Some of the Buddhist schools are called "Consciousness-only" schools as they focus on consciousness without an omnipotent deity or soul.

Idealism in the West

In his chief work Truth, Antiphon wrote: "Time is a thought or a measure, not a substance". This presents time as an ideational, internal, mental operation, rather than a real, external object.

Plato

Plato proposed an idealist theory as a solution to the problem of universals. A universal is that which all things share in virtue of having some particular property. So for example the wall, the moon and a blank sheet of paper are all white; white is the universal that all white things share. Plato argued that it is universals, The Forms, or Platonic Ideals that are real, not specific individual things. Confusingly, because this idea asserts that these mental entities are real, it is also called Platonic realism; in this sense realism contrasts with nominalism, the notion that mental abstractions are merely names without an independent existence. Nevertheless, it is a form of idealism because it asserts the primacy of the idea of universals over material things.

Plato's Allegory of the Cave relates to epistemological idealism. The mental images, or ideas, that are immediately and directly known are not the same as the exterior objects in the real world.

This world that appears to the senses has no true being, but only a ceaseless becoming; it is, and it also is not; and its comprehension is not so much a knowledge as an illusion. This is what he expresses in a myth at the beginning of the seventh book of the Republic, the most important passage in all his works .... He says that men, firmly chained in a dark cave, see neither the genuine original light nor actual things, but only the inadequate light of the fire in the cave, and the shadows of actual things passing by the fire behind their backs. Yet they imagine that the shadows are the reality, and that determining the succession of these shadows is true wisdom. -Schopenhauer, The World as Will and Representation, Vol. I, Appendix

Plotinus

Schopenhauer wrote of this Neoplatonist philosopher: "With Plotinus there even appears, probably for the first time in Western philosophy, idealism that had long been current in the East even at that time, for it taught (Enneads, iii, lib. vii, c.10) that the soul has made the world by stepping from eternity into time, with the explanation: 'For there is for this universe no other place than the soul or mind' (neque est alter hujus universi locus quam anima), indeed the ideality of time is expressed in the words: 'We should not accept time outside the soul or mind' (oportet autem nequaquam extra animam tempus accipere)." (Parerga and Paralipomena, Volume I, "Fragments for the History of Philosophy."

Descartes

Writing about Descartes, Schopenhauer claimed, "... he was the first to bring to our consciousness the problem whereon all philosophy has since mainly turned, namely that of the ideal and the real. This is the question concerning what in our knowledge is objective and what subjective, and hence what eventually is to be ascribed by us to things different from us and what is to be attributed to ourselves." (Parerga and Paralipomena, Vol. I, "Sketch of a History of the Doctrine of the Ideal and the Real") According to Descartes, we really know only what is in our own consciousnesses. We are immediately and directly aware of only our own states of mind. The whole external world is merely an idea or picture in our minds. Therefore, it is possible to doubt the reality of the external world as consisting of real objects. "I think, therefore I am" is the only assertion that can't be doubted. This is because self-consciousness and thinking are the only things that are unconditionally experienced for certain as being real. In this way, Descartes clearly presented the main problem of philosophical idealism, which is awareness of the difference between the world as an ideational mental picture and the world as a system of external objects.

Malebranche

Malebranche a student of the Cartesian School of Rationalism disagreed that if the only things that we know for certain are the ideas within our mind, then the existence of the external world would be dubious and known only indirectly. He declared instead that the real external world is actually God. All activity only appears to occur in the external world. In actuality, it is the activity of God. For Malebranche, we directly know internally the ideas in our mind. Externally, we directly know God's operations. This kind of idealism led to the pantheism of Spinoza.

Leibniz

Leibniz expressed a form of Idealism known as Panpsychism in his theory of monads, as exposited in his Monadologie. He held Monads are the true atoms of the universe, and are also entities having sensation. The monads are "substantial forms of being" They are indecomposable, individual, subject to their own laws, un-interacting, and each reflecting the entire universe. Monads are centers of force; substance is force, while space, matter, and motion are phenomenal. For Leibniz, there is an exact pre-established harmony or parallel between the world in the minds of the alert monads and the external world of objects. God, who is the central monad, established this harmony and the resulting world is an idea of the monads' perception. In this way, the external world is ideal in that it is a spiritual phenomenon whose motion is the result of a dynamic force. Space and time are ideal or phenomenal and their form and existence is dependent on the simple and immaterial monads. Leibniz's cosmology, with its central monad, embraced a traditional Christian Theism and was more of a Personalism than the naturalistic Pantheism of Spinoza.

George Berkeley

Bishop Berkeley, in seeking to find out what we could know with certainty, decided that our knowledge must be based on our perceptions. This led him to conclude that there was indeed no "real" knowable object behind one's perception, that what was "real" was the perception itself. This is characterised by Berkeley's slogan: "Their esse est aut percipi aut percipere" or "To be is to be perceived or to perceive", meaning that something only exists, in the particular way that it is seen to exist, when it is being perceived (seen, felt etc.) by an observing subject.

This subjective idealism or dogmatic idealism led to his placing the full weight of justification on our perceptions. This left Berkeley with the problem, common to other forms of idealism, of explaining how it is that each of us apparently has much the same sort of perceptions of an object. He solved this problem by having God intercede, as the immediate cause of all of our perceptions. Schopenhauer wrote: "Berkeley was, therefore, the first to treat the subjective starting-point really seriously and to demonstrate irrefutably its absolute necessity. He is the father of idealism...." (Parerga and Paralipomena, Vol. I, "Fragments for the History of Philosophy," § 12)

Arthur Collier

Arthur Collier published the same assertions that were made by Berkeley. However, there seemed to have been no influence between the two contemporary writers. Collier claimed that the represented image of an external object is the only knowable reality. Matter, as a cause of the representative image, is unthinkable and therefore nothing to us. An external world, as absolute matter, unrelated to an observer, does not exist for human perceivers. As an appearance in a mind, the universe cannot exist as it appears if there is no perceiving mind. Collier was influenced by John Norris's (1701) An Essay Towards the Theory of the Ideal or Intelligible World. The idealist statements by Collier were generally dismissed by readers who were not able to reflect on the distinction between a mental idea or image and the object that it represents.

Jonathan Edwards

Jonathan Edwards, an American theologian, went to Yale University in 1716 at the age of thirteen. After reading Locke's doctrine of ideas, he kept a notebook entitled "Mind." In it, he wrote, at the age of fourteen, that the only things that are real are minds. He contended that matter exists only as an idea in a mind. Due to his theological manner of thinking, he asserted that space is God, due to its infinity. After adolescence, he never elaborated on these early idealistic notes.

Immanuel Kant

Immanuel Kant held that the mind shapes the world as we perceive it to take the form of space-and-time. Kant focused on the idea drawn from British empiricism (and its philosophers such as Locke, Berkeley, and Hume) that all we can know is the mental impressions, or phenomena, that an outside world which may or may not exist independently creates in our minds; our minds can never perceive that outside world directly.

... if I remove the thinking subject, the whole material world must at once vanish because it is nothing but a phenomenal appearance in the sensibility of ourselves as a subject, and a manner or species of representation. –Critique of Pure Reason A383

Kant's postscript to this added that the mind is not a blank slate (contra John Locke), but rather comes equipped with categories for organising our sense impressions. This Kantian sort of idealism opens up a world of abstractions (i.e., the universal categories minds use to understand phenomena) to be explored by reason, but in sharp contrast to Plato's, confirms uncertainties about a (un)knowable world outside our own minds. We cannot approach the noumenon, the "Thing in Itself" (German: Ding an Sich) outside our own mental world. (Kant's idealism goes by the counterintuitive name of transcendental idealism.) Kant distinguished his transcendental or critical idealism from previous varieties: The dictum of all genuine idealists, from the Eleatic school to Bishop Berkeley, is contained in this formula: "All knowledge through the senses and experience is nothing but sheer illusion, and only in the ideas of the pure understanding and reason is there truth." The principle that throughout dominates and determines my idealism is, on the contrary,: "All knowledge of things merely from pure understanding or pure reason is nothing but sheer illusion, and only in experience is there truth."—Prolegomena, 374

Fichte

Johann Fichte denied Kant's noumenon, and made the claim that consciousness made its own foundation, that the mental ego of the self relied on no external, and that an external of any kind would be the same as admitting a real material. He was the first to make the attempt at a presuppositionless theory of knowledge, wherein nothing outside of thinking would be assumed to exist outside the initial analysis of concept. So that conception could be solely grounded in itself, and assume nothing without deduction from there first, what he called a

Wissenschaftslehre. (This stand is very similar to Giovanni Gentile's Actual Idealism, except that Gentile's theory goes further by denying a ground for even an ego or self made from thinking.)

Hegel

Hegel, another philosopher whose system has been called idealism, argued in his Science of Logic (1812-1814) that finite qualities are not fully "real," because they depend on other finite qualities to determine them. Qualitative infinity, on the other hand, would be more self-determining, and hence would have a better claim to be called fully real. Similarly, finite natural things are less "real"--because they're less self-determining--than spiritual things like morally responsible people, ethical communities, and God. So any doctrine, such as materialism, that asserts that finite qualities or merely natural objects are fully real, is mistaken. Hegel called his philosophy absolute idealism, in contrast to the "subjective idealism" of Berkeley and the "transcendental idealism" of Kant and Fichte, which were not based (like Hegel's idealism) on a critique of the finite. The "idealists" listed above whose philosophy Hegel's philosophy most closely resembles are Plato and Plotinus. None of these three thinkers associates their idealism with the epistemological thesis that what we know are "ideas" in our minds.

Schopenhauer

In the first volume of his Parerga and Paralipomena, Schopenhauer wrote his "Sketch of a History of the Doctrine of the Ideal and the Real". He defined the ideal as being mental pictures that constitute subjective knowledge. The ideal, for him, is what can be attributed to our own minds. The images in our head are what comprise the ideal. Schopenhauer emphasized that we are restricted to our own consciousness. The world that appears there is only a representation or mental picture of objects. We directly and immediately know only representations. All objects that are external to the mind are known indirectly through the mediation of our mind. Schopenhauer's history is an account of the concept of the "ideal" in its meaning as "ideas in a subject's mind." In this sense, "ideal" means "ideational" or "existing in the mind as an image." He does not refer to the other meaning of "ideal" as being qualities of the highest perfection and excellence. In his On the Freedom of the Will, Schopenhauer noted the ambiguity of the word "idealism" by calling it a "term with multiple meanings."

True philosophy must at all costs be idealistic; indeed, it must be so merely to be honest. For nothing is more certain than that no one ever came out of himself in order to identify himself immediately with things different from him; but everything of which he has certain, sure, and therefore immediate knowledge, lies within his consciousness. Beyond this consciousness, therefore, there can be no immediate certainty .... There can never be an existence that is objective absolutely and in itself; such an existence, indeed, is positively inconceivable. For the objective, as such, always and essentially has its existence in the consciousness of a subject; it is therefore the subject's representation, and consequently is conditioned by the subject, and moreover by the subject's forms of representation, which belong to the subject and not to the object. -The World as Will and Representation, Vol. II, Ch. 1

British Idealism

British idealism enjoyed ascendancy in English-speaking philosophy in the later part of the 19th century. F. H. Bradley of Merton College, Oxford, saw reality as a monistic whole, which is apprehended through "feeling", a state in which there is no distinction between the perception and the thing perceived. Bradley was the apparent target of G. E. Moore's radical rejection of idealism.

J. M. E. McTaggart of Cambridge University, argued that minds alone exist, and that they only relate to each other through love. Space, time and material objects are for McTaggart unreal. He argued, for instance, in The Unreality of Time that it was not possible to produce a coherent account of a sequence of events in time, and that therefore time is an illusion.

American philosopher Josiah Royce described himself as an objective idealist.

Karl Pearson

In The Grammar of Science, Preface to the 2nd Edition, 1900, Karl Pearson wrote, "There are many signs that a sound idealism is surely replacing, as a basis for natural philosophy, the crude materialism of the older physicists." This book influenced Einstein's regard for the importance of the observer in scientific measurements. In § 5 of that book, Pearson asserted that "...science is in reality a classification and analysis of the contents of the mind...." Also, "...the field of science is much more consciousness than an external world."

CRITICISM OF IDEALISM

Immanuel Kant

In the 1st edition (1781) of his Critique of Pure Reason, Kant described Idealism as such.

We are perfectly justified in maintaining that only what is within ourselves can be immediately and directly perceived, and that only my own existence can be the object of a mere perception. Thus the existence of a real object outside me can never be given immediately and directly in perception, but can only be added in thought to the perception, which is a modification of the internal sense, and thus inferred as its external cause .... In the true sense of the word, therefore, I can never perceive external things, but I can only infer their existence from my own internal perception, regarding the perception as an effect of something external that must be the proximate cause .... It must not be supposed, therefore, that an idealist is someone who denies the existence of external objects of the senses; all he does is to deny that they are known by immediate and direct perception .... —Critique of Pure Reason, A367 f.

In the 2nd edition (1787) of his Critique of Pure Reason, he wrote a section called Refutation of Idealism to distinguish his transcendental idealism from Descartes's Sceptical Idealism and Berkeley's Dogmatic Idealism. In addition to this refutation in both the 1781 & 1787 editions the section "Paralogisms of Pure Reason" is an implicit critique of Descartes Problematic Idealism, namely the Cogito. He says that just from "the spontaneity of thought" (cf. Descartes' Cogito) it is not possible to infer the 'I' as an object.

Søren Kierkegaard

Kierkegaard attacked Hegel's idealist philosophy in several of his works, but most succinctly in Concluding Unscientific Postscript (1846). In the Postscript, Kierkegaard, as the pseudonymous philosopher Johannes Climacus, argues that a logical system is possible but an existential system is impossible. Hegel argues that once one has reached an ultimate understanding of the logical structure of the world, one has also reached an understanding of the logical structure of God's mind. Climacus claims Hegel's absolute idealism mistakenly blurs the distinction between existence and thought. Climacus also argues that our mortal nature places limits on our understanding of reality. As Climacus argues: "So-called systems have often been characterized and challenged in the assertion that they abrogate the distinction between good and evil, and destroy freedom. Perhaps one would express oneself quite as definitely, if one said that every such system fantastically dissipates the concept existence.... Being an individual man is a thing that has been abolished, and every speculative philosopher confuses himself with humanity at large; whereby he becomes something infinitely great, and at the same time nothing at all."

Friedrich Nietzsche

Friedrich Nietzsche was the first to mount a logically serious criticism of Idealism that has been popularised by David Stove. He pre-empts Stove's GEM by arguing that Kant's argument for his transcendental idealism rests on a tautology and/or begging the question, and therefore is an invalid, improper argument.

In his book Beyond Good and Evil, Part 1 On the Prejudice of Philosophers Section 11, he ridicules Kant for admiring himself because he had undertaken and (thought he) succeeded in tackling "the most difficult thing that could ever be undertaken on behalf of metaphysics."

Quoting Nietzsche's prose: "But let us reflect; it is high time to do so. 'How are synthetic judgements a priori possible?' Kant asked himself-and what really is his answer? 'By virtue of a faculty' -but unfortunately not in five words,...The honeymoon of German philosophy arrived. All the young theologians of the Tübingen seminary went into the bushes all looking for 'faculties.'...'By virtue of a faculty' -he had said, or at least meant. But is that an answer? An explanation? Or is it not rather merely a repetition of the question? How does opium induce sleep? 'By virtue of a faculty,' namely the virtus dormitiva, replies the doctor in Moliére."

In addition to the Idealism of Kant, Nietzsche in the same book attacks the idealism of Schopenhauer and Descartes via a similar argument to Kant's original critique of Descartes. Quoting Nietzsche: There are still harmless self-observers who believe that there are "immediate certainties"; for example, "I think," or as the superstition of Schopenhauer put it, "I will"; as though knowledge here got hold of its objects purely and nakedly as "the thing in itself," without any falsification on the part of either the subject or the object. But that "immediate certainty," as well as "absolute knowledge" and the "thing in itself," involved a contradictio in adjecto, (contradiction between the noun and the adjective) I shall repeat a hundred times; we really ought to free ourselves from the seduction of words!

G. E. Moore

The first criticism of Idealism that falls within the analytic philosophical framework is by one of its cofounders Moore. This 1903 seminal article, The Refutation of Idealism. This one of the first demonstrations of Moore's commitment to analysis as the proper philosophical method. Moore proceeds by examining the Berkeleian aphorism esse est percipi: "to be is to be perceived". He examines in detail each of the three terms in the aphorism, finding that it must mean that the object and the subject are necessarily connected. So, he argues, for the idealist, "yellow" and "the sensation of yellow" are necessarily identical -to be yellow is necessarily to be experienced as yellow. But, in a move similar to the open question argument, it also seems clear that there is a difference between "yellow" and "the sensation of yellow". For Moore, the idealist is in error because "that esse is held to be percipi, solely because what is experienced is held to be identical with the experience of it".

Though this refutation of idealism was the first strong statement by analytic philosophy against its idealist predecessors this argument did not show that the GEM is logically invalid. Arguments advanced by Nietzsche (prior to Moore), Russell (just after Moore) & 80 years later Stove put a nail in the coffin for the "master" argument supporting idealism.

Bertrand Russell

Despite his hugely popular book The Problems of Philosophy (this book was in its 17th printing by 1943) which was written for a general audience rather than academia; few ever mention Russell's critique even though he completely anticipates David Stove's GEM both in form and content. In chapter 4 (Idealism) highlights Berkeley's tautological premise for advancing idealism.

Quoting Russell's prose (1912:42-43): "If we say that the things known must be in the mind, we are either un-duly limiting the mind's power of knowing, or we are uttering a mere tautology. We are uttering a mere tautology if we mean by 'in the mind' the same as by 'before the mind', i.e. if we mean merely being apprehended by the mind. But if we mean this, we shall have to admit that what, in this sense, is in the mind, may nevertheless be not mental. Thus when we realize the nature of knowledge, Berkeley's argument is seen to be wrong in substance as well as in form, and his grounds for supposing that 'idea'-i.e. the objects apprehended-must be mental, are found to have no validity whatever. Hence his grounds in favour of the idealism may be dismissed."

A.C. Ewing

Published in 1933 A.C. Ewing according to David Stove mounted the first full length book critique of Idealism, entitled Idealism; a critical survey. Stove does not mention that Ewing anticipated his GEM.

David Stove

The Australian philosopher David Stove argued in typically acerbic style that idealism rested on what he called "the worst argument in the world". His critique of Idealism is perhaps the most devastating critique of subjective idealism in philosophy. From a logical point of view his critique is no different from Russell or Nietzsche's but Stove has been more widely cited and most clearly highlighted the mistake of idealist proponents.

He named the form of this argument -invented by Berkeley "the GEM". Berkeley claimed that "[the mind] is deluded to think it can and does conceive of bodies existing unthought of, or without the mind, though at the same time they are apprehended by, or exist in, itself". Stove argued that this claim proceeds from the tautology that nothing can be thought of without its being thought of, to the conclusion that nothing can exist without its being thought of.

The following is Stove's homely version of Berkeley's GEM (1991:139):

(1) You cannot have trees-without-the-mind in mind, without having them in mind.

(2) Therefore, you cannot have trees-without-the-mind in mind.

   (i) Is a tautology (self-referential statement); therefore the premise of this argument is trivially true.

   (ii) Is not a trivially true conclusion. The logic flowing from 1) to 2) is valid (as this premise cannot lead to a false conclusion), but unsound because tautological premises can bring only tautological conclusions.

Refer to Stove's 1991 book The Plato Cult & Other Philosophical Follies chapter 6 Idealism: A Victorian Horror Story for numerous elucidations and numerous GEM's quoted from the history of philosophy and GEM's reconstructed in syllogistic form. For readers familiar with Nietzsche, Russell and Stove's criticism of Idealism it is clear that Stove's GEM merely repackages Russell's precise points and borrowing Nietzsche's polemics against idealism.

John Searle

In The Construction of Social Reality John Searle offers an attack on some versions of idealism. Searle conveniently summarises two important arguments for idealism. The first is based on our perception of reality:

1. All we have access to in perception are the contents of our own experiences
2. The only epistemic basis we can have for claims about the external world are our perceptual experiences therefore,
3. the only reality we can meaningfully speak of is the reality of perceptual experiences (The Construction of Social Reality p. 172)

Whilst agreeing with (2), Searle argues that (1) is false, and points out that (3) does not follow from (1) and (2).

The second argument for idealism runs as follows:

Premise: Any cognitive state occurs as part of a set of cognitive states and within a cognitive system

Conclusion 1: It is impossible to get outside of all cognitive states and systems to survey the relationships between them and the reality they are used to cognize

Conclusion 2: No cognition is ever of a reality that exists independently of cognition (The Construction of Social Reality p. 174)

Searle goes on to point out that conclusion 2 simply does not follow from its precedents.

Alan Musgrave

Alan Musgrave in an article titled Realism and Antirealism in R. Klee (ed), Scientific Inquiry: Readings in the Philosophy of Science, Oxford, 1998, 344-352 -later re-titled to Conceptual Idealism and Stove's GEM in A. Musgrave, Essays on Realism and Rationalism, Rodopi, 1999 also in M.L. Dalla Chiara et. al. (eds), Language, Quantum, Music, Kluwer, 1999, 25-35 -Alan Musgrave argues in addition to Stove's GEM, Conceptual Idealists compound their mistakes with use/mention confusions and proliferation of unnecessary hyphenated entities.

Stock examples of use/mention confusions:

Santa Claus (the person) does not exist.

'Santa Claus' (the name/concept/fairy tale) does exist; because adults tell children this every Christmas season.

The distinction in philosophical circles is highlighted by putting quotations around the word when we want to refer only to the name and not the object.

Stock examples of hyphenated entities:

things-in-itself (Immanuel Kant)

things-as-interacted-by-us (Arthur Fine)

Table-of-commonsense (Sir Arthur Eddington)

Table-of-physics (sir Arthur Eddington)

Moon-in-itself

Moon-as-howled-by-wolves

Moon-as-conceived-by-Aristotelians

Moon-as-conceived-by-Galileans

Hyphenated entities are "warning signs" for conceptual idealism according to Musgrave is because they over emphasis the epistemic (ways on how people come to learn about the world) activities and will more likely commit errors in use/mention. These entities do not exist (strictly speaking and are ersatz entities) but highlight the numerous ways in which people come to know the world.

In Sir Arthur Eddington's case use/mention confusions compounded his problem when he thought he was sitting at two different tables in his study (table-of-commonsense and table-of-physics). In fact Eddington was sitting at one table but had two different perspectives or ways of knowing about that one table. Richard Rorty and Postmodernist Philosophy in general have been attacked by Musgrave for committing use/mention confusions. Musgrave argues that these confusions help proliferate GEM's in our thinking and serious thought should avoid GEM's.

Philip J. Neujahr

"Although it would be hard to legislate about such matters, it would perhaps be well to restrict the idealist label to theories which hold that the world, or its material aspects, are dependent upon the specifically cognitive activities of the mind or Mind in perceiving or thinking about (or 'experiencing') the object of its awareness." (Kant's Idealism, Ch. 1)

Idealism in Religious Thought

A broad enough definition of idealism could include most religious viewpoints. The belief that personal beings (e.g., God and the angels) preceded the existence of insentient matter seems to suggest that an experiencing subject is a necessary reality. Also, the existence of an omniscient God suggests, regardless of the actual nature of matter, that all of nature is the object of at least one consciousness. Materialism sees no incoherence in a scenario of there being a cosmos where no sentient subject ever develops; a wholly unknown universe where neither any subject, nor any object of a subject's experience ever exists. Historically, Mechanistic Materialism has been the favorite viewpoint of Atheist philosophers. Still, idealistic viewpoints that have not included God, supernatural beings, or a post-mortem existence have sometimes been advanced.

While many religious philosophies are indeed specifically idealist, for example, some Hindu denominations view regarding the nature of Brahman, souls, and the world are idealistic, some have favored a form of substance dualism. Mahayana Buddhist denominations have usually embraced some form of idealism, while some Christian theologians have held idealist views, substance dualism has been the more common view of Christian authors, especially with the strong influence of the philosophy of Aristotle among the Scholastics. Several modern religious movements, for example the organizations within the New Thought Movement and the Unity Church, may be said to have a particularly idealist orientation.

The theology of Christian Science includes a form of subjective idealism: it teaches that all that exists is God and God's ideas; that the world as it appears to the senses is a distortion of the underlying spiritual reality. To meet Wikipedia's quality standards, this section may require cleanup.

Please discuss this issue on the talk page, and/or replace this tag with a more specific message. Editing help is available.

This section has been tagged since September 2006.

A Course in Miracles, a spiritual self-study course published in 1976, represents an explicitly idealist, pure non-dualistic thought system. In the Course, only God and His Creation, which is Spirit and has nothing to do with the world, are real. The physical universe is an illusion and does not exist. The Course compares the world of perception with a dream. It arises from the projection of the dreamer, i.e. the mind ("projection makes perception," T-21.in.1:5), according to its wishes (perception "is the outward picture of a wish; an image that you wanted to be true," T-24.VII.8:10). The purpose of the perceptual world is to ensure our separate, individual existence apart from God but avoid the responsibility and project the guilt onto others. As we learn to give the world another purpose and recognize our perceptual errors, we also learn to look past them or "forgive," as a way to awaken gradually from the dream and finally remember our true Identity in God. The Course's non-dualistic metaphysics is similar to Advaita Vedanta. What A Course in Miracles adds, is that it gives a motivation for the seeming though illusory existence of the perceptual world.

The West is inundated with physicalistic monism. There is widespread belief that everything will be explained in terms of matter/energy by science. Since we are constantly taught this it may make the idea of mentalistic monism hard to grasp. One way to begin to grasp the idea is through analogy. One analogy is the movie screen. If we next consider "Star Trek's holodeck" it takes us a step further as what appear to be physical objects are not. Next consider the movie "The Matrix". In "The Matrix" even people's bodies and identities are projected. Then replace the machine with a vast and powerful mind. A last analogy is our dreams at night. We seem to be in a world filled with other objects and other people and yet nothing of it is real. Although this is not a strict philosophical argument it does allow us to begin to think along these lines. Idealism is based on the root word "Ideal," meaning a perfect form of, and is also described as a belief in perfect forms of virtue, truth, and the absolute. (i.e., Webster's Dictionary says "conforming exactly to an ideal, law, or standard: perfect."). idealism in comparison to pragmatism

OTHER USES

In general parlance, "idealism" or "idealist" is also used to describe a person having high ideals, sometimes with the connotation that those ideals are unrealisable or at odds with "practical" life. The word "ideal" is commonly used as an adjective to designate qualities of perfection, desirability, and excellence. This is foreign to the epistemological use of the word "idealism" which pertains to internal mental representations. These internal ideas represent objects that are assumed to exist outside of the mind.

HUMAN RIGHTS

Human rights refers to inherent, universal rights of human beings regardless of jurisdiction or other factors, such as ethnicity, nationality, or sex.

The idea of human rights descended from the philosophical idea of natural rights; some recognize no difference between the two and regard both as labels for the same thing while others choose to keep the terms separate to eliminate association with some features traditionally associated with natural rights. As is evident in the United Nations Universal Declaration of Human Rights, human rights, at least in the post-war period, are conceptualized as based on inherent human dignity, retaining their universal and inalienable character.

The existence, validity and the content of human rights continue to be the subject to debate in philosophy and political science and many other forms. Legally, human rights are defined in international law and covenants, and further, in the domestic laws of many states. However, for many people the doctrine of human rights goes beyond law and forms a fundamental moral basis for regulating the contemporary geo-political order. For them, they are democratic ideals.

Human Rights Legislation

Where it has been adopted, legislation commonly contains:

- security rights that protect people against crimes such as murder, massacre, torture and rape
- liberty rights that protect freedoms in areas such as belief and religion, association, assembling and movement
- political rights that protect the liberty to participate in politics by expressing themselves, protesting, participating in a republic
- due process rights that protect against abuses of the legal system such as imprisonment without trial, secret trials and excessive punishments
- equality rights that guarantee equal citizenship, equality before the law and nondiscrimination
- welfare rights (also known as economic rights) that require the provision of education and protections against severe poverty and starvation
- group rights that provide protection for groups against ethnic genocide and for the ownership by countries of their national territories and resources

History

Appalled by the barbarism of the Second World War, the United Nations General Assembly adopted the Universal Declaration of Human Rights in 1948. While not legally binding, it urged member nations to promote a number of human, civil, economic and social rights, asserting these rights are part of the "foundation of freedom, justice and peace in the world". The declaration was the first international legal effort to limit the behavior of states and press upon them duties to their citizens following the model of the rights-duty duality. Many states wanted to go beyond the declaration of rights and create legal covenants which would put greater pressure on states to follow human rights norms. Because some states disagreed over whether this international covenant should contain economic and social rights (which usually require a greater effort to fulfill on the part of individual states), two treaties were prepared. In 1966 and 1976 respectively, the International Covenant on Civil and Political Rights and the International Covenant on Economic, Social and Cultural Rights came into force. With the Universal Declaration of Human Rights these documents form the International bill of rights.

- ...recognition of the inherent dignity and of the equal and inalienable rights of all members of the human family is the foundation of freedom, justice and peace in the world" - Preamble to the Universal Declaration of Human Rights, 1948

Since then several other pieces of legislation have been introduced at the international level:

- Convention on the Prevention and Punishment of the Crime of Genocide (entry into force: 1951)
- Convention against Torture (entry into force: 1984)
- Convention on the Elimination of All Forms of Racial Discrimination (entry into force: 1969)

- Convention on the Elimination of All Forms of Discrimination Against Women (entry into force: 1981)
- Convention on the Rights of the Child (entry into force: 1989)
- Rome Statute of the International Criminal Court (entry into force: 2002)

With the exception of the non-deformable human rights (the four most important are the right to life, the right to be free from slavery, the right to be free from torture and the right to be free from retroactive application of penal laws), the UN recognises that human rights can be limited or even pushed aside during times of national emergency -although "the emergency must be actual, affect the whole population and the threat must be to the very existence of the nation. The declaration of emergency must also be a last resort and a temporary measure". Conduct in war is governed by International Humanitarian Law.

INTERNATIONAL BODIES

The International Covenant on Civil and Political Rights created an agency, the Human Rights Committee to promote compliance with its norms. The 18 members of the committee express opinions as to whether a particular practice is a human rights violation, although its reports are not legally binding. A modern interpretation of the original Declaration of Human Rights was made in the Vienna Declaration and Programme of Action adopted by the World Conference on Human Rights in 1993. The degree of unanimity over these conventions, in terms of how many and which countries have ratified them varies, as does the degree to which they are respected by various states. The UN has set up a number of bodies to monitor and study human rights, under the leadership of the UN High Commissioner for Human Rights (UNHCHR).

Regional Legislation

There are also many regional agreements and organisations governing human rights including the European Court of Human Rights, which is the only international court with jurisdiction to deal with cases brought by individuals (rather than states); the African Commission on Human and Peoples' Rights; Inter-American Commission on Human Rights; Cairo Declaration on Human Rights in Islam; Inter-American Court of Human Rights; and Iran's Defenders of Human Rights Center.

History of Human Rights

Ur-Nammu, the king of Ur created what was arguably the first legal codex in ca. 2050 BC. Several other sets of laws were created in Mesopotamia including the Code of Hammurabi, (ca. 1780 BC) which is one of the best preserved examples of this type of document. It shows rules and punishments if those rules are broken on a variety of matters including women's rights, children's rights and slave rights.

The Persian Empire (Iran) established unprecedented principles of human rights in the 6th century BC under the reign of Cyrus the Great. After his conquest of Babylon in 539 BC, the king issued the Cyrus Cylinder, discovered in 1879 and recognized by many today as the first human rights document. The cylinder declared that citizens of the empire would be allowed to practice their religious beliefs freely. It also abolished slavery, so all the palaces of the kings of Persia were built by paid workers in an era where slaves typically did such work. These two reforms were reflected in the biblical books of Chronicles and Ezra, which state that Cyrus released the followers of Judaism from slavery and allowed them to migrate back to their land. The cylinder now lies in the British Museum, and a replica is kept at the United Nations headquarters.

Three centuries later, the Mauryan Empire of ancient India established unprecedented principles of civil rights in the 3rd century BC under the reign of Ashoka the Great. After his brutal conquest of Kalinga in circa 265 BC, he felt remorse for what he had done, and as a result, adopted Buddhism. From then, Ashoka, who had been described as "the cruel Ashoka" eventually came to be known as "the pious Ashoka". During his reign, he pursued an official policy of nonviolence (ahimsa). The unnecessary slaughter or mutilation of animals was immediately abolished, such as sport hunting and branding. Ashoka also showed mercy to those imprisoned, allowing them outside one day each year, and offered common citizens free education at universities. He treated his subjects as equals regardless of their religion, politics or caste, and constructed free hospitals for both humans and animals. Ashoka defined the main principles of nonviolence, tolerance of all sects and opinions, obedience to parents, respect for teachers and priests, being liberal towards friends, humane treatment of servants (slavery was non-existent in India at the time), and generosity towards all. These reforms are described in the Edicts of Ashoka.

Elsewhere societies have located the beginnings of human rights in religious documents. The Vedas, the Bible, the Qur'an and the Analects of Confucius are some of the oldest written sources which address questions of people's duties, rights, and responsibilities.

In 1215 King John of England issued the Magna Carta, a document forced upon him by the Pope and English barons, which required him to renounce certain rights, respect certain legal procedures and accept that the will of the king could be bound by law. Although the document did not itself limit the power of the king in the Middle Ages, its later reinterpretation in the Elizabethean and Stuart periods established it as a powerful document on which constitutional law was founded in Britain and elsewhere. In 1222, the Manden Charter in Mali was a declaration of essential human rights, including the right to life, and opposed the practice of slavery.

Several 17th and 18th century European philosophers, most notably John Locke, developed the concept of natural rights, the notion that people possess certain rights by virtue of being human. Though Locke believed natural rights were derived from divinity since humans were creations of God, his ideas were important in the development of the modern notion of rights. Lockean natural rights did not rely on citizenship nor any law of the state, nor were they necessarily limited to one particular ethnic, cultural or religious group.

Two major revolutions occurred that century in the United States (1776) and in France (1789). The United States Declaration of Independence includes concepts of natural rights and famously states "that all men are created equal, that they are endowed by their creator with certain unalienable rights, that among these are life, liberty and the pursuit of happiness."

Similarly, the Declaration of the Rights of Man and of the Citizen defines a set of individual and collective rights of the people. These are held to be universal -not only to French citizens but to all men without exception.

Philosophers such as Thomas Paine, John Stuart Mill and Hegel expanded on the theme of universality during the 18th and 19th centuries. In 1831 William Lloyd Garrison wrote in a newspaper called The Liberator that he was trying to enlist his readers in "the great cause of human rights" so the term human rights probably came into use sometime between Paine's The Rights of Man and Garrison's publication. In 1849 a contemporary, Henry David Thoreau, wrote about human rights in his treatise On the Duty of Civil Disobedience which was later influential on human rights and civil rights thinkers. United States Supreme Court Justice Davis Davis, in his 1867 opinion for Ex Parte Milligan, wrote "By the protection of the law, human rights are secured; withdraw that protection and they are at the mercy of wicked rulers or the clamor of an excited people."

Many groups and movements have managed to achieve profound social changes over the course of the 20th century in the name of human rights. In Western Europe and North America, labour unions brought about laws granting workers the right to strike, establishing minimum work conditions and forbidding or regulating child labour. The women's rights movement succeeded in gaining for many women the right to vote. National liberation movements in many countries succeeded in driving out colonial powers. One of the most influential was Mahatma Gandhi's movement to free his native India from British rule. Movements by long-oppressed racial and religious minorities succeeded in many parts of the world, among them the civil rights movement, and more recent diverse identity politics movements, on behalf of women and minorities in the United States.

CHAPTER

6 REVOLUTION: THEORY AND TYPES

INDIA'S ETHNIC SPECTRUM

India has a highly complex and colourful social mosaic. Yet, although characterized by a vast spread of cultural diversity and heterogeneity, this mosaic is not chaotic. It has a clearly discernible pattern, wherein sociocultural diversity draws its strength and sustenance from India's composite culture and civilization thrust. This culture has evolved over centuries, through a process of assimilation and amalgamation of the diverse cultural influxes coming with the hordes of invaders-the Aryans, the Sakas, the Huns, the Pathans, the Moghuls, and the Europeans. Thus, the evolved composite culture of India cannot be compared either with the melting pot of American society or with the multinational state exemplified by the now defunct Soviet Union. India's socio-cultural mosaic is the true picture of "unity in diversity," like a bouquet of flowers or vegetables in a salad bowl, where every component, while retaining its specific identity, is a part of a larger whole.

Upon this cultural diversity, within the ambit of civilization unity, is based the reality of the multi-ethnic society of India. Several cultural markers-language, race, tribe, caste, religion, and region serve as identity axes for ethnic groups and their mobilization. In most of the ethnic groups, more than one of these cultural markers are pertinent for identification. In other words, India's ethno-communities have multi-layered and multidimensional identities that impinge on each other in a non-stratified and dynamic manner. The identity composition of ethno-communities has been further complicated by the imposition of class distinctions, not only between one and another ethno-community, but also within each. Multi-layered, non-stratified identity composition has enabled ethnic groups to assert and reshuffle their cultural markers to advance their perceived objectives.

Two other commonly accepted characteristics of the spectrum of ethnic diversity in India deserve attention. One is that there is no subordinate dominant pattern between the ethnic groups. Thus, the patterns of conflicts and contradictions between ethno-communities vary along scales of time and place. Secondly, the ethnic groups do not have territories marked out for them because the cultural markers identifying such groups do not coincide with territorial boundaries. Accordingly, people belonging to specific religions, tribes, castes, races, and languages are found scattered in various territorial regions. We shall see later that not even the reorganization of states in India on linguistic lines has been able to overcome this aspect.

Potential for conflicts and their protraction

Any diversity and heterogeneity is not conflict producing per se, although it may carry a potential for conflict. India has witnessed ethnic conflicts in the process of its historical evolution, and the leadership of independent India was conscious that while India presents the picture of "unity and diversity," the possibility of conflict between the "unity" and the "diversity" could not be ruled out. Independent India's first prime minister, Jawaharlal Nehru, said:

While on the one hand, we the people of India are bound together by strong bonds of culture, common objectives, friendship and affection, on the other hand, unfortunately, there are inherent in India, separatist and disruptive tendencies... [which made India suffer in the past. In preserving its unity, India needed to]... fight communalism, provincialism, separatism, statism and casteism.

Owing to the varying parameters of the process of identity transformations and the roles of external (non-ethnic) factors, ethnic conflicts and politics in India have "waxed and waned." Even some of the raging ethnic conflicts in India have shown inconsistencies in their ideological manifestations and intensity. The conflict in the Punjab, for instance, had a dominant linguistic thrust during the mid-1960s. In the late 1970s and early 1980s it was rekindled by the rivalry between competing Sikh sects, the Nirankaris and the Akalis. To this was added intra-group political rivalries amongst the Sikhs in the Punjab. Subsequently, it assumed both religious and economic dimensions in the form of the Anandpur Sahib Resolution. At present, it is fast acquiring a Sikh fundamentalist character, with growing emphasis on the assertion of Sikh religious and cultural symbols to legitimize militancy and violence. Elements of the Punjab situation are also reflected in the Kashmir conflict, where the initial movement of the state's political and economic neglect has now clearly acquired overtones of Islamic religious assertion, to the extent of becoming fundamentalist. Accordingly, the earlier concept of Kashmir identity, or Kashmiriat, has been replaced by communal confrontation, wherein the Muslim militants have pushed Hindu Kashmiris out of the valley. India also bears witness to the fact that the precipitation and intensification of ethnic conflicts by cultural diversity is not a unilinear or irreversible process. Ethnic conflicts have been resolved and reduced, but also re-created. The conflict arising out of the demand for the Tamil language and land during the early 1960s was resolved, although potential tension between Tamil and the declared (but not imposed) national language, Hindi, still exists. In the context of the Punjab conflict, the Rajiv-Longowal accord of 1985 was a major move to contain the conflict, although it proved futile.

The initial thrust of ethnic conflict in Assam, which was directed against the influx of foreigners, experienced some respite in the mid-1980s, although now it has reemerged in violent form under the leadership of the Bodos and ULFA (United Liberation Front of Assam) groups. Similarly, some of the tribal insurgencies in the Northeast have also been politically contained. These varying patterns of conflict formation and containment (including resolution) are likely to persist in the future. For instance, a communal and fundamentalist conflict such as the clash between a temple (Hindu) and a mosque (Muslim) in Ayodhya seems to have lost its militancy and violent thrust after climaxing in 1990-91. At the same time there are signs of new conflict formations among some of the hitherto neglected tribes. The movements of Tribals in the Jharkand region (Bihar) and of Nepalis in Darjeeling and Sikkim over the language issue have become sufficiently politicized and militant to create flashpoints.

Simultaneous conflict formation and conflict containment

The inconsistent and reversible processes of ethnic conflicts can be understood in the context of India's developmental dynamics, which have been releasing simultaneously the impulses of both conflict formation and containment. Both the alienation and integration of ethnic groups have been going on side by side, a process which Arun Bose describes as "Disintegration and Reintegration." Looking at the politics of ethnicity in South Asia with reference to developmental dynamics, either of the two trends can be emphasized. On the one hand, Asaf Husain presupposed that "successful national integration would cut across structures," while on the other hand; Paul Brass highlighted a "process of nationality formation rather than state-building." The reality is that both these views are tenable since one "does not preclude the bother." It is this dual character of social development which prompts David Washbrook to say that "the politics of ethnicity have been remarkably ineffective in directing the course of modern Indian history," although many may seriously question this categorical assertion. The fact that the sharpening of ethnic boundaries and conflicts in India has been on the rise cannot be disputed. Studies have shown an increase in communal riots, and the rise in the number of persons killed in these riots has become alarming since 1985.

In 1985, rural areas which thus far had remained unaffected also accounted for 46 per cent of communal incidents. The momentum in communal violence has kept up in recent years. In 1989 there were 18 major riots, in which 1,174 persons were killed. The number of persons killed in 1986 was 418; 383 were killed in 1987, 223 in 1988, and 693 in 1990. One of the major factors behind the deterioration in the communal situation is the rise of Hindu fundamentalism and its corresponding majoritarian ethnic nationalism based on Hindutva. The temple-mosque conflict in Ayodhya was a concrete manifestation of this. Political vested interests have obviously played a decisive role in this development, which if allowed to go on unabated will worsen the situation and endanger India's unity and integrity.

As for the persistent and festering ethnic conflicts in the Punjab, Kashmir, and Assam, we have already noted that they have intensified and the extent of violence has grown. Even the character of these insurgencies, in terms of their objectives, ideologies, leadership, and methods, is becoming more strident and uncompromising. The growing violent activities of Sikh militants in the Teral region of Uttar Pradesh have become a matter of serious concern. In addition to this, other potential ethnic conflicts such as in Jharkand and the Nepali/Gurkha communities are reportedly gathering political momentum.18 In the north-eastern tribal areas, the Naga National Council (NNC) has decided to take up arms and coordinate its activities with the

National Socialist Council of Nagaland (NSCN). The tribal situation in Manipur, Tripura, and Mizoran is also moving fast towards the boil.

No less significant than this process of disintegration and conflict have been the forces of integration and mutual identification of diverse ethnic and cultural streams. We have noted earlier that the basis of the integrative process is India's composite culture, expressed in the form of secular national identity. Indian secularism did not evolve on the pattern of European secularism, which strove to detach the spiritual from the temporal. In India, all religions were accepted on an equal footing. The state gave equal rights to all religious and ethnic groups so that they could protect and promote their educational and cultural interests, by virtue of the Indian Constitution (arts. 2630). (An exception was made for scheduled castes and tribes, which were brought under the umbrella of "protective discrimination," according to Part X, arts. 30, 46, 244, 244A, and 335 of the Indian Constitution.) This secular identity was not an imposition by the state on society but a recognition of a deep-rooted social reality-that erosion of this identity would mean the disintegration of India along sectarian lines. Hence, firm constitutional provisions were made to preserve secular identity. In a way, they were necessary, owing to the trauma of India's partition.

To have a better appreciation of the dual process of integration and alienation of ethnic and national groups/identities-that is, the simultaneous occurrence of ethnic conflict formation and containment, we must look more closely at India's developmental dynamics, federalism, and democracy.

Dynamics of development

The significance of linkages between the dynamics of development and ethnic conflicts has been widely recognized. Reetz, in discussing the ethnic dilemma in Pakistan, observes that: ethnic and national group formation... could be separated from modern socioeconomic development trends of emerging capitalism. The growth of market relations at regional and national levels was the driving force behind the increasing articulation of both separate ethnic and common national interests.

This is equally relevant to the Indian situation, where the national and regional market developed much faster and more strongly than anywhere else in South Asia. The development of this market, backed by the growth of industry and commerce, brought diverse regional and ethnic interests together to interact, collaborate, and compete. As a result, regional and ethnic interests have developed stakes in expanding and strengthening the national market and linking it with the network of regional interests. Capital, technology, industry and commerce, and labour have moved from one region to another, cutting across and subordinating ethnic diversities. Diverse interest groups have come into being; industrialists, traders, transporters, and workers (trade unions). In the mixed economy of India, the process of development planning for target groups and regions has greatly helped various neglected and marginalized sections of society to join the national mainstream. Allocation of plan resources by the centre to the states has also bound them in a nexus of mutual bargaining and collaboration, notwithstanding the displeasure of the states over the amounts of resources transferred.

But these integrative pulls have not been without disintegrative implications. One of the common causes of the politicization of ethnicity and the formation of ethnic conflict is said to be the relative and perceived sense of economic deprivation by a given ethnic group. Tambiah, looking at national and international factors behind the cause of economic deprivation, says:

The present plethora of ethnic conflicts... coincides with an increasing sense of shrinking economic horizons and political battlement. Many things have gone awry with economic development: the declining terms of trade dictated by the industrialized internal bottlenecks; agricultural underemployment and migration to cities; increasing disparities of income among the expectant participants in the literacy explosion; the visible pauperisation of the urban underclass... All this has happened in the course of India's economic development. The most illustrative aspect of this development is the lopsided and uneven growth of the national market, prosperity, and income distribution, and the sensitization of underprivileged groups to their disadvantageous placement in the national division of labour. In some cases, bouts of prosperity have resulted in inflating expectations, which national resource generation and distribution mechanism have not been able to fulfill. In others, the slow pace of building prosperity has given rise to the sense of relative deprivation. Equally pertinent here is to note that corruption and family or "ethnic nepotism" have given impetus to alienation and conflict formation.

It is illustrative in this respect that economic maldevelopment has fuelled diverse ethnic insurgencies in India. Some recent studies on communal conflicts in North India show that the prosperity of Muslim artisans has given them confidence to free themselves from exploitation by Hindu traders and moneylenders, helping precipitate such conflicts. In the Punjab, it has been a problem of prosperity combined with unequal distribution of wealth resulting from the green revolution boom. The rich Punjabi farmers, in search of investing their surpluses for better returns, found it compelling to capture state power. Further marginalization of small and ladles peasants forced them into militancy for bare survival.

By contrast, the situation in Kashmir, Assam, and the Northeast has been one of economic neglect and discrimination in the perception of the affected masses. Even when national funds were allocated, they did not reach the targeted groups, because of the corruption of bureaucrats, politicians, and other mediators. In the absence of any serious attempt to correct these economic distortions, it may not be realistic to expect resolution of these raging ethnic conflicts.

Federalism

In the debate on India's national integration and ethnic tensions, the nature and functioning of the federal power structure occupies an important place. The foundations of federalism were laid down on the grounds of concern for the unity and integrity of a culturally diverse nation. In view of historical experiences of disruptive and disintegrative sectarian forces and the political context of partition prevailing at the time of independence, the founding fathers of the Indian Constitution wanted to strengthen the Union against possible disintegrative pressures. Introducing the draft Constitution in the Constituent Assembly, Dr Ambedkar said: though India was to be a federation, the federation was not the result of an agreement by the states to join in a federation.

Not being a result of an agreement, no state has the right to secede from it. Though the country and the people may be divided into different states for convenience of administration, the country is one integral whole, its people a single people living under a single imperium derived from a single source... The Drafting Committee thought it was better to make [this] clear at the outset rather than leave it to speculation... Thus the perceived basis of structuring the federation was "administrative convenience." Unlike the American and the (erstwhile) Soviet constitutions, the states had no inherent, not even notional, right to secede from the Union or demand self-determination. In fact the Union in India was empowered to frustrate any such separatist or secessionist pressures if and when they arose.

With administrative convenience the avowed guiding principle for designing the federation, not much weight was given to the need for reflecting India's cultural design. No specific provisions for religious or cultural minorities were incorporated, except that they were given equal rights. The principle of "preventive discrimination," applied in the case of scheduled castes and scheduled tribes, was designed more to undo their social and economic backwardness than to help them preserve and promote their cultural distinctiveness. The Constitution's initial provisions and subsequent amendments provided for self-government under special administrative provisions for Jammu and Kashmir (Schedule IV, article 370) and to the tribal areas of North-East (Nagas, Mizos, Manipuri, Tripura, under articles 371 and 371A-I), but the Constituent Assembly refused to endorse proposals for constituting states on a linguistic basis. Nehru even went to the extent of threatening his resignation if that was to be done, as he apprehended that such a provision would endanger India's unity and integrity. Nehru was soon to revise his position on this vital issue under the force of circumstances when, in 1953, the linguistic basis of reorganizing states was accepted and Telugu-speaking Andhra emerged as the first such state. The Commission Constituted to Reorganise States in the Indian Federation nonetheless continued to emphasize that "it is the Union of India that is the basis of our nationality." Explaining the criterion of language as the basis for constituting a state, it said:

Linguistic homogeneity provides the only rational basis for reconstituting the state, for it reflects the social and cultural pattern of living obtaining in well-defined regions of the country. The congress leadership, including Nehru, which had earlier opposed the idea, conceded, saying that, being democrats, they had to respect people's wishes. The process of linguistic reorganization of states initiated in 1953 has been carried forward under the recommendations of the States Reorganisation Commission since 1956 and was broadly completed by the end of the 1960s. This was a major development toward incorporating cultural identities into political and administrative units. The federal devolution of power strengthened this expression of cultural diversity.

The devolution of powers between the Union (or the centre) and the states was laid down in separate lists prepared for this purpose. Accordingly, the list of the states' "exclusive" powers includes: public order; police; education; local government; roads and transport; agriculture; land and land revenue; forests; fisheries; industry and trade (limited); state Public Service Commissions; and Courts (except the Supreme Court). The states can also make laws along with the centre (provided the two do not clash), on subjects included in a "Concurrent List." These subjects include: criminal laws and their administration; economic and social planning; commercial and industrial monopolies; shipping and navigation on the inland waterways; drugs; ports (limited); courts and civil procedures. The arrangement for distribution of powers between the Union and the states has remained generally stable.

One of the controversial aspects of centre-state relations has been the allocation of economic resources by the Union to the states. Such allocation is carried out by the Planning Commission in the area of developmental expenditure and has led to complaint by the states that the resources provided are inadequate. The states also have their own power to raise revenues. The "Gadgil Plan," regarding financial relations between the Union and the states, was not acceptable to the Sarkaria Commission, which was appointed to review the whole gamut of centre-state relations in view of the state's growing unhappiness in this regard. The Commission reported in 1988, but successive Finance Commissions have gradually enlarged the scope of devolution of taxes to the states. (These later Commissions were appointed under articles 280-1 of the Constitution to decide the distribution of taxes between the Union and the states as well as grants-in-aid to the states out of the Consolidated Fund of India.) The Eighth Finance Commission raised the level of such tax revenues in favour of the states from 55 to 85 per cent.

Such an elaborate structure of power devolution has combined with the linguistic basis of federal unity to facilitate the management of cultural diversity in India and help mitigate pulls toward separatism and disintegration. Centre-state relations, whether based on ethnicity or otherwise, have not been peaceful or tension-free, but the competition has tended to focus on securing resources and greater power. States of diverse languages and cultures have often joined together to enhance their bargaining power. In some cases the Indian federal structure even provides for such bargaining through bodies such as the Inter-State and National Development Councils. Examples of bargaining coalitions include that of four Southern Chief Ministers joining in 1983 to negotiate with the centre. Similarly, in 1987 a conclave of nine opposition parties held near Delhi under the leadership of the Andhra Telugu Desham leader, N.T. Rama Rao, demanded the restoration of "co-operative federalism enshrined in the Constitution."

In 1992, the Sikkim Chief Minister and his regional party, the Sikkim Sangram Parishad, asked for membership in the North-East Council (of Northeast States and Tribal Areas) for this same purpose. Some scholars have described the federal system in India as one of "coalition and administration," or one with a "high degree of collaborative partnership." In addition, both at the central and state levels, a consciously followed approach to preserve and promote the cultural specificities of diverse groups has helped such groups identify with the national mainstream. All this has contributed to the secularization of ethnicity and has thus helped strengthen integrative forces.

It is interesting to note that most of the ethnic conflicts are between one given ethnic group and the Union of India, as if there were no ethnic contradictions and incompatibilities between individual groups. As noted earlier, the issues involved in such conflicts are invariably mixed with questions of sharing economic resources and decision-making power.

The functioning of federalism has nevertheless also had undesirable implications for the ethnic scene in India. The linguistic reorganization of the states gave impetus to various groups of specific cultural markers and ethnic identities to seek political expression and legitimacy. This was because ethnic identity was provided a territory under the scheme of reorganization. The importance of ethnic territory in ethnic conflict is very crucial, as can be gathered from recent developments in the Punjab and Kashmir and earlier events in Assam. In the Punjab and Kashmir conflicts, along with the transformation of identities and issues, the territorial base of ethnicity is being perfected by driving out Punjabi-speaking Hindus from the Punjab and Kashmiri-speaking Hindus from Kashmir. The potential for conflict formation along ethnic identity lines has thus been encouraged.

This potential has been further sharpened because linguistic reorganization in a vast and diverse country like India cannot be perfectly precise. On the periphery of the newly formed linguistic states, unassimilated linguistic minorities continued to exist. Then many other linguistic groups continued to remain in the larger Hindi-speaking states without being accommodated in the new political arrangement. The dissatisfactions of some of the unrecognized minority linguistic groups also continue to simmer. Such problems exist with regard to the Konkan region of Maharasthra/Goa, Nepali-speaking groups of Darjeeling, Sikkim, and Assam, and Maithili and Avadhi language groups in Bihar. The possibility of political movements and conflict formation arising out of these problems cannot be ruled out. There are already several political parties which are ethnicity-based, and they will very willingly build their strength by exploiting the linguistic frustrations of their constituencies. The Sarkaria Commission (1988) clearly hinted at weaknesses of the linguistic reorganization of states in this respect when it said:

Very often, the sub-national sentiment which is initially based on linguistic, religious or ethnic groupings, gains strength with a blend of economic issues, such as those relating to... economic backwardness. One of the most significant developments has been the rise of linguistic chauvinism, rearrangement of the boundaries of the States on linguistic basis... resulting in fissiparous tendencies. In a very significant way, federalism has fuelled ethnic conflict through the use of the Union's special provisions over the states. The use of article 356, which provides for imposition of presidential rule in a state in the "event of the failure of constitutional machinery," has been the subject of considerable controversy and debate in this regard. Political use of this provision has been extensive, particularly by the Congress-ruled centre. It can be employed to dismiss the state government of an opposition party or to manipulate political advantages for a ruling party or a particularly favoured political leader. In such manipulative machinations, the centre-appointed governor has played a decisive role, bringing the status and integrity of the governorship into considerable disrepute. The victimized party and leaders have sought to project this abuse of power as an instance of suppression of the political rights of the dominant ethnic group in the given state.

This has been an important factor behind the alienation of the Punjab, Kashmir, and Assam. Nagaland, where presidential rule was imposed in April 1992, is a recent example of the alleged misuse of article 356. In reaction, Nagaland's Chief Minister Vamuzo, who was ousted, said:

The 'imperial character' of the Delhi government has manifested itself in its most perverted and brutal forms in the north-eastern states. The latest act of perfidy by the Congress government has come at a time when, with the knowledge and approval of Delhi, I was engaged in an effort to persuade the underground insurgents in Nagaland to give up arms and join the political process. Obviously, such efforts were not to the liking of certain sections of the political leadership in the state who have a vested interest in a violent underground movement...

Let me, however, sound a note of warning. The entire North-East is in a state of turmoil. Frustration because of unemployment is driving the educated youth of this region to desperation. The sense of alienation due to the overbearing presence of the army is being compounded by the lack of opportunity. And the denial to the people of their right to govern themselves in accordance with the Constitution is creating situations that will ultimately convince the people of the entire Northeast, from Arunachal to Mizoram, that they have no hope of a life of peace and dignity under the present dispensation.

While the abuse of some constitutional provisions by the centre against the states has tended to alienate the states-based ethnic leadership, the creation and use of other specific provisions at the local level by the army, state governments, or police have resulted in distancing the common people from the Union. (Such provisions include the Disturbed Areas Act, the Armed Forces Special Powers Act of 1958 for the Eastern region and of 1983 for Punjab and Chandigarh, and the act relating to "Terrorist Affected Disturbed Areas.") As a consequence of their application, the social bases of ethnic conflicts have widened and deepened. The Sarkaria Commission blamed those in charge of the centre for this misuse and centralization of power in the Union, saying:

Those in power at the centre, have been obliged to use diverse strategies and tactics which were not always sound from [a] long-term [point of view] to maintain their control over state level forces. Many a time, the actions of the centre, its discriminatory approach towards some states, its lack of understanding of local problems, its abject insensitiveness (sic) and the blatant misuse of authority vis-à-vis the states, have all distanced it from the people. This in turn has, it is believed, reversed the process of national integration...

Based on federal experience in India, it may not be out of place to assume that the structure of federalism and its inherent resilience can cope with the pressures of ethnicity and conflicts. It can even help resolve, or at least contain, some of these pressures, if the imperatives of federal devolution of power and obligations of mutual accommodation and adjustments are observed sincerely. The diffusion of Tamil militancy and separatism during the 1960s and instances of moderation of tribal insurgencies in the Northeast and Assam during the 1980s may be recalled in this regard. Against this, politically motivated distortions and manipulation of federal powers and institutions can worsen ethnic conflicts.

Punjab and Kashmir are painful illustrations of this. In the case of Punjab, if the political expediency of appeasing Haryana had not hamstrung the centre (irrespective of the party in power), the Rajiv-Longowal Agreement of 1985 would have been implemented to ease the conflict there, if not completely resolve it. The statement of the dismissed Nagaland Chief Minister

Vamuzo cited earlier is also relevant here. In an important way, federal relations have been vitiated by the breakdown of the Congress Party's dominance of the centre and the states since the 1960s and the emergence of political incompatibility and competition between the party ruling at the centre and in the various states. As these incompatibilities have grown, demands for redefining and restructuring these relations have been most pronounced, because the forum consisting of a single party in power everywhere could not be utilized to sort out federal tensions.

Reacting to distortions in federal relations and the abuse of powers devolved under the constitutional arrangement, some scholars have called for restructuring Indian federalism.38 That may be neither practical nor offer a real panacea, because the structure so redefined may also be misused or manipulated for political purposes. The remedy lies in the evolution and strict observance of healthy guidelines and norms in the operational aspects of federalism, which have to become a reliable instrument for containing, moderating, and resolving ethnic conflicts.

Democratic politics

Dual impulses of ethnic integration and disintegration have been released by the democratic politics of India. Democracy as an ideology and system of governance centres around the individual; hence, it underplays the ethnic specificity and group feeling of individuals. It also prescribes and permits the pursuance of multiple interests by individuals, who accordingly associate in interest groups that cut across ethnic identities. Indian experience confirms this theoretical assumption. Adult franchise and Panchayati Raj institutions in India have brought people together to communicate and interact. This has given them a sense of sharing and access to decision-making power, however ineffective and fragile this access may be. Communication and consciousness of individual rights have bound them together in non-ethnic ties and prevented the state from acquiring a specific ethnic character or bias. Seth, in discussing the problems of ethnic movements and the role of the state in pluralistic societies, holds that:

The forces generated by democratic politics prevent the state from choosing a single cultural identity, even majoritarian, [as] the basis of nationhood. Thus, the project of nation-building in a democratic polity becomes inseparable from building a civil society...

Such "civil societies" do not host ethnic conflicts or movements in any negative sense of the term. Democracy is helpful in averting ethnic precipitation in other ways, too. Freedom of expression and powerful, sensitive national media not only promote a broader national consensus but also alert and forewarn the state and society when ethnic distortions and conflict formations become imminent. There is, however, another side to democratic politics in India. Though democratic ideology focuses on the individual, political mobilization (electoral and otherwise) in a highly stratified, diverse, and clustered society like India, it has also taken place on a group basis. Accordingly, caste blocs have acted as basic and lasting "vote banks" in democratic elections. To some extent, the British legacy can be blamed for the communalization of Indian politics, because concepts like "communal representation" were introduced during the British period. But then, in independent India the reservation of elected seats and constituencies for specific caste groups (Schedule Castes and Tribes), though based on strong commitment to social justice and change, has been a persistent endorsement of politics based on social divisions. Political polarization on the Mandal Commission implementation and reservations for the Other Backward Castes (OBCs) were an outcome of this legacy. The political tallying of lower castes and ethnic loyalties has tended to encourage the upper castes and Hindu backlash emerging in the form of Hindutva politics. The root cause of the growing recourse to caste and ethnic mobilization in India's democratic politics has been the erosion of ideology and viable socioeconomic programmes around which electoral and political mobilization ought to take place. This erosion became prominent in the mid-1960s, when even the Congress Party started feeling insecure about its capacity to maintain its dominance. Mobilization along communal, caste, religious, regional, and tribal lines sought to fill in the ideological vacuum. There followed a rise, both in number and political clout, of ethnic and region-based parties.

The imperatives of federalism in India, particularly with linguistic states as a vital political category, have encouraged and strengthened regional parties. This has given impetus to the activation of ethnic identities and has contributed to the process of conflict formation along ethnic lines. There has also been a positive aspect, in the sense that no ethnic or regional party is capable of assuming power at the centre on its own. Parties have therefore endeavoured to form alliances and coalitions with national parties to evolve alternative and competing structures of power. Experiments like the Samyukt Vidhayak Dal of the 1960s, the Janata Party of the 1970s, and the National Front since the 1980s are examples. These experiments have tended to broaden and facilitate national consensus rather than hinder it. The more dangerous aspect of India's emerging democratic politics has been political parties' ruthless and cynical use of communal and ethnic contradictions for short-term, narrow political gains. Monsters of ethnic separatism and conflict were created or encouraged out of such expediency. A typical example was the building up of San Bhindrawale by the Congress (particularly Mrs Indira Gandhi and her Sikh associates like Zail Singh and Buta Singh) to contain Akali challenges in the Punjab. The encouragement of Subhas Ghiesing of the Gurkha National Liberation Front in Darjeeling to weaken the CPM's hold over West Bengal falls into the same category.45 While Bhindrawale's shadow looms large on the Punjab ethnic conflict, Ghiesing threatens to provoke a Nepali ethnic explosion. It is not only the Congress Party which has indulged in opportunistic political endeavours at the cost of national unity and ethnic peace. Unfortunately, other parties have not lagged behind. The Janata Dal's projection of the Mandal issue and the BHP's exploitation of the Ayodhya temple-mosque controversy may be recalled in this respect.

Socio-ethnic conflicts in the Northeast

Media attention, hence public awareness, including those of intellectuals and power elites in India, has traditionally been directed at events occurring in the Northwestern parts of India. It has been quite apparent since independence, except during the Sino-Indian war in 1962. The problems of Pakistan and Jammu and Kashmir have dulled Indian public and political sensitivities although more security personnel and civilians die annually due to insurgency and inter-tribal conflicts in the North-Eastern states than anywhere else. The contiguity of this region to several other countries, especially China which is India's strategic adversary, makes this region extremely sensitive. Let us take a look at an important geographical aspect which affects India's security at the strategic level. Entire North Bengal and a bit of Western Assam for about 300 km is sandwiched between Nepal, Chumbi Valley and Bhutan in the North and Bangladesh in the South. The Siliguri corridor which at its narrowest is only 30 km has an average width of about 150 km. Through this corridor all surface communications, both road and railway, to the North-Eastern region pass. Any threat to this corridor or the lower Brahmaputra Valley can seriously affect all movement in peacetime or during war. There are two major factors which are causing problems in this area. The first is the illegal immigration of aliens which is affecting the demographic balance and is a constant source of socio-economic tensions. The second is the emerging socio-ethnic conflicts among the peoples of this region. This is due to a combination of several factors such as tribal groups trying to seek a separate identity because of perceived social, political and identity because of perceived social, political and economic injustice, mainly due to the short-sighted political policies of different regional and national level parties competing for power. The emerging patterns in the states of North Bengal, Assam, Manipur and Tripura are discussed here.

North Bengal

This is a complex sector. Indian Gorkhas and Indian Muslims who form two major groups of this sector have close emotional, family and cultural links with the peoples in Nepal and Bangladesh. This, coupled with a porous border and lower economic status, provides fertile ground for illegal immigration. A senior Intelligence Bureau official posted in this region for several years revealed the following methodology of illegal entry into India in an informal conversation with the author.

People exchange property on both sides of the border and migrate. This probably refers more to Hindus from Bangladesh.Marriages take place between members of the family with links across the international border (IB) followed by the whole family migrating to live with the married members of the family on the Indian side of the IB.There is a seasonal or frequent employment migration from Bangladesh into the border belts of West Bengal, Assam and Tripura, over a period of time. This author during a study tour in 1995 found a large number of alien rickshaw pullers in Guwahati, Agartala and even in (outsider hostile) Dimapur. Apparently this state of affairs extend to head load labourers and farm labour, especially in the lower Brahmaputra Valley in Assam.People come on pilgrimage to visit various Muslim shrines or their families and do not return to Bangladesh. Our system of detection and identification of foreigners is full of loopholes. An IG-level BSF officer in charge of the IB in North Bengal bemoaned that force levels allotted to him for border security were less than half what is available for border security along the Indo-Pak border. He opined, and so does this author after visiting some fenced areas in this region, that fencing is not a solution in this type of terrain. Since the sanction is not total the fencing is in patches (about 125 km in a 1000 km stretch in West Bengal) the BSF does not know whether to guard the IB or the fence! The connivance of the lower strata police, paramilitary personnel and local officials is common for a consideration. Photographs and ration cards are prepared even before the illegal immigration. Ration cards are only a step away from getting into the voters' list, especially with political or bureaucratic help. The population increase in North Bengal is 33 per cent as against West Bengal's and the national average of 23 per cent.

DARJEELING HILL DISTRICT

This district had Siliguri, Kalimpong and Darjeeling sub-divisions. Darjeeling was ceded to British India after the Anglo-Nepal war in 1816 and therefore has predominantly ethnic Gorkhas of Nepalese origin. Kalimpong was and continues to be on perpetual lease from Sikkim Durbar; it also has a predominantly Gorkha population of Nepalese origin. However, people of both these sub-divisions are Indian citizens and so are the Gorkhas who have settled down here after service in the Indian Army. The migration of Nepalese people into Siliguri area and Jalpaiguri district has increased since 1970. In recent years, after the Nepalese settlers from the Terai region of Bhutan (Bhupatis) were driven out, the sensitivity of this area has increased. At present about 65,000 Bhupatis have been located in refugee camps in the Japa district of Eastern Nepal under UNHRC. Some of these are roaming around the Dooars area of North Bengal creating law and order problems. It is in this context that we should look into the temporarily pacified Gorkhaland agitation for the demand of a separate Gorkha state under the Indian Union. The agitation under Shri Subhash Ghising, had turned violent or a couple of years in 198788. This was the time the Sino-Indian border in the Eastern sector had become active after the Chinese intrusion into the Sumdorong Chu Valley South of the McMohan line.

Our surface communications to the Sino-Indian border in the Eastern Sector were in jeopardy. To appease the agitation leaders, as it normally happens in Indian politics, the Darjeeling District Hall Council (DGHC) was formed with limited autonomy in the social, cultural, developmental and educational. It had no power to raise revenue and had limited capability to cater for all the aspirations of the Gorkhas under DGHC. Should this continue beyond the tolerance level of the people or due to political manoeuvres of the DGHC (State and Central level) the Gorkhaland pot could be on the boil again. This time, taking advantage of the changing demographic pattern in Jalpaiguri district, they could even get "volunteers" from the nearby Bhupati refugee camp in Eastern Nepal. Shri Subhash Ghising has tried to extend his influence into Gorkha-dominated Sikkim and into Eastern Nepal. Off and on Shri Subhash Ghising drops hints of greater Gorkhaland to include Sikkim too. This is bound to result in serious resistance by Lepchas and Bhutiyas who are the original inhabitants of Sikkim. They are in minority after being swamped by ethnic Nepalese who now form nearly 80 per cent of Sikkim's population Emerging sub nationalism and socio-ethnic tensions in this sensitive area would pose problems for national security.

ASSAM

When the East India Company established their control over the Brahmaputra Valley, it started large-scale officially sponsored migration into assam from the rest of Eastern India. Better educated and emancipated Bengalis came as white collar workers les educated Bengalis, Bihari Muslims for farming, tribal labour from Orissa, Santhal Parganas and Bhihar as tea labour, and Nepalese for coal mining in the upper Assam Valley. As early as 1931 fears were expressed about the effect of this movement on Assamese identity and culture.While presenting the 1931 census report Mr C. S. Mullan said: "it is sad but by no means improbable that in another 30 years, Sibsagar district will be the only part of Assam in which Assamese will find himself at home!" Prophetic words. Today the ethnic Assamese population, i.e., Ahoms and all sections of the plain tribals form barely 30 to 40 per cent of the population, if one does not take into account certain early Bihari and Bengali Muslim settlers who adopted Assamese language and culture.

The influence of illegal Bangladeshi Muslims continues: this not only worsens the identity crisis but also poses a threat to India's national security. Today's estimate of illegal Muslim immigrants in Assam could be two to three million, bulk of them concentrated in the lower Brahmaputra Valley contiguous to Bangladesh and the illegal immigrant infected areas of North Bengal. The areas where they are being permitted to settle are in Kokrajhar, Barpeta and Nalbari.

They have been allotted pattas in the same areas which Bodos are claiming and an for an autonomous Bodoland. This has created hostility between the Bodos and Muslim setters in what Bodos perceive as their land. There is considerable connivance of the parties in power, and out of power, in legalizing the allotment of pattas of land for illegal immigrants. The latest entry into the game is Assam Ganatantra Parishad (AGP), who were the "knights in shining armour" during the Assam liberation agitation in the eighties and whose main platform for this agitation was detection, identification and deportation of foreigners, i.e., anybody other than Assamese.

Today ethnic Assamese, i.e., Ahoms, Bodos and other tribes, who do not want to be identified with Ahoms, are not in majority. Shri S. L. Shokdar, the erstwhile Chief Election Commissioner, in a conference highlighted the abnormally high rate of increase in an electoral college in Assam, especially in 1977 when within 10 months there was an increase of 10.3 per cent. The population growth during the census in 1961 and 1971 was 34.98 per cent as against the national average of 21.64 and 24.87 per cent respectively. From the late seventies to the mid-eighties the Assam liberation movement kept the Brahmaputra Valley on the boil ULFA (United Liberation Front of Assam), the militant wing of this agitation, committed political 'harakiri' with its excesses and is not a force to reckon with at present.

The Bodos, who supported the Assam liberation movement, were disillusioned after the AGP came to power, Plains tribes represented by PTCA (PlainsTribal Council of Assam) have always felt dominated by Ahoms. The undercurrent has been used by the powers that be to fragment Assamese society. The demands for autonomous councils of Karbi Anglong, Udayachal and Bodoland are all part of this process.

An autonomous council of Karbi Anglong has been formed; the Bodo Autonomous council has been accepted but is not fully functional, In the meanwhile the Bodo Security Force, the militant element of the Bodo agitation, is actively targeting Bangladeshi Muslim settlements and villages in Bodo claimed areas, like Kokrajhar, Barpeta and Nalbari. In some incidents in 1994-

95 a number of Bangladeshi Muslims have been killed and their settlements destroyed. Muslim setters are believed to be organizing village defence forces with active help from Bangladesh. If the illegal immigration continues, the situation could become dangerous in an area through which surface communications to the rest of North-Estern India pass. Currently this area is swarming with security forces operating against the Bodo Security Force whose sanctuaries extend into adjacent Bhutan. ULFA, SULFA (who surrender from ULFA), who were supplied with money and weapons by the Saikia Government and Bodo militants are extorting money from shopkeepers, truckers, tea industry workers and even common citizens. In fact this seems to have become a way of life to a generation of unemployed youth.

MANIPUR

Manipur is located in the southern part of North-East India bordering Myanmar. To its North is the Indian state of Nagaland and on its West are Indian state of Nagaland and on its West are the Indian state of Assam and Mizoram. All these states, including Northern Myanmar, have been in a state of turbulence due to sub-nationalism, resulting in insurgency for the past four decades. Manipur is a typical example of a multiethnic and multicultural society, despite living together for hundreds of years, it can be easily affected by ethnic revelry and hostility. Manipur has an area of about 22,000 sq km of which about one-third forms the Manipur valley and the balance hilly area surrounding the valley. The valley people numbering around 1.2 million, a bulk of whom are Meiteis, have been in contact with other parts of India for centuries. Meiteis follow Hindu religion (Vaishnavism) and culture. They are generally well-educated, culturally advanced and revel in many forms of art.

The hill people, about 30 different tribes, were animists till the entry of Christian missionaries in the latter half of the nineteenth century. The bulk of them are now Christians with a sprinkling of tribes following Hinduism and Buddhism. Because of their advanced cultural heritage and identification with Hindu religion, Meiteis do not come under the Scheduled Tribes (ST) status while the hill tribes, forming one-third of the population, come under the ST category and enjoy certain privileges like job reservation, protection of their lands from settlement and ownership by non-STs even if they are Manipuris. This has led to discontent among the Meiteis who perceive that the hill tribes are getting jobs disproportionate to their population, education and culture. Manipur state was a feudal state for many centuries.

When India became independent in 1947 Manipur acceded to India. It became part of the Indian Union as a 'C' state in January 1950 and became a full-fledged state on 21 January 1972. This delay was an unfortunate political error because the Meiteis the Valley people, felt that their identification with "Hindu" Indians brought them no political or economic benefits, while agitating Nagas both in Nagaland and the hill districts of Manipur benefited because of the agitation. These feelings gave encouragement to separatist tendencies; several separatist groups claimed that they were not Hindus and belonged to the old Senamai culture. Corrupt politicians and administration, economic backwardness increased the number of educated unemployed people, who acted as a catalyst.

Insurgency

The insurgency in Manipure can be classified into insurgency in the hills which is linked with insurgency in Nagaland and the Valley insurgency connected with the Meitei separatist movement. The Pan-Mongoloid movement which started in 1956-57 was the first political step of separatists for the Meities liberation from 'Hindu' India. This simmering discontent exploded in 1980 into a full-scale insurgency. There are several militant factions like the United Liberation Front (UNLF), Revolutionary Government of Manipur (RGM), People's Liberation Army (PLA), People's Revolutionary Party of Kanglupak (PREPAK), Joint Revolutionary Council (JRC) and Kangleipak Communist Party (KCP).

Each of these factions, through having similar objectives, act separately and sometimes clash with each other. "in Manipur it is as easy to launch a militant outfit as it is to launch a business project in Mumbai," says Shri Yambem Laba, a Meitei special correspondent for The Statesman (24 September 1993). Extortion from all sections of society seems to attract unemployed youth as a means of livelihood bésides giving them the macho feeling of having power over people. The Army suppressed the insurgency to controllable levels in the early eighties. But the follow-up political action was wanting because the political leaders were busy "horse trading" and shifting party alliances to stay in power. For the same reason they started covertly backing and getting the support of different militant groups. The political instability of the state has contributed considerably to the insurgency though the current turbulence in Manipur is linked more to the intertribal conflicts. The security environment of the society is also vitiated by youths brandishing arms and brand names of one organization or the other to indulge in extortion and kidnappings.

Naga-Kuki conflict

Kukis are originally inhabitants of Northern Myanmar, bordering Manipur and Mizoram. They were basically nomads but good fighters. They were recruited by Manipur kings for their army, who later settled some of them along the border with Myanmar. Some of these settled down alongside Naga villages and tilled the land owned by Nagas with the latter's concurrence. The Kukis soon started claiming these lands and this was not acceptable to the Nagas who cited the earlier tradition of Kukis handing the land back to Naga villages before they remigrated. Now the Nagas want to drive the Kukis off their lands and villages, hence the ethnic tension and the conflict.The Kukis are well-organized now: there is Kuki National Front (KNF), Kuki National Army (KNA), Kuki independent Army (KIA) and Kuki Defence Force (KDF). There is also a demand for 'Kukil' within the Indian Constitution, somewhat similar to the demand of Bodoland. In addition to all this is the struggle to control the border town of Moreh and the national highway linking Imphal to Myanmar which passes through Moreh. Moreh is the focal point for smuggling and drug traffic. Till the Kuki-Naga conflict started, NSCN (IM), a strong Naga insurgent group, controlled this town. Now the Kukis are controlling it. The NSCN (IM) is determined to drive the Kukis out of Moreh and out of Kuki settlements in Naga-dominated hill districts. Violence erupted between these tribal groups in June 1992 and till now there have been nearly 1000 killings; and about 2000 houses have been burnt. Nearly 100 villages are affected.

The killings have been brutal and the tribal tradition of sparing women and children has been forgotten. Recently there was a brutal attack on Tamil and Punjabi traders of Indian origin from Myanmar, who have settled down in the border town of Moreh. Mention has been made earlier about the ethnic tensions between the Nagas and the Meiteis of Manipur. In fact, so far as Manipur is concerned the socio-economic problems and lack of security for the general populace caused by ethnic conflict is more serious than the so-called separatist militant movement. The state's armed police and constabulary are incapable of controlling the situation as are the political and civilian agencies. The police force is generally following tribal loyalties. In fact the armed police is handing over their arms to their respective clansmen at a faster rate than the central security forces can capture. National Highways 39 and 53, the only links to Manipur from the rest of India, have become "death traps".The situation, which is essentially the result of socio-ethnic conflict, is serious. Innocent lives are being lost, properties destroyed and many security personnel are losing their lives. The politicians are playing with fire for short-term gains and lack the will and political acumen to solve these problems.

TRIPURA

Tripura is a tiny state, by Indian standards, situated in the South-West corner of the seven North-Eastern states of India. It is surrounded on three sides by Bangladesh with an international boundary of 845 km and a short corridor of contact with the mainland through Cachar district of Assam in the North. It is connected to the mainland by a National Highway and a metre gauge railway. Political changes in this part of the subcontinent, firstly by the creation of Pakistan in August 1947, and later by the birth of Bangladesh in 1971 have created upheaval in this state's demographic balance. Before August 1947, the tribal population formed two-thirds of the total population and the rest were plainsmen, most of whom were Bengalis who came in service of the king of Tripura. The situation is reversed now.

The loss of identity and pressure on the tribal land has caused serious socio-ethnic tension during the past three decades. Tripura was a princely state with its history dating back a few thousand years. It has a population (1 991 census) of about 27 lakhs in about 10,500 sq km. The 1961 census showed a decadal increase of population by 78 per cent, i.e., the aftermath of the partition as against the national figure of 21 percent. The 1971 and 1981 censuses showed a 36.28 and 31.55 per cent increase as against the national average of around 24 per cent. This could be attributed to the migration of refugees both Hindu and Muslims from Bangladesh. Herein lies the bitter pill for the 19 tribes, the natives of Tripura. The political and economic power has gone into the chands of the immigrants. In 1967 some tribes formed a political front called Tripura Upjati Juba Samiti (TUJS) whose demands were restoration of tribal lands allotted to non-tribals, creation of reserve areas for tribals and creation of Tribal Area Autonomous Councils (TADC).

The Tripura National Volunteers (TNV), a militant wing, was formed in 1980. The anti-foreigner's call given by it resulted in the Mandal massacre when about 1,800 people lost their lives, over 3,600 huts were burnt and there was heavy loss of property. The Communist Party ruled the state for 10 years between 1977 and 1987 and the Congress party for the rest of the time. The former appears to have popular support and they did provide a better administration. At present while most of Tripura is quiet, there are pockets of unrest in the tribal hill areas, astride roads illegal taxation on load-carrying vehicles is imposed, extortion by kidnappings and occasional attacks on security forces are carried out. None of the so-called insurgent/liberation forces are really strong, TUJS, TNU and National Liberation Front, Tripura (NLFT) are more prominent. Their factional fights cause law and order problems as well as casualties and loss of property of innocent tribesmen. The CPI (M) and Congress(I)'s political competition reverberates through these intra-tribal and intra-militant group's conflicts. In the meanwhile illegal Muslim immigration from Bangladesh continues though not to the extent seen in Assam and North Bengal. The international border is mostly riverine. Border fencing and the border roads being constructed at a cost of a couple of hundred crores of rupees is not likely to reduce this flow of immigrants very much. The state of Tripura should not be allowed to become a festering wound in the body politics of India.

DETERMINATION OF FORMS OF AGREEMENT; DETERMINATION OF LEGAL DISPUTES

In the cities of Sangrahana, Dronamukha, and Sthaniya, and at places where districts meet, three members acquainted with Sacred Law (dharmasthas) and three ministers of the king (amatyas) shall carry on the administration of Justice. (Valid and Invalid Transactions.) They shall hold as void agreements (vyavahara) entered into in seclusion, inside the houses, in the dead of night, in forests, in secret, or with fraud. The proposer and the accessory shall be punished with the first amercement [A fine ranging from 48 to 96 panas is called first amercement; from 200 to 500 panas, the middlemost; and from 500 to 1,000 panas the highest amercement. But agreements entered into within the hearing of others, as well as those not otherwise condemnable shall be valid. Those agreements which relate to the division of inheritance, sealed or unsealed deposits, or marriage; or those in which are concerned women who are either afflicted with disease or who do not stir out; as well as those entered into by persons who are not known to be of unsound mind shall be valid though they might be entered into inside houses.

Transactions relating to robbery, duel, marriage, or the execution of the king's order, as well as agreements entered into by persons who usually do their business during the first part of the night shall be valid though they might be done at night. With regard to those persons who live most part of their life in forests, whether as merchants, cowherds, hermits, hunters, or spies, their agreements though entered into in forests shall be valid. If fraudulent agreements, only such shall be valid as are entered into by spies. Agreements entered into by members of any association among themselves shall be valid though entered into in private. Such agreements (*i.e.*, those entered into in seclusion, etc.) except as detailed above shall be void. So also agreements entered into by dependent or unauthorised persons, such as a father's mother, a son, a father having a son, an outcast brother, the youngest brother of a family of undivided interests, a wife having her husband or son, a slave, a hired labourer, any person who is too young or too old to carry on business, a convict (abhisasta), a cripple, or an afflicted person, shall not be valid. But it would be otherwise if he were authorised.

Even agreements entered into by an authorised person shall be void if he was at the time (of making the agreements) under provocation, anxiety, or intoxication, or if he was a lunatic or a haunted person. In all these cases, the proposer, his accessory, and witnesses shall each be punished as specified above. But such agreements as are entered into in person by any one with others of his own community in suitable place and time are valid provided the circumstances, the nature, the description, and the qualities of the case are credible. Such agreements with the exception of orders (Adesa=probably a bill of exchange) and hypothecations may be binding though entered into by a third person. Thus the determination of the forms of agreement. (The Trial.)

The year, the season, the month, the fortnight (paksha), the date, the nature and place of the deed, the amount of the debt as well as the country, the residence, the caste, the gotra, the name and occupation of both the plaintiff and the defendant both of whom must be fit to sue and defend (kritasamar-thavasthayoh), having been registered first, the statements of the parties shall be taken down in such order as is required by the case. These statements shall then be thoroughly scrutinised. (The offence of Parokta.)

Leaving out the question at issue, either of the parties takes resort to another; his previous statement is not consistent with his subsequent one; he insists on the necessity of considering the opinion of a third person, though it is not worthy of any such consideration; having commenced to answer the question at issue, he breaks off at once, even though he is ordered to continue; he introduces questions other than those specified by himself; he withdraws his own statement; he does not accept what his own witnesses have deposed to; and he holds secret conversation with his witnesses where he ought not to do so. These constitute the offence of Parokta. (Punishment for Parokta.)

Fine for parokta is five times the amount (paroktadandah panchabandah). Fine for self assertion (svayamvadi = asserting without evidence) is ten times the amount (dasabandha.) (Payments for Witnesses.) Fees for witnesses (purushabhritih) shall cover 1/8th of the amount (astanga). Provision proportional to the amount sued for may also be made for the expenses incurred by witnesses in their journey. The defeated party shall pay these two kinds of costs. (Countersuits.) In cases other than duel, robbery, as well as disputes among merchants or trade-guilds, the defendant shall file no countercase against the plaintiff. Nor can there be a countercase for the defendant. (Adjournments.)

The plaintiff shall ('rejoin') reply soon after the defendant has answered the questions at issue. Else he shall be guilty of parokta, for the plaintiff knows the determining factors of the case. But the defendant does not do so. The defendant may be allowed three or seven nights to prepare his defence. If he is not ready with his defence within that time, he shall be punished with a fine ranging from 3 to 12 panas. If he does not answer even after three fortnights, he shall be fined for parokta, and the plaintiff shall recover out of the defendant's property the amount of the case. But if the plaintiff sues for a mere return of gratitude (pratyupakarana), then no (decree shall be passed).

The same punishment shall be meted out to such of the defendants as fail in their defence. If the plaintiff fails to prove his case, he shall (also) be guilty of parokta. If he fails to substantiate his case against a dead or diseased defendant, he shall pay a fine and perform the (funeral) ceremonies of the defendant, as determined by the witnesses. If he proves his case, he may be permitted to take possession of the property hypothecated to him. But if he is not a Brahman, he may, on his failure to prove his case, be caused to perform such ceremonials as drive out demons (rakshoghna rakshitakam).

- In virtue of his power to uphold the observance of the respective duties of the four castes and of the four divisions of religious life, and in virtue of his power to guard against the violation of the Dharmas, the king is the fountain of justice (dharmapravartaka).
- Sacred law (Dharma), evidence (Vyavahara), history (Charitra), and edicts of kings (Rajasasana) are the four legs of Law. Of these four in order, the later is superior to the one previously named.
- Dharma is eternal truth holding its sway over the world; Vyavahara, evidence, is in witnesses; Charitra, history, is to be found in the tradition (sangraha), of the people; and the order of kings is what is called sasana.
- As the duty of a king consists in protecting his subjects with justice, its observance leads him to heaven. He who does not protect his people or upsets the social order wields his royal sceptre (danda) in vain.
- It is power and power (danda) alone which, only when exercised by the king with impartiality and in proportion to guilt either over his son or his enemy, maintains both this world and the next.
- The king who administers justice in accordance with sacred law (Dharma), evidence (vyavahara), history (samstha) and edicts of kings (Nyaya) which is the fourth will be able to conquer the whole world bounded by the four quarters (Chaturantam mahim).
- Whenever there is disagreement between history and sacred law or between evidence and sacred law, then the matter shall be settled in accordance with sacred law.
- But whenever sacred law (Shastra) is conflict with rational law (Dharmanyaya=kings' law), then reason shall be held authoritative; for there the original text (on which the sacred law has been based) is not available.
- Self-assertion (svayamvada) on the part of either of the parties has often been found faulty. Examination (anuyoga), honesty (arjava), evidence (hetu) and asseveration by oath (sapatha)—these alone can enable a man to win his cause.
- Whenever by means of the deposition of witnesses, the statements of either of the parties are found contradictory, and whenever the cause of either of the parties is found through the king's spies to be false, then the decree shall be passed against that party.

CONCERNING MARRIAGE, THE DUTY OF MARRIAGE, THE PROPERTY OF A WOMAN, AND COMPENSATIONS FOR REMARRIAGE

Marriage precedes the other calls of life (vyavahara.) The giving in marriage of a maiden well-adorned is called Brahma-marriage. The joint-performance of sacred duties (by a man and a woman) is known as prajapatya marriage. (The giving in marriage of a maiden) for a couple of cows is called Arsha. (The giving in marriage of a maiden) to an officiating priest in a sacrifice is called Daiva. The voluntary union of a maiden with her lover is called Gandharva. Giving a maiden after receiving plenty of wealth (sulka) is termed Asura. The abduction of a maiden is called Rakshasa. The abduction of a maiden while she is asleep and in intoxication is called Paisacha marriage.

Of these, the first four are ancestral customs of old and are valid on their being approved of by the father. The rest are to be sanctioned by both the father and the mother; for it is they that receive the money (sulka) paid by the bridegroom for their daughter. In case of the absence by death of either the father or the mother, the survivor will receive the sulka. If both of them are dead, the maiden herself shall receive it. Any kind of marriage is approvable, provided it pleases all those (that are concerned in it.) (Property of Women.)

Means of subsistence (vritti) or jewellery (abadhya) constitutes what is called the property of a woman. Means of subsistence valued at above two thousand shall be endowed (on her name). There is no limit to jewellery. It is no guilt for the wife to make use of this property in maintaining her son, her daughter-in-law or herself whenever her absent husband has made no provision for her maintenance. In calamities, disease and famine, in warding off dangers and in charitable acts, the husband, too, may make use of this property. Neither shall there be any complaint against the enjoyment of this property by mutual consent by a couple who have brought forth a twin. Nor shall there be any complaint if this property has been enjoyed for three years by those who are wedded in accordance with the customs of the first four kinds of marriage. But the enjoyment of this property in the cases of Gandharva and Asura marriages shall be liable to be restored together with interest on it. In the case of such marriages as are called Rakshasa and Paisacha, the use of this property shall be dealt with as theft. Thus the duty of marriage is dealt with.

On the death of her husband a woman, desirous to lead a pious life, shall at once receive not only her endowment and jewellery (sthapyabharanam), but also the balance of sulka due to her. If both of these two things are not actually in her possession, though nominally given to her, she shall at once receive both of them together with interest (on their value.) If she is desirous of a second marriage (kutumbakama), she shall be given on the occasion of her remarriage (nivesakale) whatever either her father-in-law or her husband or both had given to her. The time at which women can remarry shall be explained in connection with the subject of long sojourn of husbands.

If a widow marries any man other than of her father-in-law's selection (svasurapratilo-myenanivishta), she shall forfeit whatever had been given to her by her fath-r-in-law and her husband. The kinsmen (gnatis) of a woman shall return to her whatever property of her own she had placed in their custody. Whoever justly takes a woman under his protection shall equally protect her property. No woman shall succeed in her attempt to establish her title to the property of her husband.

If she lives a pious life, she may enjoy it (dharmakama bhunjita). No woman with a son or sons shall be at liberty to make free use of her own property (stridhana); for that property of hers her sons shall receive.

If a woman attempts to take possession of her own property under the plea of maintaining her sons, she shall be made to endow it in their name. If a woman has many male children, then she shall conserve her own property in the same condition as she had received from her husband. Even that property which has been given her with full powers of enjoyment and disposal she shall endow in the name of her sons.

A barren widow who is faithful to the bed of her dead husband may, under the protection of her teacher, enjoy her property as long as she lives: for it is to ward off calamities that women are endowed with property. On her death, her property shall pass into the hands of her kinsmen (dayada). If the husband is alive and the wife is dead, then her sons and daughters shall divide her property among themselves. If there are no sons, her daughters shall have it. In their absence her husband shall take that amount of money (sulka) which he had given her, and her relatives shall retake whatever in the shape of gift or dowry they had presented her. Thus the determination of the property of a woman is dealt with. (Remarriage of Males)

If a woman either brings forth no (live) children, or has no male issue, or is barren, her husband shall wait for eight years, (before marrying another). If she bears only a dead child, he has to wait for ten years. If she brings forth only females, he has to wait for twelve years. Then if he is desirous to have sons, he may marry another. In case of violating this rule, he shall be made to pay her not only sulka, her property (stridhana) and an adequate monetary compensation (adhivedanikamartham), but also a fine of 24 panas to the Government. Having given the necessary amount of sulka and property (stridhana) even to those women who have not received such things on the occasion of their marriage with him, and also having given his wives the proportionate compensation and an adequate subsistence (vritti), he may marry any number of women; for women are created for the sake of sons. If many or all of them are at the same time in menses, he shall lie with that woman among them, whom he married earlier or who has a living son. In case of his concealing the fact of her being in menses or neglecting to lie with any of them after her menses, he shall pay a fine of 96 panas. Of women who either have sons or are pious or barren, or bring forth only a dead child or are beyond the age of menstruation, none shall be associated with against her liking. If a man has no inclination, he may not lie with his wife who is either afflicted with leprosy or is a lunatic. But if a woman is desirous of having sons, she may lie with men suffering from such disease.

If a husband either is of bad character or is long gone abroad or has become a traitor to his king or is likely to endanger the life of his wife or has fallen from his caste or has lost virility, he may be abandoned by his wife.

THE DUTY OF A WIFE; MAINTENANCE OF A WOMAN; CRUELTY TO WOMEN; ENMITY BETWEEN HUSBAND AND WIFE; A WIFE'S TRANSGRESSION; HER KINDNESS TO ANOTHER; AND FORBIDDEN TRANSACTIONS

Women, when twelve years old, attain their majority (praptavyavahara) and men when sixteen years old. If after attaining their majority, they prove disobedient to lawful authority (asusrushayam), women shall be fined 15 panas and men, twice the amount. (Maintenance of a woman.) A woman who has a right to claim maintenance for an unlimited period of time shall be given as much food and clothing (grasacchadana) as is necessary for her or more than is necessary in proportion to the income of the maintainer (yatha-purushaparivapam va). If the period (for which such things are to be given to her) is limited, then a certain amount of money fixed in proportion to the income of the maintainer shall be given to her; so also if she has not been given her sulka, property, and compensation (due to her for allowing her husband to remarry). If after parting with her husband, she places herself under the protection of any one belonging to her father-in-law's family (svasrakula), or if she begins to live independently, then her husband shall not be sued for (for her maintenance). Thus the determination of maintenance is dealt with. (Cruelty to women.)

Women of refractive nature shall be taught manners by using such general expressions as 'Thou, half naked; thou, fully naked; thou, cripple; thou, fatherless; thou, motherless, (nagne vinagne nyange pitrke matrke vinagne ityanirdesena vinayagrahanam). Or three beats either with a bamboo-bark or with a rope or with the palm of the hand may be given on her hips. Violation of the above rules shall be liable to half the punishment levied for defamation and criminal hurt. The same kind of punishment shall be meted out to a woman who, moved with jealousy or hatred, shows cruelty to her husband. Punishments for engaging in sports at the door of, or outside her husband's house shall be as dealt with elsewhere. Thus cruelty to women is dealt with. (Enmity between husband and wife.) A woman, who hates her husband, who has passed the period of seven turns of her menses, and who loves another shall immediately return to her husband both the endowment and jewellery she has received from him, and allow him to lie down with another woman. A man, hating his wife, shall allow her to take shelter in the house of a mendicant woman, or of her lawful guardians or of her kinsmen. If a man falsely accuses his wife of adultery with one of her or his kinsmen or with a spy—an accusation which can only be proved by eyewitnesses (drishtilinge)—or falsely accuses her of her intention to deprive him of her company, he shall pay a fine of 12 panas.

A woman, hating her husband, can not dissolve her marriage with him against his will. Nor can a man dissolve his marriage with his wife against her will. But from mutual enmity, divorce may be obtained (parasparam dveshanmokshah). If a man, apprehending danger from his wife desires divorce (mokshamichhet), he shall return to her whatever she was given (on the occasion of her marriage). If a woman, under the apprehension of danger from her husband, desires divorce, she shall forfeit her claim to her property; marriages contracted in accordance with the customs of the first four kinds of marriages cannot be dissolved. (Transgression.) If a woman engages herself in amorous sports, or drinking in the face of an order to the contrary, she shall be fined 3 panas. She shall pay a fine of 6 panas for going out at day time to sports or to see a woman or spectacles. She shall pay a fine of 12 panas if she goes out to see another man or for sports. For the same offences committed at night, the fines shall be doubled. If a woman abducts another woman while the latter is asleep or under intoxication (suptamatta-pravrajane), or if she drags her husband as far as the door of the house, she shall be fined 12 panas.

If a woman leaves her house at night, she shall pay double the above fine. If a man and a woman make signs to each other with a view to sensual enjoyment, or carry on secret conversation (for the same purpose), the woman shall pay a fine of 24 panas, and the man, double the amount. A woman, holding out her hair, the tie of her dress round her loins, her teeth or her nails, shall pay the first amercement, and a man, doing the same, twice the first amercement.

For holding conversation in suspicious places, whips may be substituted for fines. In the centre of the village, an outcaste person (chandala) may whip such women five times on each of the sides of their body. She may get rid of being whipped by paying a pana for each whip (panikam va praharam mokshayet). Thus transgression is dealt with. (Forbidden transactions.)

With regard to a man and a woman who, though forbidden to carry on any mutual transaction, help each other, the woman shall be fined 12, 24 and 54 panas respectively according as the help consists of (i) small things, of (ii) heavy things and (iii) of gold or gold-coin (hiranyasuvarnayoh); and the man, at double the above rates. With regard to similar transaction between a man and a woman who cannot mix with each other (agamvayoh), half of the above punishment shall be levied. Similar punishment shall be meted out for any forbidden transaction with any men. Thus forbidden transactions are dealt with.

Treason, transgression and wandering at will shall deprive a woman of her claim not only to (i) stridhana, some form of subsistence of above 2,000 panas and jewellery, (ii) and ahita, compensation she may have obtained for allowing her husband to marry another woman, but also (iii) to sulka, money which her parents may have received from her husband.

VAGRANCY, ELOPEMENT AND SHORT AND LONG SOJOURNMENTS

If under any other excuse than danger, a woman gets out of her husband's house, she shall be fined 6 panas. If she gets out against the order (of her husband) to the contrary, she shall be fined 12 panas. If she goes beyond her neighbouring house (prativesagrihatigatayah), she shall be fined 6 panas. If she allows into her house her neighbour, takes into her house the alms of any mendicant, or the merchandise of any merchant, she shall be fined 12 panas.

If she deals as above though expressly forbidden, she shall be punished with the first amercement. If she goes out beyond the surrounding houses (parigrihatigatayam), she shall be fined 24 panas. If under any other excuse than danger, she takes into her house the wife of another man, she shall be fined 100 panas. But she will not be guilty if the entrance is effected without her knowledge or against her orders to the contrary.

My teacher says:—With a view to avoid danger, it is no offence for women to go to any male person who is a kinsman of her husband, or is a rich and prosperous gentleman (sukhavastha), or is the headman of the village or is one of her guardians (anvadhikula), or who belongs to the family of a mendicant woman, or to any one of her own kinsmen. But Kautilya questions:— How is it possible for good women (sadhvijana) to know at least this fact that the family of her own kinsmen consisting of a number of males is good? It is no offence for women to go to the houses of kinsmen under the circumstances of death, disease, calamities, and confinement of women. Whoever prevents her going under such circumstances, shall be fined 12 panas. If a woman conceals herself under such circumstances, she shall forfeit her endowment. If her kinsmen conceal her (with a view to exempt her from giving her aid under such circumstances), they shall lose the balance of sulka, money due to them from her husband for giving her in marriage. Thus vagrancy is dealt with. (Elopement or Criminal Rendezvous.) If leaving her husband's house, a woman goes to another village, she shall not only pay a fine of 12 panas, but also forfeit her endowment and jewels (sthapyabharanalopascha). If under any other excuse than receiving her subsistence or pilgrimage (bharmadanatirthagamanabhyamanyatra), a woman goes to any other place even in company with an associable man, she shall not only pay a fine of 24 panas, but also lose all kinds of social privileges (sarvadharmalopascha). But the man who allows such a woman to accompany him in his journey shall be punished with the first amercement. If both of them (man, and woman) have similar ideals in life (tulyasreyasoh) and are of sinful life (papiyasoh), each of them shall be punished with the middle-most amercement.

If he whom a woman accompanies in her journey is her near relative, he shall not be punished. If a relative allows a woman to accompany him, though he is forbidden, he shall be punished with half the above fine (middlemost amercement). If on a road, or in the middle of a forest, or in any other concealed places a woman falls into the company of any other man, or if, with a view to enjoyment, she accompanies a suspicious or forbidden man, she shall be guilty of elopement (sangrahanam vidyat). It is no offence for women to fall into the company of actors, players, singers, fishermen, hunters, herdsmen, vintners, or persons of any other kind who usually travel with their women. If a man takes a woman with him on his journey, though forbidden to do so, or if a woman accompanies a man though she is forbidden to do so, half of the above fines shall be meted out to them. Thus elopement is dealt with. (Remarriage of women)

Wives who belong to Sudra, Vaishya, Kshatriya or Brahman caste, and who have not given birth to children should wait as long as a year for their husbands who have gone abroad for a short time; but if they are such as have given birth to children, they should wait for their absent husbands for more than a year. If they are provided with maintenance, they should wait for twice the period of time just mentioned. If they are not so provided with, their well-to-do gnatis should maintain them either for four or eight years. Then the gnatis should leave them to marry after taking what had been presented to them on the occasion of their marriages. If the husband is a Brahman, studying abroad, his wife who has no issue should wait for him for ten years; but if she has given birth to children, she should wait for twelve years.

If the husband is of Kshatriya caste, his wife should wait for him till her death; but even if she bears children to a savarna husband, (*i.e.*, a second husband belonging to the same gotra as that of the former husband) with a view to avoid the extinction of her race, she shall not be liable to contempt thereof (savarnatascha prajata na pavadam labheta). If the wife of an absent husband lacks maintenance and is deserted by well-to-do gnatis, she may remarry one whom she likes and who is in a position to maintain her and relieve her misery.

A young wife (kumari) who is wedded in accordance with the customs of the first four kinds of marriage (dharmavivahat), and whose husband has gone abroad and is heard of shall wait for him for the period of seven menses (saptatirthanya-kanksheta), provided she has not publicly announced his name; but she shall wait for him a year in case of her having announced the name of her absent husband who is heard of. In the case of a husband who is gone abroad but who is not heard of, his wife shall wait for the period of five menses, but if the absent husband is not heard of, his wife shall wait for him for the period of ten menses. In the case of a husband who is gone abroad and is not heard of, his wife shall, if she has received only a part of sulka from him, wait for him for the period of three menses; but if he is heard of, she shall wait for him for the period of seven menses. A young wife who has received the whole amount of sulka shall wait for the period of five menses for her absent husband who is not heard of; but if he is heard of, she shall wait for him for the period of ten menses. Then with the permission of judges (dharma-sthairvisrishta), she may marry one whom she likes; for neglect of intercourse with wife after her monthly ablution is, in the opinion of Kautilya, a violation of one's duty (tirthoparodho hi dharmavadha iti Kautilyah).

In the case of husbands who have long gone abroad (dirgrhapravasinah), who have become ascetics, or who have been dead, their wives, having no issue, shall wait for them for the period of seven menses; but if they have given birth to children, they shall wait for a year. Then (each of these women) may marry the brother of her husband. If there are a number of brothers to her lost husband, she shall marry such a one of them as is next in age to her former husband, or as is virtuous and is capable of protecting her, or one who is the youngest and unmarried. If there are no brothers to her lost husband, she may marry one who belongs to the same gotra as her husband's or relative. But if there are many such persons as can be selected in marriage, she shall choose one who is a nearer relation of her lost husband. If a woman violates the above rule by remarrying one who is not a kinsman (dayada) of her husband, then the woman and the man who remarry each other, those that have given her in remarriage and those who have given their consent to it shall all be liable to the punishment for elopement.

DIVISION OF INHERITANCE

Sons whose fathers and mothers or ancestors are alive cannot be independent (anisvarah). After their time, division of ancestral property among descendants from the same ancestor shall take place, calculating per sterpes (according to fathers).

Self-acquired property of any of the sons with the exception of that kind of property which is earned by means of parental property is not divisible. Sons or grandsons till the fourth generation from the first parent shall also have prescribed shares (amsabhajah) in that property which is acquired by means of their undivided ancestral property; for the line (pindah) as far as the fourth generation is uninterrupted (avichchhinnah). But those whose line or genealogy from the first ancestor is interrupted (vichchhinnapindah, *i.e.*, those who are subsequent to the fourth generation), shall have equal divisions. Those who have been living together shall redivide their property whether they had already divided their ancestral property before or they had received no such property at all. Of sons, he who brings the ancestral property to a prosperous condition shall also have a share of the profit.

If a man has no male issue, his own brothers, or persons who have been living with him, (saha jivino va), shall take possession of his movable property (dravyam); and his daughters, (born of marriages other than the first four), shall have his immovable property (riktham). If one has sons, they shall have the property; if one has (only) daughters born of such marriage as is contracted in accordance with the customs of any of the first four kinds of marriage, they shall have the property; if there are neither sons nor such daughters, the dead man's father, if living, shall have it; if he, too, is not alive, the dead man's brothers and the sons of his brothers shall have it; if there are many fatherless brothers, all of them shall divide it; and each of the many sons of such brothers shall have one share due to his father (piturekamamsam); if the brothers (sodarya) are the sons of many fathers, they shall divide it calculating from their fathers.

Among a dead man's father, brother, and brother's sons, the succeeding ones shall depend on the preceding ones if living (for their shares); likewise the youngest or the eldest claiming his own share. A father, distributing his property while he is alive, shall make no distinction in dividing it among his sons. Nor shall a father deprive without sufficient reason any of the sons of his share. Father being dead, the elder sons shall show favour to the younger ones, if the latter are not of bad character. (Time of dividing inheritance.)

Division of inheritance shall be made when all the inheritors have attained their majority. If it is made before, the minors shall have their shares, free of all debts.

These shares of the minors shall be placed in the safe custody of the relatives of their mothers, or of aged gentlemen of the village, till they attain their majority. The same rule shall hold good in the case of those who have gone abroad. Unmarried brothers shall also be paid as much marriage cost as is equal to that incurred in the marriages of married brothers (sannivishtasamamasannivishtebhyonaivesanikam dadyuh). Daughters, too, (unmarried) shall be paid adequate dowry (pradanikam), payable to them on the occasion of their marriages. Both assets and liabilities shall be equally divided.

My teacher says that poor people (nishkinchanah) shall equally distribute among themselves even the mud-vessels (udapatram). In the opinion of Kautilya, it is unnecessary to say so (chhalam); for as a rule, division is to be made of all that is in existence, but of nothing that is not in existence. Having declared before witnesses the amount of property common to all (samanya) as well as the property constituting additional shares (amsa) of the brothers (in priority of their birth), division of inheritance shall be carried on. Whatever is badly and unequally divided or is involved in deception, concealment or secret acquisition, shall be redivided. Property for which no claimant is found (adayadakam) shall go to the king, except the property of a woman, of a dead man for whom no funeral rites have been performed, or of a niggardly man with the exception of that of a Brahman learned in the Vedas. That (the property of the learned) shall be made over to those who are well-versed in the three Vedas.

Persons fallen from caste, persons born of outcaste men, and eunuchs shall have no share; likewise idiots, lunatics, the blind and lepers. If the idiots, etc., have wives with property, their issues who are not equally idiots, etc., shall share inheritance. All these persons excepting those that are fallen from caste (patitavarjah) shall be entitled to only food and clothing.

If these persons have been married (before they became fallen, etc.) and if their line is likely to become extinct, their relatives may beget sons for them and give proportional shares of inheritance to those sons.

SPECIAL SHARES IN INHERITANCE

Goats shall be the special shares of the eldest of sons, born of the same mother, among, Brahmans; horses among Kshatriyas; cows among Vaisyas; and sheep among Sudras. The blind of the same animals shall be the special shares to the middle-most sons; species of variegated colour of the same animals shall be the special shares to the youngest of sons. In the absence of quadruped, the eldest shall take an additional share of the whole property excepting precious stones; for by this act alone, he will be bound in his duty to his ancestors.

The above method is in accordance with the rules observed among the followers of Usanas.

The father being dead, his carriage and jewellery shall be the special share to the eldest; his bed, seat, and bronze plate in which he used to take his meals (bhuktakamsyam), to the middle-most;. and black grains, iron, domestic utensils, cows and cart to the youngest. The rest of the property, or the above things, too, may be equally divided among themselves. Sisters shall have no claim to inheritance; they shall have the bronze plate and jewellery of their mother after her death. An impotent eldest son shall have only 1/3rd of the special share usually given to the eldest; if the eldest son follows a condemnable occupation or if he has given up the observance of religious duties, he shall have only ¼ of the special share; if he is unrestrained in his actions he shall have nothing. The same rule shall hold good with the middlemost and youngest sons; of these two, one who is endowed with manliness (manushopetah), shall have half the special share usually given to the eldest.

With regard to sons of many wives:

Of sons of two wives of whom only one woman has gone through all the necessary religious ceremonials, or both of whom have not, as maidens, observed necessary religious rites, or one of whom has brought forth twins, it is by birth that primogenitureship is decided.

Shares in inheritance for such sons as Suta, Magadha, Vratya and Rathakara shall depend on the abundance of paternal property; the rest, *i.e.*, sons other than Suta, etc., of inferior birth, shall be dependent on the eldest for their subsistence. Dependent sons shall have equal divisions.

Of sons begotten by a Brahman in the four castes, the son of a Brahman woman shall take four shares; the son of a Kshatriya woman three shares; the son of a Vaishya woman two shares, and the son of a Sudra woman one share. The same rule shall hold good in the case of Kshatriya and Vaishya fathers begetting sons in three or two castes in order. An Anantara son of a Brahman, *i.e.* a son begotten by a Brahman on a woman of next lower caste, shall, if endowed with manly or superior qualities (manushopetah), take an equal share (with other sons of inferior qualities); similarly Anantara sons of Kshatriya or Vaishya fathers shall if endowed with manly or superior qualities, take half or equal shares (with others). An only son to two mothers of different castes shall take possession of the whole property and maintain the relatives of his father. A Palrasava son begotten by a Brahman on a Sudra woman, shall take 1/3rd share; a sapinda, (an agnate) or a kulya (the nearest cognate), of the Brahman shall take the remaining two shares, being thereby obliged to offer funeral libation; in the absence of agnates or cognates, the deceased father's teacher or student shall take the two shares. Or on the wife of such a Brahman shall a sagotra, relative bearing the same family name, or a (matribandha) relative of his mother, beget a natural son (kshetraja), and this son may take that wealth.

DISTINCTION BETWEEN SONS

My preceptor says that the seed sown in the field of another shall belong to the owner of that field. Others hold that the mother being only the receptacle for the seed (mata bhastra), the child must belong to him from whose seed it is born. Kautilya says that it must belong to both the living parents.

The son begotten by a man on his wife who has gone through all the required ceremonials is called aurasa, natural son; equal to him is the son of an appointed daughter (putrikaputra); the son begotten on a wife by another man, appointed for the purpose, and of the same gotra as that of the husband; or of a different gotra, is called kshetraja; on the death of the begetter, the kshetraja son will be the son to both the fathers, follow the gotras of both, offer funeral libations to both, and take possession of the immovable property (riktha) of both of them; of the same status as the kshetraja is he who is secretly begotten in the house of relatives and is called gudhaja, secretly born; the son cast off by his natural parents is called apaviddha and will belong to that man who performs necessary religious ceremonials to him; the son born of a maiden (before wedlock) is called kanina; the son born of a woman married while carrying is called sahodha; the son of a remarried woman (punarbhatayah) is called paunarbhava. A natural son can claim relationship both with his father and his father's relatives; but a son born to another man can have relationship only with his adopter.

Of the same status as the latter is he who is given in adoption with water by both the father and mother and is called datta. The son who, either of his own accord or following the intention of his relatives, offers himself to be the son of another, is called upagata. He who is appointed as a son is called kritaka; and he who is purchased is called krita. On the birth of a natural son, savarna sons shall have 1/3rd of inheritance while savarna sons shall have only food and clothing.

Sons begotten by Brahmans or Kshatriyas on women of next lower caste (anantaraputrah) are called savarnas; but on women of castes lower by two grades are called asavarnas. (Of such asavarna sons), the son begotten by a Brahman on a Vaishya woman is called Ambashtha; on a Sudra woman is called Nishada or Parasava. The son begotten by a Kshatriya on a Sudra woman is known as Ugra; the son begotten by a Vaishya on a Sudra woman is no other than a Sudra. Sons begotten by men of impure life of any of the four castes on women of lower castes next to their own are called Vratyas. The above kinds of sons are called anuloma, sons begotten by men of higher on women of lower castes.

Sons begotten by a Sudra on women of higher castes are Ayogava, Kshatta, and Chandala; by a Vaishya, Magadha, and Vaidehaka; and by a Kshatriya, Suta. But men of the, names, Suta and Magadha, celebrated in the Puranas, are quite different and of greater merit than either Brahmans or Kshatriyas. The above kinds of sons are pratiloma, sons begotten by men of lower on women of higher castes, and originate on account of kings violating all dharmas. The son begotten by an Ugra on a Nishada woman is called kukkuta and the same is called Pulkasa, if begotten in the inverse order. The son begotten by an Ambhashtha on a Vaidehaka woman is named Vaina; the same in the reverse order is called Kusilava. An Ugra begets on a Kshatta woman as vapaka. These and other sons are of mixed castes (Antaralas). A Vainya becomes a Rathakara, chariot-maker, by profession. Members of this caste shall marry among themselves. Both in customs and avocations they shall follow their ancestors. They may either become Sudras or embrace any other lower castes excepting Chandalas. The king who guides his subjects in accordance with the above rules will attain to heaven; otherwise he will fall into the hell. Offsprings of mixed castes (Antaralas) shall have equal divisions of inheritance. Partition of inheritance shall be made in accordance with the customs prevalent in the country, caste, guild (sangha), or the village of the inheritors.

SALE OF BUILDINGS, BOUNDARY DISPUTES, DETERMINATION OF BOUNDARIES, AND MISCELLANEOUS HINDRANCES

Rich persons among kinsmen or neighbours shall in succession go for the purchase of land and other holdings. Neighbours of good family, forty in number and different from the purchasers above mentioned, shall congregate in front of the building for sale and announce it as such. Accurate description of the exact boundaries of fields, gardens, buildings of any kind, lakes or tanks shall be declared before the elders of the village or of the neighbourhood. If, on crying aloud thrice 'Who will purchase this at such and such a price'? no opposition is offered, the purchaser may proceed to purchase the holding in question. If at this time the value of the property is increased by bidding even among persons of the same community, the increased amount together with the toll on the value shall be handed over into the king's treasury.

The bidder (vikrayapratikroshta) shall pay the toll. Bidding for a property in the absence of its owner shall be punished with a fine of 24 panas. If the owner does not come forward even on the expiration of seven nights, the bidder may take possession of the property. Sale of building, etc., (vastu) to other than the bidder shall be punished with a fine of 200 panas; if the property is other than buildings, etc., (vastu), the fine for the above offence shall be 24 panas. Thus the sale of buildings is dealt with. (Boundary disputes.) In all disputes regarding the boundary between any two villages, neighbours or elders of five or ten villages (panchagrami dasagrami va) shall investigate the case on the evidence to be furnished from natural or artificial boundary marks.

Elders among cultivators and herdsmen, or outsiders who have had the experience of former possession in the place, or one or many persons (not) personally acquainted with the boundary marks under dispute shall first describe the boundary marks, and then, wearing unusual dress (viparitaveshah), shall lead the people (to the place). If the boundary marks just described are not found, a fine of 1,000 panas shall be imposed (on the misleading or guilty person). If, however, they arrive at the exact spot, the party who have either encroached upon the boundary or have destroyed the boundary marks shall be similarly punished.

The king shall beneficially distribute among others those holdings which have no boundary-marks or which have ceased to be enjoyed by any person. (Disputes about fields.)

Disputes concerning fields shall be decided by the elders of the neighbourbood or of the village. If they are divided in their opinions, decision shall be sought for from a number of pure and respectable people, or, the disputants may equally divide the disputed holding among themselves. If both of these methods fail, the holding (vastu) under dispute shall be taken possession of by the king. The same rule shall hold good in the case of a holding for which no claimant is forthcoming; or it may beneficially be distributed among the people. Occupation of a holding (vastu) by force shall be punished as theft. If a holding is taken possession of by another on some reasonable grounds, he shall be made to pay to the owner some rent, the amount of which is to be fixed after mature considerations of what is necessary for the subsistence of the cultivator of the holding by him. Encroachment upon boundaries shall be punished with the first amercement. Destruction of boundaries shall be punished with a fine of 24 panas. The same rules shall hold good in disputes concerning hermitage in forests, pasture lands, high roads, cremation-grounds, temples, sacrificial places, and places of pilgrimage. Thus the determination of boundaries is dealt with. (Miscellaneous hindrances.)

All kinds of disputes shall depend for their settlement on the evidence to be furnished by neighbours. Of pasture lands, fields (kedara), flower gardens, a threshing-floor (khala), houses, and stables of horses (vahanakoshtha), hindrance to any one coming first in order shall be removed in preference to the one or more coming later in the series. With the exception of people in forests of Brahmans and of Soma-plants, temples, and places of sacrifice and pilgrimage, any person causing, while making use of a by-path to go to tanks, rivers, or fields, damage to the seeds sown in the fields of others, shall pay as much compensation to the sufferers as is equivalent to the damage. If the owner of any one of the following, *viz.*, wet-fields, parks, or any kinds of buildings, causes damage to the rest owned by others, the fine shall be double the value of the damage. The water of a lower tank shall not submerge the field irrigated by a higher tank.

The natural flow of water from a higher to a lower tank shall not be stopped unless the lower tank has ceased to be useful for three consecutive years. Violation of this rule shall be punished with the first amercement. The same punishment shall be meted out for emptying a tank of its water (tatakavamanam cha). Buildings of any kind (setubandha), neglected for five consecutive years shall be forfeited, except in calamities. (Remission of taxes) In the case of construction of new works, such as tanks, lakes, etc., taxes (on the lands below such tanks) shall be remitted for five years (panchavarshikah pariharah). For repairing neglected or ruined works of similar nature, taxes shall be remitted for four years. For improving or extending water-works, taxes shall be remitted for three years. In the case of acquiring such newly started works by mortgage or purchase, taxes on the lands below such works shall be remitted for two years. If uncultivated tracts are acquired (for cultivation) by mortgage, purchase or in any other way, remission of taxes shall be for two years. Out of crops grown by irrigation by means of wind power or bullocks (vatapravartiman-andinibandhayatana) or below tanks, in fields, parks, flower gardens, or in any other way, so much of the produce as would not entail hardship on the cultivators may be given to the Government. Persons who cultivate the lands below tanks, etc., of others at a stipulated price (prakraya), or for annual rent (avakraya), or for certain number of shares of the crops grown (bhaga) or persons who are permitted to enjoy such lands free of rent of any kind, shall keep the tanks, etc., in good repair; otherwise they shall be punished with a fine of double the loss. Persons, letting out the water of tanks, etc., at any other place than their sluice gate (apare), shall pay a fine of 6 panas; and persons who recklessly obstruct the flow of water from the sluice-gate of tanks shall also pay the same fine.

DESTRUCTION OF PASTURE-LANDS, FIELDS AND ROADS, AND NON-PERFORMANCE OF AGREEMENTS

Persons who obstruct, or make any kind of mischief with the flow of water intended for cultivation shall be punished with the first amercement. Construction in the sites belonging to others, of any buildings with a view to attract pilgrims thereto, of abodes of worship (chaitya), or of temples of gods; as also the sale or mortgage, or causing the sale or mortgage, of any long continued charitable building (purvanuvrittam dharmasetum) shall be punished with the middlemost amercement. Those who are witnesses to such transactions shall be punished with the highest amercement excepting in the case of neglected or ruined buildings. In the absence of claimants to dilapidated religious buildings, villagers (gramah), or charitable people (punyasilava) may repair them. (Blocking the roads.)

Forms of roads and paths have been dealt with in connection with the construction of forts. (First Chapter, Book II).

Obstruction to roads for inferior beasts or men shall be punished with a fine of 12 panas; to roads for superior beasts 24 panas; to roads for elephants or to those leading to fields, 54 panas; to those leading to any buildings or forests (setuvanapatham), 600 panas; to those for burial grounds or villages, 200 panas; to those for dronamukha, a fortress, 500 panas; and those leading to sthaniya, country parts, or pasture grounds, 1,000 panas. The same fines shall be meted out in case of ploughing the several roads too deep (atikarshane chaisham); and ¼th of the same fines for ploughing merely on their surface.

If a cultivator or a neighbour makes encroachment upon a field during the time of sowing seeds, he shall be fined 12 panas, unless the encroachment is due to evils, calamities or intolerable occurrences arising otherwise from the field (anyatra doshopanipatavishahyebhyah). (Settling in villages.)

Taxpayers shall sell or mortgage their fields to taxpayers alone; Brahmans shall sell or mortgage their Brahmadaya or gifted lands only to those who are endowed with such lands; otherwise they shall be punished with the first amercement. The same punishment shall be meted out to a taxpayer who settles in a village not inhabited by taxpayers. If a taxpayer takes the place of another taxpayer, he shall enjoy all the holdings but the house of the latter. Even the house may be given to the new settler. If a person cultivates an inalienable land of another person who does not cultivate it, such a person shall restore the same after five years enjoyment on taking a certain amount of compensation equivalent to the improvement he made on the lands. Persons who are not taxpayers and who sojourn abroad shall retain the right of ownership (bhogam) of their lands. (The Headman of the village.) When the headman of a village has to travel on account of any business of the whole village, the villagers shall by turns accompany him. Those who cannot do this shall pay 1½ panas for every yojana. If the headman of a village sends out of the village any person except a thief, or an adulterer, he shall be punished with a fine of 24 panas, and the villagers with the first amercement (for doing the same). Re-entrance into a village for a person previously sent out of it (nirastasya), is explained by 'settlement of persons in villages' (treated of above). At a distance of 800 angulas around every village, an enclosure with timber posts shall be constructed. (Trespassing cattle.) Pasture lands, plains, and forests may be availed of for grazing cattle.

For camels or buffaloes allowed to stray after grazing in pasture grounds, the fine shall be ¼th of a pana; for cows, horses, or asses, 1/8th of a pana; for inferior quadrupeds 1/16th of a pana; and for cattle found lying thereon after grazing, fines shall be double the above; for cattle ever found to live in the vicinity of pasture grounds, the fines shall be four times the above.

Bulls, let out in the name of the village deity (gramadevavrishah), cows which have not passed ten days inside the enclosure after calving, or bulls or bullocks kept for crossing cows shall not be punished. If crops are eaten away by animals, the owner or owners of them shall, if proved guilty, be made to pay twice as much as the loss. Persons driving their cattle through a field without intimating the owner shall be fined 12 panas. Any person who allows his cattle to stray shall be fined 24 panas; cowherds doing the same with the cattle under their care shall be fined half the above. The same punishment shall be meted out for letting cattle graze in flower gardens. For breaking the fence of fields, the punishment shall be double the above.

If cattle are allowed to stray and eat the grains stored in houses, a threshing floor, or a court yard, the owners of the cattle shall pay adequate compensation. If beasts maintained in reserve-forests are found grazing in a field, they shall be brought to the notice of the forest officers and the beasts shall be driven out without being hurt or killed. Stray cattle shall be driven out by the use of ropes or whips. Persons hurting them in any way shall be liable to the punishment for assault or violence. Persons who invite (cattle to graze in the fields of others) or who are caught while committing such offences shall by all means be put down. Thus the destruction of pasture lands, fields, and roads is dealt with. (Non-performance of agreement.) The fine levied on a cultivator who arriving at a village for work, does not work shall be taken by the village itself. He shall refund not only double the amount of the wages he received promising to work, but also double the value of food and drink with which he has been provided. If the work is one of sacrificial performance (prahavaneshu), then also he shall pay double the amount of the wages. Any person who does not cooperate in the work of preparation for a public show, shall, together with his family, forfeit his right to enjoy the show (preksha). If a man who has not cooperated in preparing for a public play or spectacle is found hearing or witnessing it under hiding, or if any one refuses to give his aid in a work beneficial to all, he shall be compelled to pay double the value of the aid due from him.

The order of any person attempting to do a work beneficial to all shall be obeyed. Disobedience in such a case shall be punished with a fine of 12 panas. If others unitedly beat or hurt such a person so ordering, each of them shall pay double the amount of the fine usually levied for such offence. If among the above offenders one is a Brahman or a person superior to a Brahman, he shall first be punished. If a Brahman does not take part in the combined performance of any sacrifice of his village, he shall not be violated, but may be persuaded to pay a share. The above rules shall also apply to non-performance of agreements among countries (desa), castes, families, and assemblies. Those who, with their united efforts construct on roads buildings of any kind (setubandha) beneficial to the whole country and who not only adorn their villages, but also keep watch on them shall be shown favourable concessions by the king.

RECOVERY OF DEBTS

An interest of a pana and a quarter per month per cent is just. Five panas per month per cent is commercial interest (vyavahariki). Ten panas per month per cent prevails among forests. Twenty panas per month per cent prevails among sea-traders (samudranam). Persons exceeding, or causing to exceed the above rate of interest shall be punished with the first amercement; and hearers of such transactions shall each pay half of the above fine.

The nature of the transactions between creditors and debtors, on which the welfare of the kingdom depends, shall always be scrutinised. Interest in grains in seasons of good harvest shall not exceed more than half when valued in money. Interest on stocks (prakshepa) shall be one-half of the profit and be regularly paid as each year expires. If it is allowed to accumulate owing either to the intention or to the absence abroad (of the receiver or payer), the amount payable shall be equal to twice the share or principal (mulyadvigunah). A person claiming interest when it is not due, or representing as principal the total amount of his original principal and the interest thereon shall pay a fine of four times the amount under dispute (bandhachaturgunah).

A creditor who sues for four times the amount lent by him shall pay a fine of four times the unjust amount. Of this fine, the creditor shall pay ¾ths and the debtor ¼th. Interest on debts due from persons who are engaged in sacrifices taking a long time (dirghasatra), or who are suffering from disease, or who are detained in the houses of their teachers (for learning), or who are either minors or too poor, shall not accumulate.

A creditor refusing to receive the payment of his debt shall pay a fine of 12 panas. If the refusal is due to some (reasonable) cause, then the amount free from interest (for subsequent time) shall be kept in the safe custody of others. Debts neglected for ten years, except in the case of minors, aged persons, diseased persons, persons involved in calamities, or persons who are sojourning abroad or have fled the country and except in the case of disturbances in the kingdom (rajyavibhrama), shall not be received back.

Sons of a deceased debtor shall pay the principal with interest (kusi dam). (In the absence of sons), kinsmen claiming the share of the dead man or sureties, such as joint partners of the debt, (sahagrahinah pratibhuvo va) shall pay the same. No other kind of surety is valid (na pratibhavyamanyat); a minor, as surety, is inefficient (balapratibhavyam asaram = surety of a minor is not strong).

A debt, the payment of which is not limited by time or place or both (asamkhyata-desakalam), shall be paid by the sons, grandsons or any other heirs of the dead debtor. Any debt, the payment of which is not limited by time or place or both and for which life, marriage, or land is pledged, shall be borne by sons or grandsons. (Regarding many debts against one.)

Excepting the case of a debtor going abroad, no debtor shall simultaneously be sued for more than one debt by one or two creditors. Even in the case of a debtor going abroad, he shall pay his debts in the order in which he borrowed them or shall first pay his debts due to the king or a learned Brahman. Debts contracted from each other by either a husband or wife, either a son or a father, or by any one among brothers of undivided interests shall be irrecoverable. Cultivators or government servants shall not be caught hold of for debts while they are engaged in their duties (or at work). A wife, though she has (not) heard of the debt (pratisravani), shall not be caught hold of for the debt contracted by her husband, excepting in the case of herdsmen and joint cultivators (gopalakardhasitikebhyah). But a husband may be caught for the debt contracted by his wife. If it is admitted that a man fled the country without providing for the debt contracted by his wife, the highest amercement shall be meted out; if not admitted, witnesses shall be depended upon. (Witnesses.)

It is obligatory to produce three witnesses who are reliable, honest and respected. At least two witnesses acceptable to the parties are necessary; never one witness in the case of debts.

Wife's brothers, copartners, prisoners (abaddha), creditors, debtors, enemies, maintained persons, or persons once punished by the Government shall not be taken as witnesses. Likewise persons legally unfit to carry on transactions, the king, persons learned in the Vedas, persons depending for their maintenance on villages (gramabhritaka), lepers, persons suffering from bodily erruptions, outcast persons, persons of mean avocation, the blind, the deaf, the dumb, egotistic persons, females, or government servants shall not be taken as witnesses excepting in the case of transactions in one's own community.

In dispute concerning assault, theft, or abduction, persons other than wife's brothers, enemies, and co-partners, can be witnesses. In secret dealings, a single woman or a single man who has stealthily heard or seen them can be a witness, with the exception of the king or an ascetic. On the side of prosecution masters against servants, priests or teachers against their disciples, and parents against their sons can be witnesses (nigrahanasakshyam kuryuh); Persons other than these may also be witnesses in criminal cases. If the above persons (masters and servants, etc.) sue each other (parasparabhiyoge), they shall be punished with the highest amercement. Creditors guilty of parokta shall pay a fine of 10 times the amount (dasabandha) but if incapable to pay so much, they shall at least pay five times the amount sued for (panchabandham); thus the section on witnesses is dealt with. (Taking oaths.)

Witness shall be taken before Brahmans, vessels of water and fire. A Brahman witness shall be told 'Tell the truth'; a Kshatriya or a Vaishya witness shall be told thus:—'If thou utterest falsehood, thou, do not attain the fruit of thy sacrificial and charitable deeds; but having broken the array of thy enemies in war, thou, do go a beggar with a skull in thy hand.' A Sudra witness thus:—'Whatever thy merits are, in thy former birth or after thy death, shall they go to the king and whatever sins the king may have committed, shall they go to thee, if thou utterest falsehood; fines also shall be levied on thee, for facts as they have been heard or seen will certainly be subsequently revealed.' If in the course of seven nights, witnesses are found to have unanimously made a false consert among themselves, a fine of 12 panas shall be levied. If they are thus found in the course of three fortnights, they shall pay the amount sued for (abhiyogam dadyuh).

If witnesses differ, judgment may be given in accordance with the statements of a majority of pure and respectable witnesses; or the mean of their statements may be followed; or the amount under dispute may be taken by the king.

If witnesses give testimony for a less amount, the plaintiff shall pay a fine proportional to the increased amount; if they attest to a greater amount, the excess shall go to the king. In cases where the plaintiff proves himself stupid, or where bad hearing (on the part of witnesses at the time of the transaction) or bad writing is the cause of difficulty, or where the debtor is dead, the evidence of witnesses alone shall be depended on (sakshipratyayameva syat).

"Only," say the followers of Usanas, "in those cases where witnesses prove themselves to have been stupid or senseless and where the investigation of the place, time or nature of the transaction is of no avail, the three amercements shall be levied."

"False witnesses," say the followers of Manu, "shall be fined ten times the amount which, no matter whether it is true or false, they cause to be lost."

"If," say the followers of Brihaspati, "owing to their having been stupid, they render a case suspicious, they shall be tortured to death."

"No" says Kautilya:—It is the truth that witnesses have to hear (when they are called to attest to any transaction); if they have not minded it, they shall be fined 24 panas; if they have attested to a false case (without scrutinising), they shall be fined half of the above fine.

Parties shall themselves produce witnesses who are not far removed either by time or place; witnesses who are very far removed either by time or place; witnesses who are very far, or who will not, stir out, shall be made to present themselves by the order of the judges.

CONCERNING DEPOSITS

The rules concerning debts shall also apply to deposits. Whenever forts or country parts are destroyed by enemies or wild tribes; whenever villages, merchants, or herds of cattle are subjected to the inroads of invaders; whenever the kingdom itself is destroyed; whenever extensive fires or floods bring about entire destruction of villages, or partly destroy immovable properties, movable properties having been rescued before; whenever the spread of fire or rush of floods is so sudden that even movable properties could not be removed; or whenever a ship laden with commodities is either sunk or plundered (by pirates); deposits lost in any of the above ways shall not be reclaimed.

The depositary who has made use of the deposit for his own comfort shall not only pay a compensation (bhogavetanam) to be fixed after considering the circumstances of the place and time but also a fine of 12 panas. Not only shall any loss in the value of the deposit, due to its use, be made good, but a fine of 24 panas also be paid. Deposits damaged or lost in any way shall also be made good. When the depositary is either dead or involved in calamities, the deposit shall not be sued for. If the deposit is either mortgaged or sold or lost, the depositary shall not only restore four times its value, but pay a fine of five times the stipulated value (pancbabandho dandah). If the deposit is exchanged for a similar one (by the depositary), or lost in any other way, its value shall be paid. (Pledges.) The same rules shall hold good in the case of pledges whenever they are lost, used up, sold, mortgaged, or misappropriated.

A pledge, if productive, *i.e.* (a usufructory mortgage), shall never be lost to the debtor (nadhissopakarassidet), nor shall any interest on the debt be charged; but if unproductive (*i.e.*, hypothecation), it may be lost, and interest on the debt shall accumulate. The pledgee who does not re-convey the pledge when the debtor is ready for it shall be fined 12 panas.

In the absence of the creditor or mediator (prayojahasannidhana), the amount of the debt may be kept in the custody of the elders of the village and the debtor may have the pledged property redeemed; or with its value fixed at the time and with no interest chargeable for the future, the pledge may be left where it is. When there is any rise in the value of the pledge or when it is apprehended that it may be depriciated or lost in the near future, the pledgee may, with permission from the judges (dharmasthas), or on the evidence furnished by the officer in charge of pledges (adhipalapratyayo va), sell the pledge either in the presence of the debtor or under the presidency of experts who can see whether such apprehension is justified.

An immovable property, pledged and enjoyable with or without labour (prayasabhogyhah phalabhogyova), shall not be caused to deteriorate in value while yielding interest on the money lent, and profit on the expenses incurred in maintaining it.

The pledgee who enjoys the pledge without permission shall not only pay the net profit he derived from it, but also forfeit the debt. The rules regarding deposits shall hold good in other matters connected with pledges. (Property entrusted to another for delivery to a third person.)

The same rules shall apply to orders (adesa), and property entrusted for delivery to a third person (anvadhi).

If, through a merchant, a messenger is entrusted with a property for delivery to a third person (anvadhihasta) and such messenger does not reach the destined place, or is robbed of the property by thieves, the merchant shall not be responsible for it; nor shall a kinsman of the messenger who dies on his way be responsible for the property. For the rest, the rules regarding deposits shall also hold good here. (Borrowed or hired properties.) Properties either borrowed (yachitakam) or hired (avakritakam) shall be returned as intact as they were when received. If owing to distance in time or place, or owing to some inherent defects of the properties or to some unforeseen accidents, properties either borrowed or hired are lost or destroyed, they need not be made good. The rules regarding deposits shall also apply here. (Retail sale.)

Retail dealers, selling the merchandise of others at prices prevailing at particular localities and times shall hand over to the wholesale dealers as much of the sale proceeds and profit as is realised by them. The rules regarding pledges shall also apply here. If owing to distance in time or place there occurs any fall in the value of the merchandise, the retail dealers shall pay the value and profit at that rate which obtained when they received the merchandise. Servants selling commodities at prices prescribed by their masters shall realise no profit. They shall only return the actual sale proceeds. If prices fall, they shall pay only as much of the sale proceeds as is realised at the low rate. But such merchants as belong to trade-guilds (samvyavaharikeshu) or are trustworthy and are not condemned by the king need not restore even the value of that merchandise which is lost or destroyed owing to its inherent defects or to some unforeseen accidents. But of such merchandise as is distanced by time or place, they shall restore as much value and profit as remains after making allowance for the wear and tear of the merchandise.

For the rest the rules regarding deposits shall apply here. It explains retail sale. (Sealed deposits.) The rules laid down concerning unsealed deposits (upanidhis) shall apply to sealed deposits also. A man handing over a sealed deposit to other than the real depositor shall be punished. In the case of a depositary's denial of having received a deposit, the antecedent circumstances (purvapadanam) of the deposit and (the character and social position of) the depositor are the only evidences. Artisans (karavah) are naturally of impure character. It is not an approved custom with them to deposit for some reliable reason. When a depositary denies having received a sealed deposit which was not, however, deposited for any reasonable cause, the depositor may obtain secret permission (from the judges) to produce such witnesses as he might have stationed under a wall (gudhabhitti) while depositing.

In the midst of a forest or in the middle of a voyage an old or afflicted merchant might with confidence put in the custody of a depositary some valuable article with certain secret mark, and go on his way. On his sending this information to his son or brother, the latter may ask for the sealed deposit. If the depositary does not quietly return it, he shall not only forfeit his credit, but be liable to the punishment for theft besides being made to restore the deposit.

A reliable man, bent on leaving this world and becoming an ascetic, may place a certain sealed deposit with some secret mark in the custody of a man, and, returning after a number of years, ask for it. If the depositary dishonestly denies it, he shall not only be made to restore it, but be liable to the punishment for theft. A childish man with a sealed deposit with some secret mark may, while going through a street at night, feel frightened at his being captured by the police for untimely walking, and, placing the deposit in the custody of a man, go on his way. But subsequently put into the jail, he may ask for it. If the depositary dishonestly denies, he shall not only be made to restore it, but be liable to the punishment for theft.

By recognising the sealed deposit in the custody of a man, any one of the depositor's family may probably ask not only for the deposit, but also for information as to the whereabouts of the depositor. If the custodian denies either, he shall be treated as before. In all these cases, it is of first importance to inquire how the property under dispute came in one's possession, what are the circumstances connected with the various transactions concerning the property and what is the status of the plantiff in society as to wealth (arthasamarthyam). The above rules shall also apply to all kinds of transaction between any two persons (mithassamavayah). Hence before witnesses and with no secrecy whatever, shall all kinds of agreements be entered into; either with one's own or different people, shall the circumstances of the time and place be minutely considered first.

RULES REGARDING SLAVES AND LABOURERS

The selling or mortgaging by kinsmen of the life of a Sudra who is not a born slave, and has not attained majority, but is an Arya in birth shall be punished with a fine of 12 panas; of a Vaishya, 24 panas; of a Kshatriya, 36 panas; and of a Brahman, 48 panas. If persons other than kinsmen do the same, they shall be liable to the three amercements and capital punishment respectively: purchasers and abettors shall likewise be punished. It is no crime for Mlechchhas to sell or mortgage the life of their own offspring. But never shall an Arya be subjected to slavery.

But if in order to tide over family troubles, to find money for fines or court decrees, or to recover the (confiscated) household implements, the life of an Arya is mortgaged, they (his kinsmen) shall as soon as possible redeem him (from bondage); and more so if he is a youth or an adult capable of giving help. Any person who has once voluntarily enslaved himself shall, if guilty of an offence (nishpatitah), be a slave for life. Similarly, any person whose life has been twice mortgaged by others shall, if guilty of an offence, be a slave for life. Both of these two sorts of men shall, if they are once found desirous to run away to foreign countries, be slaves for life. Deceiving a slave of his money or depriving him of the privileges he can exercise as an Arya (Aryabhava), shall be punished with half the fine (levied for enslaving the life of an Arya). A man who happens to have taken in mortgage the life of a convict, or of a dead or an afflicted man shall be entitled to receive back (from the mortgager) the value he paid for the slave.

Employing a slave to carry the dead or to sweep ordure, urine, or the leavings of food; keeping a slave naked; or hurting or abusing him; or violating (the chastity of) a female slave shall cause the forfeiture of the value paid for him or her. Violation (of the chastity) of nurses, female cooks, or female servants of the class of joint cultivators or of any other description shall at once earn their liberty for them. Violence towards an attendant of high birth shall entitle him to run away. When a master has connection with a nurse or pledged female slave against her will, he shall be punished with the first amercement; a stranger doing the same shall be punished with the middlemost amercement. When a man commits or helps another to commit rape with a girl or a female slave pledged to him, he shall not only forfeit the purchase value, but also pay a certain amount of money (sulka) to her and a fine of twice the amount (of sulka to the Government). The offspring of a man who has sold off himself as a slave shall be an Arya. A slave shall be entitled to enjoy not only whatever he has earned without prejudice to his master's work, but also the inheritance he has received from his father.

On paying the value (for which one is enslaved), a slave shall regain his Aryahood. The same rule shall apply either to born or pledged slaves. The ransom necessary for a slave to regain his freedom is equal to what he has been sold for. Any person who has been enslaved for fines or court decrees (dandapranitah) shall earn the amount by work. An Arya, made captive in war shall for his freedom pay a certain amount proportional to the dangerous work done at the time of his capture, or half the amount. If a slave who is less than eight years old and has no relatives, no matter whether he is born a slave in his master's house, or fell to his master's share of inheritance, or has been purchased or obtained by his master in any other way, is employed in mean avocations against his will or is sold or mortgaged in a foreign land; or if a pregnant female slave is sold or pledged without any provision for her confinement, his or her master shall be punished with the first amercement. The purchaser and abettors shall likewise be punished. Failure to set a slave at liberty on the receipt of a required amount of ransom shall be punished with a fine of 12 panas; putting a slave under confinement for no reason (samrodhaschakaranat) shall likewise be punished. The property of a slave shall pass into the hands of his kinsmen; in the absence of any kinsmen, his master shall take it. When a child is begotten on a female slave by her master, both the child and its mother shall at once be recognised as free. If for the sake of subsistence, the mother has to remain in her bondage, her brother and sister shall be liberated.

Selling or mortgaging the life of a male or a female slave once liberated shall be punished with a fine of 12 panas with the exception of those who enslave themselves. Thus the rules regarding slaves. (Power of Masters over their hired servants.) Neighbours shall know the nature of agreement between a master and his servant. The servant shall get the promised wages. As to wages not previously settled the amount shall be fixed in proportion to the work done and the time spent in doing it (karmakalanurupam = at the rate prevailing at the time.) Wages being previously unsettled, a cultivator shall obtain 1/10th of the crops grown, a herdsman 1/10th of the butter clarified, a trader 1/10th of the sale proceeds. Wages previously settled shall be paid and received as agreed upon. Artisans, musicians, physicians, buffoons, cooks, and other workmen, serving of their own accord, shall obtain as much wages as similar persons employed elsewhere usually get or as much as experts (kusalah) shall fix. Disputes regarding wages shall be decided on the strength of evidences furnished by witnesses. In the absence of witnesses, the master who has provided his servant with work shall be examined. Failure to pay wages shall be punished with a fine of ten times the amount of wages (dasabandhah), or 6 panas; misappropriation of wages shall be punished with a fine of 12 panas or of five times the amount of the wages (panchabandho va). Any person who, while he is being carried away by floods, or is caught in a fire, or is in danger from elephants or tigers, is rescued on his promise to offer to his rescuer not only the whole of his property, but also his sons, wife, and himself as slaves, shall pay only as much as will be fixed by experts. This rule shall apply to all cases where help of any kind is rendered to the afflicted. A public woman shall surrender her person as agreed upon; but insistence on the observance of any agreement which is ill-considered and improper shall not succeed.

RULES REGARDING LABOURERS; AND COOPERATIVE UNDERTAKING

A servant neglecting or unreasonably putting off work for which he has received wages shall be fined 12 panas and be caught-hold of till the work is done. He who is incapable to turn out work, or is engaged to do a mean job, or is suffering from disease, or is involved in calamities shall be shown some concession or allowed to get the work done by a substitute. The loss incurred by his master or employer owing to such delay shall be made good by extra work. An employer may be at liberty to get the work done by (another) provided there is no such adverse condition that the former shall not employ another servant to execute the work, nor shall the latter go elsewhere for work. An employer not taking work from his labourer or an employee not doing his employers work shall be fined 12 panas. An employee who has received wages to do a certain work which is however, not brought to termination shall not, of his own accord, go elsewhere for work. My preceptor holds that not taking work on the part of an employer from his employee when the latter is ready, shall be regarded as work done by the labourer.

But Kautilya objects to it; for wages are to be paid for work done, but not for work that is not done. If an employer, having caused his labourer to do a part of work, will not cause him to do the rest for which the latter may certainly be ready, then also the unfinished portion of the work has to be regarded as finished. But owing to consideration of changes that have occurred in time and place or owing to bad workmanship of the labourer, the employer may not be pleased with what has already been turned out by the labourer. Also the workman may, if unrestrained, do more than agreed upon and thereby cause loss to the employer. The same rules shall apply to guilds of workmen (sanghabhritah.) Guilds of workmen shall have a grace of seven nights over and above the period agreed upon for fulfilling their engagement. Beyond that time they shall find substitutes and get the work completed. Without taking permission from their employer, they shall neither leave out anything undone nor carry away anything with them from the place of work. They shall be fined 24 panas for taking away anything and 12 panas for leaving out anything undone. Thus the Rules regarding labourers.

Guilds of workmen (sanghabhritah, workmen employed by Companies) as well as those who carry on any cooperative work (sambhuya samutthatarah) shall divide their earnings (vetanam = wages) either equally or as agreed upon among themselves. Cultivators or merchants shall, either at the end or in the middle of their cultivation or manufacture, pay to their labourers as much of the latter's share as is proportional to the work done. If the labourers, giving up work in the middle, supply substitutes, they shall be paid their wages in full.

But when commodities are being manufactured, wages shall be paid out according to the amount of work turned out; for such payment does not affect the favourable or unfavourable results on the way (*i.e.*, in the sale of merchandise by peddlars).

A healthy person who deserts his company after work has been begun shall be fined 12 panas; for none shall, of his own accord, leave his company. Any person who is found to have neglected his share of work by stealth shall be shown mercy (abhayam) for the first time and given a proportional quantity of work anew with promise of proportional share of earnings as well. In case of negligence for a second time or of going elsewhere, he shall be thrown out of the Company (pravasanam). If he is guilty of a glaring offence (mahaparadhe), he shall be treated as the condemned. (Co-operation in sacrificial acts.)

Priests cooperating in a sacrifice shall divide their earnings either equally or as agreed upon excepting what is especially due to each or any of them. If a priest employed in such sacrifices as Agnishtoma, etc., dies after the ceremony of consecration, (his claimant) shall get 1/5th of the promised or prescribed present (dakshina); after the ceremony consecrating the purchase of Soma, ¼th of the present; after the ceremony called Madhyamopasad; or Pravargyodvasana, 1/3rd of the present; and after the ceremony called Maya, ½ of the share. If in the sacrifice called Sutya, the same thing happens after the ceremony called Pratassavana, ¾ths, of the share shall be paid; after the ceremony called Madhyandina, the present shall be paid in full; for by that time the payment of presents shall be over. In every sacrifice except the one called Brihaspatisavana, it is usual to pay presents. The same rule shall apply to the presents payable in Aharganas, sacrifices so called. The surviving priests carrying the balance of the present or any other relatives of a dead priest shall perform the funeral ceremony of the dead for ten days and nights.

If the sacrificer himself (he who has instituted the sacrifice) dies, then the remaining priests shall complete the sacrifice and carry away the presents. If a sacrificer sends out any priest before completing the sacrifice, he shall be punished with the first amercement. If a sacrificer sending out a priest happens to be a person who has not kept the sacrificial fire, or to be a preceptor or one who has already performed sacrifices, then the fines shall be 100, 1000, and 1000 panas respectively. As it is certain that sacrificial merits fall in value when performed in company with a drunkard, the husband of a Sudra woman, a murderer of a Brahman, or one who has violated the chastify of the wife of his preceptor, a receiver of condemnable gifts, or is a thief, or one whose performance of sacrificial acts is condemnable, it is no offence to send out such a priest.

RESCISSION OF PURCHASE AND SALE

A merchant refusing to give his merchandise that he has sold shall be punished with a fine of 12 panas, unless the merchandise is naturally bad, or is dangerous, or is intolerable.

That which has inherent defects is termed naturally bad; whatever is liable to be confiscated by the king, or is subject to destruction by thieves, fire, or floods is termed as being dangerous; and whatever is devoid of all good qualities, or is manufactured by the deceased is called intolerable.

Time for rescission of a sale is one night for merchants; 3 nights for cultivators; 5 nights for herdsmen; and with regard to the sale or barter of precious things and articles of mixed qualities (vivrittivikraye), 7 nights. Merchandise which is likely to perish sooner may, if there is no loss to others, be shown the favour of early disposal by prohibiting the sale elsewhere of similar merchandise which is not likely to perish so soon. Violation of this rule shall be punished with a fine of 24 panas or 1/10th of the value of the merchandise sold against this rule. A person who attempts to return an article purchased by him shall if the article is other than what is naturally bad, or is dangerous, or is intolerable, be punished with a fine of 12 panas. The same rescission rules that apply to a seller shall apply to the purchaser also. (Marriage Contracts)

[As regards marriages among the three higher castes, rejection of a bride before the rite of panigrahana, clasping of hands, is valid; likewise among the Sudras, observing religious rites. Even in the case of a couple that has gone through the rite of panigrahana,] rejection of a bride whose guilt of having lain with another man has been afterwards detected is valid. But never so in the case of brides and bridegrooms of pure character and high family. Any person who has given a girl in marriage without announcing her guilt of having lain with another shall not only be punished with a fine of 96 panas, but also be made to return the sulka and stridhana. Any person receiving a girl in marriage without announcing the blemishes of the bridegroom shall not only pay double the above fine, but also forfeit the sulka and stridhana (he paid for the bride). (Sale of bipeds, etc.) Sale of bipeds and quadrupeds as strong, healthy, and clean though they are either unclean or actually suffering from leprosy and other diseases, shall be punished with a fine of 12 panas. The time of rescission of sale is three fortnights for quadrupeds and one year for men; for it is possible to know by that time their good or bad condition. An assembly convened for the purpose shall, in the matter of rescending sales or gifts, decide in such a way that neither the giver nor the receiver shall be injured thereby.

RESUMPTION OF GIFTS, SALE WITHOUT OWNERSHIP AND OWNERSHIP

Rules concerning recovery of debts shall also apply to resumption of gifts. Invalid gifts shall be kept in the safe custody of some persons. Any person who has given as gift not only his whole property, his sons, and his wife, but also his own life shall bring the same for the consideration of rescissors. Gifts or charitable subscriptions to the wicked or for unworthy purposes, monetary help to such persons as are malevolent or cruel, and promise of sexual enjoyment to the unworthy shall be so settled by rescissors that neither the giver nor the receiver shall be injured thereby. Those who receive any kind of aid from timid persons, threatening them with legal punishment, defamation, or loss of money, shall be liable to the punishment for theft; and the persons who yield such aids shall likewise be punished. Co-operation in hurting a person, and showing a haughty attitude towards the king shall be punished with the highest amercement. No son, or heir claiming a dead man's property shall, against his own will, pay the value of the bail borne by the dead man (pratibhavyadanda), the balance of any dowry (sulkasesha), or the stakes of gambling; nor shall he fulfill the promise of gifts made by the dead man under the influence of liquor or love. Thus resumption of gifts is dealt with. (Sale without ownership.)

As regards sale without ownership:—On the detection of a lost property in the possession of another person, the owner shall cause the offender to be arrested through the judges of a court. If time or place does not permit this action, the owner himself shall catch hold of the offender and bring him before the judges. The judge shall put the question; how the offender came by the property. If he narrates how he got it, but cannot produce the person who sold it to him, he shall be left off, and shall forfeit the property. But the seller, if produced, shall not only pay the value of the property, but also be liable to the punishment for theft.

If a person with a stolen property in his possession runs away or hides himself till the property is wholly consumed, he shall not only pay the value, but also be liable to the punishment for theft. After proving his claim to a lost property (svakaranam kritva), its owner shall be entitled to take possession of it. On his failure to prove his title to it, he shall be fined 5 times the value of the property, (panchabandhadandah), and the property shall be taken by the king. If the owner takes possession of a lost article without obtaining permission from the court, he shall be punished with the first amercement.

Stolen or lost articles shall, on being detected, be kept in the toll-gate. If no claimant is forthcoming within three fortnights, such articles shall be taken by the king. He who proved his title to a lost or stolen biped shall pay 5 panas towards ransom (before taking possession of it). Likewise the ransom for a single-hoofed animal shall be 4 panas; for a cow or a buffalo, 2 panas, for minor quadrupeds ¼th of a pana; and for articles such as precious stones, superior or inferior raw materials, five per cent of their value. Whatever of the property of his own subjects the king brings back from the forests and countries of enemies, shall be handed over to its owner. Whatever of the property of citizens robbed by thieves the king cannot recover, shall be made good from his own pocket.

If the king is unable to recover such things, he shall either allow any self-elected person (svayamgraha) to fetch them, or pay an equivalent ransom to the sufferer. An adventurer may enjoy whatever the king graciously gives him out of the booty he has plundered from an enemy's country, excepting the life of an Arya and the property belonging to gods, Brahmans or ascetics. Thus sale without ownership is dealt with. (Ownership.) As to the title of an owner to his property:—The owners who have quitted their country where their property lies shall continue to have their title to it. When the owners other than minors, the aged, those that are afflicted with decease or calamities, those that are sojourning abroad, or those that have deserted their country during national disturbances, neglect for ten years their property which is under the enjoyment of others, they shall forfeit their title to it. Buildings left for 20 years in the enjoyment of others shall not be reclaimed. But the mere occupation of the buildings of others during the absence of the king by kinsmen, priests, or heretics shall not give them the right of possession. The same shall obtain with regard to open deposits, pledges, treasure trove (nidhi), boundary, or any property belonging to kings or priests (srotriyas).

Ascetics and heretics shall, without disturbing each other, reside in a large area. A new comer shall, however, be provided with the space occupied by an old resident. If not willing to do so, the old occupier shall be sent out. The property of hermits, (vanaprastha) ascetics (yati), or bachelors learning the Vedas (Brahmachari) shall on their death be taken by their preceptors, disciples, their brethren (dharmabhratri), or classmates in succession. Whenever hermits, etc., have to pay any fines, they may, in the name of the king, perform penance, oblation to gods, fireworship, or the ritual called Mahakachchhavardhana for as many nights as the number of panas of their fines. Those heretics (pashandah) who have neither gold nor gold-coin shall similarly observe their fasts except in the case of defamation, theft, assault and abduction of women. Under these circumstances, they shall be compelled to undergo punishment. The king shall, under penalty of fines, forbid the wilful or improper proceedings of ascetics: for vice overwhelming righteousness will in the long run destroy the ruler himself.

ROBBERY

Sudden and direct seizure (of person or property) is termed sahasa; fraudulent or indirect seizure (niranvaye'pavyayanecha) is theft. The school of Manu hold that the fine for the direct seizure of precious stones and superior or inferior raw materials shall be equal to their value. It is equal to twice the value of the articles according to the followers of Usanas. But Kautilya holds that it shall be proportional to the gravity of the crime.

In the case of such articles of small value as flowers, fruits, vegetables, roots, turnips, cooked rice, skins, bamboo, and pots (earthenware) the fine shall range from 12 to 24 papas; for articles of great value such as iron (kalayasa), wood, roping materials, and herds of minor quadrupeds, the fine shall range from 24 to 48 panas; and for such articles of still greater value as copper, brass, bronze, glass, ivory and vessels, etc., it shall range from 48 to 96 panas. This fine is termed the first amercement. For the seizure of such as big quadrupeds, men, fields, houses, gold, gold-coins, fine fabrics, etc., the fine shall range from 200 to 500 panas, which is termed the middle-most amercement.

My preceptor holds that keeping or causing to keep by force either men or women in prison, or releasing them by force from imprisonment, shall be punished with fines ranging from 500 to 1,000 panas. This fine is termed the highest amercement. He who causes another to commit sahasa after the plans prepared by himself shall be fined twice the value (of the person or property seized). An abettor who employs a hireling to comit sahasa by promising 'I shall pay thee as much gold as thou makest use of,' shall be fined four times the value.

The school of Brihaspati are of opinion that if with the promise 'I will pay thee this amount of gold,' an abettor causes another to commit sahasa, the former shall be compelled to pay the promised amount of gold and a fine. But Kautilya holds that if an abettor extenuates his crime by pleading anger, intoxication or loss of sense (moham), he shall be punished as described above.

In all kinds of fines below a hundred panas, the king shall take in addition to the fine 8 per cent more as rupa and in fines above hundred, five per cent more; these two kinds of exaction, are just inasmuch as the people are full of sins on the one hand, and kings are naturally misguided on the other.

DEFAMATION

Calumny, contemptuous talk, or intimidation constitutes defamation. Among abusive expressions relating to the body, habits, learning, occupation, or nationalities, that of calling a deformed man by his right name such as 'the blind', 'the lame', etc. shall be punished with a fine of 3 panas; and by false name 6 panas. If the blind, the lame, etc., are insulted with such ironical expressions as 'a man of beautiful eyes', 'a man of beautiful teeth', etc. the fine shall be 12 panas. Likewise when a person is taunted for leprosy, lunacy, impotency and the like. Abusive expressions in general, no matter whether true, false, or reverse with reference to the abused, shall be punished with fines ranging above 12 panas, in the case of persons of equal rank. If persons abused happen to be of superior rank, the amount of the fines shall be doubled; if of lower rank, it shall be halved. For calumniating the wives of others, the amount of the fines shall be doubled. If abuse is due to carelessness, intoxication, or loss of sense, etc., the fines shall be halved. As to the reality of leprosy and lunacy, physicians or neighbours shall be authorities. As to the reality of impotency, women, the scum of urine, or the low specific gravity of faeces in water (the sinking of faeces in water) shall furnish the necessary evidence. (Speaking ill of habits.)

If among Brahmans, Kshatriyas, Vaisyas, Sudras, and outcastes (antavasayins), any one of a lower caste abuses the habits of one of a higher caste, the fines imposed shall increase from 3 panas upwards (commencing from the lowest caste). If any one of a higher caste abuses one of a lower caste, fines imposed shall decrease from 2 panas. Contemptuous expressions such as 'a bad Brahman' shall also be punished as above. The same rules shall apply to calumnies regarding learning (sruta), the profession of buffoons (vagjivana), artisans, or musicians, and relating to nationalities such as Prajjunaka, Gandhara, etc. (Intimidation.) If a person intimidates another by using such expressions as 'I shall render thee thus', the bravado shall be punished with half as much fine as will be levied on him who actually does so. If a person, being unable to carry his threat into effect, pleads provocation, intoxication, or loss of sense as his excuse, he shall be fined 12 panas. If a person capable to do harm and under the influence of enmity intimidates another, he shall be compelled to give life-long security for the well-being of the intimidated. Defamation of one's own nation or village shall be punished with the first amercement; that of one's own caste or assembly with the middlemost; and that of gods or temples (chaitya) with the highest amercement.

ASSAULT

Touching, striking, or hurting constitutes assault. When a person touches with hand, mud, ashes or dust the body of another person below the naval, he shall be punished with a fine of 3 panas; with some but unclean things, with the leg, or spitule, 6 panas; with saliva (Chhardi), urine, faeces, etc. 12 panas. If the same offence is committed above the navel, the fines shall be doubled; and on the head, quadrupled. If the same offence is committed on persons of superior rank, the fines shall be twice as much: and on persons of lower rank, half of the above fines. If the same offence is committed on the women of others, the fines shall be doubled.

If the offence is due to carelessness, intoxication, or loss of sense, the fines shall be halved.

For catching hold of a man by his legs, clothes, hands or hair, fines ranging above 6 panas shall be imposed. Squeezing, rounding with arms, thrusting, dragging, or sitting over the body of another person shall be punished with the first amercement. Running away after making a person fall, shall be punished with half of the above fines. That limb of a Sudra with which he strikes a Brahman shall be cut off. (Striking.) For striking compensation is to be paid and half of the fines levied for touching. This rule shall also apply to Chandalas and other profane persons (committing the same offence). Striking with the hand, shall be punished with fines below 3 panas, with the leg twice as much as the above fine; and striking with an instrument so as to cause swellings shall be punished with the first amercement; and striking so as to endanger life shall be punished with the middle-most amercement. (Hurting.)

Causing a bloodless wound with a stick, mud, a stone, an iron bar, or a rope shall be punished with a fine of 24 panas. Causing the blood to gush out excepting bad or diseased blood shall be punished with double the fine. Beating a person almost to death, though without causing blood, breaking the hands, legs, or teeth, tearing off the ear or the nose, or breaking open the flesh of a person except in ulcers or boils shall be punished with the first amercement. Causing hurt in the thigh or the neck, wounding the eye, or hurting so as to impede eating, speaking, or any other bodily movements shall not only be punished with the middlemost amercement, but also be made liable to the payment (to the sufferer) of such compensation as is necessary to cure him. If time or place does not permit the immediate arrest of an offender, he shall be dealt with as described in Book IV, treating of the measures to suppress the wicked. Each one of a confederacy of persons who have inflicted hurt on another person shall be punished with double the usual fine. My preceptor holds that quarrels or assaults of a remote date shall not be complained of. But Kautilya holds that there shall be no acquittal for an offender. My preceptor thinks that he who is the first to complain of a quarrel wins inasmuch as it is pain that drives one to law.

But Kautilya objects to it; for whether a complaint is lodged first or last, it is the evidence of witnesses that must be depended upon. In the absence of witnesses, the nature of the hurt and other circumstances connected with the quarrel in question shall be evidences. Sentence of punishment shall be passed the very day that a defendant accused of assault fails to answer the charge made against him. (Robbery in quarrels.)

A person stealing anything under the tumult of a quarrel shall be fined 10 panas. Destruction of articles of small value shall be punished with a fine equal to the value of the articles besides the payment (to the sufferer) of an adequate compensation. Destruction of big things with a compensation equal to the value of the articles and a fine equal to twice the value. In the case of destruction of such things as clothes, gold, gold-coins, and vessels or merchandise, the first amercement together with the value of the articles shall be levied. Causing damage to a wall of another man's house by knocking shall be fined 3 panas; breaking open or demolishing the same shall be fined 6 panas, besides the restoration of the wall. Throwing harmful things inside the house of a man shall be fined 12 panas; and throwing such things as endanger the lives of the inmates shall be punished with the first amercement. For causing pain with sticks, etc., to minor quadrupeds one or two panas shall be levied; and for causing blood to the same, the fine shall be doubled. In the case of large quadrupeds, not only double the above fines, but also an adequate compensation necessary to cure the beasts shall be levied. For cutting off the tender sprouts of fruit-trees, flower-trees or shady trees in the parks near a city, a fine of 6 panas shall be imposed; for cutting off the minor branches of the same trees, 12 panas; and for cutting off the big branches, 24 panas shall be levied. Cutting off the trunks of the same shall be punished with the first amercement; and felling the same shall be punished with the middle-most amercement.

In the case of plants which bear flowers, fruits, or provide shade, half of the above fines shall be levied. The same fines shall be levied in the case of trees that have grown in places of pilgrimage, forests of hermits, or cremation or burial grounds. For similar offences committed in connection with the trees which mark boundaries, or which are worshipped or observed (chaityeshvalakshiteshucha,) or trees which are grown in the king's forests, double the above fines shall be levied.

GAMBLING AND BETTING AND MISCELLANEOUS OFFENCES

With a view to find out spies or thieves, the Superintendent of gambling shall, under the penalty of a fine of 12 panas if played elsewhere, centralise gambling. My preceptor is of opinion that in complaints regarding gambling, the winner shall be punished with the first amercement and the vanquished with the middle-most amercement; for though not skilful enough to win as ardently desired by him, the vanquished fellow does not tolerate his defeat. But Kautilya objects to it: for if the punishment for the vanquished were to be doubled, none would complain to the king. Yet gamblers are naturally false players. The Superintendents of gambling shall, therefore, be honest and supply dice at the rate of a kakani of hire per pair. Substitution by tricks of hand of dice other than thus supplied shall be punished with a fine of 12 panas. A false player shall not only be punished with the first amercement and fines leviable for theft and deceipt, but also be made to forfeit the stakes he has won.

The Superintendent shall take not only 5 per cent of the stakes won by every winner, and the hire payable for supplying dice and other accessories of diceplay, but also the fee chargeable for supplying water and accommodation, besides the charge for license. He can at the same time carry on the transactions of sale or mortgage of things. If he does not forbid tricks of hand and other deceitful practices, be shall be punished with twice the amount of the fine (levied from the deceitful gamblers.) The same rules shall apply to betting and challenging except those in learning and art. (Miscellaneous offences.)

As regards miscellaneous offences:

When a person does not return in required place or time the property he has borrowed or hired, or placed in his custody as a deposit, sits under the shade for more than one and a quarter of an hour (ayama) as prescribed, evades under the excuse of being a Brahman the payment due while passing military stations or crossing rivers, and bawls out or invites others to fight against his neighbours, he shall be punished with a fine of 12 panas.

When a person does not hand over the property entrusted to him for delivery to a third person, drags with his hand the wife of his brother, has connection with a public woman kept by another, sells merchandise that is under ill repute, breaks open the sealed door of a house, or causes hurt to any of the forty-house-holders or neighbours, a fine of 48 panas shall be imposed.

When a person misappropriates the revenue he collects as the agent of a household, violates by force the chastity of a widow of independent living, when an outcast (chandala) person touches an Arya woman, when a person does not run to render help to another in danger, or runs without a cause, and when a person entertains, in dinner dedicated to gods or ancestors Buddhists (sakya,) Ajivakas, Sudras and exiled persons, (pravrajita) a fine of 100 panas shall be imposed.

When an unauthorised person examines (an offender) on oath, executes Government work though not a Government servant, renders minor quadrupeds impotent, or causes abortion to a female slave by medicine, he shall be punished with the first amercement. When between father and son, husband and wife brother and sister, maternal uncle and nephew or teacher and student, one abandons the other while neither of them is an apostate; and when a person abandons in the centre of a village another person whom he brought there for his own help, the first amercement shall be levied. When a person abandons his companion in the midst of a forest, he shall be punished with the middle-most amercement. When a person threatens and abandons his companion in the midst of a forest, he shall be punished with the highest amercement.

Whenever persons who have started together on some journey abandon one another as above, half of the above fine shall be levied.

When a person keeps or causes to keep another person in illegal confinement, releases a prisoner from prison, keeps or causes another to keep a minor in confinement, he shall be punished with a fine of 1000 panas. The rates of fines shall vary in accordance with the rank of persons concerned and the gravity of the crimes. Such persons as a pilgrim, an ascetic engaged in penance, a diseased person, any one suffering from hunger, thirst, or fatigue from journey, a villager from country parts, any one that has suffered much from punishment and a money-less pauper shall be shown mercy.

Such transactions as pertain to gods, Brahmans, ascetics, women, minors, aged persons, diseased persons and helpless creatures shall, though not be complained of, be settled by the judges themselves; and in such transactions as the above, excuses due to time, place, or possession shall not be pleaded. Such persons as are noted for their learning, intelligence, bravery, high birth, or magnificent works shall be honoured. Judges shall thus settle disputes free from all kinds of circumvention, with mind unchanged in all moods or circumstances, pleasing and affable to all.

CHAPTER

7

MODERN INDIAN THOUGHT

GANDHI'S POLITICAL PHILOSOPHY

Today the world is facing the adverse effects of violence. Countries which once thrived on violence and terror are fast realising the futility of hatred. This article which was published in the Sunday Statesman, Kolkata 8 February 2004 asserts that Gandhi's philosophy of nonviolence is being accepted worldwide to create a peaceful and harmonious society.

Gandhi is now emerging as the saviour of a world threatened by superpower violence, even in Gandhi's life time great minds of the world saw in his work the promise of a new world. One of them is Romain Rolland (1866-1944) who wrote in his Mahatma Gandhi: The Man who Became One With the Universal Being (1924): "With Gandhi everything is nature, modest, simple, pure-while all his struggles are hallowed by religious serenity." Gandhi's gentle religious temper which was active in his politics was, however, observed 15 years earlier in his first biography Joseph J Doke's Gandhi, A Patriot in South Africa (1909).

If you wish to seize the essence of Gandhi's political philosophy read his presidential address at the annual session of the Indian National Congress held at Belgaum in 1924. The Mahatma said at the end of his address: "Satyagraha is search for truth; and God is Truth. Ahimsa and Nonviolence is the light that reveals that truth to me. Swaraj for me is a part of that truth.

Mahatma Gandhi is slowly but steadily emerging as a spiritual and moral hero on the international scene. The Great German existentialist philosopher, Karl Jaspers (1883-1969), wrote in his The Future of Mankind (1958) : "Today we face the question of how to escape from physical force and from war, lest we all perish by the atom bomb. Gandhi, in word and deed, gives the true answer: only a suprapolitical force can bring political salvation." This is the voice of the world conscience and this is an echo of the voice of Gandhi. The voice may not reach all ears. But they have reached at least some ears.

What is strange is that Germany, a country responsible for the Second World War, is the country which his now stressing the need for Gandhian non-violence in the modern world, Actually Germany began to understand Gandhi as early as 1931 when Rene Fullop-Miller published his Gandhi: The Holy Man. He said that political problems must be solved in the Gandhian way: "Gandhi's nationalism contains none of those elements which makes nationalist movements of the West seem a menace to peace." This is a plea for a Gandhian approach to political problems which is now, generally speaking, the German elite's view of Gandhi's nonviolence. Let us see the attitude to Gandhian nonviolence of the greatest physicist of the modern world after Einstein, Werner Heisenberg. In an essay on Gandhi he says that " Gandhi's teaching of nonviolence could prove to be stronger than the vague impersonal conception of an international court of justice. Gandhi's unique example shows that a true personal involvement together with the total rejection of force could be very successful politically."

In 1969 Dr Heimou Rau of Max Mueller Bhavan, New Delhi, edited a collection of essays which was published with the title Mahatma Gandhi As Germans See Him. It contains 16 essays by eminent German intellectuals on the life and teaching of Gandhi. The essays show how Gandhi's philosophy of nonviolence has influenced the German mind. How Gandhi's ideal has touched the soul of the Anglosaxon world we can see in Ronald J Terchek's Gandhi Struggling for Autonomy (1999). The work explains Gandhi's idea of the swaraj of our soul which along can fulfil our political and social obligations. No less important is Gandhi in His Time and Ours by David Hardiman, a professor at the University of Warwick. Hardiman seizes the essence of Gandhi's ideas when he says: "Gandhi's approach represented a state of mind and not any theory."

Gandhi's spiritual and moral approach to our political problem is particularly important today after the US declaration of war on terrorism. To realise this we have to value Gandhi's idea of reflection on our self and see what we are. The Pentagon's hitting power will not end terrorism. It will only make it more rampant. Let us hope that the people of America, once nursed on the idealism of Emerson, Thoreau and Whitman will soon begin to understand Gandhi and will abandon the spirit of revenge which now regulates the US policy of dealing with terrorists. You cannot bring peace through violence. The most effective answer to violence is nonviolence. Gandhi said in one of his articles in his Harijan (1938): " If even one great nation were unconditionally to perform the supreme act of renunciation, many of us would see in our lifetime visible peace established on earth."

GANDHIAN CONCEPT OF DECENTRALIZATION

Gandhi's greatest contribution to the social thought of this century is perhaps his insistence on decentralization of the means of production (i.e. say economic power). There are many who are ready to give thoughtful consideration to his theory because it is the only way out of the problem of unemployment in this country. They argue that it is desirable to go in for decentralization because huge capital accumulation is needed to industrialize the country through large-scale industries. They also contend that because large scale industrialization presupposes the existence of foreign markets which this country cannot have, decentralization is the only cherishable goal. In other words large-scale industrialization will be preferable in case the problem of capital formation and foreign market are solved.

Now this line of reasoning constitutes a danger to the whole theory of decentralization as put forward by Gandhi. It would be wrong to presume that Gandhi propounded his theory only to suit Indian conditions. On the other hand, Gandhiji's theory of decentralization was the result of his keen and almost prophetic insight into the numerous political, social and cultural ills which the age of large-scale industrialization has brought in its wake.

This is what Bertrand Russell has to say as regards Gandhi's concept of decentralization: "In those parts of the world in which industrialism is still young, the possibility of avoiding the horrors we have experienced still exists. India, for example is traditionally a land of village communities. It would be a tragedy if this traditional way of life with all its evils were to be suddenly and violently exchanged for the greater evils of industrialism and they would apply to people whose standard of living is already pitifully low..... "

Therefore, one has only to understand the magnitude of those "horrors" of which Russell speaks, before one can truly appreciate Gandhi's idea of decentralization. Large-scale industrialism is at the base of the centralization of political power in few hands. It is in the very nature of large-scale industries to centralize economic power in the hands of a few individuals. Under capitalism this power comes to be concentrated in the hands of individual capitalists and under socialism it is arrogated by managers, technocrats and bureaucrats. Thus the centralization of power in the State negates the very conception of democracy. This is why Gandhi did not favour the so-called democracy in the West. In his view, Western democracy was only formal. In reality it was totalitarian in so far as only a few could enjoy the political power in this system.

Apart from the political consequences, there are the evil effects of industrialization on the personality of man. Industrialism starts by snapping the naval chord of man which binds him with soil and corrosive and all-enveloping shadow of giant machineries. As a result he is reduced to a mere cog in the wheel. Since industrialization is based on the division of labour, it limits man's self-expression. The famous illustration of Adam Smith that a pin has to pass through ninety hands before it is completely manufactured only reaffirms the above charge. Hence the work loses its variety, initiative and colour. No doubt such a division increases the productivity. But it obstructs the full foliation of man's natural skill.

Not only this, industrialization does not cater to the biological needs of man. Man as a biological being requires "a specific temperature, a specific quality of climate, air, light, humidity and food." It is by working in such conditions that man maintains his bodily equilibrium. Industrialization usurps these organic needs of man. Moreover industrialization tends to gather man in the collective. This inevitably fosters the growth of totalitarian impulse in man. Man becomes oblivious of his own sovereignty. He merges his personality in the collective with the result that ultimately he is accustomed to tolerate every form of tyranny and cruelty in the name of the collective wellbeing of the society.

There are some of the most eloquent ills which result from an unchecked pursuit of industrialism. As a matter of fact, many thinkers and social reformers, Wen, Simon, Fouriser and especially Marx tired to go into the causes of these ills. According to them, therefore, the root of the malady lay in the system of ownership; all social, political and cultural ills were due to private ownership of the means of production. Once this private system of ownership was removed and instruments of production socialized they thought the malady would disappear, rather melt as if into thin air. But experience gave a lie to the rosy picture which these reforms and especially Marx had pained. Even after socialization the ills tended to appear in diverse other forms. Liberty disappeared. And the mad pursuit after power tended to reduce man to the lowest denominator of beast living as George Orwell would like to call on Animal Farm'

Where lay then the root of the disease, the fallacy in the whole approach? Undoubtedly many of the evil originated from the system of ownership. Gandhi accepted Marx in this respect. But he went a step further and delved deeper. According to him both the system of ownership and the technique of production were the real cause of the malady. Marx attacked the system of ownership in his humanistic zeal. But he left the technique of production altogether untouched. Gandhiji focused his attention to the technique also. He suggested that large-scale technique should give way to small-scale technique. This therefore forms the core of his decentralization theory. Does this mean that Gandhi was against the application of science to the instruments of production, i.e. machinery? To this he replied, "What I object to is the craze for machinery, not machinery as such....." (Young India, 1925) Indeed he favoured the application of science towards developing the small-scale technique: "I would welcome every improvement in the cottage machine", he wrote in Young India. Replying to a suggestion whether he was against all machinery he said, "My answer is emphatically No. but I am against its indiscriminate multiplication. I refuse to be dazzled by the seeming triumph of machinery. But simple tools and implements and such machinery as saves individual labour and lightens the burden of millions of cottages, I should welcome." (Young India, 1926)

We see therefore, that Gandhi was not against machinery as such. His whole approach to machinery and the use of science was radically different, deeply revolutionary and humanly conscious. A technique which tends to make man a robot, robs him of his perennial urge to freedom and makes an all-out invasion on his political, economic and social liberties is not acceptable to Gandhi. "Science in so far as it consists of knowledge, must be regarded as having value, but in so far as it consists of technique, the question whether it is to be praised or blamed depends upon the use that is made of the technique. In itself it is neutral, neither good or bad and any ultimate views that we may have about what gives value to this or that must come from some other source than science." This is what Bertrand Russell has to say about the use of scientific technique. According to Gandhi, the scientific technique, therefore, must be informed by a deep awareness of values which it is out to create. In other words, the advancement of technique and perfection must accord with the general aims. Large-Scale technique strikes at the very root of the general aims. Gandhi, therefore, does not show any quarter to it.

Communal Harmony

Mahatma Gandhi was born on the crossroads of our history and gave the country a purposeful direction. He made his mark as a reformer, as a thinker, and as a liberator. He was a practical idealist. His sense of observation, analysis, and experimentation even at a comparatively younger age gave him a distinctive mental quality and approach to the matters that he confronted. He was, as Romain Rolland remarks, "familiar with the best that Europe and America have produced." He was as familiar with the Bible as the Quran believer. Bhagavad Gita and Upanishads had a new meaning for him. He drew the best out of these. In his constructive programme, he gave the first place to communal harmony among the people of different faiths. The result was the famous book, The Way To Communal Harmony, written by Gandhi himself. in this collection of his writings and speeches, one is struck again and again by the passion and sincerity with which he pleaded for the cause of better understanding among individuals and communities. The books is a compilation of Gandhi's reflections on certain problems that divide mankind. Everywhere in the world, individuals and groups are divided because of fear, suspicion, and hatred towards each other, which further depends on whether the division expressed itself along religious, economic, political, caste, or colour lines. Whatever is the form, insecurity perhaps the major cause of individual or social dissensions. A person, who is integrated and sure of himself, fears none and consequently provokes no fear. We have examples of such heroic individuals. But we do not have till now instances of societies or communities that are fully integrated and therefore fearless.

Gandhi felt the need of community unity during his stay in South Africa. The principal question before him was harmony between Hindus and Muslims who inhabited this country. Gandhi felt that if Hindu-Muslim unity was established, unity with other communities which was already there, could easily be strengthened. He never found serious differences between the Hindus and Muslims and other minority communities like the Christians and the Sikhs, not to speak of the small community of Parsis. Naturally, therefore, he turned to the question of Hindu-Muslim unity. He insisted that the Hindus who are in a majority in the country should help the Muslims and should never entertain any idea of enforcing their rights but try to win the hearts of the minority community. He expressed : -

"I am striving to become the best cement between the two communities. My longing is to be able to cement the two with my blood, if necessary. There is nothing in either religion to keep the two communities apart. In nature there is a fundamentally unity running through all the diversity. Religions are no exception to the natural law. They are given to the mankind so as to accelerate the process of realization of fundamental unity. The need of the moment is not an establishment of a Universal religion but there is a greater need to develop mutual respect towards the different religions."

The basic principle, Truth, inspired all his thought and action. It was the realization that an inviolable harmony exists in all creation and any violation of that harmony would create disaster. He saw this principle enshrined in all religions, which led him to accord equal respect to all faiths. Vasudhaiva Kutumbakam of the Vedic tradition to him was no different from the Quranic belief that Allah the Beneficent and Merciful was the creator if all that we see and hear about and that he would dispense justice on the basis of deeds and not the professed faith of each person. Nor was it different from the Christian faith that God's love and benediction was for all without any distinction and so on. All religions insist on equality of human race and on developing a harmonious relationship with the entirety of creation around. Any violation of the principle of equality gives way to conflict and violation.

Gandhi regards Islam as a religion of peace in the same sense as Christianity, Buddhism, and Hinduism. No doubt, there are differences in degree. He says in this regard that he knew the passages that can be quoted form the Holy book Quran to the contrary. But it is possible to quote from the Vedas to the contrary. "My reading of the Quran has convinced me that the basis of Islam is not violence but is unadulterated Peace. It regards forbearance as a superior to vengeance. The very word "Islam" means Peace, which is nonviolence. My experience of all India tells me that the Hindus and the Muslims know how to live at Peace among themselves. I decline to believe that the people have said good-bye to their senses, so as to make it impossible to live at Peace with each other, as they done for generations. The enmity cannot last forever."

Gandhi had never accepted in principle the theory of the Hindus and the Muslims being two distinct nations and he tried to convince both of them of the pernicious character of this principle. He continued to the last day of his life to instill the lesson of unity among the communities of India. It is remarkable that how by his honest and fearless advocacy of communal unity he had enraged many of the Muslims and a negligible few among the Hindus. The Muslims looked upon him as an enemy, while some Hindus felt that by showing humility, respect, regard and partially for the Muslims, he was jeopardizing the cause of the Hindus. Those Hindus, who did not like his efforts, conceived the idea of getting rid of him. So he was shot to death on the prayer ground. It was a tragic end. The great leader, however, clearly saw the time coming when people belonging to different faiths will have the same regard for the other faiths that they have for their own. Just as in nature a fundamental unity running through all the existing diversity, so also in religions there is a fundamental unity, which one has to recognize and realize. In order to discover this underlying unity among all religions, Gandhi had with him a master key of Truth and nonviolence. He stressed upon universal Peace, brotherhood, an reverence for all life.

He emphatically stressed upon ethical teachings in school curriculum, as he believed that the fundamentals of ethics are common to all religions. The conflict of the creeds and religious recrimination, he detested most. he preached that we must eradicate from our midst the secret pride that our religion is truer than the other religions. Our attitude towards all other religions must be absolutely clear and sincere. He wanted unity of heart and mind among Hindus and Muslims. Communal harmony always received priority over other programmes.

All religions teach men to be good and peaceful. Intolerance is the religion of the negative. The Gita, the Quran, the Bible, the Granth Sahib, the Zend Avesta contain gems of wisdom, although the followers might belie their teachings. "The essence of true religious teaching is that one should serve and befriend all. I learnt this in my mother's lap."

M. N. ROY

M. N. Roy (1887-1954) is one of the greatest, if not the greatest, Indian philosopher of twentieth century. Unlike some other Indian thinkers of twentieth century, Roy has made a clear distinction between philosophy and religion in his thought. This alone, I think, entitles him to be recognized as the foremost Indian philosopher of twentieth century. According to Roy, no philosophical advancement is possible unless we get rid of orthodox religious ideas and theological dogmas. On the other hand, Roy has envisaged a very close relationship between philosophy and science. Secondly, Roy has given a central place to intellectual or philosophical revolution in his philosophy. According to Roy, a philosophical revolution must precede a social revolution.

Besides, Roy has, in the tradition of eighteenth century French materialist Holbach, revised and restated materialism in the light of twentieth century scientific developments. If we wish to place Roy's philosophy in the context of ancient Indian philosophy, we may place Roy in the tradition of the ancient Indian materialism, Lokayata or Charvaka. However, compared to the ancient doctrines of Lokayata, Roy's "physical realism" is a highly developed philosophy. Roy not only takes into account the then contemporary discoveries of physics in reformulating "materialism" as "physical realism", but also gives an important place to ethics in his philosophy. Moreover, Roy's philosophy has an important social and political component, which is based on his criticism of communism and "formal" parliamentary democracy. Roy called this "new philosophy of revolution", which he developed in the later part of his life, "new humanism" or "radicalism". The essence of the philosophy of new humanism is contained in Roy's "Theses on the principles of Radical Democracy" or the "Twenty-two Theses of Radical Humanism". Roy further elaborated this philosophy in his New Humanism - A Manifesto, first published in 1947.

M.N.Roy was not inclined to write his autobiography. However, after much persuasion he started writing his Memoirs in the last part of his life. Sadly, he was not able to complete it. This incomplete autobiography covers only a period of seven years from 1915 to 1922. This brief life-sketch of M. N. Roy is based mainly on V.B. Karnik's M.N. Roy, Sibnarayan Ray's introduction to Selected Works of M.N. Roy (vol. 1) and V.M. Tarkunde's Radical Humanism. I have also derived some help from Essence of Royism, compiled by G.D. Parikh, and M.N. Roy Philosopher Revolutionary, edited by Sibnarayan Ray. Besides, I have also drawn heavily from my own book M.N. Roy's New Humanism and Materialism for writing this chapter.

M.N. Roy, whose original name was Narendra Nath Bhattacharya, was born on 21 March 1887, at Arbalia, a village in 24 Parganas district in Bengal. His father, Dinabandhu Bhattacharya, was head pandit of a local school. His mother's name was Basanta Kumari. From school going age, Roy lived in Kodalia, another village in 24 Parganas.

Militant Nationalist Phase: In Search of Arms

Roy began his political career as a militant nationalist at the age of 14, when he was a school student. He joined an underground organization called Anushilan Samiti, and when it was banned, he helped in organizing Jugantar Group under the leadership of Jatin Mukherji. In course of his underground work, he was involved in many political dacoities and conspiracy cases. In 1915, after the beginning of the First World War, Roy left India for Java in search of arms for organizing an armed insurrection for overthrow of British rule in India. However, the plan failed and Roy went a second time to Java for the same purpose. Thereafter, he moved from country to country, with faked passports and different names, in his attempt to secure German arms. Finally, after wandering through Malay, Indonesia, Indo-China, Philippines, Japan, Korea and China, in June 1916, he landed at San Francisco in United States of America.

Roy's attempts to secure arms ended in a failure. In fact, Roy concluded that Germans were not serious about giving arms to the Indian revolutionaries. Besides, police repression had shattered the underground organization, which Roy had left behind. He had also come to know about the death of his leader, Jatin Mukherji, in an encounter with police.

Towards Communism

The news of Roy's arrival at San Francisco was somehow published in a local daily, forcing Roy to flee to Pao Alto, the seat of Stanford University. It was here that Roy, until then known as Narendra Nath Bhattacharya or Naren, changed his name to Manbendra Nath Roy. This change of name on the campus of Stanford University was like a new birth for Roy. As stated by him in his Memoirs, it enabled him to turn his back on a futile past and look forward to a new life of adventures and achievements. Roy's host at Pao Alto introduced him to Evelyn Trent, a graduate student at Stanford University. Evelyn Trent, who later married Roy, became his political collaborator. She accompanied him to Mexico and Russia and was of great help to him in his political and literary work. The collaboration continued until they separated in 1929.

At New York, where he went from Pao Alto, Roy met Lala Lajpat Rai, the well-known nationalist leader of India. He developed friendships with several American radicals, and frequented the New York Public Library. Roy also went to public meetings with Lajpat Rai. Questions asked by the working class audience in these meetings made Roy wonder whether exploitation and poverty would cease in India with the attainment of independence. Roy began a systematic study of socialism, originally with the intention of combating it, but he soon discovered that he had himself become a socialist! In the beginning, nurtured as he was on Bankimchandra, Vivekanand and orthodox Hindu philosophy, Roy accepted socialism "except its materialist philosophy". Later in Mexico in 1919, Roy met Michael Borodin, an emissary of the Communist International. Roy and Borodin quickly became friends, and it was because of long discussions with Borodin that Roy accepted the materialist philosophy and became a full-fledged communist. Roy was also instrumental in converting the Socialist Party of Mexico into the Communist Party of Mexico. In 1920, Roy was invited to Moscow to attend the second conference of the Communist International. Roy had several meetings with Lenin before the Conference. He differed with Lenin on the role of the local bourgeoisie in nationalist movements. On Lenin's recommendation, the supplementary thesis on the subject prepared by Roy was adopted along with Lenin's thesis by the second conference of the Communist International. The following years witnessed Roy's rapid rise in the international communist hierarchy. By the end of 1926, Roy was elected member of all the four official policy making bodies of the Comintern - the presidium, the political secretariat, the executive committee and the world congress. In 1927, Roy was sent to China as a representative of the Communist International. However, Roy's mission in China ended in a failure. On his return to Moscow from China, Roy found himself in official disfavor. In September 1929 he was expelled from the Communist International for "contributing to the Brandler press and supporting the Brandler organizations, ...". Roy felt that he was expelled from the Comintern mainly because of his "claim to the right of independent thinking."

Return to India: Prison Years

Roy returned to India in December 1930. He was arrested in July 1931 and tried for his role in the Kanpur Communist Conspiracy Case. He was sentenced to six years imprisonment. When Roy returned to India, he was still a full-fledged communist, though he had broken from the Comintern. The forced confinement in jail gave him more time than before for systematic study and reflection. His friends in Germany, especially his future wife, Ellen Gottschalk, kept providing him books, which he wanted. His letters to her from jail, published subsequently as Letters from Jail (1943), contains pointers to his reading and thinking during those years. Roy's had planned to use his prison years for writing a systematic study of 'the philosophical consequences of modern science', which would be in a way a re-examination and re-formulation of Marxism to which he had been committed since 1919. The reflections, which Roy wrote down in jail, grew over a period of five years into nine thick volumes (approximately over 3000 lined foolscap-size pages). The 'Prison Manuscripts' have not so far been published in their totality, and are currently preserved in the Nehru Memorial Museum and Library Archives in New Delhi. However, selected portions from the manuscript were published as separate books in the 1930s and the 1940s Materialism (1940), Science and Superstition (1940), Heresies of the 20th Century (1939), Fascism (1938), The Historical Role of Islam (1939), Ideal Of Indian Womanhood (1941), Science and Philosophy (1947) and India's Message (1950) are among the books that were made from these handwritten notebooks. These writings show that Roy was not satisfied with a primarily economic explanation of historical processes. He studied and tried to assess the role of cultural and ideational factors in traditional and contemporary India, in the rise and expansion of Islam, and in the phenomenon of fascism. He was particularly severe on the obscurantist professions and practices of neo-Hindu nationalism. Roy tried to reformulate materialism in the light of latest developments in the physical and biological sciences. He was convinced that without the growth and development of a materialist and rationalist outlook in India, neither a renaissance nor a democratic revolution would be possible. In a way, seeds of the philosophy of new humanism, which was later developed fully by Roy, were already evident in his jail writings.

Towards New Humanism

Immediately after his release from jail on 20 November 1936, Roy joined Indian National Congress along with his followers. He organized his followers into a body called League of Radical Congressmen. However, in December 1940, Roy and his followers left Congress owing to differences with the Congress leadership on the role of India in the Second World War. Thereafter, Roy formed the Radical Democratic Party of his own. This signaled the beginning of the last phase of Roy's life in which he developed his philosophy of new humanism. After Roy's release from jail in 1936, Ellen Gottschalk joined Roy in Bombay in March 1937. They were married in the same month. Subsequently, Ellen Roy played an important role in Roy's life, and cooperated in all his endeavors. In 1944, Roy published two basic documents, namely, People's Plan for Economic Development of India and Draft Constitution of Free India. According to V.M. Tarkunde, who played a role in drafting 'People's Plan', these "documents contained Roy's original contributions to the solution of country's economic and political problems". The Indian state, according to the draft constitution, was to be organized on the basis of countrywide network of people's committees having wide powers such as initiating legislations, expressing opinion on pending bills, recall of representatives and referendum on important national issues. According to Sibnarayan Ray, another prominent associate of Roy, "the Plan and the Constitution anticipated several of the principles which were to be formulated and developed as Radical Humanism in 1949 and the subsequent years".

Beyond Communism: Theses on Radical Humanism

Roy prepared a draft of Basic principles of Radical Democracy before the All India Conference of Radical Democratic Party held in Bombay in December 1946. The draft, in which basic ideas were put in the form of theses, was circulated among a small number of selected friends and associates of Roy including Laxman Shastri Joshi, Philip Spratt, V.M. Tarkunde, Sibnarayan Ray, G.D. Parikh, G.R. Dalvi and Ellen Roy. The "22 Theses" or "Principles of Radical Democracy", which emerged as a result of intense discussions between Roy and his circle of friends, were adopted at the Bombay Conference of the Radical Democratic Party. Roy's speeches at the conference in connection with the 22 Theses were published later under the title Beyond Communism.

In 1947, Roy published New Humanism - A Manifesto, which offered an elaboration of the 22 Theses. The draft of the manifesto was prepared by Roy, but, as Roy himself says, in the preface of New Humanism, he derived help from valuable suggestions of Philip Spratt, Sikander Choudhary and V.M.Tarkunde in improving his draft. The ideas expressed in the manifesto were, according to Roy, "developed over a period of number of years by a group of critical Marxists and former Communists." Further discussions on the 22 Theses and the manifesto led Roy to the conclusion that party-politics was inconsistent with his ideal of organized democracy. This resulted in the dissolution of the Radical Democratic Party in December 1948 and launching of a movement called the Radical Humanist Movement. At the Calcutta Conference, itself where the party was dissolved, theses 19 and 20 were amended to delete all references to party. The last three paragraphs of the manifesto were also modified accordingly. Thus, the revised versions of the 22 Theses and the manifesto constitute the essence of Roy's New Humanism.

Indian Renaissance Institute

In 1946, Roy established Indian Renaissance Institute at Dehradun. Roy was the founder-director of the Institute. In a statement prepared in 1952, Roy described the Institute as "a cultural-educational organization founded with the object of re-educating the educators and young intellectuals of India in spirit and with the ideas of Radical (or Integral) Humanism." Since 1937, Roy was editing a new weekly named Independent India. In 1949, Independent India weekly changed to The Radical Humanist weekly. The name of another quarterly journal The Marxian Way, which Roy had been publishing since 1945 in collaboration with Sudhindranath Datta, was changed to The Humanist Way in the same year.

Reason, Romanticism and Revolution

In 1948, Roy started working on his last major intellectual project. Roy's magnum opus Reason, Romanticism and Revolution is a monumental work (638 pages). The fully written, revised and typed press copy of the book was ready in April 1952. It attempted to combine a historical survey of western thought with an elaboration of his own system of ideas. As Roy says in the preface of the book: "On the basis of a humanist interpretation of cultural history, this work endeavors to outline a comprehensive philosophy which links up social and political practice with a scientific metaphysics of rationality and ethics."

International Humanist and Ethical Union

While working on Reason, Romanticism and Revolution, Roy had established contacts with several humanist groups in Europe and America, which had views similar to his own. The idea gradually evolved of these groups coming together and constituting an international association with commonly shared aims and principles. The inaugural congress of the International Humanist and Ethical Union (IHEU) was planned to be organized in Amsterdam in 1952, and Roys were expected to play an influential role in the congress and in the development of the IHEU. However, before going abroad, Roy needed some rest. He along with Ellen Roy went up for a few days from Dehradun to the hill station of Mussoorie. On June 11 1952, Roy met a serious accident. He fell fifty feet down while walking along a hill track. He was moved to Dehradun for treatment. On 25 August, he had an attack of cerebral thrombosis resulting in a partial paralysis of the right side. The accident prevented the Roys from attending the inaugural congress of the IHEU, which was held in August 1952 at Amsterdam. The congress, however, elected M.N. Roy, in absentia, as one of its vice-presidents and made the Indian Radical Humanist Movement one of the founder-members of the IHEU. On 15 August 1953, Roy had the second attack of cerebral thrombosis, which paralyzed the left side of his body. Roy's last article dictated to Ellen Roy for the Radical Humanist was about the nature and organization of the Radical Humanist Movement. This article was published in the Radical Humanist on 24 January 1954. On 25 January 1954, ten minutes before midnight, M.N. Roy died of a heart attack. He was nearly 67 at that time.

Publications

Roy was a prolific writer. He wrote many books, edited, and contributed to several journals. The Oxford University Press has published four volumes of Selected Works of M.N. Roy, edited by Sibnarayan Ray. We have already mentioned some of his works related to the final humanist phase of his life. Of these Materialism, Science and Philosophy, New Humanism and Reason, Romanticism and Revolution are of special interest to us.

Roy's Conception of Philosophy

Roy has discussed the nature of philosophy and its relationship with religion and science in his books Materialism and Science and Philosophy. "Philosophy", says Roy, quoting Pythagoras, in his book Materialism, is "contemplation, study and knowledge of the nature". Its function is "to know things as they are, and to find the common origin of the diverse phenomena of nature, in nature itself". "Philosophy", according to Roy, "begins when man's spiritual needs are no longer satisfied by primitive natural religion which imagines and worships a variety of gods as personification of the diverse phenomena of nature. The grown-up man discredits the nursery-tales, with which he was impressed in his spiritual childhood ... Intellectual growth impels and emboldens him to seek in nature itself the causes of all natural phenomena; to find in nature a unity behind its diversity." In his book Science and Philosophy, Roy defines philosophy as "the theory of life". The function of philosophy, in words of Roy, "is to solve the riddle of the Universe". Elaborating on his definition of philosophy, Roy says: Philosophy is the theory of life, because it was born of the efforts of man to explain nature and to understand his own being in relation to its surroundings; to solve the actual problems of life in the light of past experiences, so that the solution will give him an encouraging glimpse into the future.

Philosophy and Metaphysics

Roy has made a distinction between philosophy and metaphysics. According to him, metaphysics, too, begins with the desire to discover unity behind the diversity. But it leaves the ground of Philosophy in quest of a noumenon above and beyond nature, something which is distinct from phenomena. Thus it abandons the inquiry into what really exists with the object of acquiring knowledge about it, and plunges into the wilderness of speculation. It takes up the absurd task of knowing the intangible as the condition for the knowledge of the tangible. It is obvious that Roy was opposed to speculative philosophy, which set for itself the impossible task of prying into the transcendental being "above and behind" the physical universe - of acquiring the knowledge of the reality behind the appearance. In words of Roy: Speculative philosophy is the attempt to explain the concrete realities of existence in the light of a hypothetical absolute. It is the way not to truth, but to dream; not to knowledge but to illusion. Instead of trying to understand the world, the only reality given to man, speculative philosophy ends in denying of the existence of the only reality and declaring it to be a figment of man's imagination. An inquiry which denies the very existence of the object to be enquired, is bound to end in idle dreams and hopeless confusion.

Philosophy and Religion

Roy is opposed not only to speculative philosophy but also to the identification of philosophy with theology and religion. As he says in Science and Philosophy:

For the average educated man, the term philosophy has a very vague meaning, but sweeping application; it stands not only for speculative thought, but also for poetic fancy. In India, particularly, this vague, all-embracing sense is generally prevalent. Philosophy is not distinguished from religion and theology. Indeed, what is believed to be the distinctive feature of Indian philosophy is that it has not broken away from the medieval tradition, as modern western philosophy did in the seventeenth century. According to Roy, "Faith in the supernatural does not permit the search for the causes of natural phenomena in nature itself. Therefore, rejection of orthodox religious ideas and theological dogmas is the condition for philosophy." "With the assumption that the phenomena of nature are determined by the will of some supernatural being or beings," says Roy, "philosophy must make room for faith." What is supernatural, points out Roy, must be always beyond the understanding of man, who is himself a product of nature, and is, therefore, limited by the laws of nature. In this way, according to Roy, "as soon as the cause of the phenomenal world is thus placed beyond the realm of human knowledge, the world itself becomes incomprehensible." Roy is of the view that, "religion is bound to be liquidated by science, because scientific knowledge enables mankind to answer questions, confronted by which in its childhood, it was compelled to assume super-natural forces or agencies." Therefore, according to Roy, in order to perform its function, "philosophy must break away from religion" and start from the reality of the physical universe.

Philosophy and Science

On the one hand, Roy regards rejection of orthodox religious ideas and theological dogmas as the essential condition of philosophy, and on the other, he envisages a very intimate relationship between philosophy and science. In fact, according to Roy, the philosophical significance of modern scientific theory is to "render the old division of labor between science and philosophy untenable." Science is, says Roy, "stepping over the old boundary line. Digging deeper and deeper into the secrets of nature, science has come up against problems the solution of which was previously left to philosophy. Scientific inquiry has pushed into what is traditionally regarded as the 'metaphysical' realm." The problems of philosophy - cosmological, ontological and epistemological - can all be progressively solved, according to Roy, in the light of scientific knowledge. The function of philosophy is, points out Roy, to explain existence as a whole. An explanation of existence requires knowledge of existence, knowledge about the different phases of existence is gathered by the various branches of science. Therefore, in words of Roy: The function of philosophy is to coordinate the entire body of scientific knowledge into a comprehensive theory of nature and life.

Even in his Scientific Politics, which is more in the nature of a popular lecture than a philosophical treatise, Roy says, "having thus yielded position to science, philosophy can now exist only as the science of sciences - a systematic coordination, a synthesis of all positive knowledge, continuously readjusting itself to progressive enlargement of the store of human knowledge." Such a philosophy, according to Roy, has "nothing in common with what is traditionally known, particularly in this country, as philosophy. A mystic metaphysical conception of the world is no longer to be accorded the distinction of philosophy."

In Reason, Romanticism and Revolution, too, Roy repeats his conception of philosophy as a logical coordination of all the branches of positive knowledge in a system of thought to explain the world rationally and to serve as a reliable guide for life. Thus, Roy has given a secular and modern definition of philosophy. We have noted in the preface that in twentieth century the academic Indian philosophy, as taught and studied in Indian universities, has been dominated by Hindu religion, particularly advaita vedanta, in one way or another. This has been largely owing to the pervasive influence of S. Radhakrishnan. At least in twenty-first century, Indian "philosophy" must make a clean break from religion, and stop projecting "religion" as "philosophy". Otherwise, the future of "Indian philosophy" will remain bleak. Roy needs to be commended for making a clear distinction between philosophy and religion.

Roy's Materialism or Physical Realism

M.N. Roy was a strong supporter of materialist philosophy. In his book Materialism, Roy says: Strictly speaking, philosophy is materialism, and materialism is the only possible philosophy. For, it represents the knowledge of nature as it really exists - knowledge acquired through the contemplation, observation and investigation of the phenomena of nature itself.

According to Roy, materialism is not the monstrosity it is generally supposed to be. It is not the cult of "eat, drink and be merry", as it has been depicted by its ignorant or malicious adversaries. It simply maintains that "the origin of everything that really exits is matter, that there does not exist anything but matter, all other appearances being transformation of matter, and these transformations are governed necessarily by laws inherent in nature." Thus, broadly speaking, Roy's philosophy is in the tradition of materialism. However, there are some important differences between Roy's materialism and traditional materialism. In fact, Roy's "materialism" is a restatement of traditional materialism in the light of then contemporary scientific knowledge.

As Roy says: The substratum of the Universe is not matter as traditionally conceived: but it is physical as against mental or spiritual. It is a measurable entity. Therefore, to obviate prejudiced criticism, the philosophy hitherto called materialism may be renamed Physical Realism. (emphasis mine)

Restatement of Traditional Materialism

According to Roy, "materialism must be dissociated from certain notions which have been rendered untenable by the latest discoveries of science." Roy's revision and restatement of materialism embraces both the basic tenets of materialism. He has revised the concept of matter as well as that of physical determinism.

Change in the Concept of Matter

According to Roy, the discoveries of quantum physics have "made the classical notion of matter untenable". Nevertheless, Roy insists that though the substratum of the universe is "not matter as traditionally conceived" it is "physical as against mental or spiritual. It is a measurable entity". The so-called "crisis" of materialism, according to Roy, involved the conception of matter, and not its existence. The "crisis" simply exposed the inadequacy of the old atomist theory. The substance of the "crisis" was, in words of Roy, "that it appeared to reduce matter from mass to energy and radiation". However, emphasizes Roy, there cannot be any doubt about the fact that "atomic physics deals with material realities which exist objectively, outside the mind of the physicist." (emphasis mine)

Thus, in Roy's physical realism "matter" is not made up of hard and massy stone-like atoms as in traditional "mechanical materialism". The whole concept of "matter" has been revised in the light of new physics. In fact, Roy was even ready to discard the term "matter" provided a more appropriate new term could be coined. In Science and Philosophy, Roy describes "matter" as the "sole-existence". According to Roy, it is not very important what name is attached to the "substratum of existence" - matter, energy, action, vibratory motion or field. But he insists that it is a physical reality. What Roy means by calling it physical is that it exists objectively and that it is measurable. As we have seen, Roy has even renamed his revised version of materialism as "physical realism".

Revision of Physical Determinism in light of Heisenberg's Principle

Roy disagrees with the view of some thinkers that Heisenberg's Principle of Uncertainty necessitates the rejection of the doctrine of determinism. According to Roy, only a modification in the traditional conception of causality is required. Causality, in Roy's view, is not an a priori form of thought or an axiomatic law; it is physical relation inherent in the constitution of the universe.

Roy, in fact, tries to temper rigidly mechanical view of determinism by interpreting it in terms of probability. He admits plurality of possibilities and the element of contingency in the world, and tries to show that determinism and probability are not mutually exclusive. However, Roy insists that statistical methods presuppose determinism. The universe is a law-governed system, and the existence of law presupposes causality. He is emphatic that the element of uncertainty in the sub-atomic world is not to be equated with indeterminacy. Rejection of the idea that there are invariant relations in nature, maintains Roy, will blast the very foundation of science.

"Soft" Determinism

Roy also tries to reconcile freedom of will with determinism. According to him, human beings possess free will and can choose out of various alternatives in front of them. Roy, however, is not unique among materialists in recognizing free will. Epicures, among ancient Greek materialists, and Hobbes, among modern materialists, tried to accommodate free will in their philosophies. According to Roy, the vast world of biological evolution lies between the world of human beings and the world of inanimate matter, and, therefore, the world of human beings has its own specific laws, though these laws can be referred back to the general laws of the world of dead matter. Nevertheless, human will, says Roy, cannot be directly related to the laws of physical universe. Thus, Roy is not, to use the terminology of William James, a "hard" determinist like Holbach, but a "soft" determinist like Hobbes.

Objective Reality of Ideas and the Autonomy of the Mental World

Though Roy traces the origin of mental activities to the physical background of the living world, yet he also grants them an objective existence of their own. "Mind and matter", according to Roy, "can be reduced to a common denominator; as such, they are two objective realities." In Roy's view, once formed, ideas exist by themselves, governed by their own laws. Thus, Roy grants much more objectivity and autonomy to the mental world than has been traditionally granted by materialists. Roy's materialism is not an "extreme" materialism like that of the eighteenth century French materialist, Julien de la Mettrie, who regarded man to be a self-moving machine. According to Roy, on the other hand, "Man is not a living machine, but a thinking animal".

Emphasis on Ethics

Roy has given a very important place to ethics in his philosophy. According to Roy, "the greatest defect of classical materialism was that its cosmology did not seem to have any connection with ethics". Roy strongly asserts that if it is not shown that materialist philosophy can accommodate ethics, then, human spirit, thirsting for freedom, will spurn materialism. In Roy' view materialist ethics is not only possible but materialist morality is the noblest form of morality. Roy links morality with human being's innate rationality. Man is moral, according to Roy, because he is rational. In Roy's ethics freedom, which he links with the struggle of existence is the highest value. Search for truth is a corollary to the quest for freedom.

However, Roy is not unique among materialists in emphasizing the importance of ethics in his philosophy. Contrary to popular impression, ancient materialist Epicures and modern materialist Holbach, for example, accorded an important place to ethics in their philosophies. However, the details of Roy's ethics are somewhat different from these philosophies.

Roy's Physical Realism and Marxian Materialism

Roy, before he formulated and expounded his own philosophy of New Humanism, was an orthodox Marxist. In fact, Roy's revision of materialism was carried out in the context of Marxism. Thus, Roy's revision of materialism in general is also applicable to Marxian materialism to the extent Marxian materialism resembles traditional materialism. Roy's Physical Realism is, however, different from Marxian materialism in particular in three important ways. Firstly, Roy considers the Hegelian heritage a weak spot of Marxism. The simplicity and scientific soundness of materialism are marred, in Roy's view, by making its validity conditional upon dialectic. According to Roy, materialism pure, and simple, can stand on its own legs, and, therefore, he tries to de link dialectics from materialism. The validity of materialism, maintains Roy, is in no way conditional on dialectics, as there is no logical connection between the two.

Secondly, Roy rejects historical materialism and advocates a humanist interpretation of history in which he gives an important place to human will as a determining factor in history, and he recognizes the autonomy of the mental world. According to Roy, human will cannot be directly related to the laws of physical universe. Ideas, too, have an objective existence, and are governed by their own laws. The economic interpretation of history, in Roy's view is deduced from a wrong interpretation of materialism.

Thirdly, Roy's materialism is sharply different from Marxian materialism in so far it recognizes the importance of ethics and gives a prominent place to it. According to Roy, Marxian materialism wrongly disowns the humanist tradition and thereby divorces materialism from ethics. The contention that "from the scientific point of view this appeal to morality and justice does not help us an inch farther" was based, according to Roy, upon a false notion of science.

CHAPTER

8 GREEK POLITICAL THOUGHT

PLATO

Plato developed such distinct areas of philosophy as epistemology, metaphysics, ethics, and aesthetics. His deep influence on Western philosophy is asserted in the famous remark of Alfred North Whitehead: "the safest characterization of the European philosophical tradition is that it consists of a series of footnotes to Plato." He was also the prototypical political philosopher whose ideas had a profound impact on subsequent political theory. His greatest impact was Aristotle, but he influenced Western political thought in many ways. The Academy, the school he founded in 385 B.C.E., became the model for other schools of higher learning and later for European universities. The philosophy of Plato is marked by the usage of dialectic, a method of discussion involving ever more profound insights into the nature of reality, and by cognitive optimism, a belief in the capacity of the human mind to attain the truth and to use this truth for the rational and virtuous ordering of human affairs. Plato believes that conflicting interests of different parts of society can be harmonized. The best, rational and righteous, political order, which he proposes, leads to a harmonious unity of society and allows each of its parts to flourish, but not at the expense of others. The theoretical design and practical implementation of such order, he argues, are impossible without virtue.

FROM POLITICS TO PHILOSOPHY

Plato was born in Athens in c. 427 B.C.E. Until his mid-twenties, Athens was involved in a long and disastrous military conflict with Sparta, known as the Peloponnesian War. Coming from a distinguished family-on his father's side descending from Codrus, one of the early kings of Athens, and on his mother's side from Solon, the prominent reformer of the Athenian constitution-he was naturally destined to take an active role in political life. But this never happened.

Although cherishing the hope of assuming a significant place in his political community, he found himself continually thwarted. As he relates in his autobiographical Seventh Letter, he could not identify himself with any of the contending political parties or the succession of corrupt regimes, each of which brought Athens to further decline. He was a pupil of Socrates, whom he considered the most just man of his time, and who, although did not leave any writings behind, exerted a large influence on philosophy. It was Socrates who, in Cicero's words, "called down philosophy from the skies." The pre-Socratic philosophers were mostly interested in cosmology and ontology; Socrates' concerns, in contrast, were almost exclusively moral and political issues. In 399 when a democratic court voted by a large majority of its five hundred and one jurors for Socrates' execution on an unjust charge of impiety, Plato came to the conclusion that all existing governments were bad and almost beyond redemption. "The human race will have no respite from evils until those who are really philosophers acquire political power or until, through some divine dispensation, those who rule and have political authority in the cities become real philosophers."

It was perhaps because of this opinion that he retreated to his Academy and to Sicily for implementing his ideas. He visited Syracuse first in 387, then in 367, and again in 362-361, with the general purpose to moderate the Sicilian tyrants with philosophical education and to establish a model political rule. But this adventure with practical politics ended in failure, and Plato went back to Athens. His Academy, which provided a base for succeeding generations of Platonic philosophers until its final closure in C.E. 529, became the most famous teaching institution of the Hellenistic world. Mathematics, rhetoric, astronomy, dialectics, and other subjects, all seen as necessary for the education of philosophers and statesmen, were studied there.

Some of Plato's pupils later became leaders, mentors, and constitutional advisers in Greek city-states. His most renowned pupil was Aristotle. Plato died in c. 347 B.C.E. During his lifetime, Athens turned away from her military and imperial ambitions and became the intellectual centre of Greece. She gave host to all the four major Greek philosophical schools founded in the course of the fourth century: Plato's Academy, Aristotle's Lyceum, and the Epicurean and Stoic schools.

THE THREEFOLD TASK OF POLITICAL PHILOSOPHY

Although the Republic, the Statesman, the Laws and a few shorter dialogues are considered to be the only strictly political dialogues of Plato, it can be argued that political philosophy was the area of his greatest concern. In the English-speaking world, under the influence of twentieth century analytic philosophy, the main task of political philosophy today is still often seen as conceptual analysis: the clarification of political concepts. To understand what this means, it may be useful to think of concepts as the uses of words.

When we use general words, such as "table," "chair," "pen," or political terms, such as "state," "power," "democracy," or "freedom," by applying them to different things, we understand them in a certain way, and hence assign to them certain meanings. Conceptual analysis then is a mental clearance, the clarification of a concept in its meaning. As such it has a long tradition and is first introduced in Platonic dialogues.

Although the results are mostly inconclusive, in "early" dialogues especially, Socrates tries to define and clarify various concepts. However, in contrast to what it is for some analytic philosophers, for Plato conceptual analysis is not an end to itself, but a preliminary step. The next step is critical evaluation of beliefs, deciding which one of the incompatible ideas is correct and which one is wrong. For Plato, making decisions about the right political order are, along with the choice between peace and war, the most important choices one can make in politics. Such decisions cannot be left solely to public opinion, he believes, which in many cases does not have enough foresight and gets its lessons only post factum from disasters recorded in history.

In his political philosophy, the clarification of concepts is thus a preliminary step in evaluating beliefs, and right beliefs in turn lead to an answer to the question of the best political order. The movement from conceptual analysis, through evaluation of beliefs, to the best political order can clearly be seen in the structure of Plato's Republic.

THE QUEST FOR JUSTICE IN THE REPUBLIC

One of the most fundamental ethical and political concepts is justice. It is a complex and ambiguous concept. It may refer to individual virtue, the order of society, as well as individual rights in contrast to the claims of the general social order. In Book I of the Republic, Socrates and his interlocutors discuss the meaning of justice. Four definitions that report how the word "justice" (dikaiosune) is actually used, are offered. The old man of means Cephalus suggests the first definition. Justice is "speaking the truth and repaying what one has borrowed." Yet this definition, which is based on traditional moral custom and relates justice to honesty and goodness; i.e. paying one's debts, speaking the truth, loving one's country, having good manners, showing proper respect for the gods, and so on, is found to be inadequate. It cannot withstand the challenge of new times and the power of critical thinking.

Socrates refutes it by presenting a counterexample. If we tacitly agree that justice is related to goodness, to return a weapon that was borrowed from someone who, although once sane, has turned into a madman does not seem to be just but involves a danger of harm to both sides. Cephalus' son Polemarchus, who continues the discussion after his father leaves to offer a sacrifice, gives his opinion that the poet Simonides was correct in saying that it was just "to render to each his due." He explains this statement by defining justice as "treating friends well and enemies badly." Under the pressure of Socrates' objections that one may be mistaken in judging others and thus harm good people, Polemarchus modifies his definition to say that justice is "to treat well a friend who is good and to harm an enemy who is bad."

However, when Socrates finally objects that it cannot be just to harm anyone, because justice cannot produce injustice, Polemarchus is completely confused. He agrees with Socrates that justice, which both sides tacitly agree relates to goodness, cannot produce any harm, which can only be caused by injustice. Like his father, he withdraws from the dialogue. The careful reader will note that Socrates does not reject the definition of justice implied in the saying of Simonides, who is called a wise man, namely, that "justice is rendering to each what befits him," but only its explication given by Polemarchus. This definition is, nevertheless, found unclear. The first part of Book I of the Republic ends in a negative way, with parties agreeing that none of the definitions provided stands up to examination and that the original question "What is justice?" is more difficult to answer than it seemed to be at the outset. This negative outcome can be seen as a linguistic and philosophical therapy. Firstly, although Socrates' objections to given definitions can be challenged, it is shown, as it stands, that popular opinions about justice involve inconsistencies. They are inconsistent with other opinions held to be true. The reportive definitions based on everyday usage of the word "justice" help us perhaps to understand partially what justice means, but fail to provide a complete account of what is justice.

These definitions have to be supplied by a definition that will assist clarity and establish the meaning of justice. However, to propose such an adequate definition one has to know what justice really is. The way people define a given word is largely determined by the beliefs which they hold about the thing referred to by this word. A definition that is merely arbitrary or either too narrow or too broad, based on a false belief about justice, does not give the possibility of communication. Platonic dialogues are expressions of the ultimate communication that can take place between humans; and true communication is likely to take place only if individuals can share meanings of the words they use.

Communication based on false beliefs, such as statements of ideology, is still possible, but seems limited, dividing people into factions, and, as history teaches us, can finally lead only to confusion. The definition of justice as "treating friends well and enemies badly" is for Plato not only inadequate because it is too narrow, but also wrong because it is based on a mistaken belief of what justice is, namely, on the belief grounded in factionalism, which Socrates does not associate with the wise ones but with tyrants. Therefore, in the Republic, as well as in other Platonic dialogues, there is a relationship between conceptual analysis and critical evaluation of beliefs. The goals of these conversations are not merely linguistic, to arrive at an adequate verbal definition, but also substantial, to arrive at a right belief.

The question "what is justice" is not only about linguistic usage of the word "justice," but primarily about the thing to which the word refers. The focus of the second part of Book I is no longer clarification of concepts, but evaluation of beliefs. In Platonic dialogues, rather than telling them what they have to think, Socrates is often getting his interlocutors to tell him what they think. The next stage of the discussion of the meaning of justice is taken over by Thrasymachus, a sophist, who violently and impatiently bursts into the dialogue. In the fifth and fourth century B.C.E., the sophists were paid teachers of rhetoric and other practical skills, mostly non-Athenians, offering courses of instruction and claiming to be best qualified to prepare young men for success in public life. Plato describes the sophists as itinerant individuals, known for their rhetorical abilities, who reject religious beliefs and traditional morality, and he contrasts them with Socrates, who as a teacher would refuse to accept payment and instead of teaching skills would commit himself to a disinterested inquiry into what is true and just. In a contemptuous manner, Thrasymachus asks Socrates to stop talking nonsense and look into the facts.

As a clever man of affairs, he gives an answer to the question of "what is justice" by deriving justice from the city's configuration of power and making it relative to the interests of the dominant social or political group. "Justice is nothing else than the interest of the stronger." Now, by contrast to what some commentators say, the statement that Thrasymachus offers as an answer to Socrates' question about justice is not a definition. The careful reader will notice that Thrasymachus identifies justice with either maintenance or observance of law. His statement is an expression of his belief that, in the world imperfect as it is, the ruling element in the city, or as we would say today the dominant political or social group, institutes laws and governs for its own benefit. The democrats make laws in support of democracy; the aristocrats make laws that support the government of the well-born; the propertied make laws that protect their status and keep their businesses going; and so on.

This belief implies, firstly, that justice is not a universal moral value but a notion relative to expediency of the dominant status quo group; secondly, that justice is in the exclusive interest of the dominant group; thirdly, that justice is used as a means of oppression and thus is harmful to the powerless; fourthly, that there is neither any common good nor harmony of interests between those who are in a position of power and those who are not. All there is, is a domination by the powerful and privileged over the powerless. The moral language of justice is used merely instrumentally to conceal the interests of the dominant group and to make these interests appear universal. The powerful "declare what they have made-what is to their own advantage-to be just." The arrogance with which Thrasymachus makes his statements suggests that he strongly believes that to hold a different view from his own would be to mislead oneself about the world as it is. After presenting his statement, Thrasymachus intends to leave as if he believed that what he said was so compelling that no further debate about justice was ever possible. In the Republic he exemplifies the power of a dogma. Indeed he presents Socrates with a powerful challenge.

Yet, whether or not what he said sounds attractive to anyone, Socrates is not convinced by the statement of his beliefs. Beliefs shape our lives as individuals, nations, ages, and civilizations. Should we really believe that "justice [obeying laws] is really the good of another, the advantage of the stronger and the ruler, harmful to the one who obeys, while injustice [disobeying laws] is in one's own advantage." The discussion between Socrates and his interlocutors is no longer about the meaning of "justice." It is about fundamental beliefs and "concerns no ordinary topic but the way we ought to live."

Although in Book I Socrates finally succeeds in showing Thrasymachus that his position is self-contradictory and Thrasymachus withdraws from the dialogue, perhaps not fully convinced, yet red-faced, in Book II Thrasymachus' argument is taken over by two young intellectuals, Plato's brothers, Glaucon and Adeimantus, who for the sake of curiosity and a playful intellectual exercise push it to the limit. Thrasymachus withdraws, but his statement: moral skepticism and relativism, predominance of power in human relations, and non-existence of the harmony of interests, hovers over the Western mind. It takes whole generations of thinkers to struggle with Thrasymachus' beliefs, and the debate still continues. It takes the whole remainder of the Republic to present an argument in defense of justice as a universal value and the foundation of the best political order.

THE BEST POLITICAL ORDER

Although large parts of the Republic are devoted to the description of an ideal state ruled by philosophers and its subsequent decline, the chief theme of the dialogue is justice. It is fairly clear that Plato does not introduce his fantastical political innovation, which Socrates describes as a city in speech, a model in heaven, for the purpose of practical implementation. The vision of the ideal state is used rather to illustrate the main thesis of the dialogue that justice, understood traditionally as virtue and related to goodness, is the foundation of a good political order, and as such is in everyone's interest. Justice, if rightly understood, Plato argues, is not to the exclusive advantage of any of the city's factions, but is concerned with the common good of the whole political community, and is to the advantage of everyone.

It provides the city with a sense of unity, and thus, is a basic condition for its health. "Injustice causes civil war, hatred, and fighting, while justice brings friendship and a sense of common purpose." In order to understand further what justice and political order are for Plato, it is useful to compare his political philosophy with the pre-philosophical insights of Solon, who is referred to in a few dialogues. Biographical information about Plato is fairly scarce. The fact that he was related through his mother to this famous Athenian legislator, statesman and poet, regarded as one of the "Seven Sages," may be treated as merely incidental. On the other hand, taking into consideration that in Plato's times education would have been passed on to children informally at home, it seems highly probable that Plato was not only well acquainted with the deeds and ideas of Solon, but that these deeply influenced him.

The essence of the constitutional reform which Solon made in 593 B.C.E., over one hundred and fifty years before Plato's birth, when he became the Athenian leader, was the restoration of righteous order, eunomia. In the early part of the sixth century Athens was disturbed by a great tension between two parties: the poor and the rich, and stood at the brink of a fierce civil war. On the one hand, because of an economic crisis, many poorer Athenians were hopelessly falling into debt, and since their loans were often secured by their own persons, thousands of them were put into serfdom. On the other hand, lured by easy profits from loans, the rich stood firmly in defense of private property and their ancient privileges.

The partisan strife, which seemed inevitable, would make Athens even more weak economically and defenseless before external enemies. Appointed as a mediator in this conflict, Solon enacted laws prohibiting loans on the security of the person. He lowered the rate of interest, ordered the cancellation of all debts, and gave freedom to serfs. He acted so moderately and impartially that he became unpopular with both parties. The rich felt hurt by the reform. The poor, unable to hold excess in check, demanded a complete redistribution of landed property and the dividing of it into equal shares. Nevertheless, despite these criticisms from both sides, Solon succeeded in gaining social peace. Further, by implementing new constitutional laws, he set up a "mighty shield against both parties and did not allow either to win an unjust victory."

He introduced a system of checks and balances which would not favour any side, but took into consideration legitimate interests of all social groups. In his position, he could easily have become the tyrant over the city, but he did not seek power for himself. After he completed his reform, he left Athens in order to see whether it would stand the test of time, and returned to his country only ten years later.

Even though in 561 Pisistratus seized power and became the first in a succession of Athenian tyrants, and in 461 the democratic leader Ephialtes abolished the checks upon popular sovereignty, Solon's reform provided the ancient Greeks with a model of both political leadership and order based on impartiality and fairness. Justice for Solon is not an arithmetical equality: giving equal shares to all alike irrespective of merit, which represents the democratic concept of distributive justice, but it is equity or fairness based on difference: giving shares proportionate to the merit of those who receive them. The same ideas of political order, leadership, and justice can be found in Plato's dialogues.

For Plato, like for Solon, the starting point for the inquiry about the best political order is the fact of social diversity and conflicting interests, which involve the danger of civil strife. The political community consists of different parts or social classes, such as the noble, the rich, and the poor, each representing different values, interests, and claims to rule. This gives rise to the controversy of who should rule the community, and what is the best political system. In both the Republic and the Laws, Plato asserts not only that factionalism and civil war are the greatest dangers to the city, more dangerous even than war against external enemies, but also that peace obtained by the victory of one part and the destruction of its rivals is not to be preferred to social peace obtained through the friendship and cooperation of all the city's parts. Peace for Plato is, unlike for Marxists and other radical thinkers, not a status quo notion, related to the interest of the privileged group, but a value that most people usually desire. He does not stand for war and the victory of one class, but for peace in social diversity. "The best is neither war nor faction-they are things we should pray to be spared from-but peace and mutual good will."

Building on the pre-philosophical insights of Solon and his concept of balancing conflicting interests, in both the Republic and the Laws, Plato offers two different solutions to the same problem of social peace based on the equilibrium and harmonious union of different social classes. If in the Republic it is the main function of the political leadership of philosopher-rulers to make the civil strife cease, in the Laws this mediating function is taken over by laws. The best political order for Plato is that which promotes social peace in the environment of cooperation and friendship among different social groups, each benefiting from and each adding to the common good. The best form of government, which he advances in the Republic, is a philosophical aristocracy or monarchy, but that which he proposes in his last dialogue the Laws is a traditional polity: the mixed or composite constitution that reconciles different partisan interests and includes aristocratic, oligarchic, and democratic elements.

THE GOVERNMENT OF PHILOSOPHER RULERS

It is generally believed today that democracy, "government of the people by the people and for the people," is the best and only fully justifiable political system. The distinct features of democracy are freedom and equality. Democracy can be described as the rule of the free people who govern themselves, either directly or though their representatives, in their own interest. Why does Plato not consider democracy the best form of government? In the Republic he criticizes the direct and unchecked democracy of his time precisely because of its leading features. Firstly, although freedom is for Plato a true value, democracy involves the danger of excessive freedom, of doing as one likes, which leads to anarchy. Secondly, equality, related to the belief that everyone has the right and equal capacity to rule, brings to politics all kinds of power-seeking individuals, motivated by personal gain rather than public good.

Democracy is thus highly corruptible. It opens gates to demagogues, potential dictators, and can thus lead to tyranny. Hence, although it may not be applicable to modern liberal democracies, Plato's main charge against the democracy he knows from the ancient Greek political practice is that it is unstable, leading from anarchy to tyranny, and that it lacks leaders with proper skill and morals. Democracy depends on chance and must be mixed with competent leadership. Without able and virtuous leaders, such as Solon or Pericles, who come and go by chance, it is not a good form of government. But even Pericles, who as Socrates says made people "wilder" rather than more virtuous, is considered not to be the best leader. If ruling a state is a craft, indeed statecraft, Plato argues, then politics needs expert rulers, and they cannot come to it merely by accident, but must be carefully selected and prepared in the course of extensive training. Making political decisions requires good judgment. Politics needs competence, at least in the form of today's civil servants. Who then should the experts be and why? Why does Plato in the Republic decide to hand the steering wheel of the state to philosophers?

In spite of the idealism with which he is usually associated, Plato is not politically naive. He does not idealize, but is deeply pessimistic about human beings. Most people, corrupted as they are for him fundamentally irrational, driven by their appetites, egoistic passions, and informed by false beliefs. If they choose to be just and obey laws, it is only because they lack the power to act criminally and are afraid of punishment. Nevertheless, human beings are not vicious by nature. They are social animals, incapable of living alone. Living in communities and exchanging products of their labour is natural for them, so that they have capacities for rationality and goodness. Plato, as later Rousseau, believes that once political society is properly ordered, it can contribute to the restoration of morals. A good political order, good education and upbringing can produce "good natures; and [these] useful natures, who are in turn well educated, grow up even better than their predecessors."

Hence, there are in Plato such elements of the idealistic or liberal world view as the belief in education and progress, and a hope for a better future. The quality of human life can be improved if people learn to be rational and understand that their real interests lie in harmonious cooperation with one another, and not in war or partisan strife. However, unlike Rousseau, Plato does not see the best social and political order in a democratic republic. Opinions overcome truth in everyday life. Peoples' lives and the lives of communities are shaped by the prevailing beliefs. If philosophers are those who can distinguish between true and false beliefs, who love knowledge and are motivated by the common good, and finally if they are not only master-theoreticians, but also the master-practitioners who can heal the ills of their society, then they, and not democratically elected representatives, must be chosen as leaders and educators of the political community and guide it to proper ends.

They are required to counteract the destabilizing effects of false beliefs on society. Are philosophers incorruptible? In the ideal city there are provisions to minimize possible corruption, even among the good-loving philosophers. They can neither enjoy private property nor family life. Although they are the rulers, they receive only a modest remuneration from the state, dine in common dining halls, and have wives and children in common. These provisions are necessary, Plato believes, because if the philosopher-rulers were to acquire private land, luxurious homes, and money themselves, they would soon become hostile masters of other citizens rather than their leaders and allies. The ideal city becomes a bad one, described as timocracy, precisely when the philosophers neglect music and physical exercise, and begin to gather wealth. To be sure, Plato's philosophers, among whom he includes both men and women, are not those who can usually be found today in departments of philosophy and who are described as the "prisoners who take refuge in a temple." Initially chosen from among the brightest, most stable, and most courageous children, they go through a sophisticated and prolonged educational training which begins with gymnastics, music and mathematics, and ends with dialectic, military service and practical city management. They have superior theoretical knowledge, including the knowledge of the just, noble, good and advantageous, but are not inferior to others in practical matters as well. Being in the final stage of their education illuminated by the idea of the good, they are those who can see beyond changing empirical phenomena and reflect on such timeless values as justice, beauty, truth, and moderation.

Goodness is not merely a theoretical idea for them, but the ultimate state of their mind. If the life of the philosopher-rulers is not of private property, family or wealth, nor even of honour, and if the intellectual life itself seems so attractive, why should they then agree to rule? Plato's answer is in a sense a negative one. Philosophical life, based on contemplative leisure and the pleasure of learning, is indeed better and happier than that of ruling the state. However, the underlying idea is not to make any social class in the city the victorious one and make it thus happy, but "to spread happiness throughout the city by bringing the citizens into harmony with each other... and by making them share with each other the benefits that each class can confer on the community." Plato assumes that a city in which the rulers do not govern out of desire for private gain, but are least motivated by personal ambition, is governed in the way which is the finest and freest from civil strife. Philosophers will rule not only because they will be best prepared for this, but also because if they do not, the city will no longer be well governed and may fall prey to economic decline, factionalism, and civil war. They will approach ruling not as something really enjoyable, but as something necessary.

Objections against the government of philosopher-rulers can be made. Firstly, because of the restrictions concerning family and private property, Plato is often accused of totalitarianism. However, Plato's political vision differs from a totalitarian state in a number of important aspects. Especially in the Laws he makes clear that freedom is one of the main values of society. Other values for which Plato stands include justice, friendship, wisdom, courage, and moderation, and not factionalism or terror that can be associated with a totalitarian state. The restrictions which he proposes are placed on the governors, rather than on the governed. Secondly, one can argue that there may obviously be a danger in the self-professed claim to rule of the philosophers. Individuals may imagine themselves to be best qualified to govern a country, but in fact they may lose contact with political realities and not be good leaders at all.

If philosopher-rulers did not have real knowledge of their city, they would be deprived of the essential credential that is required to make their rule legitimate, namely, that they alone know how best to govern. Indeed, at the end of Book VII of the Republic where philosophers' education is discussed, Socrates says: "I forgot that we were only playing, and so I spoke too vehemently," as if to imply that objections can be made to philosophical rule. As in a few other places in the dialogue, Plato throws his political innovation open to doubt. However, in Plato's view, philosopher-rulers do not derive their authority solely from their expert knowledge, but also from their love of the city as a whole and their impartiality and fairness. Their political authority is not only rational but also substantially moral, based on the consent of the governed. They regard justice as the most important and most essential thing. Even if particular political solutions presented in the Republic may be open to questioning, what seems to stand firm is the basic idea that underlies philosophers' governance and that can be traced back to Solon: the idea of fairness based on difference as the basis of the righteous political order. A political order based on fairness leads to friendship and cooperation among different parts of the city.

For Plato, as for Solon, government exists for the benefit of all citizens and all social classes, and must mediate between potentially conflicting interests. Such a mediating force is exercised in the ideal city of the Republic by the philosopher-rulers. They are the guarantors of the political order that is encapsulated in the norm that regulates just relations of persons and classes within the city and is expressed by the phrase: "doing one's own work and not meddling with what isn't one's own." If justice is related to equality, the notion of equality is indeed preserved in Plato's view of justice expressed by this norm as the impartial, equal treatment of all citizens and social groups. It is not the case that Plato knew that justice meant equality but made it inequality, as Karl Popper believed. In the ideal city all persons and social groups are given equal opportunities to be happy, i.e. pursue happiness, but not at the expense of others. Their particular individual, group or class happiness is limited by the need of the happiness for all.

The happiness of the whole city is not for Plato the happiness of an abstract unity called the polis, or the happiness of the greatest number, but rather the happiness of all citizens derived from a peaceful, harmonious, and cooperative union of different social classes. According to the traditional definition of justice by Simonides from Book I, which is reinterpreted in Book IV, as "doing one's own work," each social class receives its proper due in the distribution of benefits and burdens. The philosopher-rulers enjoy respect and contemplative leisure, but not wealth or honours; the guardian class, the second class in the city, military honours, but not leisure or wealth; and the producer class, family life, wealth, and freedom of enterprise, but not honours or rule.

Then, the producers supply the city with goods; the guardians, defend it; and the philosophers, attuned to virtue and illuminated by goodness, rule it impartially for the common benefit of all citizens. The three different social classes engage in mutually beneficial enterprise, by which the interests of all are best served. Social and economic differences, i.e. departures from equality, bring about benefits to people in all social positions, and therefore, are justified. In the Platonic vision of the Republic, all social classes get to perform what they are best fit to do and are unified into a single community by mutual interests. In this sense, although each are different, they are all friends.

POLITICS AND THE SOUL

It can be contended that the whole argument of the Republic is made in response to the denial of justice as a universal moral value expressed in Thrasymachus' statement: "Justice is nothing else than the interest of the stronger." Moral relativism, the denial of the harmony of interests, and other problems posed by this statement are a real challenge for Plato for whom justice is not merely a notion relative to the existing laws instituted by the victorious factions in power. In the Laws a similar statement is made again, and it is interpreted as the right of the strong, the winner in a political battle. By such interpretation, morality is denied and the right to govern, like in the "Melian Dialogue" of Thucydides, is equated simply with might. The decisions about morals and justice which we make are for Plato "no trifle, but the foremost thing."

The answer to the question of what is right and what is wrong can entirely determine our way of life, as individuals and communities. If Plato's argument about justice presented in both the Republic and the Laws can be summarized in just one sentence, the sentence will say: "Justice is neither the right of the strong nor the advantage of the stronger, but the right of the best and the advantage of the whole community." The best, as explained in the Republic, are the expert philosophical rulers. They, the wise and virtuous, free from faction and guided by the idea of the common good, should rule for the common benefit of the whole community, so that the city will not be internally divided by strife, but one in friendship. Then, in the Laws, the reign of the best individuals is replaced by the reign of the finest laws instituted by a judicious legislator.

Throughout this dialogue Plato's guiding principle is that the good society is a harmonious union of different social elements that represent two key values: wisdom and freedom. The best laws assure that all the city's parts: the democratic, the oligarchic, and the aristocratic, are represented in political institutions: the popular Assembly, the elected Council, and the Higher Council, and thus each social class receives its due expression.

Still, a democratic skeptic can feel dissatisfied with Plato's proposal to grant the right to rule to the best, either individuals or laws, even on the basis of tacit consent of the governed. The skeptic may believe that every adult is capable of exercising the power of self-direction, and should be given the opportunity to do so. He will be prepared to pay the costs of eventual mistakes and to endure an occasional civil unrest or even a limited war rather than be directed by anyone who may claim superior wisdom. Why then should Plato's best constitution be preferable to democracy? In order to fully explain the Platonic political vision, the meaning of "the best" should be further clarified.

In the short dialogue Alcibiades I, little studied today and thought by some scholars as not genuine, though held in great esteem by the Platonists of antiquity, Socrates speaks with Alcibiades.

The subject of their conversation is politics. Frequently referred to by Thucydides in the History of the Peloponnesian War, Alcibiades, the future leader of Athens, highly intelligent and ambitious, largely responsible for the Athenian invasion of Sicily, is at the time of conversation barely twenty years old. The young, handsome, and well-born Alcibiades of the dialogue is about to begin his political career and to address the Assembly for the first time. He plans to advise the Athenians on the subject of peace and war, or some other important affair. His ambitions are indeed extraordinary. He does not want just to display his worth before the people of Athens and become their leader, but to rule over Europe and Asia as well. His dreams resemble that of the future Alexander the Great.

His claim to rule is that he is the best. However, upon Socrates' scrutiny, it becomes apparent that young Alcibiades knows neither what is just, nor what is advantageous, nor what is good, nor what is noble, beyond what he has learned from the crowd. His world-view is based on unexamined opinions. He appears to be the worst type of ignorant person who pretends that he knows something but does not. Such ignorance in politics is the cause of mistakes and evils.

What is implied in the dialogue is that noble birth, beautiful looks, and even intelligence and power, without knowledge, do not give the title to rule. Ignorance, the condition of Alcibiades, is also the condition of the great majority of the people. Nevertheless, Socrates promises to guide Alcibiades, so that he becomes excellent and renowned among the Greeks. In the course of further conversation, it turns out that one who is truly the best does not only have knowledge of political things, rather than an opinion about them, but also knows one's own self and is a beautiful soul. He or she is perfect in virtue. The riches of the world can be entrusted only to those who "take trouble over" themselves, who look "toward what is divine and bright," and who following the supreme soul, God, the finest mirror of their own image, strive to be as beautiful and wealthy in their souls as possible. The best government can be founded only on beautiful and well-ordered souls.

In a few dialogues, such as Phaedo, the Republic, Phaedrus, Timaeus, and the Laws, Plato introduces his doctrine of the immortality of the soul. His ultimate answer to the question "Who am I?" is not an "egoistic animal" or an "independent variable," as the twentieth century behavioural researcher blatantly might say, but an "immortal soul, corrupted by vice and purified by virtue, of whom the body is only an instrument." Expert political knowledge for him should include not only knowledge of things out there, but also knowledge of oneself. This is because whoever is ignorant of himself will also be ignorant of others and of political things, and, therefore, will never be an expert politician. Those who are ignorant will go wrong, moving from one misery to another. For them history will be a tough teacher, but as long they do not recognize themselves and practice virtue, they will learn nothing.

Plato's good society is impossible without transcendence, without a link to the perfect being who is God, the true measure of all things. It is also impossible without an ongoing philosophical reflection on whom we truly are. Therefore, democracy would not be a good form of government for him unless, as it is proposed in the Laws, the element of freedom is mixed with the element of wisdom, which includes ultimate knowledge of the self. Unmixed and unchecked democracy, marked by the general permissiveness that spurs vices, makes people impious, and lets them forget about their true self, is only be the second worst in the rank of flawed regimes after tyranny headed by a vicious individual. This does not mean that Plato would support a theocratic government based on shallow religiosity and religious hypocrisy. There is no evidence for this. Freedom of speech, forming opinions and expressing them, which may be denied in theocracy, is a true value for Plato, along with wisdom. It is the basic requirement for philosophy. In shallow religiosity, like in atheism, there is ignorance and no knowledge of the self either. In Book II of the Republic, Plato criticizes the popular religious beliefs of the Athenians, who under the influence of Homer and Hesiod attribute vices to the gods and heroes. He tries to show that God is the perfect being, the purest and brightest, always the same, immortal and true, to whom we should look in order to know ourselves and become pure and virtuous. God, and not human beings, is the measure of political order.

PLATO'S ACHIEVEMENT

Plato's greatest achievement may be seen firstly in that he, in opposing the sophists, offered to decadent Athens, which had lost faith in her old religion, traditions, and customs, a means by which civilization and the city's health could be restored: the recovery of order in both the polis and the soul.

The best, rational and righteous political order leads to the harmonious unity of a society and allows all the city's parts to pursue happiness but not at the expense of others. The characteristics of a good political society, of which most people can say "it is mine" are described in the Republic by four virtues: justice, wisdom, moderation, and courage. Justice is the equity or fairness that grants each social group its due and ensures that each "does one's own work." The three other virtues describe qualities of different social groups. Wisdom, which can be understood as the knowledge of the whole, including both knowledge of the self and political prudence, is the quality of the leadership. Courage is not merely military courage but primarily civic courage: the ability to preserve the right, law-inspired belief, and stand in defense of such values as friendship and freedom on which a good society is founded. It is the primary quality of the guardians. Finally, moderation, a sense of the limits that bring peace and happiness to all, is the quality of all social classes. It expresses the mutual consent of both the governed and the rulers as to who should rule.

The four virtues of the good society describe also the soul of a well-ordered individual. Its rational part, whose quality is wisdom, nurtured by fine words and learning, should together with the emotional or spirited part, cultivated by music and rhythm, rule over the volitional or appetitive part. Under the leadership of the intellect, the soul must free itself from greed, lust, and other degrading vices, and direct itself to the divine. The liberation of the soul from vice is for Plato the ultimate task of humans on earth. Nobody can be wicked and happy. Only a spiritually liberated individual, whose soul is beautiful and well ordered, can experience true happiness. Only a country ordered according to the principles of virtue can claim to have the best system of government. Plato's critique of democracy may be considered by modern readers as not applicable to liberal democracy today. Liberal democracies are not only founded on considerations of freedom and equality, but also include other elements, such as the rule of law, multiparty systems, periodic elections, and a professional civil service.

Organized along the principle of separation of powers, today's Western democracy resembles more a revised version of mixed government, with a degree of moderation and competence, rather than the highly unstable and unchecked Athenian democracy of the fourth and fifth century B.C.E., in which all governmental policies were directly determined by the often changing moods of the people. However, what still seems to be relevant in Plato's political philosophy is that he reminds us of the moral and spiritual dimension of political life.

He believes that virtue is the lifeblood of any good society. Moved by extreme ambitions, the Athenians, like the mythological Atlantians described in the dialogue Critias, became infected by "wicked coveting and the pride of power."

Like the drunken Alcibiades from the Symposium, who would swap "bronze for gold" and thus prove that he did not understand the Socratic teaching, they chose the "semblance of beauty," the shining appearance of power and material wealth, rather than the "thing itself," the being of perfection. "To the seen eye they now began to seem foul, for they were losing the fairest bloom from their precious treasure, but to such who could not see the truly happy life, they would appear fair and blessed."

They were losing their virtuous souls, their virtue by which they could prove themselves to be worthy of preservation as a great nation. Racked by the selfish passions of greed and envy, they forfeited their conception of the right order. Their benevolence, the desire to do good, ceased. "Man and city are alike," Plato claims. Humans without souls are hollow. Cities without virtue are rotten. To those who cannot see clearly they may look glorious but what appears bright is only exterior. To see clearly what is visible, the political world out there, Plato argues, one has first to perceive what is invisible but intelligible, the soul. One has to know oneself. Humans are immortal souls, he claims, and not just independent variables.

They are often egoistic, but the divine element in them makes them more than mere animals. Friendship, freedom, justice, wisdom, courage, and moderation are the key values that define a good society based on virtue, which must be guarded against vice, war, and factionalism. To enjoy true happiness, humans must remain virtuous and remember God, the perfect being. Plato's achievement as a political philosopher may be seen in that he believed that there could be a body of knowledge whose attainment would make it possible to heal political problems, such as factionalism and the corruption of morals, which can bring a city to a decline. The doctrine of the harmony of interests, fairness as the basis of the best political order, the mixed constitution, the rule of law, the distinction between good and deviated forms of government, practical wisdom as the quality of good leadership, and the importance of virtue and transcendence for politics are the political ideas that can rightly be associated with Plato. They have profoundly influenced subsequent political thinkers.

ARISTOTLE

Born at Stagira in northern Greece, Aristotle was the most notable product of the educational program devised by Plato; he spent twenty years of his life studying at the Academy. When Plato died, Aristotle returned to his native Macedonia, where he is supposed to have participated in the education of Philip's son, Alexander (the Great). He came back to Athens with Alexander's approval in 335 and established his own school at the Lyceum, spending most of the rest of his life engaged there in research, teaching, and writing. His students acquired the name "peripatetics" from the master's habit of strolling about as he taught. Although the surviving works of Aristotle probably represent only a fragment of the whole, they include his investigations of an amazing range of subjects, from logic, philosophy, and ethics to physics, biology, psychology, politics, and rhetoric. Aristotle appears to have thought through his views as he wrote, returning to significant issues at different stages of his own development. The result is less a consistent system of thought than a complex record of Aristotle's thinking about many significant issues.

The aim of Aristotle's logical treatises (known collectively as the Organon) was to develop a universal method of reasoning by means of which it would be possible to learn everything there is to know about reality. Thus, the Categories proposes a scheme for the description of particular things in terms of their properties, states, and activities. On Interpretation, Prior Analytics, and Posterior Analytics examine the nature of deductive inference, outlining the system of syllogistic reasoning from true propositions that later came to be known as categorical logic. Though not strictly one of the logical works, the Physics contributes to the universal method by distinguishing among the four causes which may be used to explain everything, with special concern for why things are the way they are and the apparent role of chance in the operation of the world. In other treatises, Aristotle applied this method, with its characteristic emphasis on teleological explanation, to astronomical and biological explorations of the natural world

POLITICAL THEORY

Aristotle was a Greek philosopher, logician, and scientist. Along with his teacher Plato, Aristotle is generally regarded as one of the most influential ancient thinkers in a number of philosophical fields, including political theory. Aristotle was born in Stagira in northern Greece, and his father was a court physician to the king of Macedon. As a young man he studied in Plato's Academy in Athens. After Plato's death he left Athens to conduct philosophical and biological research in Asia Minor and Lesbos, and he was then invited by King Philip II of Macedon to tutor his young son, Alexander the Great. Soon after Alexander succeeded his father, consolidated the conquest of the Greek city-states, and launched the invasion of the Persian Empire. Aristotle returned as a resident alien to Athens, and was close friend of Antipater the Macedonian viceroy.

At this time (335-323 BC) he wrote or at least completed some of his major treatises, including the Politics. When Alexander died suddenly, Aristotle had to flee from Athens because of his Macedonian connections, and he died soon after. Aristotle's life seems to have influenced his political thought in various ways: his interest in biology seems to be expressed in the naturalism of his politics; his interest in comparative politics and his sympathies for democracy as well as monarchy may have been encouraged by his travels and experience of diverse political systems; he criticizes harshly, while borrowing extensively, from Plato's Republic, Statesman, and Laws; and his own Politics is intended to guide rulers and statesmen, reflecting the high political circles in which he moved.

POLITICAL SCIENCE IN GENERAL

The modern word 'political' derives from the Greek politikos, 'of, or pertaining to, the polis'. (The Greek term polis will be translated here as 'city-state'. It is also translated as 'city' or 'polis', or simply anglicized as 'polis'. City-states like Athens and Sparta were relatively small and cohesive units, in which political, religious, and cultural concerns were intertwined. The extent of their similarity to modern nation-states is controversial.) Aristotle's word for 'politics' is politike, which is short for politike episteme or 'political science'. It belongs to one of the three main branches of science, which Aristotle distinguishes by their ends or objects. Contemplative science (including physics and metaphysics) is concerned with truth or knowledge for its own sake; practical science with good action; and productive science with making useful or beautiful objects. Politics is a practical science, since it is concerned with the noble action or happiness of the citizens (although it resembles a productive science in that it seeks to create, preserve, and reform political systems.) Aristotle thus understands politics as a normative or prescriptive discipline rather than as a purely empirical or descriptive inquiry.

In Nicomachean Ethics I.2 Aristotle characterizes politics as the most authoritative science. It prescribes which sciences are to be studied in the city-state, and the other capacities--such as military science, household management, and rhetoric--fall under its authority. Since it governs the other practical sciences, their ends serve as means to its end, which is nothing less than the human good. "Even if the end is the same for an individual and for a city-state, that of the city-state seems at any rate greater and more complete to attain and preserve. For although it is worthy to attain it for only an individual, it is nobler and more divine to do so for a nation or city-state." Aristotle's political science encompasses the two fields which modern philosophers distinguish as ethics and political philosophy. Political philosophy in the narrow sense is roughly speaking the subject of his treatise called the Politics.

CHARACTERISTICS AND PROBLEMS OF ARISTOTLE POLITICS

The work which has come down to us under this name appears to be less an integrated treatise than a collection of essays on various topics in political philosophy, which may have been compiled by a later editor rather than by Aristotle. The following topics are discussed in the eight books:

I. Naturalness of the city-state and of the household

II. Critique of ostensibly best constitutions

III. General theory of constitutions

IV. Inferior constitutions

V. Preservation and destruction of constitutions

VI. Further discussion of democracy and oligarchy

VII-VIII. Blueprint of the best constitution

This ordering of the books reflects, very roughly, the program for the study of constitutions which concludes the Nicomachean Ethics:

First, then, if any particular point has been treated well by those who have gone before us, we must try to review it; then from the constitutions that have been collected we must try to see what it is that preserves and destroys each of the constitutions, and for what reasons some city-states are well governed and others the reverse. For when these things have been examined, we will perhaps better understand what sort of constitution is best, and how each is structured, and which laws and customs it uses. Let us then begin our discussion.

However, scholars have raised problems with the Politics as we have it. The first concerns the intended order of its eight books. Some have questioned the traditional ordering, arguing that the discussion of the best constitution should follow directly after book III. Indeed, book III concludes with a transition to a discussion of the best constitution (although this may be due to a later editor). However, cross-references between various passages of the Politics indicate that books IV-V-VI form a connected series, as do books VII-VIII, but these series do not refer to each other. However, both series refer back to book III which in turn refers to book I. With some oversimplification, the Politics is comparable to a tree trunk supporting two separate branches: the root system is I, the trunk is II-III, and the branches are IV-V-VI and VII-VIII.

The second problem concerns the order in which the books were actually written. If they were composed at very different dates, they might represent discordant stages in the development of Aristotle's political philosophy. For example, Werner Jaeger argued that books VII-VIII contain a youthful utopianism, motivating Aristotle to emulate his teacher Plato in erecting "an ideal state by logical construction." In contrast, books IV-VI are based on "sober empirical study." Other scholars have seen a more pragmatic, even Machiavellian approach to politics in books IV-VI. A difficulty for this interpretation is that in book IV Aristotle regards the business of constructing ideal constitutions as perfectly compatible with that of addressing actual political problems. Although much ink has been spilled since Jaeger attempted to discern different chronological strata in the Politics, it has not resulted in a clear scholarly consensus. Because there is no explicit evidence of the dates at which the various books of the Politics were written, argument has turned on alleged inconsistencies between different passages.

This leads to the third problem, whether there are major inconsistencies of doctrine or method in the Politics. For example, Aristotle's account of the best constitution assumes his theory of justice, a moral standard which cannot be met by the actual political systems (democracies and oligarchies) of his own day. He does discuss practical political reforms in books IV-VI but more in terms of stability than justice. This raises the question of whether books IV-VI mark a radical departure from the political philosophy of the other books. Resolution of this problem requires careful study of the Politics as a whole

ARISTOTLE'S VIEW OF POLITICS

Political science studies the tasks of the politician or statesman (politikos), in much the way that medical science concerns the work of the physician. It is, in fact, the body of knowledge that such practitioners, if truly expert, will also wield in pursuing their tasks. The most important task for the politician is, in the role of lawgiver (nomothetes), to frame the appropriate constitution for the city-state. This involves enduring laws, customs, and institutions (including a system of moral education) for the citizens. Once the constitution is in place, the politician needs to take the appropriate measures to maintain it, to introduce reforms when he finds them necessary, and to prevent developments which might subvert the political system. This is the province of legislative science, which Aristotle regards as more important than politics as exercised in everyday political activity such as the passing of decrees. Aristotle frequently compares the politician to a craftsman. The analogy is imprecise because politics, in the strict sense of legislative science, is a form of practical wisdom or prudence, but valid to the extent that the politician produces, operates, and maintains a legal system according to universal principles. In order to appreciate this analogy it is helpful to observe that Aristotle explains production of an artifact in terms of four causes: the material, formal, efficient, and final causes. For example, clay (material cause) is molded into a vase shape (formal cause) by a potter (efficient or moving cause) so that it can contain liquid (final cause).

One can also explain the existence of the city-state in terms of the four causes. It is a kind of community (koinonia), that is, a collection of parts having some functions and interests in common. Hence, it is made up of parts, which Aristotle describes in various ways in different contexts: as households, or economic classes (e.g., the rich and the poor), or demes (i.e., local political units). But, ultimately, the city-state is composed of individual citizens, who, along with natural resources, are the "material" or "equipment" out of which the city-state is fashioned.

The formal cause of the city-state is its constitution (politeia). Aristotle defines the constitution as "a certain ordering of the inhabitants of the city-state." He also speaks of the constitution of a community as "the form of the compound" and argues that whether the community is the same over time depends on whether it has the same constitution. The constitution is not a written document, but an immanent organizing principle, analogous to the soul of an organism. Hence, the constitution is also "the way of life" of the citizens. Here the citizens are that minority of the resident population who are adults with full political rights.

The existence of the city-state also requires an efficient cause, namely, its ruler. On Aristotle's view, a community of any sort can possess order only if it has a ruling element or authority. This ruling principle is defined by the constitution, which sets criteria for political offices, particularly the sovereign office. However, on a deeper level, there must be an efficient cause to explain why a city-state acquires its constitution in the first place. Aristotle states that "the person who first established [the city-state] is the cause of very great benefits." This person was evidently the lawgiver (nomothetes), someone like Solon of Athens or Lycurgus of Sparta, who founded the constitution. Aristotle compares the lawgiver, or the politician more generally, to a craftsman (demiourgos) like a weaver or shipbuilder, who fashions material into a finished product. The notion of final cause dominates Aristotle's Politics from the opening lines:

Since we see that every city-state is a sort of community and that every community is established for the sake of some good (for everyone does everything for the sake of what they believe to be good), it is clear that every community aims at some good, and the community which has the most authority of all and includes all the others aims highest, that is, at the good with the most authority. This is what is called the city-state or political community. Soon after, he states that the city-state comes into being for the sake of life but exists for the sake of the good life. The theme that the good life or happiness is the proper end of the city-state recurs throughout the Politics.

To sum up, the city-state is a hylomorphic (i.e., matter-form) compound of a particular population (i.e., citizen-body) in a given territory (material cause) and a constitution (formal cause). The constitution itself is fashioned by the lawgiver and is governed by politicians, who are like craftsmen (efficient cause), and the constitution defines the aim of the city-state.

PRESUPPOSITIONS OF ARISTOTLE'S POLITICS

Aristotle's political philosophy is distinguished by its underlying philosophical doctrines. Of these the following four principles are especially noteworthy:

The principle of teleology Aristotle begins the Politics by invoking the concept of nature. In the Physics Aristotle identifies the nature of a thing above all with its end or final cause. The end of a thing is also its function, which is its defining principle. On Aristotle's view plants and animals are cardinal examples of natural existents, because they have a nature in the sense of an internal causal principle which explains how it comes into being and behaves. For example, an acorn has an inherent tendency to grow into an oak tree, so that the tree exists by nature rather than by craft or by chance. The thesis that human beings have a natural function has a fundamental place in the Eudemian Ethics II.1, Nicomachean Ethics I.7, and Politics I.2. The Politics further argues that it is part of the nature of human beings that they are political or adapted for life in the city-state. Thus teleology is crucial for the political naturalism which is at the foundation of Aristotle's political philosophy.

The principle of perfection Aristotle understands good and evil in terms of his teleology. The natural end of the organism (and the means to this end) is good for it, and what defeats or impedes this end is bad. For example, he argues that animals sleep in order to preserve themselves, because "nature operates for the sake of an end, and this is a good," and sleeping is necessary and beneficial for entities which cannot move continuously. For human beings the ultimate good or happiness (eudaimonia) consists in perfection, the full attainment of their natural function, which Aristotle analyzes as the activity of the soul according to reason (or not without reason), i.e., activity in accordance with the most perfect virtue or excellence.

This also provides a norm for the politician: "What is most choiceworthy for each individual is always the highest it is possible for him to attain." This ideal is to be realized in both the individual and the city-state: "that way of life is best, both separately for each individual and in common for city-states, which is equipped with virtue." However, Aristotle recognizes that it is generally impossible to fully realize this ideal, in which case he invokes a fall-back principle: it is best to attain perfection, but, failing that, a thing is better in proportion as it is nearer to the end.

Aristotle's perfectionism was opposed to the subjective relativism of Protagoras, according to which good and evil is defined by whatever human beings happened to desire. Like Plato, Aristotle maintained that the good was objective and independent of human wishes. However, he rejected Plato's own theory that the good was defined in terms of a transcendent form of the good, holding instead that good and evil are in a way relative to the organism, that is, to its natural end.

The principle of community Aristotle maintains that the city-state is the most complete community, because it attains the limit of self-sufficiency, so that it can exist for the sake of the good life. Individuals outside of the city-state are not self-sufficient, because they depend on the community not only for material necessities but also for education and moral habituation. "Just as, when perfected, a human is the best of animals, so also when separated from law and justice, he is the worst of all." On Aristotle's view, then, human beings must be subject to the authority of the city-state in order to attain the good life. The following principle concerns how authority should be exercised within a community.

Principle of rulership Aristotle believes that the existence and well-being of any system requires the presence of a ruling element: "Whenever a thing is established out of a number of things and becomes a single common thing, there always appears in it a ruler and ruled.... This [relation] is present in living things, but it derives from all of nature."

Just as an animal or plant can survive and flourish only if its soul rules over its body, a human community can possess the necessary order only if it has a ruling element which is in a position of authority, just as an army can possess order only if it has a commander in control. Although Aristotle followed Plato on this principle, he rejected Plato's further claim that one form of rule is appropriate for all. For Aristotle different forms of rule are necessary for different systems: e.g., political rule for citizens and despotic rule for slaves. The imposition of an inappropriate type of rule results in disorder and injustice.

The aforementioned principles account for much of the distinctive flavour of Aristotle's political philosophy, and they also indicate where many modern theorists have turned away from him. Modern philosophers such as Thomas Hobbes have challenged the principles of teleology and perfectionism, arguing against the former that human beings are mechanistic rather than teleological systems, and against the latter that good and bad depend upon subjective preferences of valuing agents rather than on objective states of affairs. Liberal theorists have criticized the principle of community on the grounds that it cedes too much authority to the state. Even the principle of rulership which Aristotle, Plato, and many other theorists thought self-evident has come under fire by modern theorists like Adam Smith and F. A. Hayek who argued that social and economic order may arise spontaneously as if by an "invisible hand." Modern neo-Aristotelian political theorists are committed to defending one or more of these doctrines against such criticisms. It is in these terms that Aristotle understands the fundamental normative problem of politics: What constitutional form should the lawgiver and politician establish and preserve in what material for the sake of what end?

GENERAL THEORY OF CONSTITUTIONS AND CITIZENSHIP

Aristotle states that "the politician and lawgiver is wholly occupied with the city-state, and the constitution is a certain way of organizing those who inhabit the city-state." His general theory of constitutions is set forth in Politics III. He begins with a definition of the citizen (polites), since the city-state is by nature a collective entity, a multitude of citizens. Citizens are distinguished from other inhabitants, such as resident aliens and slaves; and even children and seniors are not unqualified citizens (nor are most ordinary workers). After further analysis he defines the citizen as a person who has the right (exousia) to participate in deliberative or judicial office. In Athens, for example, citizens had the right to attend the assembly, the council, and other bodies, or to sit on juries. The Athenian system differed from a modern representative democracy in that the citizens were more directly involved in governing. Although full citizenship tended to be restricted in the Greek city-states (with women, slaves, foreigners, and some others excluded), the citizens were more deeply enfranchised than in modern representative democracies because they were more directly involved in governing. This is reflected in Aristotle's definition of the citizen (without qualification). Further, he defines the city-state (in the unqualified sense) as a multitude of such citizens which is adequate for a self-sufficient life.

Aristotle defines the constitution as a way of organizing the offices of the city-state, particularly the sovereign office. The constitution thus defines the governing body, which takes different forms: for example, in a democracy it is the people, and in an oligarchy it is a select few (the wealthy or well born). Before attempting to distinguish and evaluate various constitutions Aristotle considers two questions. First, why does a city-state come into being? He recalls the thesis, defended in Politics I.2, that human beings are by nature political animals, who naturally want to live together. For a further discussion of this topic, see the following supplementary document:

POLITICAL NATURALISM

Aristotle lays the foundations for his political theory in Politics book I by arguing that the city-state and political rule are "natural." The argument begins with a schematic, quasi-historical account of the development of the city-state out of simpler communities. First, individual human beings combined in pairs because they could not exist apart. The male and female joined in order to reproduce, and the master and slave came together for self-preservation. The natural master uses his intellect to rule, and the natural slave uses his body to labour. Second, the household arose naturally from these primitive communities in order to serve everyday needs. Third, when several households combined for other needs a village emerged also according to nature. Finally, "the complete community, formed from several villages, is a city-state, which at once attains the limit of self-sufficiency, roughly speaking. It comes to be for the sake of life, and exists for the sake of the good life." Aristotle defends three claims about nature and the city-state: First, the city-state exists by nature, because it comes to be out of the more primitive natural associations and it serves as their end, because only it attains self-sufficiency. Second, human beings are by nature political animals, because nature, which does nothing in vain, has equipped them with speech, which enables them to communicate moral concepts such as justice which are formative of the household and city-state. Third, the city-state is naturally prior to the individuals, because individuals cannot perform their natural functions apart from the city-state, since they are not self-sufficient. However, these three claims are immediately followed by a fourth: the city-state is a creation of human intelligence. "Therefore, everyone naturally has the impulse for such a [political] community, but the person who first established [it] is the cause of very great benefits." This great benefactor is evidently the lawgiver, for the legal system of the city-state makes human beings just and virtuous and lifts them from the savagery in which they would otherwise languish.

Aristotle's political naturalism presents the difficulty that he does not explain how he is using the term "nature" (phusis). In the Physics nature is understood as an internal principle of motion or rest. If the city-state were natural in this sense, it would resemble a plant or an animal which grows naturally to maturity out of a seed. However, this cannot be reconciled with the important role which Aristotle also assigns to the lawgiver as the one who established the city-state. For on Aristotle's theory a thing either exists by nature or by craft; it cannot do both. Aristotle can seemingly escape this dilemma only if it is supposed that he speaks of the city-state as "natural" in another sense of the term. For example, he might mean that it is "natural" in the extended sense that it arises from human natural inclinations (to live in communities) for the sake of human natural ends, but that it remains unfinished until a lawgiver provides it with a constitution.

He then adds that "the common advantage also brings them together insofar as they each attain the noble life. This is above all the end for all both in common and separately." Second, what are the different forms of rule by which one individual or group can rule over another? Aristotle distinguishes several types. He first considers despotic rule, which is exemplified in the master-slave relationship.

Aristotle thinks that this form of rule is justified in the case of natural slaves who (he asserts without evidence) lack a deliberative faculty and thus need a natural master to direct them. Although a natural slave allegedly benefits from having a master, despotic rule is still primarily for the sake of the master and only incidentally for the slave. (Aristotle provides no argument for this: if some persons are congenitally incapable of self-governance, why should they not be ruled primarily for their own sakes?) He next considers paternal and marital rule, which he also views as defensible: "the male is by nature more capable of leadership than the female, unless he is constituted in some way contrary to nature, and the elder and perfect [is by nature more capable of leadership] than the younger and imperfect."

Aristotle is persuasive when he argues that children need adult supervision because their rationality is "imperfect" (ateles) or immature. But he also alleges (without substantiation) that, although women have a deliberative faculty, it is "without authority" (akuron), so that females require male leadership. (Aristotle's arguments about slaves and women appear so weak that some commentators take them to be ironic. However, what is obvious to a modern reader need not have been so to an ancient Greek, so that it is not necessary to suppose that Aristotle's discussion is ironic.) It is noteworthy, however, that paternal and marital rule are properly practiced for the sake of the ruled (for the sake of the child and of the wife respectively), just as arts like medicine or gymnastics are practiced for the sake of the patient. In this respect they resemble political rule, which involves equal and similar citizens taking turns in ruling for one another's advantage. This sets the stage for the fundamental claim of Aristotle's constitutional theory: "constitutions which aim at the common advantage are correct and just without qualification, whereas those which aim only at the advantage of the rulers are deviant and unjust, because they involve despotic rule which is inappropriate for a community of free persons."

The distinction between correct and deviant constitutions is combined with the observation that the government may consist of one person, a few, or a multitude. Hence, there are six possible constitutional forms (Politics I.7):

	Correct	**Deviant**
One Ruler	Kingship	Tyranny
Few Rulers	Aristocracy	Oligarchy
Many Rulers	Polity	Democracy

This six-fold classification (which is adapted from Plato's Statesman) sets the stage for Aristotle's inquiry into the best constitution, although it is modified in various ways throughout the Politics. For example, he observes that the dominant class in oligarchy (literally rule of the oligoi, i.e., few) is typically the wealthy, whereas in democracy (literally rule of the demos, i.e., people) it is the poor, so that these economic classes should be included in the definition of these forms. Also, polity is later characterized as a kind of "mixed" constitution typified by rule of the "middle" group of citizens, a moderately wealthy class between the rich and poor.

Aristotle turns to arguments for and against the different constitutions, which he views as different applications of the principle of distributive justice. Everyone agrees, he says, that justice involves treating equal persons equally, and treating unequal persons unequally, but they do not agree on the standard by which individuals are deemed to be equally (or unequally) meritorious or deserving. He assumes his own analysis of distributive justice set forth in Nicomachean Ethics V.3: Justice requires that benefits be distributed to individuals in proportion to their merit or desert. The oligarchs mistakenly think that those who are superior in wealth should also have superior political rights, whereas the democrats hold that those who are equal in free birth should also have equal political rights.

Both of these conceptions of political justice are mistaken in Aristotle's view, because they assume a false conception of the ultimate end of the city-state. The city-state is neither a business association to maximize wealth (as the oligarchs suppose) nor an agency to promote liberty and equality (as the democrats maintain). Instead, Aristotle argues, "the good life is the end of the city-state," that is, a life consisting of noble actions. Hence, the correct conception of justice is aristocratic, assigning political rights to those who make a full contribution to the political community, that is, to those with virtue as well as property and freedom. This is what Aristotle understands by an "aristocratic" constitution: literally, the rule of the aristoi, i.e., best persons. Aristotle explores the implications of this argument in the remainder of Politics III, considering the rival claims of the rule of law and the rule of a supremely virtuous individual. Here absolute kingship is a limiting case of aristocracy. Again, in books VII-VIII, Aristotle describes the ideal constitution in which the citizens are fully virtuous.

STUDY OF SPECIFIC CONSTITUTIONS

The purpose of political science is to guide "the good lawgiver and the true politician." Like any complete science or craft, it must study a range of issues concerning its subject matter. For example, gymnastics (physical training) studies what sort of training is advantageous for what sort of body, what sort of training is best or adapted to the body that is naturally the best, what sort of training is best for most bodies, and what capacity is appropriate for someone who does not want the condition or knowledge appropriate for athletic contests.

Political science studies a comparable range of constitutions: first, the constitution which is best without qualification, i.e., "most according to our prayers with no external impediment"; second, the constitution that is best under the circumstances "for it is probably impossible for many persons to attain the best constitution"; third, the constitution which serves the aim a given city-state population happens to have, i.e., the one that is best "based on a hypothesis": "for [the political scientist] ought to be able to study a given constitution, both how it might originally come to be, and, when it has come to be, in what manner it might be preserved for the longest time; I mean, for example, if a particular city happens neither to be governed by the best constitution, nor to be equipped even with necessary things, nor to be the [best] possible under existing circumstances, but to be a baser sort."

Hence, Aristotelian political science is not confined to the ideal system, but also investigates the second-best constitution, the one which is the best that most city-states are capable of supporting. For it is the closest approximation to full political justice which the lawgiver can attain under the circumstances. Although Aristotle's political views were influenced by his teacher Plato, he is very critical of the ideal city-state set forth in Plato's Republic on the grounds that it overvalues political unity, it embraces a system of communism that is impractical and inimical to human nature, and it neglects the happiness of the individual citizens. In contrast, in Aristotle's own "best constitution" each and every citizen will possess moral virtue and the equipment to carry it out in practice, and thereby attain a life of excellence and complete happiness.

All of the citizens will hold political office and possess private property because "one should call the city-state happy not by looking at a part of it but at all the citizens." Moreover, there will be a common system of education for all the citizens, because they share the same end. But if (as is the case with most city-states) the population lacks the capacities and resources for complete happiness, the lawgiver must be content with fashioning a suitable constitution. The second-best system typically takes the form of a polity (in which citizens possess an inferior, more common grade of virtue) or mixed constitution (combining features of democracy, oligarchy, and aristocracy, so that no group of citizens is in a position to abuse its rights).

In addition, the political scientist must understand existing constitutions even when they are bad. Aristotle adds that "to reform a constitution is no less a task [of politics] than it is to establish one from the beginning," and in this way "the politician should also help existing constitutions." The political scientist should also be cognizant of forces of political change which can undermine an existing regime. Aristotle criticizes his predecessors for excessive utopianism and neglect of the practical duties of a political theorist. However, he is no Machiavellian. The best constitution still serves as a regulative ideal by which to evaluate existing systems.

These topics occupy the remainder of the Politics. Books IV-VI are concerned with the existing constitutions: that is, the three deviant constitutions, as well as polity or the mixed constitution, the best attainable under most circumstances. The whole of book V investigates political change and revolution. Books VII-VIII are devoted to the ideal constitution. As might be expected, Aristotle's attempt to carry out this program involves many difficulties, and scholars disagree about how the two series of books (IV-VI and VII-VIII) are related to each other: for example, which were written first, which were intended to be read first, and whether they are ultimately consistent with each other. For a further discussion of this topic, see the following supplementary document:

Aristotle's Politics did not have an immediate impact because it defended the Greek city-state, which was already becoming obsolete in his own lifetime.

For similar reasons much of his discussion of particular political institutions is not directly applicable to modern nation-states (apart from his objectionable defenses of slavery, female subservience, and disenfranchisement of the working classes). Even so, Aristotle's Politics has had a deep influence on political philosophy until the present day, because it contains deep and thought-provoking discussions of perennial concerns of political philosophy: the role of human nature in politics, the relation of the individual to the state, the place of morality in politics, the theory of political justice, the rule of law, the analysis and evaluation of constitutions, the relevance of ideals to practical politics, the causes and cures of political change and revolution, and the importance of a morally educated citizenry.

POSITIVE AND NEGATIVE LIBERTY

Negative liberty is the absence of obstacles, barriers or constraints. One has negative liberty to the extent that actions are available to one in this negative sense. Positive liberty is the possibility of acting-or the fact of acting-in such a way as to take control of one's life and realize one's fundamental purposes. While negative liberty is usually attributed to individual agents, positive liberty is sometimes attributed to collectivities, or to individuals considered primarily as members of given collectivities. The idea of distinguishing between a negative and a positive sense of the term 'liberty' goes back at least to Kant, and was examined and defended in depth by Isaiah Berlin in the 1950s and '60s. Discussions about positive and negative liberty normally take place within the context of political and social philosophy. They are distinct from, though sometimes related to, philosophical discussions about free will. Work on the nature of positive liberty often overlaps, however, with work on the nature of autonomy.

As Berlin showed, negative and positive liberty are not merely two distinct kinds of liberty; they can be seen as rival, incompatible interpretations of a single political ideal. Since few people claim to be against liberty, the way this term is interpreted and defined can have important political implications. Political liberalism tends to presuppose a negative definition of liberty: liberals generally claim that if one favours individual liberty one should place strong limitations on the activities of the state. Critics of liberalism often contest this implication by contesting the negative definition of liberty: they argue that the pursuit of liberty understood as self-realization or as self-determination (whether of the individual or of the collectivity) can require state intervention of a kind not normally allowed by liberals.

Many authors prefer to talk of positive and negative freedom. This is only a difference of style, and the terms 'liberty' and 'freedom' can be used interchangeably. Although some attempts have been made to distinguish between liberty and freedom, these have not caught on. Neither can they be translated into other European languages, which contain only the one term, of either Latin or Germanic origin (e.g. liberte, Freiheit), where English contains both.

TWO CONCEPTS OF LIBERTY

Imagine you are driving a car through town, and you come to a fork in the road. You turn left, but no one was forcing you to go one way or the other. Next you come to a crossroads. You turn right, but no one was preventing you from going left or straight on. There is no traffic to speak of and there are no diversions or police roadblocks. So you seem, as a driver, to be completely free. But this picture of your situation might change quite dramatically if we consider that the reason you went left and then right is that you're addicted to cigarettes and you're desperate to get to the tobacconists before it closes. Rather than driving, you feel you are being driven, as your urge to smoke leads you uncontrollably to turn the wheel first to the left and then to the right. Moreover, you're perfectly aware that your turning right at the crossroads means you'll probably miss a train that was to take you to an appointment you care about very much. You long to be free of this irrational desire that is not only threatening your longevity but is also stopping you right now from doing what you think you ought to be doing.

This story gives us two contrasting ways of thinking of liberty. On the one hand, one can think of liberty as the absence of obstacles external to the agent. You are free if no one is stopping you from doing whatever you might want to do. In the above story you appear, in this sense, to be free. On the other hand, one can think of liberty as the presence of control on the part of the agent. To be free, you must be self-determined, which is to say that you must be able to control your own destiny in your own interests. In the above story you appear, in this sense, to be unfree: you are not in control of your own destiny, as you are failing to control a passion that you yourself would rather be rid of and which is preventing you from realizing what you recognize to be your true interests. One might say that while on the first view liberty is simply about how many doors are open to the agent, on the second view it is more about going through the right doors for the right reasons.

In a famous essay first published in 1958, Isaiah Berlin called these two concepts of liberty negative and positive respectively (Berlin 1969). The reason for using these labels is that in the first case liberty seems to be a mere absence of something (i.e. of obstacles, barriers, constraints or interference from others), whereas in the second case it seems to require the presence of something (i.e. of control, self-mastery, self-determination or self-realization). In Berlin's words, we use the negative concept of liberty in attempting to answer the question "What is the area within which the subject-a person or group of persons-is or should be left to do or be what he is able to do or be, without interference by other persons?", whereas we use the positive concept in attempting to answer the question "What, or who, is the source of control or interference that can determine someone to do, or be, this rather than that?"

It is useful to think of the difference between the two concepts in terms of the difference between factors that are external and factors that are internal to the agent. While theorists of negative freedom are primarily interested in the degree to which individuals or groups suffer interference from external bodies, theorists of positive freedom are more attentive to the internal factors affecting the degree to which individuals or groups act autonomously. Given this difference, one might be tempted to think that a political philosopher should concentrate exclusively on negative freedom, a concern with positive freedom being more relevant to psychology or individual morality than to political and social institutions. This, however, would be premature, for among the most hotly debated issues in political philosophy are the following: Is the positive concept of freedom a political concept? Can individuals or groups achieve positive freedom through political action? Is it possible for the state to promote the positive freedom of citizens on their behalf? And if so, is it desirable for the state to do so? The classic texts in the history of western political thought are divided over how these questions should be answered: theorists in the classical liberal tradition, like Constant, Humboldt, Spencer and Mill, are typically classed as answering 'no' and therefore as defending a negative concept of political freedom; theorists that are critical of this tradition, like Rousseau, Hegel, Marx and T.H. Green, are typically classed as answering 'yes' and as defending a positive concept of political freedom.

In its political form, positive freedom has often been thought of as necessarily achieved through a collectivity. Perhaps the clearest case is that of Rousseau's theory of freedom, according to which individual freedom is achieved through participation in the process whereby one's community exercises collective control over its own affairs in accordance with the 'general will'. Put in the simplest terms, one might say that a democratic society is a free society because it is a self-determined society, and that a member of that society is free to the extent that he or she participates in its democratic process. But there are also individualist applications of the concept of positive freedom. For example, it is sometimes said that a government should aim actively to create the conditions necessary for individuals to be self-sufficient or to achieve self-realization. The negative concept of freedom, on the other hand, is most commonly assumed in liberal defences of the constitutional liberties typical of liberal-democratic societies, such as freedom of movement, freedom of religion, and freedom of speech, and in arguments against paternalist or moralist state intervention. It is also often invoked in defences of the right to private property, although some have contested the claim that private property necessarily enhances negative liberty.

After Berlin, the most widely cited and best developed analyses of the negative concept of liberty include Hayek (1960), Day (1971), Oppenheim (1981), Miller (1983) and Steiner (1994). Among the most prominent contemporary analyses of the positive concept of liberty are Milne (1968), Gibbs (1976), C. Taylor (1979) and Christman (1991, 2005).

THE PARADOX OF POSITIVE LIBERTY

Many liberals, including Berlin, have suggested that the positive concept of liberty carries with it a danger of authoritarianism. Consider the fate of a permanent and oppressed minority. Because the members of this minority participate in a democratic process characterized by majority rule, they might be said to be free on the grounds that they are members of a society exercising self-control over its own affairs. But they are oppressed, and so are surely unfree. Moreover, it is not necessary to see a society as democratic in order to see it as self-controlled; one might instead adopt an organic conception of society, according to which the collectivity is to be thought of as a living organism, and one might believe that this organism will only act rationally, will only be in control of itself, when its various parts are brought into line with some rational plan devised by its wise governors (who, to extend the metaphor, might be thought of as the organism's brain). In this case, even the majority might be oppressed in the name of liberty.

Such justifications of oppression in the name of liberty are no mere products of the liberal imagination, for there are notorious historical examples of their endorsement by authoritarian political leaders. Berlin, himself a liberal and writing during the cold war, was clearly moved by the way in which the apparently noble ideal of freedom as self-mastery or self-realization had been twisted and distorted by the totalitarian dictators of the twentieth century-most notably those of the Soviet Union-so as to claim that they, rather than the liberal West, were the true champions of freedom. The slippery slope towards this paradoxical conclusion begins, according to Berlin, with the idea of a divided self. To illustrate: the smoker in our story provides a clear example of a divided self, for she is both a self that desires to get to an appointment and a self that desires to get to the tobacconists, and these two desires are in conflict.

We can now enrich this story in a plausible way by adding that one of these selves-the keeper of appointments-is superior to the other: the self that is a keeper of appointments is thus a 'higher' self, and the self that is a smoker is a 'lower' self. The higher self is the rational, reflecting self, the self that is capable of moral action and of taking responsibility for what she does. This is the true self, for rational reflection and moral responsibility are the features of humans that mark them off from other animals. The lower self, on the other hand, is the self of the passions, of unreflecting desires and irrational impulses. One is free, then, when one's higher, rational self is in control and one is not a slave to one's passions or to one's merely empirical self. The next step down the slippery slope consists in pointing out that some individuals are more rational than others, and can therefore know best what is in their and others' rational interests.

This allows them to say that by forcing people less rational than themselves to do the rational thing and thus to realize their true selves, they are in fact liberating them from their merely empirical desires. Occasionally, Berlin says, the defender of positive freedom will take an additional step that consists in conceiving of the self as wider than the individual and as represented by an organic social whole-"a tribe, a race, a church, a state, the great society of the living and the dead and the yet unborn". The true interests of the individual are to be identified with the interests of this whole, and individuals can and should be coerced into fulfilling these interests, for they would not resist coercion if they were as rational and wise as their coercers. "Once I take this view", Berlin says, "I am in a position to ignore the actual wishes of men or societies, to bully, oppress, torture in the name, and on behalf, of their 'real' selves, in the secure knowledge that whatever is the true goal of man... must be identical with his freedom."

Those in the negative camp try to cut off this line of reasoning at the first step, by denying that there is any necessary relation between one's freedom and one's desires. Since one is free to the extent that one is externally unprevented from doing things, they say, one can be free to do what one does not desire to do. If being free meant being unprevented from realizing one's desires, then one could, again paradoxically, reduce one's unfreedom by coming to desire fewer of the things one is unfree to do. One could become free simply by contenting oneself with one's situation. A perfectly contented slave is perfectly free to realize all of her desires. Nevertheless, we tend to think of slavery as the opposite of freedom. More generally, freedom is not to be confused with happiness, for in logical terms there is nothing to stop a free person from being unhappy or an unfree person from being happy. The happy person might feel free, but whether they are free is another matter (Day, 1971). Negative theorists of freedom therefore tend to say not that having freedom means being unprevented from doing as one desires, but that it means being unprevented from doing whatever one might desire to do.

Some theorists of positive freedom bite the bullet and say that the contented slave is indeed free-that in order to be free the individual must learn, not so much to dominate certain merely empirical desires, but to rid herself of them. She must, in other words, remove as many of her desires as possible. As Berlin puts it, if I have a wounded leg 'there are two methods of freeing myself from pain. One is to heal the wound. But if the cure is too difficult or uncertain, there is another method. I can get rid of the wound by cutting off my leg'. This is the strategy of liberation adopted by ascetics, stoics and Buddhist sages. It involves a 'retreat into an inner citadel'-a soul or a purely noumenal self-in which the individual is immune to any outside forces. But this state, even if it can be achieved, is not one that liberals would want to call one of freedom, for it again risks masking important forms of oppression. It is, after all, often in coming to terms with excessive external limitations in society that individuals retreat into themselves, pretending to themselves that they do not really desire the worldly goods or pleasures they have been denied.

Moreover, the removal of desires may also be an effect of outside forces, such as brainwashing, which we should hardly want to call a realization of freedom.

Because the concept of negative freedom concentrates on the external sphere in which individuals interact, it seems to provide a better guarantee against the dangers of paternalism and authoritarianism perceived by Berlin. To promote negative freedom is to promote the existence of a sphere of action within which the individual is sovereign, and within which she can pursue her own projects subject only to the constraint that she respect the spheres of others. Humboldt and Mill, both defenders of the negative concept of freedom, compared the development of an individual to that of a plant: individuals, like plants, must be allowed to grow, in the sense of developing their own faculties to the full and according to their own inner logic. Personal growth is something that cannot be imposed from without, but must come from within the individual.

TWO ATTEMPTS TO CREATE A THIRD WAY

Critics, however, have objected that the ideal described by Humboldt and Mill looks much more like a positive concept of liberty than a negative one. Positive liberty consists, they say, in exactly this growth of the individual: the free individual is one that develops, determines and changes her own desires and interests autonomously and from within. This is not liberty as the mere absence of obstacles, but liberty as self-realization. Why should the mere absence of state interference be thought to guarantee such growth? Is there not some third way between the extremes of totalitarianism and the minimal state of the classical liberals-some non-paternalist, non-authoritarian means by which positive liberty in the above sense can be actively promoted?

Much of the more recent work on positive liberty has been motivated by a dissatisfaction with the ideal of negative liberty combined with an awareness of the possible abuses of the positive concept so forcefully exposed by Berlin. John Christman (1991), for example, has argued that positive liberty concerns the ways in which desires are formed-whether as a result of rational reflection on all the options available, or as a result of pressure, manipulation or ignorance. What it does not regard, he says, is the content of an individual's desires. The promotion of positive freedom need not therefore involve the claim that there is only one right answer to the question of how a person should live, nor need it allow, or even be compatible with, a society forcing its members into given patterns of behaviour. Take the example of a Muslim woman who claims to espouse the fundamentalist doctrines generally followed by her family and the community in which she lives.

On Christman's account, this person is positively unfree if her desire to conform was somehow oppressively imposed upon her through indoctrination, manipulation or deceit. She is positively free, on the other hand, if she arrived at her desire to conform while aware of other reasonable options and she weighed and assessed these other options rationally. Even if this woman seems to have a preference for subservient behaviour, there is nothing necessarily freedom-enhancing or freedom-restricting about her having the desires she has, since freedom regards not the content of these desires but their mode of formation. On this view, forcing her to do certain things rather than others can never make her more free, and Berlin's paradox of positive freedom would seem to have been avoided.

It remains to be seen, however, just what a state can do, in practice, to promote positive liberty in Christman's sense without encroaching on any individual's sphere of negative liberty: the conflict between the two ideals seems to survive his alternative analysis, albeit in a milder form. Although not coercing individuals into specific patterns of behaviour, a state interested in promoting autonomy in Christman's sense might still be allowed considerable space for intervention of an informative and educational nature, perhaps subsidizing some activities (in order to encourage a plurality of genuine options) and financing this through taxation. Liberals might criticize this on anti-paternalist grounds, objecting that such measures will require the state to use resources in ways that the supposedly heteronomous individuals, if left to themselves, might have chosen to spend in other ways. Some liberals will make an exception in the case of the education of children (in such a way as to cultivate open minds and rational reflection), but even here other liberals will object that the right to negative liberty includes the right to decide how one's children should be educated.

Other theorists of freedom have remained closer to the negative conception of freedom but have attempted to go beyond it, saying that freedom is not merely the enjoyment of a sphere of non-interference but the enjoyment of certain conditions in which such non-interference is guaranteed. These conditions may include the presence of a democratic constitution and a series of safeguards against a government wielding power arbitrarily, including the exercise of civic virtues on the part of citizens. As Berlin admits, on the negative view of freedom, I am free even if I live in a dictatorship just as long as the dictator happens, on a whim, not to interfere with me. There is no necessary connection between negative freedom and any particular form of government. On the alternative view sketched here, I am free only if I live in a society with the kinds of political institutions that guarantee the independence of each citizen from exercises of arbitrary power. Quentin Skinner has called this view of freedom 'neo-Roman', invoking ideas about freedom both of the ancient Romans and of a number of Renaissance and early modern writers. Philip Pettit has called the same view 'republican', and this label has tended to dominate in the recent literature.

Republican freedom can be thought of as a kind of status: to be a free person is to enjoy the rights and privileges attached to the status of republican citizenship, whereas the paradigm of the unfree person is the slave. Freedom is not simply a matter of non-interference, for a slave may enjoy a great deal of non-interference at the whim of her master. What makes her unfree is her status, such that she is permanently liable to interference of any kind. Even if the slave enjoys non-interference, she is, as Pettit puts it, 'dominated', because she is permanently subject to the arbitrary power of her owner.

Contemporary republicans therefore claim that their view of freedom is quite distinct from the negative view of freedom. As we have seen, one can enjoy non-interference without enjoying non-domination; conversely, according to Pettit, one can enjoy non-domination while nevertheless being interfered with, just as long as the interference in question is constrained, through republican power structures, to track one's interests. Only arbitrary power is inimical to freedom, not power as such. On the other hand, republican freedom is also distinct from positive freedom as expounded and criticized by Berlin. First, republican freedom does not consist in the activity of virtuous political participation; rather, that participation is seen as instrumentally related to freedom as non-domination. Secondly, the republican concept of freedom cannot lead to anything like the oppressive consequences feared by Berlin, because it has a commitment to non-domination and to liberal-democratic institutions already built into it.

It remains to be seen, however, whether the republican concept of freedom is ultimately distinguishable from the negative concept, or whether republican writers on freedom have not simply provided good arguments to the effect that negative freedom is best promoted, on balance and over time, through certain kinds of political institutions rather than others. While there is no necessary connection between negative liberty and democratic government, there may nevertheless be a strong empirical correlation between the two. Ian Carter and Matthew H. Kramer have argued, along these lines, that republican policies are best argued for empirically on the basis of the standard negative ideal of freedom, rather than on the basis of a conceptual challenge to that ideal.

An important premise in their argument is that the degree to which a person is negatively free depends, in part, on the probability with which he or she will be constrained from performing future acts or act-combinations. People who are subject to arbitrary power are, according to Carter and Kramer, less free in the negative sense even if they do not actually suffer interference, because the probability of their suffering constraints is always greater (ceteris paribus, as a matter of empirical fact) than it would be if they were not subject to that arbitrary power.

CHAPTER

9 CONTEMPORARY POLITICAL THOUGHT

RAWLS'S POLITICAL THOUGHT

John Rawls has been hailed recently as "the most distinguished political philosopher" of the twentieth century (Nussbaum 1999, 424). In large part, this accolade is based on the Harvard philosopher's originality as a political thinker. Rawls's Theory of Justice ([1971] 1999) single-handedly revived the tradition of "grand theory" at a time when political philosophy as a constructive, creative enterprise was widely viewed as "dead in the water." Moreover, Rawls provided a sophisticated and novel account of justice that captured the imagination of an entire generation of scholars and students. Indeed, no single work has had a wider impact or greater influence on formal political thinking over the past thirty years than A Theory of Justice. As a result, Rawls's leading tenets-"justice as fairness," "the difference principle," "fair equality of opportunity," "equal basic liberties," "the original position," "the veil of ignorance"-have become permanent fixtures in the lexicon of academic political discourse. Like many of his famous predecessors in the field of political speculation, Rawls owes his notoriety as much to his critics as to his admirers.

On sheer volume alone, the critical responses to A Theory of Justice suggest that its author had something important, provocative, and original to say. An inventory of these responses confirms this suspicion because no thinker of common metal could have generated the heated, voluminous, and sustained outpouring of debate that has surrounded Rawls's chief work. Agree or disagree with its teaching, A Theory of Justice has attained the status of a political classic, an honor that rests in large part on the originality of its author's philosophical achievement. Although studies of Rawls continue apace, the leading tenets of Theory have received serious, sustained, and comprehensive examination. I am not claiming that nothing remains to be said, for by definition a classic provides an inexhaustible supply of grist for the mill. On the whole, however, it is questionable that another critique of the "original position," the "difference principle," and so forth will yield much of scholarly interest or value. In fact, the better-known and more original of Rawls's doctrines have been scrutinized ad nauseam, and further inquiry along conventional lines runs the risk of irrelevance and redundancy.

One original feature of Theory, however, has escaped the notice of readers for the most part-namely, that Rawls's theory of justice "leaves open the question whether its principles are best realized by some form of property-owning democracy or by a liberal socialist regime" ([1971] 1999, xv). "Justice as fairness" theory does not entail the determination of specific economic arrangements or even take up the matter of ownership of the means of production (242).

At first glance, this omission may appear unimportant. Why should the status of property relations necessarily be part of a theory of justice? Is it not possible indeed, reasonable-to assume that justice is compatible with either a capitalist economy or a socialist economy? This position, which Rawls takes, deserves more scrutiny than it has received. Perhaps he is perfectly justified in excluding property relations from his account of "justice as fairness," but given the importance of property in the history of political philosophy, the exclusion cries out for an explanation. At the least, it would seem apposite to provide a rationale for leaving this important question open-ended. We may then consider whether this rationale is internally consistent with Rawls's principles of justice. Finally, we may ask if a theory of justice that fails to deal with the vital issue of property relations qualifies as a political philosophy in the comprehensive sense.

Rawls's Basic View of Property Relations

In the first chapter of Theory, Rawls asserts that the topic of his book "is . . . social justice." He then provides a summary of that subject: For us the primary subject of justice is the basic structure of society, or more exactly, the way in which the major social institutions distribute fundamental rights and duties and determine the division of advantages from social cooperation. By major institutions I understand the political constitution and the principal economic and social arrangements. Thus the legal protection of freedom of thought and liberty of conscience, competitive markets, private property in the means of production, and the monogamous family are examples of major social institutions. Taken together as one scheme, the major institutions define men's rights and duties and influence their life prospects. . . . The basic structure is the primary subject of justice because its effects are so profound and present from the start. ([1971] 1999, 6-7)

From Rawls's summary we learn that "justice" involves political as well as economic arrangements and that "private property in the means of production" exemplifies a major social institution. We learn also that economic arrangements are part of the "basic structure" of society and fall under the subject of justice owing to their "profound" impact on people's lives. The notion that "[t]he primary subject of the principles of justice is the basic structure of society" (47) is repeated throughout Theory, therefore creating the impression that the determination of economic arrangements (including property relations) constitutes a vital and necessary component of justice. This impression is strengthened by the fact that Rawls invariably links "the arrangement of major social institutions" to the basic structure, or the "primary subject of justice." "Our concern," he writes, "is solely with the basic structure of society and its major institutions and therefore with the standard cases of social justice" (50). Such statements appear to indicate clearly that "justice as fairness" will include, at the very least, a consideration of the merits of basic economic arrangements. Insofar as the principles of justice will "regulate the choice of a political constitution and the main elements of the economic and social system" (7, emphasis added), we may reasonably expect Rawls to specify the relation between justice and the "main elements" (that is, the property relations) of economic arrangements. The expectation is piqued by the first formulation of Rawls's "two principles of justice." The first principle states that "each person is to have an equal right to the most extensive scheme of equal basic liberties compatible with a similar scheme of liberties for others" (53).

Among the basic liberties, Rawls includes "the right to hold personal property," a right he justifies on the basis of individual autonomy and integrity. The second principle pertains to economic issues more directly: "social and economic inequalities are to be arranged so that they are both (a) reasonably expected to be to everyone's advantage, and (b) attached to positions and offices open to all" (53). Implicit in this principle is the toleration of economic inequality, the condition in which some persons possess more wealth and income than others. As long as such inequalities are mutually advantageous and do not involve exclusion from any remunerative position, they are consistent with "justice as fairness."

At this point in the argument, one may suspect that Rawls is providing a rationale for the inequalities that exist in capitalist democracies. His critics on the left often read him in this way. The reader need only turn the page, however, to discover that Rawls, though unequivocally committed to democracy, is by no means committed to capitalism. As noted earlier, he includes "the right to hold personal property" under the basic liberties but excludes "the right to own certain kinds of property (e.g., means of production) and freedom of contract as understood by the doctrine of laissez-faire" (54).

For Rawls, such rights "are not basic; and so they are not protected by the priority of the first principle [of justice]" (54). The exclusion of property rights beyond personal items from the list of basic liberties raises a number of important questions. If such rights are not basic to liberty, what is their relation to liberty, if any? Is there any right to property beyond personal holdings? If so, what is the basis of this right, and how may it be justified?

If no such right exists, does this lack imply that justice requires public ownership of the means of production? If so, how far may the right of personal ownership extend before it encroaches on the right of public ownership? Furthermore, on what basis does the "right" of public ownership stand? Rawls does provide something like answers to these questions in the form of the "difference principle" (the second principle of justice), but for the moment let us defer consideration of this controversial aspect of his thought.

Property Relations and Economic Equality

The assertion that private ownership beyond personal property is not a basic liberty is a red flag for readers who suspect Rawls is "privileging" capitalism. Indeed, any hopes (or fears) that Rawls aims to defend private ownership tout court are immediately dashed by his "general conception of justice," which states that "[a]ll social values," including "income and wealth," "are to be distributed equally," but he completes the sentence with a caveat: "unless an unequal distribution . . . is to everyone's advantage" (54). As we shall see, this qualification is a crucial (perhaps the crucial) element in his theory of justice. Significant in the present context, however, is that the initial presumption rests on the side of an equal distribution of wealth and income. Only the inequality thereof (however slight) requires justification, a position that places Rawls firmly in the socialist camp of political thinkers. This characterization is confirmed later

in Theory, where he argues that an equal distribution of "primary goods" including wealth and income) is not only "reasonable," but self-evident: "Since it is not reasonable for him [the hypothetical person or an unbiased person] to expect more than an equal share in the division of social primary goods, and since it is not rational for him to agree to less, the sensible thing is to acknowledge as the first step a principle of justice requiring an equal distribution. Indeed, this principle is so obvious given the symmetry of the parties that it would occur to everyone immediately" (130).

Here Rawls is describing the reasoning process that takes place in the "original position," a hypothetical scenario in which the parties aim to reach a consensus on the first principles of justice. To ensure that the choice of principles is not influenced by bias or morally irrelevant factors, persons in the "initial situation" have no knowledge of their social circumstances, natural endowments, or life chances. Rawls argues that it would be rational for the parties operating behind this "veil of ignorance" to agree to an equal distribution of everything of basic value, including material goods. Such a distribution presumably would constitute justice par excellence, for the veil of ignorance eliminates all those "factors which are so arbitrary from a moral point of view" (63) and permits the parties to choose those (egalitarian) principles most consistent with the principle of fairness. Why, then, does Rawls reject this solution to the problem of distributive justice? What could possibly justify a deviation from an unbiased, rational, and unanimous decision to divide shares equally? As noted earlier, Rawls states that inequalities of wealth and income are defensible only when they are to everyone's advantage. This condition is the famous "difference principle" that has attracted so much attention among students of Theory.

The difference principle is based on three basic assumptions. First, the leading principle of justice (equal basic liberties) is prior in that it is never justifiable to sacrifice basic liberties in exchange for greater economic advantages. Second, parties in the original position "normally prefer more primary social goods rather than less," and "it is rational" to do so (123). Finally, the difference principle assumes that everyone (including the least fortunate) will be better off if economic institutions are arranged on the basis of "efficiency" (57), including "a division of a labor" (244). With these assumptions in place, Rawls can abandon the economic equality that seems so "reasonable" to parties in the original position because it is presumably more reasonable to procure additional social goods even when those goods are divided unequally. The special conditions attached to economic inequality make the difference principle even more "attractive" to the least fortunate because inequalities are justified only when they are "to everyone's advantage" and where no formal barriers obstruct positions of monetary gain ("fair equality of opportunity"). Given these assumptions and safeguards, Rawls argues that parties in the original position would opt unanimously for the difference principle as a pillar of justice.

Whatever the merit of this argument, Rawls makes clear that the integrity of the difference principle does not depend on specific economic arrangements or property relations. He does assume, however, "that the economy is roughly a free market system, although the means of production may or may not be privately owned" (57).

Although the notion that a "free market system" is equally compatible with either capitalist or socialist property relations may sound odd, it presents no real difficulty for Rawls. In fact, he takes far greater pains to defend against egalitarian attacks on the difference principle than to justify his glib neutrality with respect to the issue of private versus public ownership. After outlining the difference principle, Rawls observes that although his "liberal conception seems clearly preferable to the system of natural liberty, intuitively it still appears defective" (63-64) because "it still permits the distribution of wealth and income to be determined by the natural distribution of abilities and talents. . . . D]istributive shares are decided by the outcome of the natural lottery; and this outcome is arbitrary from a moral perspective" (64).

The idea that injustice exists if persons of greater abilities and talents procure a greater share of wealth and income will appear peculiar to many. May we accurately or reasonably characterize this state of affairs as "arbitrary from a moral perspective," even with the difference principle in place? Strictly speaking, according to Rawls we

may, for "[t]here is no more reason to permit the distribution of income and wealth to be settled by the distribution of natural assets than by historical and social fortune" (64). Unfortunately, it is impossible to secure equal chances for the acquisition of equal goods, "at least as long as some form of the family exists."

In lieu of perfect "fair equality of opportunity," Rawls looks to the difference principle as the "best choice" among the alternatives he considers. In this sense, the difference principle represents a "second-best" solution to the problem of justice (247), an imperfect approximation of the ideal, similar in spirit to Plato's "second-best" state in The Laws. And just as Plato clung to the ideal of the Republic, Rawls remains attached to the justice of economic equality because "unless there is a distribution that makes both persons [i.e., the less and more fortunate] better off . . . an equal distribution is to be preferred" (65-66).

The foregoing discussion suggests that economic equality has a moral priority for Rawls. He never attempts to defend it, but he assumes that on the whole it is more just to distribute wealth and income equally than to permit inequalities that do not benefit the least advantaged. As we have seen, Rawls goes to notable lengths to defend inequality-one might fairly describe his efforts as an apologia. Still, for him, inequality is regrettable and unfair insofar as it results from life's "natural lottery." By implication, then, nature itself is unfair because it distributes talents and abilities unevenly, thus giving some persons an undue advantage that is totally "undeserved" (86). Even so, Rawls hopes to show how inequality can be made legitimate, much in the manner that Rousseau believed he could show the legitimacy of man's social "chains." Yet not even Rousseau (or for that matter any of the classical political philosophers) believed that doing so required overturning "the arbitrariness found in nature" (88).

Capitalist Versus Socialist Property Relations

For the first half of Theory, Rawls ignores almost completely the question of property relations. He does assume the presence of a free market or "competitive economy" (137), but he expresses no concern as to whether the ownership of the means of production is public or private. Only near the middle of Theory does he consider this question in a sustained manner. At the beginning of the chapter titled "Distributive Shares," Rawls reiterates that "the choice between a private-property owning economy and socialism is left open; from the standpoint of justice alone, various basic structures would appear to satisfy its principles" (228). In itself, Rawls's neutrality on economic systems seems consistent with his difference principle. Difficulties would arise, however, if one system can produce greater economic advantages than another for all persons. Moreover, what if inequalities in the more prosperous society are not to everyone's benefit, but the least fortunate are still better off than in the society where the difference principle prevails? Rawls considers neither question directly, but his theory of distributive justice would seem to require an answer. Instead, he simply leaves the determination of economic arrangements to individual circumstances; it is a matter "best left to the course of events to decide" (230).

Those committed to a market or a socialist or a mixed economy will find Rawls's lack of interest in this question alarming. If "justice as fairness" establishes equal basic liberties once and for all, regardless of social or cultural conditions, should it not establish something more definitive about the economic institutions that have such a "profound" impact on people's lives? Rawls repeatedly observes that economic arrangements are part of the basic structure, which is the "primary subject of justice" (82). Why then should the decision be left to "circumstances, institutions, and historical traditions" (248)? Might not the same be said with regard to political rights and liberties? Why, for example, are political rights noncontingent and absolute, on the one hand, but property relations contingent and relative, on the other?

Rawls appears to have a fourfold response. First, he claims agnosticism: "There is presumably no answer to this question" of private versus public ownership of the economy (242). Second, he pleads ignorance: "The theory of justice does not include these matters" (242). Third, he invokes historicism: the choice of economic arrangements "depends in large part upon the traditions, institutions, and social forces of each country, and its particular historical circumstances" (242). Finally, Rawls argues that a socialist economy is consistent with free-market principles and is potentially as productive as a capitalist system. As for the last of these points, the philosopher-cum-economist assures his readers that "there is no essential tie between the use of free markets and private ownership of the instruments of production" (239); on the contrary, he maintains, there is a basic "consistency of market arrangements with socialist institutions" (241). Moreover, inasmuch as "socialist systems normally allow for the free choice of occupation and of one's place of work" (239), they do not violate the first principles of justice. Indeed, "it is clear that, in theory anyway, a liberal socialist regime can also answer to the two principles of justice. We have only to suppose that the means of production are publicly owned and that firms are managed by workers' councils say, or by agents appointed by them" (248). (Just how worker-managed firms meet the requirements of equal basic liberties and the difference principle is unclear, however.) Accordingly, because a socialist regime can embody "justice as fairness" as well as a capitalist system, "[t]he theory of justice does not by itself favor either form of regime" (248). The question of private, public, or mixed ownership of land, farms, businesses, industry, and natural resources is not one of principle, but one of practice. It is a matter for "political judgment," a question of "which variation is most likely to work out best in practice" (242).

On the surface, Rawls's "response" to the proponents of market, socialist, or mixed economic systems appears reasonable and complete. As long as the two principles of justice are satisfied, each society should be free to work out its economic destiny in accordance with its particular circumstances. Considerations of justice will play a "necessary part" in the process, but "justice as fairness" does not provide a "sufficient" basis for selecting any particular set of economic arrangements (242). Of course, Rawls can define justice or limit its scope in any manner he chooses. Still, in taking the question of economic arrangements off the table, does he not truncate his conception of justice, which takes the "basic structure" (including economic arrangements) as the "primary subject of justice"? His answer to this objection is that economic policy (including property relations) is a second-order question left to the determination of the "constitutional" or "legislative" stages of social formation.

Here (and not at the initial stage of deliberation) is where persons "ascertain how the principles of justice apply" to economic arrangements (229). Yet by Rawls's own account, such principles will be largely relative insofar as they depend on the "traditions, institutions, and social forces of each country" (242). And what if these traditions do not honor the difference principle, or if the existing institutions exhibit pervasive inequalities yet enjoy widespread support, or if existing social forces oppose Rawlsian policies of economic justice? Is a society then simply "unjust" in spite of itself? One further caveat: If in the "original position" Rawls is willing to settle the matter of distributive justice (equal shares), why should he be unwilling to do so once the "veil of ignorance" is removed? He is not necessarily required to give a definitive answer to the question of public, private, or mixed ownership, of course, but ignoring it altogether leaves a curious gap in his political philosophy.

That Rawls himself was not entirely satisfied with this lacuna is suggested in the preface he added to Theory in 1999, where he observes that in hindsight he would have "distinguish[ed] more sharply the idea of a property-owning democracy . . . from the idea of a welfare state" (xiv). The need to underscore this distinction presumably stems from the common (mis)conception that Rawls was advancing an argument for the modern welfare state. Given his call for a "social minimum," progressive taxation, reallocation of resources, and other features commonly associated with welfarism, it is not difficult to see how readers arrived at this conclusion. Yet Rawls insists that the model he advanced in Theory was not the welfare state, which permits unjustifiable inequalities in exchange for a social minimum, but an "ideal property-owning system" (242), which satisfies the two principles of justice. A careful reading of sections 41-43 makes this distinction apparent if not entirely clear (hence the proposed "revision" mentioned in the preface). First,

Rawls eschews the phrase "welfare economics" because of its association with utilitarianism (228-29), which he explicitly rejects as a philosophical framework for working out his theory of justice. Next, he argues that neither a capitalist nor a socialist system is, ceteris paribus, more consistent with the principles of justice than the other. (He does go to great lengths, however, to prove that, "theoretically at least, a socialist regime can avail itself of the advantages of this [free-market] system" [240].) Finally, he provides a sketch of an "ideal scheme" of economic arrangements for a "property-owning democracy" (242). Again, lest it be thought that he is "privileging" capitalism in selecting this model, he hastens to add that his choice of schemes springs simply from the fact that "this case is likely to be better known": it is not, however, "intended to prejudge the choice of regimes in particular cases" (242).

Although this disclaimer would appear sufficient, Rawls seeks to distance himself further from capitalist societies and their "grave injustices." Just because we can imagine "an ideal property-owning system that would be just does not imply that historical forms are just, or even tolerable" (242). Rawls admits that "the same is true of socialism" (242), but he is far more concerned (here and elsewhere) with disavowing any preference for capitalism than with distancing himself from socialism. As we have seen, Rawls provides a spirited defense of socialism as a viable economic system. In his originalist defense of "equal shares," his a priori belief that political liberty is fully consistent with public ownership of the means of production, and his implicit attack on the "grave injustices" of capitalist societies, he seems to express a tacit preference for socialism, "in theory anyway."

Rawls's "Ideal" Economic Democracy

The principal difference between a welfare state and a property-owning democracy is that the latter ensures "the widespread ownership of productive assets and human capital (educated abilities and trained skills)" (xv). More specifically, basic institutions must from the outset put in the hands of citizens generally, and not only of a few, the productive means to be fully cooperating members of a society. The emphasis falls on the steady dispersal over time of the ownership of capital and resources by the laws of inheritance and bequest, on fair equality of opportunity secured by provisions for education and training, and the like, as well as on institutions that support the fair value of the political liberties. . . . [The purpose of such arrangements is to] put all citizens in a position to manage their own affairs and to take part in social cooperation on a footing of mutual respect and under appropriately equal conditions. (xv)

Whatever else may be said of Rawls's "ideal" democracy, he is certainly correct in distinguishing it from the welfare state. In Theory, Rawls provides a few details regarding property rights, the regulation of business, taxation, education, and welfare. Here, too, the aims are to "prevent concentrations of power" and to "encourage the wide dispersal of property" (245). Indeed, only by "gradually and continually . . .correct[ing] the distribution of wealth" is it possible to ensure "the fair value of political liberty and fair equality of opportunity" (245). I have yet to discuss these terms, but they are central to Rawls's theory of justice and contribute substantially to its novelty. By adding fair to these familiar concepts, Rawls aims to give political liberty and equality of opportunity a greater substantive (as opposed to a merely formal) value. Although he is characteristically short on specifics, by fair he means something more than the mere absence of legal discrimination or arbitrary barriers to positions and offices. Just what this condition would mean in practice, however, is unclear. What is clear is that Rawls believes that "fairness" is not possible in a society that fails to institute the widespread (re)distribution of wealth and income. He might well have specified (if only approximately) how wide the "dispersal" of capital and resources must be in order to qualify as fair or just. His failure to do so raises an important question. Would considerations of efficiency limit the degree of economic decentralization, or would "fairness" considerations trump efficiency? The same might be asked with regard to taxation-cum-redistribution policies. In any event, Rawls clearly suggests that the concentration of economic power would be a perennial problem even under ideal arrangements. As noted earlier, policymakers would be required "gradually and continually to correct the distribution of wealth and to prevent concentrations of power" (245, emphasis added). The implication is that the concentration of wealth is "natural" in a capitalist economy, even when the means of production are widely dispersed. A further implication is that the widespread dispersal of the means of production would be notably inefficient. If so, would it be necessary for the Rawlsian state to subsidize inefficient or noncompetitive firms in the interest of maintaining economic pluralism and the "fairness" it serves?

Just how the economic arrangements of Rawls's "ideal" democracy would affect the principles of efficiency, productivity, innovation, and incentive is not immediately clear, but one need not be an economist to suspect a negative result for each. More important, Rawls shows no signs of recognizing this prospect, which perhaps is not surprising in light of his faith in the efficacy of market socialism. Perhaps he simply is willing to sacrifice efficiency, productivity, and so forth in the interest of his "strongly egalitarian" (65) conception of justice. This reading would be consistent with Rawls's belief that in choosing between economic systems, "[c]onsiderations of efficiency are but one basis of decision and often relatively minor at that" (229). Because the decision "involves some view of the human good," it "must . . . be made on moral and political as well as on economic grounds" (229). This position is certainly reasonable and fully consistent with his view that justice has a priority over efficiency, just as liberties have a privilege above economic advantages. Nevertheless, it is reasonable to ask: To what degree should efficiency be sacrificed in the name of justice? Is there not a point at which a disregard for efficiency in the name of fairness encroaches on justice itself? Rawls does not consider this possibility, but it is curious that although minimizing the importance of efficiency when raising the question of choice of economic systems, he proceeds to defend the market system on the basis of its "efficiency" (240).

The reader concerned about the status of property rights in Theory may presume that in Rawls's "property-owning democracy"-where "private ownership of capital and natural resources" is admitted (243)-individual property rights are secure. Such, however, does not appear to be the case. In discussing the "allocation branch" (one of five proposed governmental "background institutions"-the others are the "stabilization," "transfer," "distribution," and "exchange" branches),

Rawls notes that one of its chief functions is to effect "changes in the definition of property rights" (244). Ironically, the purpose of such changes (along with affecting "reasonably full employment," the task of the "stabilization" branch) is "to maintain the efficiency of the market economy generally" (244). Similarly, Rawls proposes "necessary adjustments in the rights of property" in order to "preserve an approximate justice in distributive shares" (245), the task of the "distribution" branch. (The "transfer" branch is charged with maintaining a "social minimum," and the "exchange" branch considers measures outside the scope of justice.)

Even in Rawls's "property-owning democracy," then, private-property rights (outside of "personal property") clearly are not secure. The heavy tax rates Rawls proposes on inheritance and income apparently suffice to ensure a distribution of wealth consistent with the "fair value" of liberty and opportunity demanded by "justice" (246-47). Property itself is made subject to redistribution whenever its accumulation is perceived to violate the canons of "fairness," but Rawls (conveniently) leaves unstated precisely how such a determination would be made. More to the point, the prospect that property rights in the means of production will be subject to continual "adjustments" strongly suggests that they are not "rights" at all-at least not in the conventional sense. Furthermore, the practical consequences of this conception of property appear disturbing at best and disastrous at worst.

A government authorized to "redefine" and "readjust" property relations in the ways Rawls suggests (for example, through redistribution of privately owned capital and natural resources) is ill-suited to gain the confidence of those whose fortunes are tied to private enterprise (owners and workers), much less to encourage an entrepreneurial spirit. The insecurity of property rights and the shadowy nature of property relations under Rawls's scheme would more likely create a climate of uncertainty, distrust, and complacency. In lieu of clearly defined property rights and stable relations in property, individuals would have little incentive to behave in a manner consistent with the principles of efficiency, productivity, and innovation. Unless Rawls envisages a relatively stagnant economy in which productive capacities are held in check by heavy taxes and the threat of expropriation, his provisions for a "property-owning democracy" are likely to be self-defeating. Indeed, given these provisions, is he not misleading readers in calling his scheme a property-owning democracy? Insofar as Rawls's model aspires to a condition of economic equality through the "steady dispersal" of collective assets over time, should it not be more accurately characterized as a species of socialism?

A Complete Political Theory?

Having surveyed Rawls's remarks on property and economic systems, we are now in a position to consider whether the teaching in Theory constitutes a political philosophy in the comprehensive sense. Before doing so, however, it may be advisable to consult Rawls's other major treatise, Political Liberalism (1993). Because this book restricts itself to a "political conception of justice" (as opposed to the comprehensive moral doctrine articulated in Theory), we might expect that property relations (and economic arrangements generally) will receive more substantial and definitive treatment there. This expectation is disappointed, however. We find only a restatement of the position taken in Theory: that private ownership beyond "personal property" is not a "basic right" (1993, 338); that "the question of private property in the means of production or their social ownership . . . [is] not settled at the level of the first principles of justice, but depend[s] upon the traditions and social institutions of a country and its particular problems and historical circumstances" (338); and that the determination of property relations is left to the "legislative stage" of social formation (339). Rawls's rationale for taking this position is based on the limits of "[p]hilosophical argument" to persuade others of the "correct" view of ownership of the means of production (338, 339). (He does not consider, however, the notion that empirical considerations might be relevant to the question.) He does add that the two principles of justice provide "a possible common court of appeal for settling the question of property" (339), but (as in Theory) the relation between the imperative of "justice as fairness" and the reality of historical contingency remains unexplored. In fine, the question of "private-property democracy versus liberal socialism" is left "on all fours" (416).

Inasmuch as Political Liberalism (or the subsequent Justice as Fairness: A Restatement [2001]) adds nothing new to Rawls's view of property relations, we may proceed to our final query. To rephrase the question: Does "justice as fairness" qualify as a complete political theory even though it fails to specify the nature of property relations or economic arrangements? More specifically, can Rawls's theory qualify as comprehensive when it remains totally agnostic on matters widely acknowledged as central to considerations of prudence, efficiency, and justice? Given the mass of available evidence from the work of economists and economic historians, is it acceptable for a political philosophy that aspires to completeness to express no preference whatsoever for a particular economic system or to abjure a consideration of the merits of various economic systems? Is it sufficient simply to stipulate, as Rawls does in Theory, that "justice as fairness includes no natural right of private property in the means of production . . . nor a natural right to worker-owned and -managed firms" ([1971] 1999, xvi) and leave the matter there?

The answer to these questions hinges on two considerations. First, property relations are arguably as vital a concern to citizens and as critical to the well-being of a society as political rights and civil liberties. As Rousseau wrote in his Discourse on Political Economy, "the right to property is the most sacred of all the citizens' rights, and more important in certain respects than liberty itself. . . . [P]roperty is the true foundation of civil society and the true guarantee of the citizens' commitments" (qtd. in Cress 1987, 127). Like Rawls, Rousseau denied a "natural right" to private property and grounds its legitimacy in convention and positive title. Yet Rousseau (who was no less an egalitarian than Rawls) clearly recognized that property rights are foundational in a sense that Rawls apparently fails to appreciate. By this statement, I mean that the right of ownership is not something simply to be juxtaposed with liberty (as Rawls does); it lies at the very heart of liberty. This observation is hardly new; political philosophers and philosophical economists have voiced it for centuries. The belief that private ownership is central to liberty per se does not imply, however, that it is a "natural" right or justify a right to unlimited accumulation. It does create, nonetheless, a presumption that property constitutes a species of liberty and should not be sequestered from political rights as Rawls has done.

Reference to the history of political thought provides a second standard for assessing the status of Rawls's political philosophy. Those familiar with the canon of political classics (and with the history of political theory generally) know that questions of property relations have figured importantly (and sometimes prominently) in the works of nearly all the major political philosophers. Plato, Aristotle, Cicero, Aquinas, Machiavelli, Hobbes, Locke, Montesquieu, Hume, Rousseau, Publius, Kant, Burke, Hegel, Marx, and Mill had something significant (and often something definite) to say about property in one form or another. As Howard Williams, a Kant scholar, writes: "That the concept of property has been a central concern of political philosophy from classical times onward is not surprising in view of the fact that the way in which wealth and goods are held determines a great deal of the structure and make-up of a community. Property relations go to the root of any social system" (1983, 77).

The main point is that no major political thinker (nor a host of lesser figures) believed that the determination of basic property relations lies beyond the fundamental concerns of political speculation. To leave such a profound question-whether a society is to be capitalist or socialist- "on all fours" would have struck most of them as a fatal omission. Similarly, to say that considerations of justice alone can tell us nothing about the desirability of radically different economic systems would have elicited perplexity, and perhaps disdain. That Rawls does provide a characterization of society that includes a discussion of economic arrangements (his "property-owning democracy") might mitigate such responses, yet, as we have seen, his ideal makes no claim to priority or privilege over a "liberal socialist regime." If either system is privileged, it is socialism, for the reasons given earlier. This position creates an interesting (and largely unobserved) tension in Rawls's political thought. It also speaks to what is perhaps the greatest frustration surrounding his philosophy: his sphinxlike silence on the relation of his theory of justice to existing societies and on the matter of his political commitments. On the basis of the foregoing analysis, one is tempted to implore:

"Professor Rawls, come out of your ivory closet, check your fancy philosophy at the door, and confirm that you are, indeed, a 'bourgeois socialist'" (Bayer 1990, 574)! Such a revelation would be the first step in elevating Rawls's status as the creator of a comprehensive political philosophy. It would not only comport with the principles outlined in Theory, but free Rawls to commit himself on the matter of property. In doing so, he then might justifiably claim his place among the titans of political thought. Short of this confession, however, John Rawls must remain in the second tier of political authors who, notwithstanding their fame and influence, articulate only a partial philosophy of politics.

Of course, we might read Rawls's "original omission" on the subject of property in other ways. It is possible to represent the exclusion of property relations as an advance in political speculation that, on one hand, serves to direct the focus of political philosophy toward (formal) questions of justice "transcending" specific economic arrangements and that, on the other hand, subordinates economics to the requirements of justice, thus providing a rational-cum-moral basis for assessing a whole range of economic arrangements. Although justice tout court cannot settle the matter of property relations, we might argue that it can "set out in a schematic way the outlines of a just economic system that admits of several variations" (Rawls [1971] 1999, 242). Whether Rawls's (admittedly "limited") construction of justice constitutes an advance over the tradition of political philosophy (or merely a valid alternative) must be left ultimately to each observer. Yet even if we grant the legitimacy of Rawls's "omission," there remains the matter of his "ideal" scheme, which entails widespread distribution of (nonpersonal) property, progressive rates of taxation, marked restrictions of the right of bequest, ongoing "adjustments" in property rights, and the redistribution of income, capital, and natural resources. As suggested earlier, this scheme-along with other facets of his theory of justice-suggests that his putative neutrality on economic systems actually veils a discernable preference for principles, policies, and outcomes closely associated with the socialist tradition. He even defends his adoption of free-market principles (in part) on the basis of its consistency with public ownership of the means of production. In fine, Rawls's capitalist model of democracy looks suspiciously like a species of socialism insofar as it truncates property rights, widely redistributes wealth and income, and aims to place the means of production in the hands of "the people." If his "property-owning democracy" represents capitalism under "justice as fairness," one can only conclude that his "liberal socialist regime" would impose further restrictions on property rights and intensify redistributivist policies. In light of these considerations, we may conclude that perhaps Rawls has not omitted the question of property after all and that "justice as fairness" naturally leads to a society of a distinctively socialist caste, "theoretically at least."

ROBERT NOZICK (1938-2002)

A thinker with wide-ranging interests, Robert Nozick is one of the most important and influential political philosophers, along with John Rawls, in the Anglo-American analytic tradition. His first and most celebrated book, Anarchy, State, and Utopia (1974), has brought about, along with his Harvard colleague John Rawls' A Theory of Justice (1971), the revival of the discipline of social and political philosophy within the analytic school. Rawls' influential book is a systematic defense of egalitarian liberalism, but Nozick's Anarchy, State, and Utopia is a compelling defense of free-market libertarianism.

Unlike Rawls, Nozick neglected political philosophy for the rest of his philosophical career. He moved on to address other philosophical questions and made significant contributions to other areas of philosophical inquiry. In epistemology, Nozick developed an externalist analysis of knowledge in terms of counterfactual conditions that provides a response to radical skepticism. In metaphysics, he proposed a "closest continuer" theory of personal identity.

His final work, Invariances (2001), offers a theory of objective reality. His other significant contributions to analytic philosophy notwithstanding, Nozick's defense of libertarianism remains his most notable intellectual mark on philosophical inquiry.

Life

Robert Nozick was born in Brooklyn, New York in 1938, and he taught at Harvard University until his death in January 2002. He was a thinker of the prodigious sort who gains a reputation for brilliance within his chosen field while still in graduate school, in his case at the Princeton of the early 1960's, where he wrote his dissertation on decision theory under the supervision of Carl Hempel. He was also, like so many young intellectuals of that period, drawn initially to the politics of the New Left and to the socialism that was its philosophical inspiration. But encountering the works of such defenders of capitalism as F.A. Hayek, Ludwig von Mises, Murray Rothbard, and Ayn Rand eventually led him to renounce those views, and to shift his philosophical focus away from the technical issues then dominating analytic philosophy and toward political theory. The result was his first and most famous book, Anarchy, State, and Utopia (1974), an ingenious defense of libertarianism that immediately took on canonical status as the major right-wing philosophical counterpoint to his Harvard colleague John Rawls's influential defense of social-democratic liberalism, A Theory of Justice (1971).

Like Rawls's book, Nozick's generated lively debate and an enormous secondary literature. But where Rawls made the development of his theory of justice and its defense against critics his life's work, Nozick took little interest either in responding to critics of Anarchy, State, and Utopia in particular or in continuing to do systematic work in political philosophy in general. Instead, he moved on to produce groundbreaking work in several other areas of philosophical inquiry, particularly in epistemology and metaphysics. His development of an externalist theory of knowledge and his "closest continuer" account of personal identity have been particularly influential. It remains to be seen what impact on philosophy will be made by the general theory of objective truth developed in his last book, Invariances (2001), published shortly before his untimely death from stomach cancer.

In any case, it seems clear, judging from the disproportionate amount of attention that it has received relative to the rest of his writings, that it is his early work in political theory that will stand as his most significant and lasting contribution.

Anarchy, State, and Utopia and Libertarianism

Anarchy, State, and Utopia is, together with Rawls's A Theory of Justice, generally regarded as one of the two great classics of twentieth-century analytic political philosophy. Indeed, these two works essentially revived the discipline of political philosophy within the analytic school, whose practitioners had, until Rawls and Nozick came along, largely neglected it. Nozick's book also revived interest in the notion of rights as being central to political theory, and it did so in the service of another idea that had been long neglected within academic political thought, namely libertarianism.

Libertarianism is a political philosophy holding that the role of the state in society ought to be severely limited, confined essentially to police protection, national defense, and the administration of courts of law, with all other tasks commonly performed by modern governments - education, social insurance, welfare, and so forth - taken over by religious bodies, charities, and other private institutions operating in a free market.

Many libertarians appeal, in defending their position, to economic and sociological considerations - the benefits of market competition, the inherent mechanisms inclining state bureaucracies toward incompetence and inefficiency, the poor record of governmental attempts to deal with specific problems like poverty and pollution, and so forth. Nozick endorses such arguments, but his main defense of libertarianism is a moral one, his view being that whatever its practical benefits, the strongest reason to advocate a libertarian society is simply that such advocacy follows from a serious respect for individual rights.

Self-Ownership, Individual Rights, and the Minimal State

Nozick takes his position to follow from a basic moral principle associated with Immanuel Kant and enshrined in Kant's second formulation of his famous Categorical Imperative: "Act so that you treat humanity, whether in your own person or in that of another, always as an end and never as a means only." The idea here is that a human being, as a rational agent endowed with self-awareness, free will, and the possibility of formulating a plan of life, has an inherent dignity and cannot properly be treated as a mere thing, or used against his will as an instrument or resource in the way an inanimate object might be.

In line with this, Nozick also describes individual human beings as self-owners (though it isn't clear whether he regards this as a restatement of Kant's principle, a consequence of it, or an entirely independent idea). The thesis of self-ownership, a notion that goes back in political philosophy at least to John Locke, is just the claim that individuals own themselves - their bodies, talents and abilities, labor, and by extension the fruits or products of their exercise of their talents, abilities and labor. They have all the prerogatives with respect to themselves that a slaveholder claims with respect to his slaves. But the thesis of self-ownership would in fact rule out slavery as illegitimate, since each individual, as a self-owner, cannot properly be owned by anyone else. (Indeed, many libertarians would argue that unless one accepts the thesis of self-ownership, one has no way of explaining why slavery is evil. After all, it cannot be merely because slaveholders often treat their slaves badly, since a kind-hearted slaveholder would still be a slaveholder, and thus morally blameworthy, for that. The reason slavery is immoral must be because it involves a kind of stealing - the stealing of a person from himself.)

But if individuals are inviolable ends-in-themselves (as Kant describes them) and self-owners, it follows, Nozick says, that they have certain rights, in particular (and here again following Locke) rights to their lives, liberty, and the fruits of their labor. To own something, after all, just is to have a right to it, or, more accurately, to possess the bundle of rights - rights to possess something, to dispose of it, to determine what may be done with it, etc. - that constitute ownership; and thus to own oneself is to have such rights to the various elements that make up one's self. These rights function, Nozick says, as side-constraints on the actions of others; they set limits on how others may, morally speaking, treat a person. So, for example, since you own yourself, and thus have a right to yourself, others are constrained morally not to kill or maim you (since this would involve destroying or damaging your property), or to kidnap you or forcibly remove one of your bodily organs for transplantation in someone else (since this would involve stealing your property). They are also constrained not to force you against your will to work for another's purposes, even if those purposes are good ones. For if you own yourself, it follows that you have a right to determine whether and how you will use your self-owned body and its powers, e.g. either to work or to refrain from working.

So far this all might seem fairly uncontroversial. But what follows from it, in Nozick's view, is the surprising and radical conclusion that taxation, of the redistributive sort in which modern states engage in order to fund the various programs of the bureaucratic welfare state, is morally illegitimate. It amounts to a kind of forced labor, for the state so structures the tax system that any time you labor at all, a certain amount of your labor time - the amount that produces the wealth taken away from you forcibly via taxation - is time you involuntarily work, in effect, for the state. Indeed, such taxation amounts to partial slavery, for in giving every citizen an entitlement to certain benefits (welfare, social security, or whatever), the state in effect gives them an entitlement, a right, to a part of the proceeds of your labor, which produces the taxes that fund the benefits; every citizen, that is, becomes in such a system a partial owner of you (since they have a partial property right in part of you, i.e. in your labor). But this is flatly inconsistent with the principle of self-ownership.

The various programs of the modern liberal welfare state are thus immoral, not only because they are inefficient and incompetently administered, but because they make slaves of the citizens of such a state. Indeed, the only sort of state that can be morally justified is what Nozick calls a minimal state or "night-watchman" state, a government which protects individuals, via police and military forces, from force, fraud, and theft, and administers courts of law, but does nothing else.

In particular, such a state cannot regulate what citizens eat, drink, or smoke (since this would interfere with their right to use their self-owned bodies as they see fit), cannot control what they publish or read (since this would interfere with their right to use the property they've acquired with their self-owned labor - e.g. printing presses and paper - as they wish), cannot administer mandatory social insurance schemes or public education (since this would interfere with citizens' rights to use the fruits of their labor as they desire, in that some citizens might decide that they would rather put their money into private education and private retirement plans), and cannot regulate economic life in general via minimum wage and rent control laws and the like (since such actions are not only economically suspect - tending to produce bad unintended consequences like unemployment and housing shortages - but violate citizens' rights to charge whatever they want to for the use of their own property).

Refuting the Anarchist

It might be thought that given Nozick's premises, no state at all, minimal or otherwise, could be justified, that full-blown anarchism is what really follows from the notion of self-ownership. For the activities of even a minimal state would need to be funded via taxation. Wouldn't this taxation also amount to forced labor and partial slavery? Nozick thinks not. Indeed, in his view it turns out that even if an anarchistic society existed, not only could a minimal state nevertheless arise out of it in a way that violates no one's self-ownership rights, in fact such a state would, morally speaking, have to come into existence.

Suppose there is a certain geographical area in which no state exists, and everyone must protect his own rights to life, liberty, and property, without relying on a government and its police and military to do so. Given that doing so would be costly, difficult, and time-consuming, people would, Nozick says, inevitably band together to form voluntary protection associations, agreeing to take turns standing watch over each others' property, to decide collectively how to punish rights-violators, and so forth. Eventually some members of this anarchistic community would decide to go into the protection business full-time, instituting a private firm that would offer protection services to members of the community in exchange for a fee. Other members of the community might start competing firms, and a free market would develop in protection services.

Inevitably, Nozick argues, this process will (via a kind of "invisible hand" mechanism of the sort discussed by economists) give rise to either a single dominant firm or a dominant confederation of firms. For most people will surely judge that where protection of their lives and property is concerned, nothing short of the biggest and most powerful provider of such protection will do, so that they will flock to whatever firm is perceived as such; and the "snowball" effect this will create will ensure that that firm ends up with an overwhelming share of the market. Even if multiple large firms come into being, however, they are likely to form a kind of single dominant association of firms.

For there will be occasions when the clients of different firms come into conflict with one another, one client accusing the other of violating his rights, the other insisting on his innocence. Firms could go to war over the claims of their respective clients, but this would be costly, especially if (as is likely) such conflicts between clients became frequent. More feasible would be an agreement between firms to abide by certain common rules for adjudicating disputes between clients and to go along with the decisions of arbitrators retained by the firms to interpret these rules - to institute, that is, a common quasi-legal system of sorts. With the advent of such a dominant protection agency (or confederation of agencies) - an organization comprised essentially of analogues of police and military forces and courts of law - our anarchistic society will obviously have gone a long way toward evolving a state, though strictly speaking, this agency is still a private firm rather than a government.

How will the dominant protection agency deal with independents - those (relatively few) individuals who retain no protection firm and insist on defending their rights themselves - who attempt to mete out justice to those of its clients they accuse of rights violations? Will it allow them to try and punish its clients as they see fit? Nozick argues that the dominant agency will not allow this and, morally speaking, must not. For the agency was hired to protect its clients' rights, and that includes a right not to be arrested, tried, or punished unjustly or, where one really is guilty of a rights violation, to be punished more harshly than one deserves. Of course, its clients might really be guilty; but the point is, so long as the dominant agency doesn't itself know that they are, it cannot allow them to be punished. The dominant agency must, accordingly, generally prohibit independents from defending their own rights against its clients; it must take upon itself the exclusive right to decide which of its clients is worthy of punishment, and what sort of punishment that ought to be. In doing so, however, it has taken on one of the defining features of a state, viz. a monopoly on the legitimate use of force. It has become what Nozick calls an "ultra-minimal state."

In doing so, however, the dominant agency seems to have jeopardized the rights of independents - for though it has (rightly) prohibited those independents from exacting justice on its own clients, lest they inflict unjust punishments, it has thereby also left them unable to defend their own rights. To avoid committing an injustice against independents, then, the dominant agency or ultra-minimal state must compensate them for this - it must, that is, defend their rights for them by providing them the very protection services it affords its own clients. It can, Nozick says, legitimately charge them for this protection, but only the amount that they would have spent anyway in defending themselves. The end result of this process, though, is that the ultra-minimal state has taken on another feature of a state, namely the provision of protection to everyone within its borders. Moreover, in charging everyone for this protection it engages, in effect, in a kind of taxation (though this taxation - and only this taxation - does not violate self-ownership rights, because the original clients of the agency pay voluntarily, while the later, formerly independent, clients are charged only an amount they would have spent anyway for protection). The ultra-minimal state has thus become a full-fledged minimal state.

A minimal state would thus inevitably arise out of an originally anarchic society, given both practical circumstances and the moral requirements - concerning the prohibition of potentially rights-violating self-defense and compensation for this prohibition - binding on any agency acting to enforce the rights of others. And it would do so in a way that violates no one's rights of self-ownership. So the anarchist can have no principled objection to it.

Nozick's conception of the origins of the state is reminiscent of the social contract tradition in political thought represented by Hobbes, Locke, Rousseau, and, in contemporary thought, Rawls. For insofar as the state arises out of a process that begins with the voluntary retention by individuals of the services of an agency that will inevitably take on the features of a state, it can be seen to be the result of a kind of contract. The details of the state-originating process in Nozick's account are very different from those of other social contract accounts, however; and, most importantly, for Nozick, unlike other social contract theorists, individual rights do not result from, but exist prior to, any social contract, and put severe constraints on the shape such a contract can take. Furthermore, the parties to the contract in Nozick's conception are to be imagined very much on the model of human beings as we know them in "real life," rather than along the lines of the highly abstractly conceived rational agents deliberating behind a "veil of ignorance" in Rawls's "original position" thought experiment.

Distributive Justice

Most critics of the libertarian minimal state don't complain that it allows for too much government; they say that it allows for far too little. In particular, they claim that a more-than-minimal state is necessary in order to fulfill the requirements of distributive justice. The state, it is held (by, for instance, Rawls and his followers), simply must engage in redistributive taxation in order to ensure that a fair distribution of wealth and income obtains in the society it governs. Nozick's answer to this objection constitutes his "entitlement theory" of justice.

Talk about "distributive justice" is inherently misleading, Nozick argues, in that it seems to imply that there is some central authority who "distributes" to individuals shares of wealth and income that pre-exist the distribution, as if they had appeared like "manna from heaven." Of course this is not really the way such shares come into existence, or come to be "distributed," at all; in fact they come to be, and come to be held by the individuals who hold them, only through the scattered efforts and transactions of these innumerable individuals themselves, and these individuals' efforts and transactions give them a moral claim over these shares. Talk about the "distribution of wealth" covers this up, and unjustifiably biases most discussions of distributive justice in a socialist or egalitarian liberal direction.

A more adequate theory of justice would in Nozick's view enumerate three principles of justice in holdings. The first would be a principle of justice in acquisition, that is, the appropriation of natural resources that no one has ever owned before. The best-known such principle, some version of which Nozick seems to endorse, is the one enshrined in Locke's theory of property, according to which a person (being a self-owner) owns his labor, and by "mixing his labor" with a previously unowned part of the natural world (e.g. by whittling a stick found in a forest into a spear) thereby comes to own it. The second principle would be a principle of justice in transfer, governing the manner in which one might justly come to own something previously owned by another. Here Nozick endorses the principle that a transfer of holdings is just if and only if it is voluntary, a principle that would seem to follow from respect for a person's right to use the fruits of the exercise of his self-owned talents, abilities, and labor as he sees fit. The final principle would be a principle of justice in rectification, governing the proper means of setting right past injustices in acquisition and transfer.

Anyone who got what he has in a manner consistent with these three principles would, Nozick says, accordingly be entitled to it - for, his having abided by these principles, no one has any grounds for complaint against him. This gives us Nozick's entitlement theory of distributive justice: a distribution of wealth obtaining in a society as a whole is a just distribution if everyone in that society is entitled to what he has, i.e. has gotten his holdings in accordance with the principles of acquisition, transfer, and rectification.

And it is therefore just however equal or unequal it happens to be, and indeed however "fair" or "unfair" it might seem intuitively to be. Standard theories of distributive justice, Nozick says, are either ahistorical "end-state" or "end-result" theories, requiring that the distribution of wealth in a society have a certain structure, e.g. an egalitarian structure (regardless of how the distribution came about or how people got what they have); or they are historical theories requiring that the distribution fit a certain pattern reflecting such historical circumstances as who worked the hardest or who deserves the most. The entitlement theory of justice is historical yet unpatterned: The justice of a distribution is indeed determined by certain historical circumstances (contrary to end-state theories), but it has nothing to do with fitting any pattern guaranteeing that those who worked the hardest or are most deserving have the most shares. What matters is only that people get what they have in a manner consistent with the three principles of justice in holdings, and this is fully compatible with some people having much more than others, unlucky hard workers having less than lazier but luckier ones, morally repulsive individuals having higher incomes than saints, and so forth.

Nozick illustrates and defends the entitlement theory in a famous thought-experiment involving the basketball player Wilt Chamberlain. Imagine a society in which the distribution of wealth fits a particular structure or pattern favored by a non-entitlement conception of justice - suppose, to keep things simple, that it is an equal distribution, and call it D1. Nozick's opponent must of course grant that this distribution is just, since Nozick has allowed the opponent himself to determine it. Now suppose that among the members of this society is Wilt Chamberlain, and that he has as a condition of his contract with his team that he will play only if each person coming to see the game puts twenty-five cents into a special box at the gate of the sports arena, the contents of which will go to him. Suppose further that over the course of the season, one million fans decide to pay the twenty-five cents to watch him play. The result will be a new distribution, D2, in which Chamberlain now has $250,000, much more than anyone else - a distribution which thereby breaks the original pattern established in D1. Now, is D2 just? Is Chamberlain entitled to his money? The answer to these questions, Nozick says, is clearly "Yes." For everyone in D1 was, by hypothesis, entitled to what he had; there is no injustice in the starting point that led up to D2. Moreover, everyone who gave up twenty-five cents in the transition from D1 to D2 did so voluntarily, and thus has no grounds for complaint; and those who did not want to pay to see Chamberlain play still have their twenty-five cents, so they have no grounds for complaint either. But then no one has any grounds for a complaint of injustice; and thus there is no injustice.

What this shows, in Nozick's view, is that all non-entitlement theories of justice are false. For all such theories claim that it is a necessary condition for a distribution's being just that it have a certain structure or fit a certain pattern; but the Wilt Chamberlain example (which can be reformulated so that D1 is, instead of an egalitarian distribution, a distribution according to hard work, desert, or whatever) shows that a distribution (such as D2) can be just even if it doesn't have a particular structure or pattern.

Moreover, the example shows that "liberty upsets patterns," that allowing individuals freely to use their holdings as they choose will inevitably destroy any distribution advocated by non-entitlement theories, whether they be socialist, egalitarian liberal, or some other theory of distribution. And the corollary of this is that patterns destroy liberty, that attempts to enforce a particular distributional pattern or structure over time will necessarily involve intolerable levels of coercion, forbidding individuals from using the fruits of their talents, abilities, and labor as they see fit. As Nozick puts it, "the socialist society would have to forbid capitalist acts between consenting adults." This is not merely a regrettable side-effect of the quest to attain a just distribution of wealth; it is a positive injustice, for it violates the principle of self-ownership.

Distributive justice, properly understood, thus does not require a redistribution of wealth; indeed, it forbids such a redistribution. Accordingly, the minimal state, far from being inconsistent with the demands of distributive justice, is in fact the only sure means of securing those demands.

Utopia

The minimal state might seem, even to those sympathetic to the arguments for it, to make for a rather austere vision of political life. But Nozick insists that we ought to see it as "inspiring, as well as right." Indeed, the minimal state constitutes in his view a kind of utopia. For, among all models of political order, it alone makes possible the attempt to realize every person's and group's vision of the good society.

It is often thought that libertarianism entails that everyone must live according to a laissez faire capitalist ethos, but this is not so; it requires only that, whatever ethos one is committed to, one not impose it by force on anyone else without his consent.

If some individuals or groups want to live according to socialist or egalitarian principles, they are free to do so as far as Nozick is concerned; indeed, they may even establish a community, of whatever size, within the boundaries of the minimal state, and require that everyone who comes to live within it must agree to have a portion of his wealth redistributed. All they are forbidden from doing is forcing people to join or contribute to the establishment of such a community who do not want to do so.

The minimal state thus constitutes a "framework for utopia" - an overarching system within the boundaries of which any number of social, moral, and religious utopian visions may be realized. It thereby provides a way for people even of radically opposed points of view - socialists and capitalists, liberals and conservatives, atheists and religious believers, whether Jews, Christians, Muslims, Buddhists, Hindus - to make a go of implementing their conceptions of how life ought to be lived, within their own communities, while living side by side in peace. This gives us, in Nozick's view, a further reason to endorse it.

Epistemology

Nozick's most influential contributions to philosophy outside of political theory have been in epistemology and the metaphysics of personal identity. In the case of the former, he is best known for his version of an "externalist" theory of knowledge, developed in his second book, Philosophical Explanations (1981).

Traditional theories of knowledge hold that a knower S knows a proposition p if and only if S believes p, p is true, and S is justified in believing p.

The third condition has always been the most problematic: the logical possibility of skeptical scenarios in which the would-be knower is the hapless victim of an omnipotent, omniscient, and deceiving Cartesian demon, or a brain in a vat hooked up by mad scientists to a virtual reality supercomputer feeding it non-stop hallucinations, threaten to make the justification of almost any belief impossible. Examples of the sort made famous by Edmund Gettier - wherein S has a justified true belief (say, a belief that it is now 5:00, based on S's glance at a nearby clock) that nevertheless does not plausibly amount to knowledge (say, because the clock is broken, and just by chance happens to be displaying the correct time) - also cast doubt on the adequacy of the traditional analysis of knowledge, whatever one says about the threat of skepticism.

These supposed inadequacies in the traditional view of knowledge are often said by its critics to stem from its "internalism" - the assumption that the factors that warrant S's claim to knowledge must be factors of which S is aware: factors internal to the set of his consciously held beliefs.

But these inadequacies can, it is argued, be remedied by adopting an externalist perspective instead, on which the factors that warrant S's belief, and make it genuine knowledge rather than mere belief, may well be factors of which S is entirely unaware, and which are external to his conscious cognitive processes.

One such factor (emphasized by "reliabilist" versions of externalism) might be a belief's having been produced by a reliable belief-producing mechanism: a mechanism of the existence and operations of which S might be utterly ignorant.

Nozick's unique contribution to the externalist approach is to suggest that the conditions that make S's true belief that p count as knowledge are the counterfactuals: (a) that were p not true S would not believe it (the "variation" condition), and (b) that were p still true in somewhat different circumstances, S would still believe it and would not believe that not-p (the "adherence" condition).

A belief that fulfills these conditions is one that, in Nozick's expression, "tracks the truth." (S's belief that it is 5:00 in the example above would fail to meet these conditions, and thus fails to track the truth: had it in fact been 4:55 when S looked at the broken clock, he would still have believed that it is 5:00; and had the clock been stopped at 4:55 instead, S would not believe that it is 5:00, and indeed would believe that it is not 5:00.)

Nozick applies this analysis to answering skepticism as follows. We ought to concede to the skeptic that S cannot know that he is not in fact a brain in a vat, for his belief that he isn't is not one that tracks the truth (since the variation condition can't be met - if it were not true that S is not a brain in a vat, S would still believe he isn't).

But though this might appear to give away the store to skepticism, in fact it does not. For what the skeptic claims to threaten are everyday beliefs such as, e.g., S's belief that he is driving in his car - for obviously, if S is actually a brain in a vat, he isn't really driving in his car. Nozick argues that S can indeed know that he is driving and know that if he is driving then he isn't a brain in a vat, even though he cannot know that he isn't a brain in a vat.

For it may well be that S's belief that he is driving tracks the truth (it might, for instance, be produced by a reliable belief-forming process) even if his belief that he isn't a brain in a vat doesn't; and if so, then it is at least possible, contra the skeptic, to know, for example, that one is driving in one's car. In taking this position, Nozick famously, and controversially, denies what is known among epistemologists as the "closure principle," the principle that if S knows that p and that p entails q, then S knows that q.

Personal Identity

Nozick's contribution to the debate over personal identity is his "closest continuer" theory, also presented in Philosophical Explanations. Philosophical puzzles over personal identity arise from various bizarre thought experiments that seem to present genuine logical possibilities.

For instance, there is Locke's famous example of the prince and the cobbler, wherein the man who wakes up in the cobbler's body one morning appears to have all the memories of the prince, and none of the memories of the cobbler.

So who is the man actually in the cobbler's body, the prince or the cobbler himself? Or we can imagine a person A stepping into a teleportation machine of the sort described in science-fiction stories, and, due to some glitch in the machine's operation, not one but two persons similar to A, call them B and C, appearing in the spot where the machine was supposed to send A. Which, if either, is the "real" A?

Nozick's answer to such questions is that it is the later person who "most closely continues" the earlier one who is the one who is truly identical to the latter. What counts as closeness in this context is not susceptible of a simple, cut and dried answer.

If we take psychological properties to be of greater importance to personhood than bodily ones, the closest continuer of the prince in Locke's example would be the man who wakes up in the cobbler's body, even though he has none of the prince's bodily traits (and indeed, even though the prince's body may still exist, and especially if someone else - the cobbler, say -seems to be in the prince's body now). If instead we take bodily properties to be of greatest importance, then the closest continuer of the prince would be the person in the prince's body, whatever memories, if any, that person has. In any case, part of what counts as contributing to closeness is, in Nozick's view, going to be determined by a person's own self-conception, by what a person himself takes to be most important to his identity.

What about the case where two or more individuals seem equally close continuers of an earlier person, as in the transporter example? Here Nozick's view is that, in the latter case, neither B nor C is identical to A - since there is no single closest continuer - and thus A no longer exists; though had only one person arrived in the spot to which the machine was supposed to send A, A would have continued to exist. Personal identity thus depends in part on factors extrinsic to the person himself.

Conclusion

Nozick made contributions to other areas of philosophy as well, developing a complex theory of rationality in The Nature of Rationality (1993) and meditating on the meaning of life in The

Examined Life (1989), though these works received nothing like the attention garnered by Anarchy, State, and Utopia. But his work in epistemology and metaphysics has been nearly as controversial as his work in political philosophy, and has generated as large a literature.

Time will tell whether similar controversy will be generated by his final work, Invariances, wherein he developed a theory of objective reality on which the mark of the objectively real or true, whether in science, metaphysics, or ethics, is "invariance under transformations," a property of the sort exhibited by the relationships between the numbers we use to measure the temperature, relationships which remain constant or "invariant" whether we use the Fahrenheit or centigrade scales, despite the various differences these scales exhibit in other respects.

In any event, it is almost certain that it is Nozick's defense of libertarianism that will stand as his most significant contribution to philosophy..

BIBLIOGRAPHY

Atri, Ajit : *Gandhi's View of Legal Justice*, New Delhi, Deep and Deep Pub., 2007.

Bakshi, S.R. : *Rabindra Nath Tagore and the Challenges of Today*, New Delhi, Om Publications, 2001.

Barman, Suren Deb : *Rabindranath Tagore and Tripura*, Kolkata, Minerva, 2006.

Bhattacharya, Sabyasachi : *Vande Mataram : The Biography of a Song*, New Delhi, Penguin, 2003.

Bourai, Himanshu : *Gandhi and Modern Indian Liberals*, Delhi, Abhijeet Pub., 2004.

Chakrabarti, Mohit : *Rabindranath Tagore : A Miscellany,* New Delhi, Kanishka Pub., 2003.

Chatterjee, Indira : *A Thematic Study of Tagore's Novels,* Gurgaon, Shubhi Pub., 2007.

Dalton, Dennis : *Gandhi's Power : Nonviolence in Action*, New Delhi, OUP, 2001.

Datta, P.K. : *Rabindranath Tagore's The Home and the World : A Critical Companion,* Delhi, Permanent Black, 2003.

Desai, Mahadev : *Gandhi and Indian Villages*, New Delhi, Mohit Pub., 2002.

Gupta, S.P. Das : *Rabindranath Tagore : Thought Relics: New Expanded Version*, Kolkata, Sadesh, 2007.

Jain, P.C. : *Gandhi in Stamps : The Courier of Truth and Non-violence*, New Delhi, Aravali, 2002.

Krishnan, Anita : *Gandhian Satyagrah in South Africa*, New Delhi, Alfa Pub., 2008.

Lal, Ananda : *Rabindranath Tagore : Three Plays*, New Delhi, Oxford University Press, 2001.

Mahmud, Jafar : *Mahatma Gandhi : A Multifaceted Person*, New Delhi, APH, 2004.

Mohit Chakrabarti : *Religion and Rabindranath,* New Delhi, Kalpaz Pub., 2008.

Pandey, Janardan : *Gandhi and 21st Century*, 1998.

Sanyal, Bandana : *Achalayatan : The Petrified Place, Rabindranath Tagore*, New Delhi, Rupa, 2006.

Sharma, S.R. : *Life and Works of Rabindranath Tagore,* Jaipur, Book Enclave, 2003.

Singh, Ramjee : *Gandhi and The New Millennium*, Delhi, Commonwealth, 2000.

Sinha, Biswajit : *Rabindranath Tagore*, Delhi, Raj, 2003.

Tagore, Saumyendranath : *Rabindranath Tagore : Philosophy of Life and Aesthetics*, Kolkata, Aparna Book, 2006.

Yeats, W.B. : *Gitanjali : Song Offerings/Rabindranath Tagore*, New Delhi, Mahaveer, 2005.

INDEX

A

Achievement, 218, 219, 238.
Agreements, 10, 11, 34, 82, 84, 104, 138, 158, 159, 172, 174, 179.
Aristotle, 1, 18, 21, 100, 101, 110, 135, 206, 207, 220, 221, 222, 223, 224, 225, 226, 227, 228, 229, 230, 249.
Associations, 15, 16, 33, 41, 59, 78, 227, 254.

B

Bureaucracy, 24, 25, 30, 48, 105.
Bureaucratic Politics, 24.

C

Citizenship, 137, 139, 226, 236.
Constitutions, 15, 43, 52, 53, 54, 59, 61, 62, 74, 75, 81, 89, 90, 91, 94, 95, 96, 97, 104, 105, 106, 107, 108, 109, 110, 111, 112, 113, 115, 146, 221, 222, 226, 228, 229, 230.
Crops, 172, 182, 186, 193.
Culture, 7, 16, 17, 23, 50, 101, 116, 143, 144, 146, 156, 157, 158.

D

Diplomacy, 7, 8, 9, 10, 11, 12, 104, 120.

E

Economy, 1, 17, 25, 30, 32, 33, 35, 38, 40, 42, 49, 50, 144, 239, 242, 243, 246, 247, 248.

F

Freedoms, 12, 13, 15, 17, 109, 137.

G

Gandhi, 151, 190, 191, 192, 193, 194, 195.
Governments, 2, 3, 12, 20, 33, 43, 44, 100, 102, 103, 104, 107, 110, 113, 114, 115, 116, 149, 207, 251.

H

Historiography, 2, 4, 5, 6, 7.
Human Rights, 12, 16, 109, 117, 124, 136, 137, 138, 139, 140.

I

Industrialization, 19, 191, 192.
Islamic World, 2, 6.

J

Justice, 17, 18, 20, 23, 104, 110, 137, 140, 150, 158, 160, 191, 194, 205, 208, 209, 210, 211, 212, 214, 215, 216, 218, 219, 222, 225, 227, 228, 229, 230, 238, 239, 240, 241, 242, 243, 244, 245, 246, 247, 248, 249, 250, 251, 254, 255, 256, 257, 258.

L

Laws, 14, 15, 16, 17, 21, 25, 27, 43, 44, 47, 52, 54, 78, 80, 88, 101, 102, 103, 104, 106, 107, 108, 110, 111, 112, 127, 136, 138, 140, 146,

147, 202, 203, 204, 205, 207, 210, 211, 212, 213, 214, 216, 217, 221, 222, 223, 242, 249, 257.
Local Government, 14, 146.

M

Maintenance, 23, 39, 161, 163, 165, 166, 175, 210.
Market Economy, 32, 38, 50, 247.
Mechanism, 10, 11, 23, 35, 43, 48, 71, 72, 74, 75, 76, 146, 255, 261.

N

Neorealism, 120, 121, 122, 123.

O

Ownership, 30, 31, 32, 33, 42, 49, 51, 137, 155, 173, 183, 184, 192, 193, 239, 240, 242, 243, 244, 245, 246, 248, 250, 252, 253, 255, 257.

P

Performance, 161, 172, 174, 182.
Philosophy, 1, 17, 18, 19, 20, 21, 23, 46, 100, 115, 118, 123, 126, 127, 129, 130, 131, 132, 133, 134, 135, 136, 190, 191, 195, 196, 197, 198, 200, 201, 202, 203, 204, 205, 206, 207, 208, 211, 214, 218, 219, 220, 221, 222, 224, 225, 230, 231, 232, 238, 239, 244, 247, 248, 249, 250, 251, 252, 258, 260, 261.
Plato, 1, 17, 18, 21, 101, 125, 129, 133, 206, 207, 208, 209, 211, 212, 213, 214, 215, 216, 217, 218, 219, 220, 222, 225, 229, 242, 249.
Political Culture, 100.
Political Freedom, 12, 13, 232.
Political Ideologies, 48, 104.
Political Philosophy, 1, 17, 18, 19, 20, 21, 23, 46, 100, 123, 190, 207, 208, 211, 219, 221, 222, 224, 225, 230, 232, 238, 239, 244, 247, 248, 249, 250, 251, 252, 261.
Political Power, 38, 44, 45, 47, 101, 102, 116, 117, 192, 207.
Political Thought, 1, 18, 19, 20, 21, 23, 101, 206, 220, 232, 249, 251, 255.
Politics, 1, 2, 3, 8, 17, 18, 19, 21, 23, 24, 44, 45, 46, 47, 50, 53, 58, 76, 78, 79, 83, 84, 88, 89, 90, 91, 93, 94, 95, 97, 100, 101, 111, 115, 117, 118, 121, 122, 137, 139, 140, 142, 143, 150, 151, 153, 154, 158, 190, 199, 200, 202, 203, 206, 207, 208, 213, 216, 217, 219, 220, 221, 222, 223, 224, 225, 226, 227, 228, 229, 230, 231, 249, 250, 251.
Powers, 3, 8, 9, 12, 22, 25, 42, 43, 44, 45, 58, 105, 108, 109, 112, 113, 114, 115, 116, 117, 122, 140, 146, 147, 149, 150, 154, 162, 199, 219, 253.
Proportional Elections, 63, 81, 89, 95, 96, 97.
Proportionalism, 62, 63, 64, 68, 71, 72, 73, 74, 85.

R

Relations, 1, 2, 3, 7, 10, 12, 19, 32, 77, 78, 80, 87, 89, 90, 93, 118, 119, 121, 122, 123, 124, 144, 147, 150, 204, 210, 215, 239, 240, 242, 243, 244, 247, 248, 249.
Research, 4, 5, 6, 32, 87, 120, 121, 123, 124, 220, 222.
Revolution, 9, 11, 19, 20, 22, 23, 30, 107, 141, 145, 196, 198, 200, 202, 230.

T

Terminology, 59, 64, 80, 81, 85, 89, 208.
Treatment, 81, 111, 118, 139, 200, 216, 248.

W

Women's Rights, 124, 138, 140.

□□□